OXFORD GEOGRAPHICAL AND
ENVIRONMENTAL STUDIES

Editors: Gordon Clark, Andrew Goudie, and Ceri Peach

GLOBALIZATION AND URBAN CHANGE

Globalization and Urban Change

Capital, Culture, and Pacific Rim Mega-Projects

Kris Olds

OXFORD

UNIVERSITY PRESS

OXFORD
UNIVERSITY PRESS

Great Clarendon Street, Oxford OX2 6DP

Oxford University Press is a department of the University of Oxford.
It furthers the University's objective of excellence in research, scholarship,
and education by publishing worldwide in

Oxford New York

Athens Auckland Bangkok Bogotá Buenos Aires Cape Town
Chennai Dar es Salaam Delhi Florence Hong Kong Istanbul Karachi
Kolkata Kuala Lumpur Madrid Melbourne Mexico City Mumbai
Nairobi Paris São Paulo Shanghai Singapore Taipei Tokyo Toronto Warsaw
with associated companies in Berlin Ibadan

Oxford is a registered trade mark of Oxford University Press
in the UK and in certain other countries

Published in the United States
by Oxford University Press Inc., New York

British Library Cataloguing in Publication Data
Data available

Library of Congress Cataloging-in-Publication Data
Olds, Kris, 1961–
Globalization and urban change : capital, culture, and Pacific Rim mega-projects/Kris Olds.
p.cm.—(Oxford geographical and environmental studies)
Includes bibliographical references and index.
1. Urban economics. 2. City planning. 3. Globalization. I. Title. II. Series.
HT321 .O53 2000   307.76—dc21   00-058038
ISBN 0-19-823361-2

1 3 5 7 9 10 8 6 4 2

Typeset in Times
by Best-set Typesetter Ltd., Hong Kong
Printed in Great Britain by
Biddles Ltd., Guildford & Kings Lynn

EDITORS' PREFACE

Geography and environmental studies are two closely related and burgeoning fields of academic enquiry. Both have grown rapidly over the past two decades. At once catholic in its approach and yet strongly committed to a comprehensive understanding of the world, geography has focused upon the interaction between global and local phenomena. Environmental studies, on the other hand, have shared with the discipline of geography an engagement with different disciplines, addressing wide-ranging environmental issues in the scientific community and the policy community of great significance. Ranging from the analysis of climate change and physical processes to the cultural dislocations of post-modernism and human geography, these two fields of enquiry have been in the forefront of attempts to comprehend transformations taking place in the world, manifesting themselves in a variety of separate but interrelated spatial processes.

The new 'Oxford Geographical and Environmental Studies' series aims to reflect this diversity and engagement. It aims to publish the best and original research studies in the two related fields and in doing so, to demonstrate the significance of geographical and environmental perspectives for understanding the contemporary world. As a consequence, its scope will be international and will range widely in terms of its topics, approaches, and methodologies. Its authors will be welcomed from all corners of the globe. We hope the series will assist in redefining the frontiers of knowledge and build bridges within the fields of geography and environmental studies. We hope also that it will cement links with topics and approaches that have originated outside the strict confines of these disciplines. Resulting studies will contribute to frontiers of research and knowledge as well as representing individually the fruits of particular and diverse specialist expertise in the traditions of scholarly publication.

Gordon Clark
Andrew Goudie
Ceri Peach

This book is dedicated to Janice Haller and our two sons (Thomas and Liam) for their love, support and inspiration.

Loving thanks to my parents, my sister, and the rest of my family for the inspirational support and encouragement over the many years.

ACKNOWLEDGEMENTS

This book is derived from a Ph.D. dissertation that was completed in late 1995. The text was revised in 1997, 1998, and 1999 in the midst of two new jobs (in Bristol and Singapore) involving three overseas moves, a new baby (Liam Olds, b. 10 December 1998), personal tragedies (the loss of dear friend Jane Herman and her unborn baby), ongoing research projects and publications, the turmoil of living through the 'Asian economic crisis' in Singapore, other assorted personal experiences, and the emergence of a flood of books and articles on globalization. In short, the process of transforming a Ph.D. dissertation on issues related to globalization and urban change in the Pacific Rim into monograph form was not exactly ideal! However, the process of trying to revise text in the midst of all of these changes has reinforced (to me at least) the significance of publishing the book. First, while there is now a flood of material on globalization in academia, much of it does not deal with the relationship between globalization and urban change, especially in a manner that focuses on the *construction* of global flows. Secondly, the regional (i.e., Pacific Rim) focus of the book continues to be underrepresented given the North American and European bias to most texts on globalization (or globalization and urban change). And thirdly, the somewhat reflexive and situated account presented herein is rarely adopted in texts on globalization (or globalization and urban change). The vast majority of texts continue to be written as if the author were the omnipotent viewer from above, casting a universal eye over the proceedings of economic, political, social, and cultural change in the late twentieth-century city. Enough said on the rationale for the book at this stage: a more detailed exposition is contained within Chapters 1 and 3 of this text.

Before progressing, it is important to note that I could not have written this book without receiving substantial assistance from a wide range of people and institutions, many of whom will have to remain unnamed (for lack of space here, or reasons of privacy). The vast majority of them are listed in the Appendices (under my list of resource people and institutions). However, I should acknowledge the following institutions up-front. Funding or other significant assistance was provided by: the Association of Commonwealth Universities and the British Council (via a Commonwealth Scholarship); the Social Sciences and Humanities Research Council of Canada (via doctoral and post-doctoral fellowships); the University of Bristol; the University of British Columbia Centre for Human Settlements (via their Canadian International Development Agency (CIDA) Centre of Excellence Project); Tongji University (College of Architecture and Urban Planning); and the Chinese University of Hong Kong (Hong Kong Institute of Asia-Pacific Studies). I would also like to acknowledge support from 1996 on via the Vancouver Centre for the Study of Immigration and the Metropolis ⟨http://riim.metropolis.net⟩, which is funded by the Government of Canada, and the National University of Singapore (via research project RP970013).

I would also like to acknowledge that parts of the following articles are reprinted or revised (with permission) and folded into Chapters 1 to 5 of this book: *Environment and Planning A*, 27: 1713–43 (Pion Limited, London); *Progress in Human Geography*, 20(3): 311–37 (Arnold Publishers); *Cities*, 14(2): 109–23 (Elsevier Science); *Urban Geography*, 19(4): 360–85 (V. H. Winston & Sons, Inc.). Numerous other people, companies, and institutions have permitted me to incorporate data into this book. I would particularly like to thank Concord Pacific Group Inc.; KARO Design; the Shanghai Lujiazui Central Area International Planning and Urban Design Consultation Committee; the Richard Rogers Partnership; BC Stats; Citizenship and Immigration Canada; CY Leung; FPD Savills; Jones Lang Wootton (now known as Jones Lang LaSalle); Morgan Stanley, Baring Securities (now known as ING Barings), and Ronald Skeldon. I sincerely apologize if I have omitted anyone, and will take steps to rectify the situation if and when contacted.

Of the many individuals I owe a debt to, I would particularly like to thank: Jacques Guaran of the French Ministère de l'Équipement, des Transports et du Tourisme and the Shanghai Lujiazui Central Area International Planning and Urban Design Consultation Committee; Zhao Min of Tongji University; and Thomas Hutton, You-tien Hsing, and Aprodicio Laquian of the UBC Centre for Human Settlements. My field work would have been much more difficult without the assistance the five of you provided. David Ley and Terry McGee of UBC's Geography Department, and Katharyne Mitchell of the University of Washington's Geography Department have also helped to shape this text, in more ways than they know. However, none of the above people is in anyway responsible for the content or opinions contained in this book.

At the University of Bristol, I would like to thank my two supervisors—Nigel Thrift and Keith Bassett—for their consistent encouragement and support. My stay at the Bristol Geography Department (and in England) was made truly enjoyable through the kind hospitality of Paul Cloke, Ian Cook, Mike Crang, Emily Gilbert, Paul Glennie, Annie Hughes, Owain Jones, Dave Kilham, James Kneale, Andrew Leyshon, Paul Longley, Phil McManus, Richard Smith, Lorraine Thorne, Sara Whatmore, Dave the janitor, and many others. Simon Godden and Tony Philpott provided excellent graphic assistance. Thanks as well to Chris Hamnett and Andrew Leyshon for their constructive and supportive feedback during my Ph.D. viva in November 1995.

At the National University of Singapore, I would like to acknowledge the support and collegial inspiration offered by many people, including Tim Bunnell, Neil Coe, Shirlena Huang, Phil Kelly, Lily Kong, Victor Savage, Peta Sanderson, David Taylor, Teo Siew Eng, Peggy Teo, Brenda Yeoh, and Henry Yeung. The inspirational presence of Jane, Chris, Adam, and Ortrud in our Singaporean adventures must also be noted—I/we miss you all in so many ways.

At Oxford University Press, I would sincerely like to thank Andrew Lockett, Dorothy McLean, and especially Dominic Byatt for their understanding during the many phases of change I went through while trying to generate the manuscript. I would also like to thank the anonymous reviewer of my draft manuscript for OUP—the insightful comments that he or she offered were very useful in revising the text.

Finally, while he is tragically no longer with us in person, the spirit of my close friend (and critical urbanist) Doug Konrad ripples through these pages.

K.O.

Singapore
December 1999

CONTENTS

LIST OF FIGURES

LIST OF TABLES

LIST OF ABBREVIATIONS

AA	Architectural Association	EEC	European Economic Community
ADB	Asian Development Bank		
AIG	American International Group	EIU	Economist Intelligence Unit
APEC	Asia Pacific Economic Cooperation	EJV	Equity Joint Venture
		EPAD	L'Etablissement Public d'Aménagement de La Défense
APFC	Asia-Pacific Foundation of Canada		
API	Asia Pacific Initiative	ESCAP	Economic and Social Commission for Asia and the Pacific
BC	British Columbia		
BCEC	British Columbia Enterprise Corporation		
		FDI	foreign direct investment
BHP	Brooke Hillier Parker	FEC	foreign exchange certificates
BIE	Bureau of International Expositions		
		GATT	General Agreement on Tariffs and Trade
BIS	Bank for International Settlements		
		GDP	gross domestic product
BURA	British Urban Regeneration Association	GIC	Global Intelligence Corps
		GLOBE	Global Opportunities for Business and the Environment
CADD	Computer Aided Design and Drafting		
CBD	central business district	GNP	gross national product
CCP	Chinese Communist Party	GVRD	Greater Vancouver Regional District
C$	Canadian dollar		
CEF	Canadian Eastern Finance	HIC	Habitat International Coalition
CHS	UBC Centre for Human Settlements		
		HKCBA	Hong Kong–Canada Business Association
CIAM	Congrès Internationaux d'Architecture Moderne		
		HKTDC	Hong Kong Trade Development Council
CIBC	Canadian Imperial Bank of Commerce		
		IAURIF	Institut d'Aménagement et d'Urbanisme de la Région Ile de France
CIDA	Canadian International Development Agency		
CJV	contractual or cooperative joint venture	IBG	Institute of British Geographers
		IDD	International direct dial
COPE	Coalition of Progressive Electors	IDRC	International Development Research Centre
CPR	Canadian Pacific Railway		
DAE	developing Asian economies	IFC	International Financial Centre Vancouver
DERA	Downtown Eastside Residents Association	IIP	Immigrant Investor Program
ECADI	East China Architecture and Design Institute	IMC	International Maritime Centre

IMF	International Monetary Fund	Rmb	reminbi
INTA	International Urban Development Association	SCMP	*South China Morning Post*
		SEHK	Stock Exchange of Hong Kong
IRPP	Institute for Research on Public Policy	SEZ	special economic zone
		SFU	Simon Fraser University
ISDN	Integrated services digital network	SLDC	Shanghai Lujiazui Development Company
JLW	Jones Lang Wootton	SLFTZDC	Shanghai Lujiazui Finance and Trade Zone
KLCC	Kuala Lumpur City Centre		Development Company
LCFD	Lujiazui Central Finance District	SMG	Shanghai Municipal Government
LICP	Lujiazui International Consultation Process	SSE	Shanghai Stock Exchange
MIPIM	annual international property market fair	SUPDI	Shanghai Urban Planning and Design Institute
MNC	Multinational Corporation	TEAM	The Electors Action Movement
NGO	non-governmental organization	TNC	transnational corporation
NIC	newly industrializing country	UBC	University of British Columbia
NIDL	new international division of labour	UMP	urban mega-project
		UNCHS	United Nations Centre for Human Settlements
NPA	Non-partision Association	UNCRD	United Nations Centre for Regional Development
ODP	official development plan		
OECD	Organization for Economic Cooperation and Development	UNCTAD	United Nations Conference on Trade and Development
OPEC	Organization of Petroleum Exporting Countries	UNDP	United Nations Development Programme
O&Y	Olympia and York	WFOE	wholly foreign-owned enterprise
PRC	People's Republic of China	WTO	World Trade Organization
RIBA	Royal Institute of British Architects	YDUS	Yangtze Delta Urban System
RICS	Royal Institution of Chartered Surveyors		

1

Introduction: Globalizing Networks, Globalizing Cities

Now, I want to make one simple point here, and that is about what one might call the power-geometry of it all; the power-geometry of time-space compression. For different social groups and different individuals are placed in very distinct ways in relation to these flows and interconnections. This point concerns not merely the issue of who moves and who doesn't, although that is an important element of it; it is also about power in relation to the flows and the movement. Different social groups have distinct relationships to this anyway differentiated mobility: some are more in charge of it than others; some initiate flows and movement, others don't; some are more on the receiving end of it than others; some are effectively imprisoned by it.

(*Massey*, 1994: 149)

The real significance of the growth of the transnational cultures, however, is often not the new cultural experience that they can offer people—for it is frequently rather restricted in scope and depth—but their mediating possibilities. The transnational cultures are bridgeheads for entry into other territorial cultures. Instead of remaining with them, one can use the mobility connected with them to make contact with the meanings of other rounds of life, and gradually incorporate this experience into one's personal perspective.

(Hannerz, 1990: 245)

Actors constantly strive to enrol (human and non-human) entities in a network by channeling and stabilizing their behaviour in the desired direction, such that they gain new and stable identities or attributes within the network. This power is seen as depending on the strength of associations between actors, which, in turn, will depend on the ability to use a network to enrol the force of others and speak for them. In other words, power is the action of others. If actors are successful they will be able to build, maintain and expand these networks so that they can act at considerable distances.

(*Amin and Thrift*, 1995a: 51)

Surveying the landscape, we find inspiration and purpose.

(*Cheung Kong (Holdings) Ltd*, 1999,
⟨http://www.ckh.com.hk/market/⟩, accessed 13 Aug. 1999)

Introduction

Let me[1] take you on a brief tour through a condominium unit in *The Concordia*, part of the Pacific Place mega-project on the North Shore of False Creek in Vancouver, Canada. The unit, and the project it is situated in, are elegant markers of the intersection of a burgeoning trans-Pacific residential property market with trans-Pacific migration, and succession plans within one of the world's leading ethnic Chinese corporate groups (the Cheung Kong Group)—three factors that both constitute and are constituted by the processes driving globalization. The unit, and the project, are generated by networks that span across the Pacific Ocean at a specific time in world history, linking social formations in the two Pacific Rim cities of Vancouver and Hong Kong.

We start the tour on the fifteenth floor (see Fig. 1.1) and make our way into a unit in the range of 1,100 sq. ft. of 'timeless elegance and sophistication' creating 'a new standard in home design'—priced between C$200,000 and $300,000 at this floor level. 'Finely crafted with care and attention', your home offers views of the water, southern exposure to the sun, and your choice of select materials and equipment to outfit and decorate the unit. The unit and *The Concordia* express an 'ambiance', a 'distinctive residence', in a 'classic estate' on an 'exclusive seafront'. But, this is no pedestrian condominium unit, for it is connected with 'state of the art fiber optics providing enhanced personal communications' enabling you to carry out a multitude of activities such as: working at home through the exchange of high speed text, audio, video and graphic information with people from around the world; calling home to turn on the oven or adjust room temperature; ordering videos to be 'piped in'; and, surveillance through the use of high definition video monitoring equipment to simultaneously view up to four different locations (by splitting your television screen into quadrants) in the private, semi-public, and public spaces in and around *The Concordia*.

The Concordia itself is situated on a 'sheltered Pacific inlet' at the 'heart of a great international centre of fashion and finance'—Vancouver—the 'Pacific Coast's most dynamic city'. In short, you are now a resident of Concord Pacific Place, the 'pre-eminent planned community on the Pacific Rim'.[2]

This unit did not actually exist in physical reality until mid-1995—two years after the field research that this passage is based upon. We have been inside the display unit of a CDN $2 million presentation centre where the 'pre-sale' process takes place. In the pre-sale process prospective purchasers of condo-

---

[1] A narrative style and first person form is used in many sections of this book. See Appendix A for further details.

[2] All of the above quotations are taken from one promotional brochure titled *The Concordia at David Lam Park* which was published in February 1994 and distributed at Concord Pacific's presentation centre on the Pacific Place project site. The themes are in keeping with other materials published by Concord Pacific Developments Ltd., and the concepts expressed by the firm's representatives in both formal interviews and casual discussions with me between 1992 and 1997.

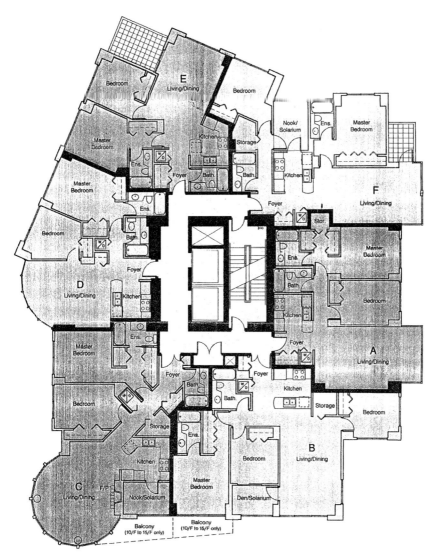

Fig. 1.1. Floor plan of units in *The Concordia*, Pacific Place, Vancouver

Source: Concord Pacific Developments Ltd.

minium units examine mock suites, graphic images such as Figure 1.1, models of condominium towers, a model of the entire project site, a large map of the Pacific Rim, and numerous other types of information including mortgage arrangement details with banks in Vancouver or Hong Kong. The atmosphere of a market-place prevails, with large crowds at certain times of the week. You can mingle with representatives of the development company, fellow buyers, and researchers such as myself. Glass-enclosed meeting rooms permit you to see deals in the making, and each closure is followed by the placing of a red sticker on a graphic of the condo tower announcing SOLD. Full page announcements of the sale of new condominium towers such as *The Concordia* are also placed in all of Vancouver's major English and Chinese language newspapers, as well as in select Asian newspapers (see Fig. 1.2).

If you prefer a more distanciated mode of viewing the condominium units being built at Pacific Place, log on to the World Wide Web (WWW) and key in Concord Pacific's internet address ⟨http://www.concordpacific.com⟩. Through the vehicle of communications technology you will be able to examine floor plans, take yacht trips down False Creek, and find out the latest company-sponsored public events planned for the site.

This style of buying property is a relatively recent phenomenon in Vancouver. It emerged as a common sales method in the early 1990s when projects such as Pacific Place were being developed and sold in the context of a globalizing residential property market, driven by increasing linkages between Vancouver and Hong Kong. Indeed, the Vancouver Information Centre in Hong Kong acted (until 1997) as a virtual replica to this one, albeit on the twentieth floor of the China Tower, Central Hong Kong. Pre-sale is the most common method of residential property development in the hyperactive temple of money worship—Hong Kong, also known as Mammon's Temple.[3] Pre-sale provides the developer with 'capitalism's ultimate fantasy—the world's first perpetual money machine' (Newman, 1993: 36) where risk is shifted to the buyer from the seller, where turnover time, gearing levels, and carrying costs are significantly reduced, and where future speculative goals can be more carefully weighed.

I've taken you for a brief walk through this condominium plan and presentation centre *circa* 1994 because they are fascinating indicators of the increasing interconnectedness of Vancouver and Hong Kong. Global flows of capital, people, images, ideas, and commodities are binding these two cities together, and in the process transforming the nature of urban life. Networks of a global scale are linking together processes of change within seemingly separate cities, generating new forms of interdependencies, intertwined futures, hybrid social practices, and built forms representative of a plethora of competing and complementary agendas and rationalities. And while it is obvious to anyone living in Vancouver that the nature of urbanity is changing, and that Hong Kong is playing a key role in this process of change (see e.g. Mitchell, 1993a, 1995; Olds, 1998a), it is very difficult to make sense of the social and relational dynamics behind these changes. Other cities on the 'Pacific Rim' such as Shanghai are also hooked up to Hong Kong, though the nature of the connections between

---

[3] This term was used by several senior international financiers during conversations with me during my field work in Hong Kong. The degree of money worship in Hong Kong, evident during all stages of the colonial period, was hyperactive in the 1990s with capitalists in the city benefiting from unprecedented flows of capital and goods in and out of China.

The Concordia
at David Lam Park

REMEMBER EXPO 86?
NOW YOU CAN LIVE IN A NEIGHBOURHOOD
THAT INVITED THE WORLD

**Preview
Exhibition**

*Saturday,
February 12th
and Sunday,
February 13th
from 12 noon
to 7 p.m.*

*The waterfront is
yours for life.
The opportunity
is now.*

*For further
information visit
the Presentation
Centre
1088 Pacific
Boulevard
or telephone
899-8800.*
PROMPTON PROPERTY
MANAGEMENT INC.

This weekend, discover the West Coast lifestyle at Concord Pacific Place. Visit the Pacific Rim's pre-eminent planned community, set in the heart of Vancouver.

Concord Pacific Place is the newest address of distinction in a city emerging as an international centre of finance and culture.

Now, The Concordia is creating a new standard in elegant, functional, urban home design with 2 & 3 bedroom condominiums and townhomes.

Your home at The Concordia is one of a limited number of exclusive residences. Discover the ultimate waterfront home.

CONCORD PACIFIC
PLACE

Fig. 1.2. Advertisement for The *Concordia* in the *Vancouver Sun* (11 Feb. 1994, p. D5)

Source: Courtesy of Concord Pacific Developments Ltd., and KARO Design.

these two cities is considerably different (as is the scale of urban change). More-over, both cities have a plethora of connections to other places; connections that wax and wane, diverge and converge.

Towards a Relational Geography

The main aim in writing this book is to examine the implications of contemporary globalization processes for Pacific Rim cities. This topic is approached by using two urban mega-projects (UMPs) in Vancouver and Shanghai as vehicles through which to explore the processes underlying urban change. UMPs such as the Pacific Place project briefly described above, are large scale (re)development projects composed of a mix of commercial, residential, retail, industrial, leisure, and infrastructure uses. They are developed primarily in the inner city, on large tracts of former port, railway, industrial, military or racetrack lands, or on 'under-utilized' suburban, agricultural, swamp, or island land within the extended metropolitan region. London's Docklands and *La Défense* in Paris are two well-known examples of mega-projects.

UMPs are increasingly being developed around the world (Hall, 1995: 27; Olds, 1995; Ford, 1998). As part of an ongoing global scan of urban development trends around the world I have identified over three dozen projects in the process of being developed in Europe, North America, Asia, and Australia. Dozens of other UMPS are likely to be under way right now as well.

Although by no means homogeneous, it is apparent that many UMPs are often:

(1) developed with a myriad of capital sources that change over time;

(2) modelled on each other;

(3) developed and planned by architects, financiers, engineers, and planners who have experience of working on and/or knowledge of previous or ongoing mega-projects in other cities around the world;

(4) developed with both explicit and implicit internationalization strategies in mind;

(5) marketed to overseas firms and high income individuals for subsequent lease or purchase; and

(6) designed to symbolize a global urban 'utopia' for the twenty-first century.

Many projects include conspicuous high-profile buildings that quickly reorient the international imagery of a city (witness Canary Wharf in London, or the Petronas twin towers in Kuala Lumpur) (Sudjic, 1993*a*; King, 1996; Ford, 1998; Bunnell, 1999). A number of UMPs are also fitted with elaborate artificial light schemes to appeal to our modern highly visual culture (Jay, 1992;

Thrift, 1994).[4] These projects are therefore highly implicated in the contemporary globalization processes that are reshaping cities.

Although some research has been conducted on individual UMPs, particularly the port redevelopment projects in the UK, Australia, New York, and Toronto (e.g. Desfor *et al.*, 1988; Brownill, 1990), few analyses move beyond simple abstract assertions regarding the global flows underlying these projects (exceptions, primarily focused on Battery Park in New York and London Docklands, include: Crilley, 1993*a*, 1993*b*; Zukin, 1992*a*, 1992*b*; Fainstein, 1994). This is unfortunate because the development of new urban spaces in many cities (particularly Pacific Rim cities) is strongly linked to contemporary globalization processes. For example, as implied earlier in this chapter, the process of development, nature, and interpretation of Vancouver's Pacific Place project is shaped by global networks linking Hong Kong and Vancouver. To paraphrase Appadurai (1996: 18), UMPs are the 'sites' suitable for the examination of how 'locality emerges in a globalizing world' (Appadurai, 1996: 18).

A social constructionist approach to the analysis of UMPs is adopted in this book. Through two empirical case studies, I explore the processes through which global connections are being forged in the social production of new urban spaces on the Pacific Rim. The development processes of two mega-projects in Vancouver and Shanghai are situated within the larger 'global cultural economy' (Appadurai, 1996), thereby highlighting how the urban (re)development process is increasingly articulated by the *space of flows* operating at a global scale (Castells, 1996).

The book is predicated upon a belief that, as has been discussed with increasing frequency in the social sciences literature (e.g. Harris, 1986; Henderson, 1989; Appadurai, 1990*a*, 1996; Emirbayer, 1997), there is a need to move beyond binary concepts such as centre–periphery, North–South, East–West, First World–Third World, and so on when we conduct our analyses. Even at urban and regional scale analysts such as Mike Douglass and Terry McGee (in the case of Southeast Asia and East Asia) have highlighted the problems associated with 'urban/rural conceptualizations', and new (perhaps less Eurocentric) concepts such as the Bahasa Indonesian term *desakota* are being worked with as an alternative (see Douglass, 1998*a*; Forbes, 1996; McGee, 1989, 1991, 1994). As I hope to demonstrate, one way of comprehending in a more interactive and complex world is to develop a non-functionalist geography of linkage, interdependence, connections, mutuality—a relational geography focused on *networks* and *flows* (Abu-Lughod, 1989; Castells, 1989,

---

[4] The *La Defénse* project in Paris was the setting for a Jean Michel Jarré concert in 1990. The concert drew over two million people and it involved monumental laser systems with image projection on the sides of various *La Defénse* structures. Similar concerts have been staged by Jarré in London Docklands (1988), and in downtown Houston (1986). On the general subject of light and the city see Thrift (1994) and Virilio (1991, 1994).

1996; Appadurai, 1990*a*, 1990*b*, 1996; Virilio, 1991; Clifford, 1992; Hannerz, 1992*a*; Luke, 1997; Thrift, 1994, 1996; Bingham, 1996; Amin and Hausner, 1997; Murdoch, 1997; Massey *et al.*, 1999). This is a relational geography that recognizes the contingent, historically specific, uneven, and dispersed nature of material and non-material flows; a relational geography that approaches the subject of globalization in a complex, uncertain, and messy manner (Whatmore, 1999).

This book is situated within ongoing debates about globalization and the production of new urban spaces, especially in the Pacific Rim. Clearly, no one can deny that flows of money, capital, people (labour, migrants, tourists, professionals), information, images, technologies, and products are increasing in scale and velocity throughout the world, often beyond the national scale, though still shaped by national regulatory regimes (Held *et al.*, 1999). These flows have effectively become 'deterritorialized', that is, 'separated from their original local and national settings, but only to reappear in places as new influences blending in with existing myths, memories and beliefs (Smith, 1990)' (Amin and Thrift, 1994: 5). Such global flows are also being recognized for their 'complexly multilinear' and uneven nature (Pred and Watts, 1992: p. xv). In other words, globalization is not a homogeneous and unmediated process. While the forces of globalization derive much of their strength and vigour from powerful institutions with bases in the West, these forces are not sweeping through the cities of the Pacific Rim depositing a purely foreign product. Globalization is a contingent, non-uniform, and temporal mesh of processes that do not, contrary to popular opinion, lead to simple homogenization; globalization *must* initiate a myriad of local interpretations and transformations (Amin and Thrift, 1994: 2). Or, as Appadurai (1996: 18) puts it, locality is 'itself a historical product' and the 'histories through which localities emerge are eventually subject to the dynamics of the global'.

Another key assumption running through this book is that the global space of flows does not float in ethereal space, guided by a transcendental logic of its own, dropping from place to place in a 'footloose' and unexpected manner (though see Harvey, 1994*a*). Global *flows* of objects and subjects are processes designed by nctworks of human beings (via non-human entities like the telephone, fax, academic journal, or book). The majority of these flows are formulated, activated, and legitimized by powerful human beings who are unevenly spread across the world in (primarily) global cities (Sassen, 1991; Hamnett, 1995). These actors, within their broader relational systems, draw themselves and others into the same 'social space' and the same 'historical time' in order to implement their goals (the transformation of urban space in this case). This cosmopolitan network of humans (Hannerz, 1992*a*, 1996) is a continually evolving social space constructed by dynamic 'networks of social relationships stretched across the globe' (Allen, 1995*a*: 135; Amin and Thrift, 1994: 6; Thrift, 1996); peopled with the resources (material and otherwise) to maintain and enhance such social spaces. The concept of 'extended social relations', enables us to 'reevaluate' the concepts of 'global' and 'local' and recognize that they offer 'points of view on networks that are by their very nature neither global nor local, but more or less long and more or less connected' (Latour, 1993: 122; Amin and Thrift, 1994: 6).

The adoption of a network perspective on the 'global' implies that I do not subscribe to the geological metaphor of the global and the local, one scale dominating the other (on this metaphor see Beauregard, 1995 or Dirlik, 1999). Rather, the analysis that informs this book adopts many of the principles of the emerging 'relational materialist' and 'associationalist' approaches to geography and sociology (see Abu-Lughod, 1989; Amin and Hausner, 1997; Grabher and Stark, 1997; Murdoch, 1997; Thrift, 1997; Whatmore and Thorne, 1997; Massey *et al.*, 1999); an approach often (but not always) influenced by the writings of prominent actor-network theorists such as Bruno Latour and John Law. In these approaches modernist binaries are rejected (e.g. global/local) with greater attention devoted to the 'associations' which give rise to so-called 'purified outcomes' (i.e. the 'role of the analyst is to follow' networks as they 'stretch through space and time, localizing and globalizing along the way'). This is a geography in which research is focused on 'how associations and networks are built and maintained' (i.e. the production of global flows is a *performative* act which has as much capacity to fail as to it does to succeed) (Murdoch, 1997: 334–5). As Whatmore and Thorne (1997: 290) put it, 'global reach' is a 'laboured, uncertain, and above all, contested process of "acting at a distance" '; an approach to analysis which is at odds with the 'peculiarly modernist geographical imagination that casts globalisation as a colonisation of surfaces which, like a spreading ink stain, progressively colours every spot on the map' (p. 287). They carry on:

Rather than conceptualising the spatial orderings of economic activity in territorial terms—a globalisation of surfaces—this approach implies a conception of the spatial ordering of economic activity in mobile terms—a globalisation of flows. It shifts concern from a predictable unfolding of social structures in space to the means whereby networks of actors construct space by using certain forms of ordering which mobilise particular rationalities, technological and representational devices, living beings (including people), and physical properties. More than this, unlike the filled in surfaces of globalisation, this approach opens up space-time to the coexistence of multiple cross-cutting networks of varied length and durability. . . . (p. 302)

With a focus on the ordering of global flows, greater attention needs to be devoted to the creation and operation of networks. As Lash and Urry (1994: 24) note:

The movement, the flows of capital, money, commodities, labour, information and images across time and space are only comprehensible if 'networks' are taken into account because it is through networks that these subjects and objects are able to gain mobility. Whatever form of institutional governance is dominant, whether markets, hierarchies, the state or corporatism, the subjects and objects which are governed must be mobile through networks . . . The issue for us in this context is what are becoming the modal changes in this mapping of the post-organized capitalist order; that is, where and what sort of the 'cobwebs' of connections on these maps are becoming denser, and which are becoming sparser.

Greater attention also needs to be devoted to the specific role of the city in the process of globalization. This is because the global space of flows is primarily controlled by networked actors situated within a 'cosmopolitan and international network of global cities' (Lash and Urry, 1994: 26); in other words, real people, living in real cities—not abstract inhuman 'global forces' that forge through cities, driven by a 'colossal logos outside or above the social fray' (Whatmore, 1999: 27). The terms 'global' and 'local' retain their usefulness if they are associated with extended social relations across space in real time which are linked to the what, how, and why of a flow. The global space of flows does not operate at a hypermobile atmospheric level, delinked from human action and ready to pummel and dismember 'the local', should the flows' 'functional logic' (Castells, 1989) suggest so. Rather, the global space of flows is profoundly bound up with human-directed action within cities, and global social relations between cities; these flows are social constructs with the inherent complexities that such a conception obviously entails.

While the adoption of such a focus on the global space of flows is leading to some interesting insights on contemporary globalization processes (e.g. Weyland, 1993) much of the literature on flows is reckless in failing to clarify how the term is used, how the flows are mobilized, what the flows actually consist of, and how the flows are interpreted—in other words, the enormously complex nature of the term and the process. As Mitchell (1995: 371) notes in relation to Castells's use of the 'space of flows' concept:

Although he is careful to note that 'information is based upon culture, and information processing is, in fact, symbol manipulation' (1991: 15), Castells's economistic emphasis precludes a serious discussion as to what information actually is, how it is used, where, by whom, and with what specific meanings and effects. By focusing on the process of power consolidation through the social action of bureaucratic organization or through access to technological innovation, he effectively removes the discussion from the realm of culture, where information itself, rather than the control of information, is primary. Furthermore, the power to direct these 'space of flows' is construed as a top down structural domination, maintained through an abstracted threat of violence rather than through the processes and practices of everyday life.

What I seek to do in order to escape from simplifying the complex nature of the global space of flows is to focus, through empirical research, on the processes underlying the material and non-material flows associated with two urban redevelopment projects on the Pacific Rim. While there is a growing volume of literature on the global space of flows, there is a noticeable lack of detailed empirical work conducted on the subject (Murdoch, 1997: 332). The analysis in this book also situates the flows within a multi-level historical context, discusses the myriad of manners in which the flows are specifically structured by networked actors, takes into account the many influences on the formulation process (including what perceptions the actors have regarding the destination of the flows), and accounts for the articulation process (where the flows are transformed and moulded as they become further enmeshed with the locality they have been directed to).

The analysis of the global space of flows must be situated and grounded in empirical research practice to contextualize the argumentation and offer new insights. Modernist arguments, contextless abstracted arguments, are dangerous and self-defeating in that they prevent propositions from being validated (Ley and Mills, 1993: 271), they oversimplify the processes of globalization, and they lead to the priorization of 'hyperspace', as evidenced in the writings of Castells (1989) and Harvey (1989a) in a Western context, and Luke (1997) in an Asia-Pacific context. Such discourses of globalization propagate the concept of hypermobile 'footloose' capital (Cox, 1992, 1997; Leyshon, 1997), aiding and abetting a development model that these self-perceived critics dislike. Rather, all stages of global flow formation and articulation are subject to severe contingencies which need to be addressed (Whatmore and Thorne, 1997).

The Research Focus

The specific processes to be addressed (these processes drive any international property development project) are: (1) flows of capital and development expertise, and (2) flows of images and development expertise. More specifically, the key processes are examined in detail using inter-related yet non-comparative case studies on two *transnational cultures*:[5]

Elite Chinese Property Tycoons and the Pacific Place Project (Vancouver, Canada—late 1980s to mid-1990s). This case study is an examination of flows of capital and property development expertise which are predominantly shaped by Hong Kong-based ethnic Chinese property tycoons;[6] tycoons responsible for initiating the development of one of North America's largest

---

[5] The term 'transnational cultures' is one of several that could have been adopted to describe the network of élites I am focusing on in this book. Alternatives include 'cosmopolitans', 'transnational capitalist class', 'global cultures', 'third cultures', and 'globalized business élites'—people and their networks that are starting to receive increasing attention in books and articles by analysts such as Hannerz (1992b, 1996), A. Jones (1998), Mitchell (1997a, 1997b), Sklair (1995, 1997), and A. Smith (1990). I decided to use transnational cultures as the network of élites I am focusing on are not necessarily capitalists and they straddle a variety of worlds/cultures/communities during the course of both work and leisure. The UK-based Transnational Communities project ⟨http://www.transcomm.ox.ac.uk⟩ is another source of material on these concepts and groups.

[6] The term 'tycoon' is used as it best describes the social, economic, and political status of the élite ethnic Chinese entrepreneurs who control firms such as Cheung Kong, Henderson Land, or New World Development. These men (for they are all men) are not developers *per se*; rather they

private urban redevelopment projects. These flows are intertwined with flows of migrants, images, and other capital flows from Hong Kong, as well as with capital flows from a variety of Canadian sources. The built form, under construction at the time of writing, reflects an evolving articulation process whereby flows guided by the developer are moulded by the regulatory arm of the local state in a process involving both conflict and complementarity. Key to the handling of this global property market transaction is a network of extended social relations across the Pacific Ocean that is linked to the formation of a dense web of local, provincial, and national (Canadian) social networks—all revolving around the Vancouver-based representatives of the tycoons. This 'economic' process is embedded within distinct social relations that are stretched across the Pacific at a particular historical moment, thereby creating new time–space configurations.

Elite Professional Architects and Lujiazui Central Finance District (Pudong, Shanghai, PR China—early 1990s).   This case study is an examination of flows of urban development concepts (and associated images) that were formulated by predominantly European architectural professionals (hereafter called the 'Global Intelligence Corps' (GIC) following Rimmer, 1991*a*).[7] These flows were directed to Shanghai in the early 1990s with the aim of initiating the planning for one of the world's largest new international financial centres (Lujiazui Central Finance District). These flows were initiated and guided by representatives of the Shanghai Municipal Government (SMG), in association with Paris-based representatives of the French state. Following a period of conceptual planning for the site, the flows of expertise and images to Shanghai were effectively halted in 1992. From that point on the SMG took complete control for planning, guiding, and marketing the development of Lujiazui; a process dependent upon waves of speculative property capital directed from Hong Kong, Taiwan, and various arms of the Chinese state. The concepts and images produced via the consultative process were also directed into the discursive field associated with the architectural profession and discipline, furthering a variety of autonomous professional goals from 1992 to the date of writing.

In short, this book focuses on the transnational cultures which formulate the global flows, and shape the global networks, that play a key role in constituting what we define as 'globalization'. However, it is important for me to emphasize that this is not a book simply about 'big men'—heroic actors able to stamp their vision onto the face of the city with little difficulty. Rather, this

---

strategize, socialize, and do deals, leaving the management of the property 'development' process to their family members and non-family member employees. The term does not have derogatory connotations in Asia, and is only used in the English language.

   [7] See Rimmer's (1991*a*) article 'The global intelligence corps and world cities: engineering consultancies on the move' for further details. The GIC term refers to the firms which provide services to the international financial institutions that are 'engaged in reshuffling ownership and control of productive assets on a global scale' (p. 67).

book is suffused with an understanding that the Chinese tycoons and élite architects I focus on have only become influential people because of their power to facilitate and shape (to their advantage) their relationships within a multitude of networks (spanning distances from the local to the global). Human beings, like Li Ka-shing and Richard Rogers are 'mediators', 'weavers' (Thrift, 1996: 26), 'enrolling actors' (Murdoch, 1995. 747), they are people with the capacity to shape, in a very influential manner, the ongoing constitution of networks that reach across space via the circulation of intermediaries. In other words, these powerful actors are made powerful through their relations, their associations—their power is contained in relationships that are bound up in ever-shifting networks. Even then though, as we will see in the Shanghai case in particular, their power to achieve goals has to be performed and implemented with considerable effort, and their successes are by no means guaranteed.

Such broad questions regarding the development of two UMPs in such diverse contexts obviously constitute a very complex story, and four more detailed research questions can be delineated.

1. What are the key factors leading these transnational cultures to extend their reach over space into Vancouver and Shanghai between the late 1980s and early to mid-1990s? Answering this question entails attempting to understand: (*a*) the business and personal dynamics of the key actors involved with these global flows, set within a broader political-economic context; (*b*) the meaning and significance of the cities of Vancouver and Shanghai to the actors; and (*c*) the significance and multiple functions of this type of property development project—the UMP—to the actors.

2. How did the transnational cultures extend their reach and control over space in order to formulate and activate the global flows associated with these two UMPs? This question is bound up with: (*a*) the construction of social relationships across space of variable depths that play a role in constituting the actual nature of the flows; and (*b*) the construction of social relationships across space of variable depths that play a role in guiding the distanciating process.

3. What is the role of the state in each of the UMP development processes? More specifically, what is the role of the state in enabling, structuring, or contesting the global flows associated with these transnational cultures? The local and national state plays a very different role in the Vancouver and Shanghai projects, yet, there are also many interesting commonalities. Addressing this question involves: (*a*) focusing on the nature of the relationship between the state and the developers in the Vancouver case, and with the GIC (in the Shanghai case); (*b*) the level of state dependency on flows of capital and/or immigrants to fulfil state objectives; (*c*) the role of specific government officials and politicians in influencing the development process; and (*d*) the nature of state–society relations. This research question, as does the fourth, attempts to develop a more persuasive argument that addresses the issue of how people (including state representatives) respond to global flows, recognizing that there are a myriad of uncertainties involved in this process (Hannerz, 1992*a*: 243), rather than neglecting the issue or offering mere assertions (as is very common in most of the political economy literature on globalization).

4. What roles does the global city play in the activities of the transnational cultures in general, and in these initiatives in particular? This question is bound up with: (*a*) the strategy of the property tycoons and élite architects to situate their firms at socio-spatial nodes through which global flows pass in order to exploit these flows; (*b*) the importance of global city institutions to the activities of transnational cultures; and (*c*) the presence of the 'global ecumene'—a cosmopolitan city of people characterized by a 'single field of persistent interaction and exchange between cultures' (Hannerz, 1992*c*, 1996).

An Outline of the Book

There are five subsequent chapters in this book and the text is designed to follow the schema outlined below.

Chapter 2 is a substantive discussion about globalization and urban spatial change in the Pacific Rim. First, a definition of globalization is delineated. Secondly, five key dimensions of contemporary globalization processes are outlined that have significant impacts on the production of urban space. And thirdly, an overview of the development trends in the production of Pacific Rim UMPs is provided, set within a general discussion of spatial change in the Pacific Rim. Chapter 2 is designed to provide the overall context that Chapters 4 and 5 need to be viewed within.

Chapter 3 begins with a continuation of the discussion about the global space of flows that was initiated in Chapter 1. After an overview of several approaches to analysing the global space of flows in the urban context, I provide a detailed exposition of my adopted theoretical framework. There are two layers to the framework I am implementing, and these are explained in Chapter 3. To briefly foreshadow, the foundation of my conceptual framework is Arjun Appadurai's (1990*a*, 1990*b*, 1996) concept of the five 'scapes' (ethnoscape; mediascape; technoscape; finanscape; ideoscape) that make up the global cultural economy—the overlapping disjunctive scapes through which global flows pass. These global flows are inextricably bound to the perspectives and imaginations of geographically and historically situated actors. Appadurai's approach is effectively a decentred form of world-systems theory that reflects the influence of chaos theory. Following this relatively abstract discussion, I then draw upon complementary insights from socio-economic literature (in geography and sociology) to explain how the actors associated with global flows need to be 'situated' and 'embedded' in multiple networks

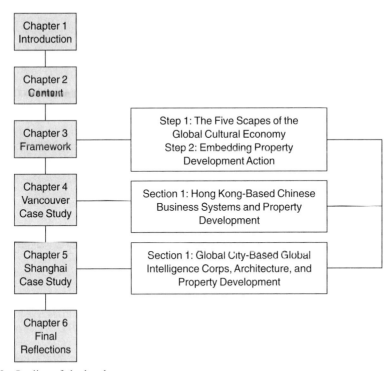

Fig. 1.3. Outline of the book

and institutions (as Appadurai suggests you have to). The basic theme of this latter section is that the production of global flows is a form of social action, a social construct that can be more subtly analysed through provisional accounts focused on specific actors, institutions, and events.

The discussion of situated actors in Chapter 3 is then extended in Section 1 of the two case study chapters (Chapter 4 and Chapter 5). Section 1 of Chapter 4 is a general analysis of the nature of Hong Kong-based ethnic Chinese business systems, while Section 1 of Chapter 5 is an analysis of the nature of global city-based GIC professional systems. Both of these analyses touch upon the main features of the institutions and networks that these transnational cultures are embedded in, and the importance of understanding how each transnational culture uses extended social networks and property development projects to achieve short- and long-term goals. This discussion should be conceived of as the initial application of the multi-level conceptual framework to the subject (see Fig. 1.3).

Following this relatively general analysis in Section 1 of the two case study chapters, Sections 2 of both Chapter 4 and Chapter 5 provide empirical case studies of the global flows associated with the Vancouver and Shanghai UMPs.

Chapter 6 provides a summary of the main findings of the research process, while also highlighting some implications for future theorization and research on the implications of globalization processes for urban change in cities.

The Appendix consists of a review of the research methodology I adopted in collecting and analysing data for the book. A substantial discussion on the role of *multi-locale* field research in conducting research on globalization processes is provided, along with a description of the specific techniques I employed to acquire data. I also explain the rationale for the narrative form that is employed in this book (the case study chapters in particular). The inclusion of a lengthy discussion on research methods is designed to highlight how 'grounded research' can (and should) be conducted on the processes globalizing cities.

2

Globalization and the Development of Pacific Rim Mega-Projects

Introduction

The nature of economic activity and social life is being reshaped in our 'globalizing era'. National societies and economies are becoming increasingly interdependent, albeit in a highly uneven manner. This is particularly true in the Pacific Rim—a 'region' experiencing unprecedented forces of change in a multitude of dimensions (Dirlik, 1993; Olds *et al.*, 1999).

This chapter provides a brief overview of the substantive context to this study of globalization and urban change in the Pacific Rim. More specifically, the confusing concept of globalization is discussed, five dimensions of contemporary globalization processes (all of which have significant impacts on the production of urban space) are delineated, and some background detail on the spatial context of the rise of contemporary Pacific Rim urban mega-projects is provided. This chapter is designed to lay the context for a more theoretical discussion of globalization in Chapter 3— indeed, in some ways this chapter provides fodder for a reassessment of how to understand globalization, particularly from perspectives that focus on the formation of networks and relations that reach across space; networks and relations that facilitate the rapid transformation of urban space.

Globalization

Throughout the 1980s and early 1990s, there has been an explosion of analyses of globalization processes from various theoretical perspectives (e.g. Castells, 1989, 1996; Harvey, 1989*a*; Featherstone, 1990*a*; Giddens, 1990, 1994; Held, 1991, 1993, 1996; Helleiner, 1992; McGrew, 1992*a*, 1992*b*; King, 1993; Massey, 1993; Amin and Thrift, 1994; Lash and Urry, 1994; Allen and Hamnett, 1995; Featherstone *et al.*, 1995; Waters, 1995; Appadurai, 1996; Hirst and Thompson, 1996; Mittelman, 1996; Sassen, 1996; Cox, 1997; Dicken *et al.*,

1997; Dicken, 1998; Kayatekin and Ruccio, 1998; Herod *et al.*, 1998; Held *et al.*, 1999; Kelly, 1999). Academic disciplines from business to geography have grappled with the implications of this concept for 'traditional' theories; theories often based upon analytical frameworks which conceptualize objects of study from the neighbourhood to the city to the nation in a bounded self-determinatory manner (Appadurai, 1996; Amin and Hausner, 1997). Concepts such as time–space compression (Harvey, 1989*a*), time–space distanciation (Giddens, 1990, 1994), time–space convergence (Janelle, 1969), and the global city (Sassen, 1991) have required the reformulation of theories for, as Lash and Urry (1994: 223) suggest, the ' "stretching" of social relations associated with globalization processes means that there has to be a profound redrawing of conventional academic boundaries, particularly between sociology, geography and history'. This is especially true at the urban level since 'whoever studies cities today, in any part of the world, is aware that what happens in a local neighbourhood is likely to be influenced by many factors— such as world money and commodity markets—operating at indefinite distance away from that neighbourhood itself' (Giddens, 1990: 64). Moreover, apart from the impact of globalization on cities, cities also play a key economic, socio-cultural, and political role in the *constitution* of globalization processes (Amin and Thrift, 1992; Sassen, 1994, 1999; Knox, 1995; UNCHS, 1996).

By globalization I mean (following Giddens, 1994: 4) the *process* of the transformation of space and time through 'action at distance'. Globalization refers to two distinct phenomena (Held, 1991: 145):

1) political, economic and social activity is becoming world-wide in scope; and

2) there has been an intensification of levels of interaction and interconnectedness between states and societies which make up an international society.

To be more concise, I follow Held *et al.*'s (1999: 16) definition of globalization as:

a process (or set of processes) which embodies a transformation in the spatial organization of social relations and transactions—assessed in terms of their extensity, intensity, velocity and impact—generating transcontinental or interregional flows and networks of activity, interaction, and the exercise of power.

While globalization is certainly not a new force (Wallerstein, 1974, 1979, 1983; Abu-Lughod, 1989; Held, 1996; Hirst and Thompson, 1996), it is the *nature* of contemporary globalization processes which are novel, with social relations stretching and intensifying 'in and through new dimensions of activity—technological, organizational, administrative and legal, among others' (Held, 1996: 340; also see Dicken *et al.*, 1997, Jessop, 1999, and United Nations Development Programme, 1999, on this issue). Equally important, people today are much more conscious of the world as a whole, and of global scale processes of change (Robertson, 1992). The near worldwide adoption of neoliberal policy prescriptions is an additional factor underlying the stretching and deepening of global-scale processes (Biersteker, 1995; Mittelman, 1996; Kelly, 1999).

As the above definitions imply, globalization must be seen as a multi-dimensional phenomena, involving 'highly intricate interactions between a whole variety of social, political and economic institutions across a spectrum of geographical scales' (Dicken *et al.*, 1997: 3; Jessop, 1999). Economistic analyses of globalization (e.g. see Hirst and Thompson, 1996) narrowly capture this multi-dimensional phenomenon with globalization shrinking the 'distance between elites', shifting 'key relations between producers and consumers', breaking down the 'many links between labor and family life', and obscuring the 'lines between temporary locales and imaginary national attachments' (Appadurai, 1996: 9–10).

Globalization should therefore be conceived of as a contingent and multi-centric mesh of interactive processes that operate at a variety of scales (Jessop, 1999). As such, 'local, and even personal, contexts of social experience' are implicated in the wider systemic changes taking place in the late 20th century (Giddens, 1994: 5; also see Beck *et al.*, 1994): one only has to link the commodity chain between the sweater on your body or your child's plastic rattle to the factories and workshop practices of coastal China to recognize this point. With the forces of globalization unevenly experienced across time and space, seemingly uniform flows of ideas, images, or capital are interpreted to an infinite degree creating diverse impacts in similar localities at the same time, or in the same locality at a different time. Thus, the processes that we define as globalization 'often act in contradictory ways, producing conflicts, disjunctures, and new forms of stratification' (Giddens, 1994: 5).

Finally, globalization is also a discourse of knowledge that is created and used to legitimize certain practices such as the framing of policy prescriptions. This discourse is a social construction, used by actors and institutions of all ideological shades to 'understand, explain and legitimize experiences' (Kelly, 1997: 4). The discourse of globalization shapes perspectives on which scale (or scales) of analysis it is important to focus on. As in all decisions over analysis, the choice of scale (e.g. the 'global', the 'local', or 'glocalization') is:

neither an ontologically given and a priori definable geographical territory nor a politically neutral discursive strategy in the construction of narratives. Scale, both in its metaphorical use and material construction, is highly fluid and dynamic, and both processes and effects can easily move from scale to scale and affect people in different ways, depending on the scale at which the process operates. . . . Scale is, consequently, not socially or politically neutral, but embodies and expresses power relationships. (Swyngedouw, 1997: 140)

In short, globalization is a discourse of knowledge that elevates awareness of the links between various scales of social life. It is also a contested discourse exhibiting many variants. However, some variants are clearly more influential than others (Leyshon, 1997; Marcuse, 1997a; Thrift, 1999a).

Globalization and the Production of Urban Space: Five Dimensions

In order to examine the subject of globalization with respect to the production of urban space (and the two case study UMPs in particular) five key dimensions of contemporary globalization processes are outlined: the development and restructuring of the international financial system; the globalization of property markets; the changing role of the transnational corporation; the stretching of social relations, transnational/epistemic communities; and travelling and networking. Each of these five interwoven dimensions plays an important (albeit uneven) role in the processes which influence the nature of the Vancouver and Shanghai development projects.

The Development and Restructuring of the International Financial System

All sectors of the world economy have been deeply affected by recent developments in the international financial system. The nature, form, pace, and scale of finance capital availability has shifted with the introduction or restructuring of equity and debt financial instruments such as mutual funds, the trend towards market deregulation and standardization, the lowering of barriers on cross-border capital flows into previous off-limits sectors including property, increasingly rapid currency rate fluctuations, and the continued development and use of 'offshore' financial centres. Moreover, financial sectors are also affected by the coordinating activities of supra-national institutions such as the International Monetary Fund (IMF), the World Bank, and the World Trade Organization (WTO).

Finance and credit is increasingly available on a global 'private' scale beyond the bounds of national control (Strange, 1988; Leyshon and Thrift, 1992; World Bank, 1993a, 1996a, 1996b; BIS, 1996, 1997, 1998; Sassen, 1999); a trend that was accentuated in the 1980s as governments around the world have chosen (or were convinced/pushed) to 'throw in the towel' and embrace 'liberalization as a doctrine' (Akyüz, 1993: 1; also see Biersteker, 1995). For example, a World Bank (1993a: 1) report notes that there has been a 'radical shift in the pattern of external financial flows to developing countries in the early 1990s, from debt to equity financing and from bank to non bank sources' such as international equity and bond markets. This trend has been particularly evident in the Asia-Pacific region, and it helped generate some of the causal factors associated with the late 1990s 'Asian economic crisis' (Henderson, 1999; Paderanga, 1999).

These changes have enabled a diverse array of actors to become involved in worldwide speculative activities such as property investment, or large-scale property development projects (Sassen, 1999). For example, Shanghai Municipal Government can access 'concession funds from foreign credit agen cies for its projects' (Sender, 1993: 72), thereby loosening dependence upon the central government. However, it should be noted that access to such sources of international capital is far from equitable.

One of the consequences of such developments in this multi-centred financial system has been an unprecedented growth in the volume, complexity, and pace of international financial transactions. Official grants and official loans, private loans, foreign direct investment, derivatives trading, and portfolio equity investment (comprising external stock offerings in the form of depository receipts, country funds, and direct equity investments by foreign investors) have all grown rapidly throughout the 1980s and most of the 1990s (IMF, 1992; Ahmed and Gooptu, 1993; World Bank, 1993*a*; BIS, 1996). For example, international capital markets turned over approximately US$75 trillion per year in 1992, and international trade amounted to some $2.5 to $3 trillion per year in the first half of the 1990s (Ruggie, 1993: 141). Even more startling, foreign exchange transactions amounted to approximately US$1.2 trillion per day in 1995, and then increased again to an estimated daily average of $1.5 trillion in April 1998, up from $590 billion in 1989. Of this amount in 1995, $464 billion was traded in London, $244 billion in New York, and $161 billion in Tokyo (BIS, 1996: 96; 1999).

Foreign direct investment (FDI) flows grew rapidly in terms of volume and complexity during the 1980s and the first half of the 1990s. Global outflows peaked in the late 1980s, declined slightly from 1990–4 (the main period of focus in this book), rose from 1995 on, and then were drastically reshaped by the 'Asian economic crisis' that started in 1997 (BIS, 1995; UNCTAD, 1996, 1998; Kelly and Olds, 1999). Throughout this period key investment roles have been played by 'developed' countries, especially the USA, the UK, and Japan.

Regionally, FDI flows into developing countries increased between the mid-1980s and 1997, with Asian nations taking an increasingly larger share (see Table 2.1). Further, while the 'Asian economic crisis' that started in 1997 dramatically reduced the scale of portfolio investment flows to Asia, levels of FDI have been maintained at relatively significant rates (International Chamber of Commerce and UNCTAD, 1998; UNCTAD, 1998).

The first half of the 1990s was also a period marked by significant inward investment to North America from Asian countries such as Japan or Hong Kong (Douglass, 1987; Davis, 1992; Edgington, 1992, 1994; OECD, 1992). Overall investment flows have slightly decreased since that time, and FDI geographical and sectoral distribution has changed towards intra-regional flows (EC/Japan–Asia), a growth of Developing Asian

Table 2.1. Regional distribution of inward and outward FDI stock, 1985, 1990, 1995, and 1997 (per cent)

Region/country	Inward FDI stock				Outward FDI stock			
	1985	1990	1995	1997	1985	1990	1995	1997
Developed countries	72.3	79.3	70.6	68.0	95.7	95.6	91.5	90.2
Western Europe	33.6	44.1	39.1	36.9	44.4	50.8	51.1	50.4
European Union	31.2	41.5	36.3	34.6	40.6	46.3	45.1	45.1
Other Western Europe	2.3	2.7	2.8	2.3	3.8	4.5	5.9	5.3
USA	24.4	22.7	20.5	20.9	36.4	25.5	25.6	25.6
Japan	0.6	0.6	1.2	1.0	6.4	11.8	8.5	8.0
Developing Countries	27.7	20.6	28.1	30.2	4.3	4.4	8.4	9.7
Africa	3.1	2.2	2.1	1.9	0.9	0.7	0.5	0.5
Latin America and the Caribbean	10.1	7.1	10.2	10.9	1.1	0.7	0.9	1.0
Developing Europe	0.1	0.1	0.1	0.1	—	—	—	—
Asia	14.3	11.1	15.6	17.2	2.3	2.9	6.9	8.2
West Asia	5.7	2.8	2.1	1.7	0.3	0.4	0.3	0.3
Central Asia	—	—	0.1	0.2	—	—	—	—
South, East, and Southeast Asia	8.6	8.3	13.4	15.3	2.0	2.6	6.4	7.9
The Pacific	0.2	0.1	0.1	0.1	—	—	—	—
Central and Eastern Europe	—	0.1	1.3	1.8	—	—	0.1	0.2
World	100	100	100	100	100	100	100	100

Source: UNCTAD (1998, table 1.3, p. 5).

Economies (DAE) investment abroad, a greater emphasis on investment in services (spurred by worldwide privatization initiatives), and higher value-added manufacturing industries (OECD, 1992, 1993; Allen, 1995*b*). Obviously, credit availability and the state of the world economy is a critical factor in FDI flow (see Strange, 1988, on the important role of structural power over credit formation).

Capitalization levels in 'emerging'[1] equity markets literally exploded in the 1980s and the first half of the 1990s. While the market value of quoted firms was only $100 billion in 1983, it reached nearly $1 trillion by October 1993 (IMF, 1994*a*: 26). As in most industrial countries, 'financial intermediation through capital markets' in developing countries (especially in the Asia-Pacific region) 'has increased in importance relative to intermediation through banks' (BIS, 1996: 120). Further, in relation to GDP, the stock market capitalization

---

[1] The general consensus of international investors in the early 1990s is that 'emerging markets' are stockmarkets in the developing countries of Asia, Latin America, and Eastern Europe. The term 'emerging market' is used with some reservation as it implies a North-centred conceptual framework wherein 'development' (modernization) occurs in stages over time as increasing numbers of countries fall under the orbit of the formal international financial system. See Ó Tuathail (1997*b*) and Sidaway and Pryke (2000) for critical geographical perspectives on 'emerging markets'.

of developing countries such as China, Hong Kong, Malaysia, and Singapore grew significantly in the late 1980s and first half of the 1990s (BIS, 1995: 151), though the late 1990s Asian economic crisis led to drastic falls in capitalization levels. At a sectoral level, the proportion of total stock market capitalization represented by property companies is very large in developing countries. This feature is even more pronounced in the Asia-Pacific region where, for example, 31 per cent of the constituent companies (by capitalization value) in the Hong Kong stock exchange are from the property sector (The Stock Exchange of Hong Kong, 1997: 15). These 'emerging stock markets' effectively provide the Hong Kong-based property tycoons active in Vancouver with access to the global capital flows that their firms need to develop mega-projects (Olds and Yeung, 1999).

The Globalization of Property Markets

Property markets are one sector that is being radically transformed by the globalization of finance and the restructuring of FDI. Property markets have traditionally been analysed from a local or national perspective and, in contrast to 'goods' such as securities or sectors such as manufacturing, they have received very little academic attention (exceptions include: Goldberg, 1985, 1989, 1991*a*, 1993; Thrift, 1986, 1987; Berry and Huxley, 1992; Edgington, 1992, 1994; Logan, 1993; Berry, 1994; Coakley, 1994; Lizieri and Doblias, 1995; Lizieri and Finlay, 1995; Seek, 1996; Haila, 1997; Mitchell and Olds, 2000). This is unfortunate as property makes up one of three major factors in the production process (land, labour, and capital), and real estate represents much of the world's wealth (somewhere between 20 and 60 per cent according to Mueller, 1992).

Property markets have become increasingly integrated into the fluxes of the global economy and regional development processes. With the deregulation of financial markets (especially international lending), the growth and geographical expansion of pension fund investing, the emergence of new mechanisms to link real estate financing more closely to broader capital markets (securitization), the lowering of barriers to foreign investment in land, and the development of vastly improved information databases on property markets, global real-estate strategies are now being pursued with vigour (Logan, 1993; Lizieri and Doblias, 1995; EIU, 1997; Haila, 1997). Today one cannot make sense of the downtown residential and commercial property markets in cities such as Hong Kong, Sydney, London, Shanghai, or Vancouver without 'taking sophisticated account of the very complex fiscal and investment flows' that link national economies through a 'global grid of currency speculation and capital transfer' (Appadurai, 1990*a*: 8).

As with stocks or bonds, investors are seeking to diversify their investment portfolios in both a sectoral and a geographic sense and property offers a perceived opportunity to improve risk-adjusted returns. Particular sectors of the property market that are focused on include high class ('Grade A') office space, 'trophy buildings', luxury condominium housing, hotels, vacant suburban tracts of land, rental housing, and industrial land, with strategic planning for both development and marketing phases often conducted 'in the world context' (Rosehaugh Stanhope Developments, 1991; Haila, 1997). Given their economic size and cultural make-up, transnational property firms tend to be interested in larger projects which offer better economies of scale while also enabling the developers to produce an UMP which symbolizes their global image and reach (Haila, 1997). Moreover, in countries such as China, there has been a massive influx of foreign capital in the late 1980s and early 1990s spurred on by urban land-market reform experiments which have been used to develop residential and commercial property, particularly in the coastal regions (Dowall, 1993*a*; Ho, 1993; Jones Lang Wootton, 1993*b*; Seek, 1996; Colliers Jardine, 1997). The majority of the investment capital in Chinese property is derived from Hong Kong and Taiwanese firms, Chinese state enterprises (often 'round routed' through Hong Kong to take advantage of tax incentives) and, of late, global pension-funds driven by a herd instinct towards the world's latest 'sexy' destination. While the attraction of property markets in places like Shanghai started waning in approximately 1995, it is clear that in an overall sense, global capital has been flowing into Asia-Pacific property markets, linking together cities and engendering relationships of uneven interdependencies across space. Such flows ultimately facilitate the *building* (in a material sense) of the global city (Sassen, 1991; Haila, 1997).

The Transnational Corporation

The main actor both instigating and taking advantage of the restructuring of the global financial system and of the development of world property markets is the transnational corporation (TNC). The TNC, alone or acting as a partner with the state, has played a critical role in UMP developments throughout the world. TNCs are developing property to serve both domestic and foreign markets as they seek to play cyclical markets (with varying degrees of success) in growth regions spurred on by access to credit from an array of sources. Both global and regional strategies have been developed, often built upon existing economic and cultural linkages with particular cities or regions. For example, companies such as Bangkok Land, Kumagai Gumi, Cheung Kong, Henderson Land, Hang Lung Development, and New World Development are playing a prominent role in the development of large-scale tracts of land in Thailand and China, as they seek to take advantage of rapid economic growth, the rise of domestic incomes, and the opening up of new areas of cities and regions through infrastructure provision (*The Economist*, 18 July 1992: 21–4; Sender, 1993; Morgan Stanley, 1994). The scale of such developments is breathtaking. For example, by November 1994, New World Development had acquired land in China for the development of property totalling (gross floor area) 214 million sq. ft., and Henderson Land was developing 35 million sq. ft. (Morgan Stanley, 1994: 13–14). By 1996, New World Development had invested HK$9.2 billion in China, 41 per cent of which was directed into property (UBS Global Research, 1995: 30).

Transnational firms also play a key role in providing background support work for the projects. Chartered surveyors such as FPD Savills, Jones Lang LaSalle, or Colliers Jardine provide services including the development or evaluation of corporate property strategies, market analysis, the facilitation of necessary planning consents, leasing, and property management (Thrift, 1986, 1987; Leyshon *et al.*, 1987; Haila, 1997). Jones Lang LaSalle, for example, has a highly integrated network operating in 34 countries around the world, and it maintains some of the largest private databases in the world, including the ability to model central business districts in key global cities on CADD. The company provides wide-ranging integrated expertise on a local, regional, and global level to owners, occupiers, and investors. In Hong Kong, FPD Savills, CY Leung & Company Limited, and Brooke Hiller Parker are rapidly expanding their activities into Chinese cities such as Shanghai, while others such as Vigers and Colliers Jardine are concentrating on the facilitation of Hong Kong investment into Vancouver's property market. In all cases, chartered surveyors work in close liaison with legal firms, accountancy firms, and banks while guiding the investment of capital flows into foreign property markets.

The Stretching of Social Relations, World Social Networks, and Epistemic Communities

The stretching of social relations, world social networks, and epistemic communities is a dimension often overlooked by some of the more economistic analyses of globalization. Globalization implies the 'stretching out over space of relations of power, and of relations imbued with meaning and symbolism' (Massey, 1992: 4). Or, in Giddens's (1990: 64) words, globalization entails the 'intensification of worldwide social relations which link distant localities in such a way that local happenings are shaped by events occurring miles away'. Increasingly, social life is being reordered (and extended) across time and space—time–space distanciation—and analysts need to pay greater attention to 'the complex relations between *local involvements* (circumstances of copresence) and *interaction across distance* (the connections of presence and absence)' (emphasis in original).

The processes of globalization are effectively dependent upon the role of 'expert' knowledge with respect to the development and transition of the spheres of production, circulation, and consumption (Strange, 1988; Giddens, 1990; Corbridge *et al.*, 1994; Lash and Urry, 1994). These 'expert systems' not only enable the intensification of worldwide social relations to occur, but they also work through the formation of such relations.

Pacific Rim UMPs, for example, are activated by extended and reflexive social networks associated with transnational actors who have the power, agility, and interest to operate on the global stage (Olds, 1997; Mitchell and Olds, 2000). The globalization of property development capital, development expertise, and urban design images are all dependent upon the knowledge and social relations of professionals working in the producer services sector in cities around the world (Sassen, 1994; Dicken, 1998). Lash and Urry (1994: 254) suggest that the development of such expert systems is related to the nature of modernity where social relations are:

disembedded from local contexts of action (see Giddens, 1991a: 209). Disembedding means the 'lifting out' of social relations from local involvements and their recombination across larger spans of time and space. Such disembedding depends upon trust. People need to have faith in institutions or processes of which they possess only limited knowledge. Trust arises from the development of expert or professional knowledge, which gives people faith, including the forms of transport which convey them through time-space.

Analysts are increasingly paying attention to the role of worldwide social networks of knowledge-based experts who have the resources and power (or access to power) to impact on decisions in arenas such as foreign policy, economic policy, or in this particular case, property development and planning. Sometimes called 'epistemic communities', these social structures are 'a network of professionals with recognized expertise and competence in a particular domain and an authoritative claim to policy-relevant knowledge within that domain or issue-area' (Haas, 1992: 3). In sectoral terms, this is the new 'professional-managerial class' which is associated with information-processing activities related to the restructuring of the world economy (Castells, 1989: 348). In more sociological terms, these are the 'emerging sets of "third cultures"', which themselves are conduits for all sorts of diverse cultural flows; a 'coterie of new specialists and professionals' who work outside the 'traditional professional and organizational cultures of the nation states' (Featherstone, 1990a: 1, 8). These are cosmopolitan people who revel in travel; they are hybridized transnational intellectuals 'who keep in touch via global cultural flows and who are not only at home in other cultures, but seek out and adopt a reflexive, metacultural or aesthetic stance to divergent cultural experiences' (Featherstone, 1990a: 9; also see Hannerz, 1990, Friedman, 1997, and Mitchell, 1997b). The geographical imaginations of these people orients them beyond 'home', beyond their nation state, towards new and 'exotic' frontiers. However, given their background, professional skills, and need to engage in profit-oriented ventures, their imagination only directs them to places and issues integrally bound up with the global space of flows.

There is an emerging (and amazingly small) epistemic community of developers, architects, planners, and academics who draw upon each other (or each other's work) in planning and building UMPs throughout the world. These actors (the GIC) work within architectural, engineering, and property development TNCs, and they are building up a critical mass of expertise and know-how which facilitates the extremely complex, lengthy, and risky UMP development process. Government officials within cities where UMPs have been developed are also gaining expertise, and it is a common trend for them to be 'headhunted' by private sector developers, to work within their home city, or to work on UMPs in other cities around the world. Such a knowledge base clearly has positive impacts for the companies as well, and it is an important factor in the global expansion of engineering firms such as the Ove Arup Partnership (Rimmer, 1991*a*); a process linked to the dissemination of urban development models (Rimmer, 1991*c*). Section 1 of Chapter 5 discusses the nature of the GIC in considerable detail, while Section 2 examines their involvement and impacts in the planning of Shanghai's new international financial centre in Pudong.

In a related sense, the social and financial networks of the *Chinese diaspora*[2]—ethnic Chinese living outside mainland China—plays a critical role in much of the restructuring taking place in the Pacific Rim. This is a trend which Western financial and state institutions are only now beginning to systematically comprehend (East Asia Analytical Unit, 1995; Gereffi, 1996; Olds and Yeung, 1999). Numbering only some 55 million people (including those living in Hong Kong and Taiwan), the ethnic Chinese diaspora is associated with access to formal and informal capital sources, a complex and worldwide social network, an historically close relationship to property, and a preference for 'deal-making' (Goldberg, 1985; Redding, 1990; Mitchell, 1993*a*). Chinese developers such as Li Ka-shing and family are developing a vast array of property and infrastructure projects throughout the Pacific Rim, including Vancouver's UMP, and major port and property developments in Shanghai. While the huge sources of capital are clearly significant, the major property development projects of the overseas Chinese firms depend upon the nurturing of social networks for strategic positioning in the development and execution of investment deals (UBS Global Research, 1995). Section 1 of Chapter 4 discusses ethnic Chinese business systems in greater detail, while Section 2 examines the role of prominent Chinese tycoons in the planning and development of Vancouver's largest ever downtown redevelopment project.

---

[2] See Chapter 3 for a discussion of the use of the term 'ethnic Chinese' and 'overseas Chinese'. I would also add that the Chinese diaspora is incredibly complex in historic, cultural, linguistic, class, and gender senses, and the concept is best used in provisional accounts (such as a case study). Ien Ang's (1994) article 'On not speaking Chinese: postmodern ethnicity and the politics of diaspora' is a sharp critique of analyses which decontextualize and flatten difference when speaking of the Chinese diaspora.

Travelling and Networking

Travelling and networking is the final dimension worth noting. Apart from the usual emphasis on tourism growth figures, it is important to highlight the increasing amount of travel being undertaken by politicians, developers, architects, and planners who visit cities throughout the world where UMPs are being developed. For example, one Tokyo Metropolitan Government planner passed through Vancouver in 1989 during the midst of a two month North American tour to every single waterfront development project. His task was to generate innovative ideas for their Tokyo Bay waterfront projects. In another case, the British Urban Regeneration Association (BURA) sponsored a 1992 tour of UK planners, academics, and developers to several Japanese cities to examine waterfront mega-projects in Tokyo. Real estate programmes in North America frequently sponsor 'international' field trips for their students to visit more well-known cities and development projects such as *La Défense* in Paris, or Docklands in London. Travel permits the acquisition of direct knowledge about the sites from a wider array of sources than would be the case otherwise, and it is deemed worthwhile (*vis-à-vis* expenses) because of the scale of the UMP developments, and the vast resources committed to them. Similarly, there has been a spate of conferences in the 1990s which comparatively examined international urban development policies and projects, and these events have aided the dissemination process. The UN is also involved in supporting the analysis and dissemination of UMPs and associated 'mega-infrastructure' through the UN Centre for Regional Development (UNCRD) which is based in Nagoya (see the summer 1993 issue of the UNCRD's *Regional Development Dialogue*). At all of these events, it is common for the more well-known mega-project architects, planners, and developers to speak about their experiences, and their visions for the future.

Mega-Projects, the Pacific Rim, and New Forms of Urbanity

These broad dimensions of globalization have contributed to the formation of new configurations in the social and spatial systems of the Pacific Rim. In very general terms, the spatial context for the emergence of late twentieth-century UMPs in the Pacific Rim has been described by the geographer Peter Rimmer (1991*b*, 1994) as one of mega-cities, multi-layered networks, and development corridors. UMPs are one component of:

(1) the rapid growth of urban areas, where levels of urbanization have increased because of natural population growth, rural–urban migration, the reclassification (or annexation) of previously 'external' areas, and international migration (Jones, 1991);

competition (Castells, 1989; Harvey, 1989*b*; Lee and Schmidt-Marwede, 1993; Fainstein, 1994; Hall and Hubbard, 1998). At the local level when the state does not have access to political jurisdiction and significant capital, generic policy emphasis tends to be directed to the development of more streamlined planning approval procedures (Beazley, 1994; also see Thornley, 1993, in the European context), programmes, and projects to alter the image of the city to meet the value system of international investors (e.g. an emphasis on business tourism facilities such as convention centres, festival market-places, luxury hotels, aesthetically pleasing CBDs). In short, a 'global city discourse' has emerged and this discourse is being used by political and business groups to ensure urban policy is formulated in a market-friendly environment (Machimura, 1998). In such a context, the proposal of an UMP from an outside investor is generally supported since it is perceived as an opportunity to benefit from inward investment, regenerate the city, and act as a symbolic indicator of a 'robust' local and regional economy (Singapore's Suntec City, or Pacific Place in Vancouver is clearly this type of space). However, there are obviously variations between places in terms of what (if any) incentives the state will offer (e.g. in the Vancouver case direct tax incentives were not offered to attract foreign investment, though the provincial government did offer to take responsibility for 'toxic soil' clean-up expenses).

In contrast, when the local state has a tradition of proactive development, political jurisdiction, political impetus, *and* access to major sources of capital (via savings, the issuance of bonds, inter-governmental transfer, and/or partnerships with senior levels of government and the private sector) they commonly coordinate the development of the UMP themselves. This is particularly the case in Asia-Pacific where the state plays a crucial role in economic development initiatives (on the 'developmental state' see: Amsden, 1989; Haggard, 1990; Douglass, 1994; Castells, 1992; Harris, 1992; Appelbaum and Henderson, 1992; Woo-Cumings, 1999). The perception of the forces of globalization exhorts the state to focus on *local* space in an effort to provide both a real and a symbolic node, a state of the art command and control centre, to 'hook up' to the global economy, thereby theoretically improving city, regional, and national comparative advantage in a global sense. The UMP, in this sense, could be conceived of as 'the formation of space for global control functions' (Machimura, 1992: 123) or a 'functioning way-station for the space of money flows' (Corbridge and Thrift, 1994: 15). The Sudirman Central Business District in Jakarta or Lujiazui Central Finance District in Shanghai is clearly this type of space.

The production of urban space in such a monumental style reflects the specificities of each locality's history, and the 'complex interplay' with the global flows driving the restructuring process (King, 1993: 89; Lash and Urry, 1994: 321). The nature of the 'distant voices' in these places is changing in the short and long term for, as Amin and Thrift (1994:

10) remark: 'Globalization . . . represents a redefinition of places as juxta-positions of intersecting, overlapping, and unconnected global flows and historical fixities. It characterizes localities as territories living with differ-ent bits and pieces of the transnational division of labour as well as their own inherited industrial traditions.'

Understanding the refashioning of space and place in the context of the global space of flows requires analytical approaches which mirror the complex and multi-layered processes at work in our cities today. Or, as Massey (1993: 68) justly suggests, a 'progressive sense of place' would understand that the 'char-acter of a place' can 'only be constructed by linking that place to places beyond' and that what we need is a 'global sense of the local, a global sense of place' (also see Hannerz, 1992*a*, 1992*b*, 1992*c*, 1996; Murdoch, 1997; Whatmore and Thorne, 1997). It is this 'relational' challenge from Doreen Massey that I seek to address in developing my conceptual framework, and in the theoretically informed empirical analyses presented in Chapters 4 and 5.

Summary

The development processes of UMPs are deeply implicated in globalization processes. Although there are significant differences between the nature of UMPs in different cities and countries, they are all being influenced by the forces and perceptions of the restructuring of the international financial sys-tem, the globalization of property markets, the changing role of the TNC, the development of global-scale social networks, and the increasing importance (and ease) of travelling and networking.

The opening up of land for the development of UMPs is related to the restructuring of the economy, and the growth of the tertiary and quaternary sectors of the economy. Most UMPs are developed on waterfront land in for-mer industrial and transport (port and rail) districts. Large tracts of state-owned land in the city has also become available via privatization initiatives. In short, UMPs fill the gaping wounds of the 'postmodern city'; a city integrated into the processes of global systemic restructuring.

Some UMPs are designed to be the functional and symbolic 'command and control centres' of the world economy; and as such they are composed of significant amounts of 'Grade A' commercial space which is wired with the latest telecommunications infrastructure. Other UMPs are consumption-oriented, and they tend to consist of expensive condominium buildings and retail centres designed for, and marketed to, the burgeoning professional-managerial class.

The finance, design, construction, and marketing phases of these projects are structured by the agents of contemporary globalization processes—global property developers, including ethnic Chinese property tycoons, and professional élites, including the GIC. These transnational cultures have developed a comprehensive knowledge base and understanding of current and future trends in the design and commodification of built space for the global stage (in the purest marketing sense). Local influences are incorporated where they augment the overall aims of the projects, though such projects must be seen as the manifestation of the intentional global(izing) city.

3

The Social Construction
of Global Flows

Introduction

This chapter outlines a multi-level theoretical framework that is heavily influenced by the writings of Arjun Appadurai (1990a, 1990b, 1996) and a broad group of geographers and sociologists working in the 'socio-economic' school of analysis. The basic aim of the chapter is to highlight how I analyse the intertwined material and non-material global flows which are associated with Pacific Place in Vancouver, and Lujiazui Central Finance District, Shanghai.

The first section of this chapter is a critical overview of the development of the 'global space of flows' concept. I subsequently explain why my adopted conceptual framework was chosen, and then work through the specifics of how the framework can be applied in the Vancouver and Shanghai case studies. As noted in Chapter 1, two steps of the framework are outlined here, and they specifically inform the third step (which is Section 1 in both Chapter 4 and Chapter 5).

Interrogating the Human Geography
of the Global Space of Flows

The contemporary world is being impacted in an uneven manner by global flows of capital, people (labour, migrants, tourists, professionals), information, images, technologies, and products. Held *et al.* (1999), among many analysts, note that flows are increasing in scale and velocity; they are increasingly organized beyond the national scale; they are increasingly independent, yet still shaped by the national state; and they do not originate from all parts of the world equally (on this last point see Sklair, 1991; Lash and Urry, 1994; Allen and Hamnett, 1995; Cox, 1997; UNDP, 1999). While space limitations preclude a full summary of the writings about 'global flows' suffice it to say the vast majority of the literature is focused on economic flows (capital in particular) from both political economy and neoclassical perspectives.

In the context of expanding global flows, an increasing number of analysts are reimagining the city and emphasizing the need for an ontology of movement, and new conceptualizations of the 'space of flows' (Castells, 1989, 1993a, 1993b, 1996). The urban anthropologist Ulf Hannerz (1990, 1992a, 1992b, 1992c, 1996), for example, writes of the historical increase in global 'cultural flows', the emergence of the global ecumene—'a single field of persistent interaction and exchange between cultures'—and the enabling role of the world city in the formation of such 'open ramifying networks'. Sociologists Scott Lash and John Urry (1994) analyse 'asymmetrical' flows of subjects and objects at a global scale—the people, ideas, images, technologies, and capital which make up the modern economies of signs and space (which shape the dynamics of 'disorganized capitalism'). They pay particular attention to the role of the global city as a 'switching' centre of 'information, knowledge, images and symbols' (1994: 220) where global flows are mediated by networked institutions employing highly skilled, cosmopolitan, and reflexive professionals. Kevin Robins (1991: 12–13) summarizes several other writers who focus on flows and the city:

Now . . . the city has become integrated not only into more complex, international transportation systems, but also into global information and communications networks. We can now talk of a process of globalization or transnationalization in the transformation of urban space and form. Manuel Castells describes the advent of the 'informational city', and identifies 'the historical emergence of the space of flows, superseding the space of places'. Others have described this same process in similar ways. Suggesting that 'things are not defined by their physical boundaries any more', the [deconstructionist] architect Bernard Tschumi points to the advent of the 'exploded city'. Paul Virilio calls it the 'overexposed city': 'In the place of a discrete boundary in space, demarcating distinct spaces, one sees spaces co-joined by semi-permeable membranes, exposed to flows of information in particular ways'.

As Robins notes, Manuel Castells is one of the analysts most commonly associated with the terminology 'the space of flows', and his influential writings on the development of the informational city are relevant for this research topic. In a joint essay with Jeffrey Henderson (Castells and Henderson, 1987), the two authors attempt to outline the main contours of a new model of capitalist development, and the implications of this model for urban and regional development processes. They focus on the interaction of global economic restructuring, technological revolution (the rise and impact of new information technologies), and the emergence of socio-political processes (where 'the economy (under capitalism) structures society') (1987: 3). With the emergence of truly *global* restructuring processes, there is a 'tendency for a space of flows to supersede the space of places' where 'the actual dynamics of a given territory rely mainly on the connection of the population and activities of that territory to activities and decisions that go far beyond the boundaries of each locality' (ibid.). In such a process the 'dominant logic is based upon flows' where places (communities) tend to be opposed to an 'abstract, flow-oriented logic of worldwide organizations and interests'. They carry on (1987: 17) to note that the contemporary territorial dynamics 'tend to be organized around the contradiction between placeless power and powerless places', although a note at the end of the essay clarifies that 'placeless power' was a phrase meant to emphasize that information-flow technologies are transforming our world at a global scale, and being used by global actors to 'increasingly' penetrate and determine the lives of local populations (i.e. they realize power will 'always originate from within particular places').

Later publications by Castells (1989, 1993*a*, 1993*b*, 1996) extend this focus on the space of flows in the context of the development of an 'informational mode of development'. The informational mode of development is conceived of as a complex and interacting system of technological and organizational processes which underlie economic growth and social change—a 'techno-organizational system' (1989: 19). This system is formed through the rapid development of new information technologies, and related organizational shifts (the concentration of knowledge in powerful organization; the shift towards flexibility; moves towards decentralization) and it interacts and articulates with the restructuring of capitalism (after the oil crisis of the early 1970s) to create 'the framework shaping the dynamics of our society and our space' (1989: 28). In the new informational mode of development: 'the source of productivity lies in the technology of knowledge generation, information processing, and symbol communication . . . what is specific about the informational mode of development is the action of knowledge upon knowledge itself as the main source of productivity' (Castells, 1996: 17).

As a result, major social transformations have occurred, including the rise of the *informational society*—'a society whose sources of economic productivity, cultural hegemony, and political-military power depend, fundamentally, on the capacity to retrieve, store, process, and generate information and knowledge' (Castells, 1993*b*: 248–9; also see Castells, 1996). Economically, a truly global economy has emerged which 'works in real time at a planetary scale. It is an economy where capital flows, labour markets, commodity markets, information, raw materials, management and organization are internationalized and fully interdependent throughout the planet' (1993*b*: 249); it is also an economy where the production of surplus is increasingly derived through information processing and knowledge generation via the networked enterprise.

Spatially, we see, among other things, the emergence of the *informational city*, a nodal point connecting global networks (i.e. this is a conception of the city as 'process' versus the city as 'form') (Castells, 1996: 410). The informational city is increasingly dependent upon information-processing activities, and it is characterized by the development of concentrated business centres (including UMPs), decentralized 'back offices', and social polarization related to dualistic labour markets. The informational city is derived out of a spatial logic that:

is determined by the pre-eminence of the *space of flows* over the space of places. By space of flows, I refer to the system of exchange—of information, capital and power—that structures the basic processes of societies, economies, and states among different localities, regardless of localization. I call it 'space' because it does have a spatial materiality. This is comprised of the directional centres located in a few selective areas of a few, selected localities; the telecommunication system dependent upon telecommunication facilities and services unevenly distributed in the space, thus marking a telecommunicated space; the advanced transportation system, that makes such nodal points dependent upon major airports and airline services, upon freeway systems, upon high-speed trains; the security systems necessary for the protection of such directional spaces, surrounded by a potentially hostile world; and the symbolic marking of such spaces by the new monumentality of abstraction, making the locales of the space of flows meaningfully meaningless, both in their internal arrangement and in their architectural form. The space of flows, superseding the space of places, epitomizes the increasing differentiation between power and experience [place], the separation of meaning [place] from function (Castells, 1993*b*: 254, emphasis added).

The actors behind this dynamic yet destructive process (the 'new managerial-technocratic-political élite') seek to form a suitable architecture to the space of flows, just as they achieve their power by working through and extracting from the space of flows. These mutually supportive goals which, according to Castells, are derived from *a* functional logic [capital accumulation] are approached through the formation of networks of interaction (using the space of flows) between relevant actors such as the state, international financial firms, international property developers, and international architectural firms. In his words, 'there is a shift, in fact, from the centrality of the organizational unit to the network of information and decision. In other words, *flows, rather than organizations*, become the units of work, decision, and output accounting' (1989: 142; emphasis in original).

While there is insufficient space to highlight the full arguments within influential texts such as Castells's *The Informational City* or *The Network Society*, it is clear that the analysis of Castells (1989, 1996) and many others (e.g. Sassen, 1991, 1994; Lash and Urry, 1994) is fundamentally based upon a series of dualisms:

Future	Past
Flows	Places
Function	Experience
Power	Culture
Global	Local

much like Zukin's (1991) division between 'market' and 'place', with the left column superseding the right. From Castells's (1989: 169–70) perspective, for example, the networked organizations (such as Hong Kong-based property conglomerates) structuring the global space of flows, and the material and non-material flows which shift along this spatial architecture, are organizationally placeless, and increasingly independent from a place-bound societal logic. In other words the spatial dimension of the space of flows develops out of the logic of organizations (which are large-scale information-processing complexes) which prizes access to the network of flows above all other goals (Castells, 1996).

While there are considerable insights in Castells's analysis of the processes constituting 'globalization', and the restructuring of space and place, his account is far too ambitious and abstract. It could be argued that such conceptualizations of placeless organizational logics, all-powerful organizations restructuring static places to facilitate flows, are too firm, too grand, and lacking in the dynamism that might be evident in more provisional accounts about globalization (M. P. Smith, 1994; Thrift, 1995; Dicken *et al.*, 1997). As Thrift (1995: 34–35) argues, the 'space of flows' can be: 'revealed as a partial and contingent affair, just like all other human enterprises, which are not abstract or abstracted but consists of social networks, often of quite limited size even though they might span the globe'.

Can we simply assume that 'movement and flow' are overwhelming the 'identity of place' as Robins (1991: 13) and Castells suggest? Perhaps so in some cases, though in many cases flows may be simply transforming the identity of places which have *always* been intersected by flows from a variety of scales (Massey, 1993; Allen *et al.*, 1999). This situation may be even more true in Shanghai and Vancouver—two port cities with long histories of contact with 'external' forces, and diverse cultures. Or perhaps the global space of flows takes considerably more effort to bring into effect than Castells implies.

More specifically, much discussion about the global space of flows (from Castells and others) falls into six main traps. First, narratives about the flows are fundamentally abstracted, decontextualized, and dehumanized. These narratives are written as if the flows were formulated by homogeneous actors (including developers, architects, planners) who 'conceive' of space and formulate objectified representations of space in a Lefebvrian (1991) sense, and then set associated flows free to accelerate and shift across space and time which then pulverize place in the process of creative destruction (see e.g. Zukin, 1991). These are fundamentally disembodied flows since the subjective views of the formulators, funnellers, and skimmers of the global flows are merely assumed rather than examined. If the subjective perception of the actors is examined, it is rarely situated or problematized, and it is also assumed that agents of flows operate according to a global logic (i.e. 'Space is commanded and appropriated by capital and represents the realm of a rootless, fluid reality consisting of flows of capital, commodities, money and information that may take on global dimensions' (Merrifield, 1993: 103)). Such analyses (including those on property capital flows) are ultimately reflective of Western perspectives on development processes. For example, the vast majority of neoclassical property market analyses (e.g. Baum and Schofield, 1991; RICS, 1993) are rooted in the catechisms of self-equilibrating markets, the workings of 'natural' laws, and efficient price-setting markets. More critical analysts working under the urban political economy rubric (e.g. Harvey, 1982, 1989*a*; Badcock, 1984; Berry and Huxley, 1992; Merrifield, 1993) perform analyses using different terms, but with many functional similarities, universal causal tenets, and foci (Healey, 1991). The applicability of both approaches to a property development project (like Pacific Place) driven by Asian Asia-based developers needs to be questioned.

Secondly, the content of the global flows is homogenized and distanced from the fundamental ordering and signification processes associated with the authors of the flows. Commonly associated with the hypermobility of capital thesis, these arguments are 'dangerously overgeneralized', they encourage many forms of defeatism at the local level (Cox, 1992, 1997), and they support dominant discourses that portray globalization as a monolithic, inevitable, and unstoppable force (Gibson-Graham, 1996; Leyshon, 1997). For example, narratives on the flow of money tend to assume that money equals money, that it serves one obvious and clear purpose (capital accumulation) which does not change over time, and that the goal of capital accumulation can be satisfied on an isotropic plain of increasingly global scale. As Mitchell (1997*a*: 104) puts it, research that focuses on globalization 'often relies on a homogeneous vision of global processes' where:

Capitalism, money, information and a hegemonic narrative of modernity are assumed as standards—standards which are, of course, transformed in various ways upon contact with local regions, but which nevertheless contain a form and explanatory potential that is inviolate. The origins of these processes recede from view, and their power and ability to expand and diffuse take on the characteristic of the self-evident.

Thirdly, non-material flows such as information, expertise, and images are rarely examined in contrast to flows of capital or goods, even though these factors play a crucial role in the formulation of material products. Much of the discussion to date has been too narrowly economistic (Lash and Urry, 1994; Appadurai, 1996).

Fourthly, in the rush to revel in the rapid explosion of the global space of flows, be the writers of a critical (e.g. Pred and Watts, 1992) or supportive disposition (e.g. Dowall, 1993*a*, 1993*b*; World Bank, 1993*a*), few analyses are provided of how flows are mobilized: in other words, what are the key mechanisms by which the process of *flowing* is enacted in a coordinated manner to serve the short-and long-term goals of the agents (be it the state, a TNC, a small firm, or an individual person) who guide the process. The spatial relational architecture associated with the activation and extension of flows (across space) is not being addressed. This is a weakness that may be related to the dominance of 'representational' theories of globalization versus theories of practice *vis-à-vis* the *constitution* of globalization (i.e. non-representational theory) (see Thrift, 1997, 1999*b*, on 'non-representational' theory).

Fifthly, while some analysts recognize the importance of the global city as the 'cotter pin' of the global space of flows (e.g. Sassen, 1991, 1994, 1998), few analyses examine the specific interrelations between the social, cultural, economic, and political dimensions of the global city as an enabling context for the production of flows. Furthermore, little attention has been devoted to understanding how the 'cross-border network' of global cities actually works as the 'key scaffolding for the management, coordination, and servicing' of the global space of flows (Sassen, 1998: 131).

And sixthly, few analyses provide provisional accounts of the concrete 'articulations' that accompany the processes of global flows as 'they unfold under geographically and historically specific conditions' (Pred and Watts, 1992: p. xiii; also see Appadurai, 1996). For example, my Vancouver case study needs to be historically specific because the globalization of ethnic Chinese corporate groups is very much a recent phenomenon (see Yeung and Olds, 2000); it also needs to be socially and geographically specific in that Chinese business activity is largely associated with the ethnic Chinese diaspora and their geographical concentration in specific Pacific Rim cities such as Vancouver or Sydney. Moreover, provisional accounts enable us the perceive the uneven nature of the global space of flows, the many problems associated with constructing a spatial architecture to coordinate the flows (i.e. these organizations are not as uniformly powerful as some academics would have us believe), and the processes of contestation as other organizations (e.g. the local state, community organizations) seek to limit or alter the impacts of the power of flows (Murdoch, 1997; Whatmore and Thorne, 1997; Mitchell and Olds, 2000).

These analytical gaps are related to, and compounded by, the steady retreat into heavily theoretical work as researchers make little effort to access global élites, global networks, and link these actors and networks to transformations at the local level (Mitchell, 1997*a*; Ong, 1999). In such a context, this book is one small contribution towards deepening and socializing the analysis of the global space of flows, by linking the flows to the actors who formulate them, and by interrogating the internal ever-shifting nature of the space of flows. The rationale is to construct a socialized discussion of urban mega-project development by examining actors (including groups and institutions within their broader societal context(s)) and their discourses in order to humanize the account of global change. The analysis of intentional acting people within their interwoven 'social and historical context' (Ley, 1989*b*: 234–5), in the cause of global change is too rarely examined, since, in 'the rush to structure, what Pollner has charmingly dubbed "the extraordinary organization of the ordinary" (1987, p. xvii) is entirely lost', leading to a 'largely lifeless view of human society' (Boden, 1994: 5). While such analyses provide important insights, 'lost in process is the important intersection of action and structure or, more simply, people and their history' (ibid.; also see Whatmore and Thorne, 1997). What is needed, in the opinion of Deidre Boden and others (e.g. Giddens, 1990, 1994; Massey, 1993; Murdoch, 1997) is work which seeks to link details of local action, and articulates these 'on a scale with the pace of global history in the making' (Boden, 1994: 6), realizing of course that these are episodic changes, and with the briefest passing of time, they are unlikely to articulate in the *exact* same manner again even in the same locale. One additional outcome of such a perspective, is the deflating of methodologically useful (but empirically unobservable) concepts such as 'micro' and 'macro', since reality is conceived of as a 'seamless web of actions, reactions and inactions' in which all actions are 'embedded in a continuous stream of social relationships, which, in turn, are framed by a historical context' (Boden, 1994: 214; Thrift, 1996).

Theory, Field Work, and the Adoption of a Conceptual Framework

During the course of the heaviest phase of my field work (from 1992 to 1996) I was aware of various approaches to the subject of globalization and the global space of flows, and they informed my *in-situ* analyses and my decisions on which types of data to acquire. I must be totally honest, however, and admit that I did not adopt an explicit 'theoretical framework' (or even a synthesis of frameworks) before I conducted field work. My multi-locale travels (see Appendix A) were also undertaken at the theoretical level throughout the whole research process; partly out of a desire to see what I discovered in the 'field' before confirming a theoretical framework, and principally because of the pragmatics of time and uncertainty in relation to field work for the Shanghai case study. The efforts to set up my research project in 1992/3 far outweighed my expectations, and I constantly felt mired in ('dragged deeper' is perhaps a more appropriate phrase!) the day to day realities of academic responsibilities (contact formation, letter writing, faxing, meetings with relevant academics and business people), and personal concerns (including a first year 'adjustment to a new country' phase after moving from Vancouver to Bristol in 1992 to begin a doctoral programme). Successful field work in Asia is critically dependent upon locating an appropriate host in each city, and the efforts to consolidate my temporary Shanghai base were extremely time consuming. Communications with China are still slower than with many Asian countries (e.g. Tongji University, my host university in Shanghai, had only one central fax machine in 1993). More importantly, I was attempting to receive approval, resource commitments, guidance, and formal liaison assistance through the University of British Columbia Centre for Human Settlements in Vancouver and this simply took time; time when I should have (ideally) been working through key theoretical literatures.

After returning to Bristol in May 1994 the search for an appropriate theoretical framework was mixed in with further responsibilities with respect to: transcribing and reading my interviews; further data acquisition in Paris;

further data acquisition through correspondence (many field-work days were simply spent locating appropriate contacts for subsequent correspondence); repaying obligations to overseas field contacts (e.g. thank you letters, gifts, numerous photocopied articles); maintaining these contacts (further letters); and personal responsibilities on the employment and pregnancy/childbirth fronts.[1] In effect, this permitted seven months of field-work experiences to blend in with my knowledge of relevant issues before beginning the research phase, and a myriad of post-field-work activities including reading and thinking before adopting a framework.

The real conundrum for me then was how to analyse what many academics have been calling, in very cold and distanced language, 'global flows of capital and images' when I recognized (after my field work) the complexity and totally human character of the people I had been meeting with and interviewing. How could I conduct a *global* study in a somewhat humble manner? How should I make sense of the man I met at the World Property Market Exhibition in Hong Kong in September 1993 who recently guided over US$1 billion of private equity into Shanghai's property market? His animated comments during our impromptu conversation (triggered when he noticed me staring at his garish red shoes) focused on how Shanghai was being restructured and the reasoning behind why he would only sink capital into certain areas of the city. The conversation was fascinating for its many social dimensions. His strategy in Shanghai was based on a complex mixture of financial estimates, gut instinct, regular trips to the city from Hong Kong, and a knowledge of regional (Asia-Pacific) and global trends in flows of capital and people to both Shanghai and Hong Kong (their main profit-generating centre)—all underlain by strong social and cultural connections with key decision-makers in Shanghai and Beijing. A logic and a method? No. Instead, a multitude of shifting influences, an awareness of distinct and overlapping flows, and strategic positioning in the midst of extended social networks formed through common cultural backgrounds.

The Foundation of a Conceptual Framework: Step 1—The Five Scapes of the Global Cultural Economy

Given the above, and at this post-field work stage, it seems to me that the work of the anthropologist Arjun Appadurai on the global cultural economy provides the most appropriate framework for the analysis of the subject, providing his 'situated' actors are indeed situated (embedded) within their diasporic and professional systems; systems which are intrinsically linked to the nature and functioning of global cities. In my opinion, Appadurai addresses the contemporary global space of flows in a flexible, insightful, and subtle manner. As

---

[1] Our first child (Thomas) was born on 29 January 1995. This research project (the field-work phase in particular) would not have been conducted in the same manner if we were parents of a baby in 1993 and 1994. Multi-locale field work can be demanding upon family relationships.

Massey (1993: 68) notes in relation to the issue of globalization, the production of space and place, and the erroneous (in her view) conception of place as 'static' withering under the postmodern hyperspace of flexible accumulation, more subtle and gentle approaches are required:

An approach which focused on cultural relations or flows (see for instance, Appadurai 1990) rather than, or as well as, culture areas [bounded territories] might make this point easier to appreciate since individual 'places' are precisely located differentially in the global network of such relations. Further, the specificity of place also derives from the fact that each place is the focus of a distinct *mixture* of wider and more local social relations and, further, that the juxtaposition of these relations may produce effects that would not happen otherwise. And, finally, all these relations interact with and take a further element of specificity from the accumulated history of a place, with that history itself conceptualized as the product of layer upon layer of different sets of linkages both local and to the wider world. (emphasis in original)

In a landmark article, Arjun Appadurai (1990*a*, 1990*b*) outlines the rudimentary 'bare bones of a general approach to a general theory of global cultural processes' (1990*a*: 19). He focuses on the processes of contemporary 'cultural transactions' associated with deterritorialization, and the formation of large-scale interactions of 'cultural material' (e.g. money, ideas) at the global scale. Appadurai suggests that the 'new global cultural economy has to be understood as a complex, overlapping, disjunctive order, which cannot any longer be understood in terms of existing centre-periphery models (even those that might account for multiple centres and peripheries)' (1990*b*: 296). Rather, we must come to terms with what Lash and Urry (1987) call 'disorganized capitalism' and recognize that the current global economy is unprecedently complex due to 'certain fundamental disjunctures between economy, culture and politics which we have barely begun to theorize' (Appadurai, 1990*b*: 296).

To address the lacunae in knowledge caused by these disjunctures, he proposes an 'elementary framework' which examines the relationship between 'five dimensions of global cultural flow' (1990*b*: 296). The five dimensions are outlined in Fig. 3.1 for the sake of brevity. It is important to recognize that the suffix *scape* indicates 'first of all that these are not objectively given relations which look the same from every angle of vision, but rather that they are deeply perspectival constructs, inflected very much by the historical, linguistic and political situatedness of different sorts of actors' (down in scale from the nation state to the individual, and including diaspora communities), and that these landscapes are irregularly shaped and fluid (1990*b*: 296). Appadurai suggests that these landscapes are 'navigated' by actors (agents) who 'both experience and constitute larger formations, in part by their own sense of what these landscapes offer' (ibid.). This mode of thought is clearly sympathetic to the concept of the duality of structure and agency, and Giddens's structuration theory.

Type of landscape	Key characteristics
Ethnoscapes	The landscape of mobile people within the global system including tourists, immigrants, and refugees, and those who have to move, or those fulfilling the fantasies of wanting to move. Ethnoscapes involve tension between motion and stability, and such groups can rarely let their imaginations rest for long.
Mediascapes	The image-centred landscapes offering print and electronic-mediated narrative accounts (or 'strips of reality') of human lives and places within the global system. Such narratives blur the 'real' and the fictional in the construction of imaginative and idealized commodities, peoples, and places.
Technoscapes	The landscape of mobile technology, moving at high speed across national boundaries, organized by multinational companies and/or governments. Such processes are driven by increasingly complex relationships between political openings, money flows, and the availability of capital and labour.
Finanscapes	The mysterious landscape of global capital associated with currency markets, equity markets, commodity markets, and property markets.
Ideoscapes	Politically centred ideologically derived world-views, involving key concepts such as modernization, freedom, democracy, sovereignty. These ideoscapes are increasingly derived in distinctive manners from the Western master-narrative of the Enlightenment and its 'keywords' (Williams, 1976). They travel differential paths via distinctive sets of communicative genres (e.g. print, TV, the architectural press, planning documents).

Fig. 3.1. Appadurai's concept of the 'global cultural economy'

Source: Derived from Appadurai (1990*a*, 1990*b*) and Holton (1992: 234).

Each of these landscapes is subject to unique 'incentives' and 'constraints' which change over time and space leading them to follow 'non-isomorphic' (i.e. they do not have the same form and relations) paths. As the landscapes are also fundamentally disjunctive (involving separation; disjoining in an increasingly fluid and uncertain manner) they can intersect in a 'profoundly unpredictable', uneven, and chaotic manner (Appadurai, 1990*b*: 298; B. Smart, 1993: 149). What Appadurai means by disjunctive is (1990*a*: 11):

people, machinery, money, images, and ideas follow increasingly non-isomorphic paths: of course, at all periods in human history, there have been some disjunctures between the flows of these things, but the sheer speed, scale and volume of each of these flows is now so great that the disjunctures have become central to the politics of global culture. The Japanese are notoriously hospitable to ideas and are stereotyped as inclined to export (all) and import (some) goods, but they are also notoriously closed to immigration, like the Swiss, the Swedes and the Saudis. Yet the Swiss and Saudis accept populations of guestworkers, thus creating labor diasporas of Turks, Italians and other circum-Mediterranean groups.

Following this logic, the more culturally oriented scapes (the ideoscape, the mediascape) are not *necessarily* subordinate to, nor directly associated with, the more economically oriented scapes (the technoscape, the finanscape) (Holton, 1992: 233–4). In other words, the restructuring of global capitalism is leading to the reinscription of relations of power 'in a new, more complex configuration, for example, through a disarticulation of the economic and the cultural as sites of power' (Ang and Stratton, 1996: 28). In the case of this research subject, for example, the Chinese government is opening their cities to extraordinary flows of investment capital and migrant workers to facilitate the construction of massive skyscrapers, yet they are inhospitable to flows of ideas regarding 'democracy' and the human rights of forcibly relocated residents. Even more relevant with respect to the Shanghai experience, Chinese officials view Western concepts related to 'sustainable cities' with distaste, while Western icons of resource-consuming development (the skyscraper and expressways) are wholeheartedly welcomed (see Chapter 5).

Together, these landscapes structure and are structured by the imaginations of 'historically situated persons and groups spread around the world'— they are the 'building blocks' of what, extending Benedict Anderson (1983), Appadurai calls 'imagined worlds' (Appadurai, 1990*b*: 296). Riding the waves of a globalized world economy, moored in the 'irregularities that now characterize "disorganized capital" ', Appadurai feels we should now conceive of 'the world as one, large, interactive system, composed of many complex sub-systems' (1990*b*: 306). This is a world characterized by increasingly 'delicate' state capacities to regulate the space of flows; a world which resonates as disjunctive global flows intersect in random manner, become 'absorbed into local political and cultural economies,' and then become 'repatriated' as heterogeneous flows and so on (1990*b*: 307).

In Appadurai's mind, the critical importance of understanding uncertainty, fragmentation, and difference on a global scale should force the reevaluation of all-encompassing modernist theoretical frameworks such as Marxist-derived world-systems analysis which is most often associated with Immanuel Wallerstein (1974, 1979, 1983), or neoclassical economics (though he seeks to 'retain the narrative authority of the Marxist tradition') (1990*b*: 308 n. 1). Appadurai critically dismantles Wallerstein's world-systems theory in order to make sense of the contemporary polymorphic global system; a system where complex, volatile, plural, and distinct flows operate to form a 'multitude of deterritorialized globalist-localisms that operate above and below the level of the nation state' (Buell, 1994: 316). As with Janet Abu-Lughod (1989), he suggests that theoretical and methodological advances can be made by decentring world-systems theory and injecting into it an element of quantum and chaos theory; a stance closely linked to his awareness of the enabling capacities of the technological explosion and the associated rise of the global electronic media (Buell, 1994: 313). More specifically:

What I would like to propose is that we begin to think of the configuration of cultural forms in today's world as fundamentally fractal, that is as possessing no Euclidean boundaries, structures, or regularities. Second, I would suggest that these cultural forms, which we should strive to represent as fully fractal, are also overlapping, in ways that have been discussed only in pure mathematics (in set theory for example) and in biology (in the language of polythetic classifications). Thus we need to combine a fractal metaphor for the shape of cultures (in the plural) with a polythetic account of their overlaps and resemblances. Without this latter step, we shall remain enmired in comparative work which relies on clear separation of the entities to be compared, before serious comparison can begin. How are we to compare fractally shaped cultural forms which are also polythetically overlapping in their coverage of terrestrial space? (Appadurai, 1990*a*: 20)

Through Appadurai's framework we see a world system that is 'no longer unitary, but rather both one and many (heterogeneous, conflicting, cooperating, overlapping) systems at the same time' (Buell, 1994: 316). Given the posited changes, the fundamental research question to be asked—what are the dynamics of the system?—takes place in the context of flow and uncertainty, rather than 'order, stability and systemacity' (Appadurai, 1990*a*: 20).

The approach outlined above is relevant for the purposes of this research project because it addresses the social construction of an uneven and evershifting global space of flows. The implication of this approach is that modernist metanarratives and 'objective' viewpoints need to be challenged (B. Smart, 1993: 146; Whatmore, 1999). These landscapes are bound up with the human imagination, and observations on global flows, as well as the flows themselves, are:

inflected very much by the historical, linguistic and political situatedness of different sorts of actors: nation-states, multinationals, diasporic communities, as well as subnational groupings and movements (whether religious, political or economic), and even intimate face-to-face groups, such as villages, neighbourhoods and families. Indeed, the individual actor is the last locus of this perspectival set of landscapes . . . These landscapes . . . are the building blocks of . . . 'imagined worlds', that is the multiple worlds which are constituted by the historically situated imaginations of persons and groups spread around the world (Appadurai cited in Smart, 1993: 146–7).

Similarly, Buell (1994: 314) notes:

In this view the imagination is no longer the superstructure of an economic base; it has become equally determinative with economic factors in a world that is now 'a complex transnational construction of imaginary landscapes.' In this world, imagination no longer represents transcendence or escape, but is crucial—indeed, the most crucial—form of social construction, of productive work.

This is not to suggest that Appadurai is an idealist.[2] He simply recognizes that greater attention to the imaginations of actors will help us make clearer sense

---

[2] An idealist philosophy 'claims the world is only made known through, and is therefore constituted by, our "ideas" (and this term refers to senses, perceptions and interpretations)' (Cloke *et al.*, 1991: 132).

of the processes of globalization in a material world that is becoming increasingly fragmented yet also interconnected. The imagination has a basis in very real social, cultural, and political circumstances. The global flows unleashed by actors are both constituted by and constitutive of a greater material reality (also see Walton, 1995, on idealism).

Buell (1994: 314, 316) suggests that the fusion of the terms global *cultural economy* is a symbolic statement of the 'crucial significance of the notion of imagined communities'—a series of unevenly deterritorialized yet 'specifically situated "actors"' who exercise their perspectival constructs, their multiple global imaginations, to propel a myriad of global flows in a polymorphic manner. These flows are not unencumbered either, for the imagination, in relation to the processes of formulation and funnelling, is formed in historically and geographically specific multi-level contexts; contexts with unique social, cultural, economic, and political dimensions.

Indeed, here I can see the direct relevance of Appadurai's framework as it enables me to link the actions of the ethnic Chinese developers and the GIC (derived from their global imaginary) to their production of global flows associated with urban mega-projects in the context of other distinct, overlapping, and disjunctive flows. In the Shanghai case, for example, the massive financial flows impacting the city are directed from Hong Kong, and they are associated with (and overlap on) cultural and linguistic relations formed by the ethnoscapes associated with the 1949 communist revolution. These are not unitary and wooden subjects acting according to a functional (read purely economic) logic drip-fed into them by 'capital' in a tightly knit world-system. The fatalism of world-systems theory is shattered by the existence of dynamic, complex, and situated actors who, at the local level, can formulate flows that may 'cascade catastrophically' into large disturbances in the global system, 'depending on what else is happening throughout the system' (Buell, 1994: 321).

Reformulating and Applying Appadurai's Global Cultural Economy Framework

The basic framework outlined above is used in this book to formulate the subsequent narrative I provide on the global flows of capital, development models, expertise, and images which structure the development of Pacific Place in Vancouver and Lujiazui Central Area in Shanghai. As Appadurai's framework cannot be rigidly applied like a grid forcing data to fit within conceptual boxes, nor even displayed in diagrammatic form, Appadurai's insights are used to inform my mind as I construct the narrative, and they underlie all of the subsequent text in the two case studies.

However, Appadurai's approach needs to be complemented by other theoretical approaches in order to provide a fuller more nuanced analysis.

Fortunately, his is an approach which provides the reformulator with the opportunity to nest complementary theoretical approaches focused on the actors associated with the flows.

The basic approach adopted in this analysis of Pacific Rim mega-projects and the global cultural economy is to focus on the dynamics of the systems which are producing these monumental urban spaces. This is accomplished by performing an analysis of the nature and impacts of the overlapping and intertwined flows associated with each of the mega-projects. This analysis takes place in two subsequent steps within the rest of this chapter, and in Section 1 of Chapters 4 and 5 (as outlined in Fig. 1.3).

The Foundation of a Conceptual Framework: Step 2—'Embedding' Property Development Action

The development of large property projects such as the UMP requires significant flows of capital. In a standard economic sense, this would involve the investment of capital from a firm in a city such as Hong Kong to Vancouver or Shanghai—a source which could be tabulated as FDI. Most property analysts would conceive of this process as being reflective of the search by a firm (or capitalists) for profit (capital accumulation) in response to perceived demand (a rent gap). Aggregated, the ongoing interaction of these firms (capitalists) forms a property market, subject of course to state regulations at a variety of levels (from local to national). In short, this 'straightforward' economic analysis would be applicable for the universal property investor from Canada to Hong Kong to the Czech Republic.

Similarly, the development of large property projects requires significant flows of images and expertise from service providers. In turn, the information and images are subsequently used by both the clients and by the service-providing firms to achieve a variety of direct and indirect goals such as the marketing of the project or the city the project is based in. In a standard business sense, most economists or economic geographers would conceive of this process as reflecting the search by a firm for profit in response to perceived demand for its services—another case of straightforward economic rationale.

In contrast to the above approaches, the rationale underlying this analysis is the need to problematize conceptions of *economic* action (property development action) as if it can be disentangled from the cultural, the social, or the political; one sphere determining the other. Rather, this analysis assumes that economic action by a firm—the ethnic Chinese property developers in the Vancouver case, and the GIC in the Shanghai case—is socially constructed.[3] More-

---

[3] As noted in Jackson and Penrose (1993: 2), social construction theory is 'concerned with the ways in which we think about and use categories to structure our experience and analysis of the world. Social construction theory rejects the longstanding view that some categories are "natural", bearing no trace of human intervention'. Categories such as 'race', 'gender', 'nature', and 'market' are acknowledged to be *created* by social beings and their technologies, while also generating uneven

over, these actors must also be situated within their historically specific social, cultural, and professional contexts, for they work in institutionalized and networked environments which both 'constrain and buttress their involvement in economic activity' (Gereffi and Hamilton, 1991: 7). In other words, the formulation, funnelling, and skimming of global flows is a form of economic action which is socially and culturally embedded, time- and space-bound, and hence impossible to analyse in isolation from issues related to temporally specific socio-cultural relations (Granovetter, 1985; Grabher, 1993; Amin and Hausner, 1997). In the context of the global space of flows described earlier, however, this account must also address the deterritorialization of cultural flows, and associated signs, meanings, and identities in today's thoroughly 'complex, overlapping', and 'disjunctive order' (Appadurai, 1990*b*: 296; Amin and Thrift, 1994; Ó Tuathail, 1997*a*).

This perspective is developed through the application of insights from what is broadly termed the 'economic sociology' or 'socio-economic' paradigm, along with insights from economic and cultural geographers who are addressing similar issues (though with a firmer understanding of the spatial dimensions of change).[4] This paradigm is related to the 'new institutionalism in organizational analysis' approach (e.g. Powell and DiMaggio, 1991) and the 'new institutional economics' (e.g. Hodgson, 1994). These writers (e.g. Granovetter, 1985; Block, 1990; Redding, 1990, 1994; Zukin and Dimaggio, 1990; Gereffi and Hamilton, 1991; Ghirardo, 1991; Hamilton, 1991*a*, 1992, 1994; Whitley, 1991, 1992*a*, 1994, 1999; Amin and Thrift, 1992, 1994, 1995*a*, 1995*b*; Dicken and Thrift, 1992; Granovetter and Swedberg, 1992; Grabher, 1993; Larson, 1993, 1994; Portes and Sensenbrenner, 1993; Mitchell, 1995; Yeung, 1998; Gereffi, 1999; Mitchell and Olds, 2000) develop a 'socio-organizational' approach to the operation of capitalism in distinct time–space contexts, which (ideally) can be used to complement political economic approaches. On complementarity, Zukin and DiMaggio (1990: 23) note:

While the political-economy approach has always accepted *structure* as the expression of determination by forces that are larger-than-life and outside any individual's control,

material implications. Furthermore, it is assumed that all social beings are embedded in multi-layered social relations and networks that are themselves socially constructed and culturally defined at specific space-times. Social constructionist perspectives (of diverse types) have been developed, adopted and critiqued by a wide variety of social scientists (e.g. Berger and Luckmann, 1966; Burningham and Cooper, 1999), including social and cultural geographers (e.g. Anderson, 1991; Jackson and Penrose, 1993; Kobayashi, 1994; Bonnett, 1996; Jackson, 1998; Whatmore, 1999), environmental and historical geographers (e.g. Demeritt, 1996; Proctor, 1998), and economic geographers (Amin and Thrift, 1995*a*; Leyshon and Thrift, 1996, 1999; Yeung, 1998; Amin, 1999).

[4] Economic sociology as it is defined now is derived out of the classic writings of Marx, Weber, Schumpeter, Veblen, and Polanyi (a disparate group which explains variations in the analyses produced under this banner). Still, all recognized the importance of starting analyses at the central 'institutional order that comprises a society's cultural and economic infrastructures' (Zukin and DiMaggio, 1990: 2; see Smelser and Swedberg, 1994*a*, for a detailed overview of the intellectual tradition of economic sociology).

the social-organizational approach emphasizes the *variability* of institutions that are formed by conscious action or historical accretion. Though capital, moreover, is the *driving force and major resource* of the economy in the political economy view, capital ordinarily remains *implicitly embedded* in the socio-organizational approach to the economy. Inquiry that combines these approaches pursues two objectives.

One the one hand it studies macroeconomic, cultural, and societal *frameworks* in which people act; on the other hand, it studies the organizational variables that enhance their *capacity* to produce different outcomes. The distinctive contribution of the new studies in economic sociology is their emphasis on the interconnectedness of structures and capital—*in* other words, of power, culture and organization. (emphasis in original)

While there is considerable diversity within these writings, the main propositions (Swedberg and Granovetter, 1992: 6) of economic sociology and 'socio-economic geography', as it has been practised to date, are:

1. Economic action is a form of social action;
2. Economic action is socially situated; and
3. Economic institutions are social constructions.

These propositions are expanded upon in some detail below (Table 3.1) as adapted from Smelser and Swedberg's (1994*a*: 4) table, and augmented by other writers to reflect my concern with two particular business enterprises— Hong Kong-based ethnic Chinese property development firms, and global city-based GIC firms.

Clearly, the main concept running through the above propositions is the *social* construction of economic activity, and the embeddedness of economic actors (including the firm) in networks and institutions. However, it is important to be wary of simplistic statements about the 'social' and about 'embeddedness'. In empirical research, analyses should delineate the '*historically specific constitution* of the social dimensions of the economy' with respect to the particular regime(s) under attention (see A. Smart, 1994: 11; emphasis added). Therefore this analysis addresses: the nature of Hong Kong-based ethnic Chinese business systems in the late 1980s and first half of the 1990s (for the Vancouver case study); and the nature of the global city-based GIC in the first half of the 1990s (for the Shanghai case study).

The above approach clearly recognizes that the identities and social nature of these actors are provisional constructs, articulated in specific contexts (M. P. Smith, 1994). However, it is also important to recognize that these actors also exhibit a *deterritorialized* nature. The nature of how these transnational cultures specifically organize material and non-material flows through time and space in the creation of the global space of flows is inextricably linked to their capacity to excel in a shifting world of flows and extended social relations. The answer to the juxtaposition of the seemingly separate qualities of territorialization and deterritorialization lies in the relationship of these transnational cultures to the global city, and this relationship will be addressed in greater detail in the case study chapters. Overall, this second step is very important to the

Table 3.1. Economic sociology and socio-economic geography: principal propositions

Issue	Main points
The structural context	• The analysis of business enterprises should be conceptualized as being endogenous (positioned within) a structural context (i.e. the capitalist production system) (Dicken and Thrift, 1992: 284). The capitalist system or world economy is composed of a multiplicity of 'institutional environments' (from families to TNCs to states)—it is not a monolithic entity. There are 'multiple modes of incorporation into the world economy' and the 'continuous reproduction of different institutional structures is part of the way the world economy changes over time' (Gereffi and Hamilton, 1991: 5).
	• Structural change underpins the changing nature of the actors who formulate the global flows. Changes in the nature of global flows 'correspond to (and attempt to make sense of) structural changes lived through and perceived by strategically located groups of people' (the powerful coordinators of firms) (Larson, 1993: 6).
Concept of the actor	• The actor is influenced by other actors and is part of groups, networks, and society.
	• There is considerable diversity in terms of the organization of economic action across time and space. It is impossible to make tight, universal generalizations about the form of business organizations.
	• Socio-cultural factors heavily influence the construction and restructuring of economic actors (e.g. the firm) and economic processes.
	• The dividing line between the business enterprise and the environment is porous and constantly changing (Powell, 1990 in Amin and Thrift, 1994: 11). Rather than conceiving of the firm as an autonomous entity, it should be conceived of as a dynamic and shifting amalgam of interconnections spread across legal and spatial boundaries.
	• The success of the business enterprise in meeting its goals depends in great part upon the nature of the 'institutional atmosphere' within which it operates. 'Successful firms' devote considerable resources in 'constructing' this institutional atmosphere; a process involving a wide array of activities including the formation of networks and alliances (Amin and Thrift, 1994; Redding, 1990; Whitley, 1992*a*; Yeung, 1998).
Economic action	• Many different types of economic action are used, including rational ones; rationality is variable and multiple.
	• Economic action is embedded in a historically situated, socially constructed institutional environment (Hamilton, 1992: 20).
	• Larger business enterprises should be represented as networks (rather than hierarchies) of intra- and interfirm relationships of power and influence. These constantly shifting networks will reflect the specific socio-cultural context(s) within which they are formed and operate (Amin and Thrift, 1994; Granovetter, 1985; Yeung, 1998).

Table 3.1. (*cont.*)

Issue	Main points
	• Business enterprises and markets are 'territorially embedded in social and cultural relations and dependent upon: processes of cognition (different forms of rationality); culture (different forms of shared understanding or collective consciousness); social structure (networks of interpersonal relationships); and politics (the way in which economic institutions are shaped by the state, class forces, etc.)' (Amin and Thrift, 1994: 16–17; Amin and Hausner, 1997). More precisely, economic behaviour is 'clearly embedded in networks of interpersonal relations' and institutions (Granovetter, 1985: 506), and these networks are 'continuously constructed and reconstructed during interaction' (Grabher, 1993: 4).
	• The globalization of economic activity is associated with, and dependent upon, the formation of extended networks across space (Gereffi and Hamilton, 1991; Olds and Yeung, 1999). These networks, in association with 'expert-systems' and an array of technologies help actors identify and interpret the shifting political-economic contexts within which they are operating, or expect to operate. This process of identification and interpretation is increasingly important in the context of globalization where the environment is characterized by enhanced complexity and risk (Giddens, 1990; Amin and Thrift, 1992, 1994).
	• Organization and control is exercised through networks in a diffuse contingent manner subject to improvization and 'ad-hocery' (Amin and Thrift, 1995*b*: 99; Law, 1994; Whatmore and Thorne, 1997).
	• The formation of trust, and the provision of relevant, timely, and 'correct' information between actors is the 'glue' which links key networks in the organization of economic activity (Amin and Thrift, 1994; Grabher, 1993; Hamilton, 1991*a*; Yeung, 1998). Trust is a social and cultural construct, and it is conceived of differently in different cultural contexts (Wong, 1991). Moreover, systems of 'generalized reciprocity and trust tend to rest on organizational foundations of dense interaction which reduce information costs and enhance capacities for mutual monitoring' (DiMaggio, 1994: 38).
Constraints on the action	• Economic actions are constrained by the scarcity of resources (including information), by social structures, and by meaning structures.
The economy and the state in relation to society and culture	• The economy is seen as an integral part of society; society is always the basic reference. Economic processes are intertwined with social, cultural, and political processes, and one process cannot be separated out, or registered as universally dominant.
	• Culture constitutes actors and economic institutions, it defines the meaning of 'rationality', it defines the 'ends and means of action', the 'boundaries between state and market' (A. Smart, 1994) and it regulates 'the relationship between means and ends' (DiMaggio, 1994: 47).

analysis, and it informs the subsequent step (step 3) of 'embedding property development action' in relation to the two global cultures. Again, this discussion takes place in Section 1 of each of the case study chapters (Chapters 4 and 5).

In keeping with the propositions outlined above, I should also mention that the case study narratives are constructed in a manner which recognizes the broader political economic context. Given this, I draw upon insights from the 'development studies' and 'urban political economy' literatures in the production of the two case study chapters (as I did in when I prepared Chapter 2). Key issues to be addressed within these chapters include: the 'pivotal role' of cities in the economic, political, social, and cultural interrelations between the global, regional, national, and urban systems (e.g. Kirkby, 1985; Douglass, 1989, 1998*b*; Sassen, 1991, 1994; Simon, 1992, 1993); the economic expansion of the Asia-Pacific region, and the changing nature of political and economic relations between this region and the rest of the world (e.g. Applebaum and Henderson, 1992; Dirlik, 1993; Yabuki, 1995; Olds *et al.*, 1999); the role of the 'developmental state' in the Asia-Pacific region (e.g. Castells, 1992; Douglass, 1994; Woo-Cumings, 1999); the nature of interurban competition, urban entrepreneurialism, and property-led urban redevelopment processes (e.g. Harvey, 1989*b*; Hall and Hubbard, 1998); the structural dynamics of the urban economy, the social division of labour (including a growing producer services sector), and the implications for urban form (Castells, 1989, 1996; Daniels, 1993; King, 1990*a*, 1990*b*); the contested processes related to the inscription of meaning and symbolism in the city (e.g. Davis, 1991; Merrifield, 1993; Jacobs, 1994; King, 1996; Cartier, 1999); and the formation of urban growth coalitions between indigenous élites (state and non-state) and the global actors associated with these flows (e.g. Molotch, 1993; Peck, 1995).

I enable these literatures to inform my narrative because global flows of capital, ideas, images, and expertise are constituted in, and constitutive of, the broader political economic context. These global flows are formulated by actors who are unevenly aware of their multi-level political economic context; in turn these flows are contributing to the changing nature of this context. This is an ever-changing process which is taking on increasingly global, complex, and unstable dimensions. This is also a process which reflects *difference* where:

such differences are the complex interplay between each society's history and the current flows of capital, technologies, people, ideas and images, where those flows are also seen as having a history and a geography and where there are certain local nodes in particular societies involved in the propagation or reproduction of particular flows. (Lash and Urry, 1994: 321)

Summary

To address the implications of contemporary globalization processes for cities, this research project focuses on the transnational cultures associated with the global flows of capital, images, and property development expertise that underlie the production of new urban spaces. An analytical narrative is constructed in the subsequent two chapters through the application of Arjun Appadurai's concept of the global cultural economy. Appadurai suggests that we need to focus on the nature and impact of five overlapping and disjunctive 'landscapes' through which global flows pass: global 'ethnoscapes' associated with increasingly mobile people; global 'mediascapes' associated with flows of electronic-mediated accounts of human lives and places; global 'technoscapes' associated with flows of technological systems and components; global 'finanscapes' associated with flows of capital into a myriad of markets; and global 'ideoscapes' associated with flows of ideologically derived world-views. This framework, a decentred, dismantled, and fundamentally reassembled version of world-systems theory, implies that it is important to take account of the perspectives and imaginations of the situated actors who formulate, funnel, skim, and use material and non-material global flows.

The final step of constructing the overall conceptual framework is to 'situate' the actors associated with these global flows by drawing upon select economic sociology, economic geography, international business, architectural sociology, and architectural geography literatures. The global flows examined in this book are social constructs; they are formulated by actors who are socially and culturally embedded in networks and institutions. These actors have the capacity to exercise their power as they are enrolled in transnational networks that are territorialized within distinct social spheres associated with the global city. Ultimately, it is the ability of these actors to activate and operate within such relational networks which enables them to reach across space as they seek to implement their goals. It is the construction of such relational geographies to which we turn our attention now.

4

Liquid Aƨƨcƚƨ: Producing the Pacific Rim Consumptionscape in Vancouver, Canada

Section 1

> On the world map Hong Kong, Singapore and Taiwan are easy to locate, but Chinese capitalism is, I believe, less so, because it is not readily confined to a time in history, to a place in the world, or even to what we might think of as a capitalist mode of production. Hamilton (1996: 330)

Situating the Actors: Hong Kong-Based Chinese Business Systems and Property Development

Chinese capitalism is playing an important albeit overlooked role in the economic development of numerous Pacific Rim cities and nations.[1] Section 1 of this chapter examines the nature of 'Chinese capitalism', relevant features of Hong Kong-based Chinese business systems (including the importance of property to Chinese firms), and the significance of Hong Kong as the 'node' through which Chinese firms hook into the capital and knowledge base of the contemporary global economy. Understanding the nature of the Pacific Place development process in Vancouver depends, to a significant degree, on understanding the factors outlined above. This is because the actors who are backing and ultimately guiding the development of the Pacific Place project in Vancouver are deeply embedded in networks and institutions that revolve around Hong Kong, and that stretch out across the Pacific.

---

[1] See, for example, a major World Bank (1993c) report *The East Asian Miracle*, or the summary of the same report by Page (1994), which does not discuss the historical and contemporary significance of the ethnic Chinese to the economic development of the East Asian region.

The Nature of Chinese Business Systems

The 'overseas Chinese' (ethnic Chinese living outside of mainland China) number some 55 million people, and control liquid assets (excluding securities) of approximately US$2 trillion (*The Economist*, 18 July 1992; Seagrave, 1995).[2] While there is considerable ethnic and linguistic diversity among the ethnic Chinese living outside mainland China, most analysts have recognized that racial and cultural linkages play a critical role in explaining the nature of economic activity and its geographical consequences in East and Southeast Asia (Redding, 1990, 1994, 1995; Smart and Smart, 1991; Mackie, 1992; Hsing, 1993, 1994, 1998; Seagrave, 1995; Yeung, 1998; Yeung and Olds, 2000), and beyond (Mitchell, 1993a, 1995). Moreover, it is becoming increasingly apparent that the most economically powerful of the ethnic Chinese are generating their wealth both directly and indirectly in the *city*—directly through the provision of mass housing projects, commercial complexes, and forms of collective consumption, and indirectly, through the listing of public firms on Asian stock markets, and through access to global bond markets.

Detailed accounts of ethnic Chinese business systems are offered by many analysts so it does not make sense to redescribe their work. However, for the purposes of the Vancouver case study, I will highlight several relevant features of the operation and spread of Chinese capitalism.

One common feature of the wealth-generation process of the ethnic Chinese living in the Asia-Pacific region, historically and to the present date, is the development and strategic use of flexible social networks at a variety of culturally conceived levels and geographical scales. It is important to note, however, that the strength of Chinese capitalism is set within and integral to the development and changing nature of the modern world economy; contemporary globalization processes are merely creating new forms of complexity, rather than dissolving and unifying all forms of capitalism (Hamilton, 1992, 1996; Whitley, 1992a; Redding, 1994). In other words, the dynamics of Chinese capitalism, as it incorporates aspects of Vancouver's property sector, depends fundamentally on the machinations of East Asian economies; economies that are in turn integrated into the modern global economy (e.g. see Olds and Yeung, 1999). The turmoil and tumult of global economic change generates the context in which such flexible social networks form and

---

[2] The term 'overseas Chinese' is problematic according to some scholars (Greenhalgh, 1994; Dirlik, 1995, 1997; Ong, 1999). The term is related to the Chinese term *huaqiao* (Chinese national abroad) which has been sharply criticized for its implications that Chinese born abroad with status as a citizen in another country are still China Chinese in essence. Consequently, at least in some academic circles, *huaren* (ethnic Chinese) has become more politically acceptable. In English, overseas Chinese is usually used to include *huaqiao*, *huaren*, and residents of Taiwan, Hong Kong, and Macau (*tong bao*) who are considered to be compatriots living in parts of the territory of China temporarily outside mainland Chinese control. Throughout this book, I will generally refer to 'ethnic Chinese' or to specific groups (e.g. Hong Kong entrepreneurs) rather than 'overseas Chinese' in their discussions of research materials. But references to the literature sometimes require usage of the term 'overseas Chinese'.

dissolve. In turn these social networks help constitute the forces driving global economic change.

Following Hamilton (1992: 17–18) there are a variety of flexibly defined social networks in Chinese capitalism which relate to each other, and which are applied in the capital accumulation process. The first and most important set of relationships are derived from the bonds of kinship (ethnic ties) which can extend to incorporate family members who are not related by blood (ibid.; Redding, 1994). The second set of relationships includes people with regional and sub-ethnic ties (*tongxiang guanxi*) which would include people from the same region, city, or village, and people who speak the same language and thereby share similar cultural traditions. The third level is that of relational ties (*guanxi*) and this, the loosest form of relationships, can include people who are connected through educational history, or common business and social contacts.

The main function and influence of social networks in the economic development process is the encouragement of personal particularistic (as opposed to system universalistic) *trust*, which then encourages cooperation, loyalty, obedience, duty, stability, adaptiveness, and legitimacy in the short and long term (see Wong, 1991*a*, and Hamilton, 1991*a*, who draw upon Weber, Luhmann, and other sociologists in their analyses of trust). These are the common features that underpin Chinese capitalism with its dynamism, leading to both success and failure (Smart and Smart, 2000). At a deeper level, such features are thought (by some analysts) to be derived from Confucian thought which is rooted in the concept of harmony; a harmony built upon five 'cardinal relations' which are fundamental for ensuring social order: ruler/subject, parent/child, husband/wife, senior/junior, and peer/peer (see Redding, 1990; Hamilton, 1991*a*; and Cazal, 1994, for a fuller discussion of the role of Confucianism in the formation of social networks which influence the structure and workings of Chinese business networks).

While there are a myriad of interpretations of the specific role of Confucian thought in guiding Chinese business relationships and behaviour, particularly in the context of cultural assimilation processes in host countries of the Chinese, many recent analyses support Redding's recent statement that 'the Confucian ideals of authority and cooperation have ensured that, while the borrowed ideas have been inordinately well used, the end product remains an essentially Confucian structure' (Redding, 1994: 116; also see Wong, 1991, and Hamilton, 1992, more generally). Since the Confucian doctrine effectively encourages personal rather than institutional (system) ties, as noted above (also see Mackie, 1992: 42), this leads to a reliance on networked personal relations to formulate and propel the economic development process.

It should be noted, however, that other recent studies of Chinese capitalism cast doubt and considerable criticism on such conventional wisdom (e.g. Greenhalgh, 1994; Hodder, 1996; Dirlik, 1997; Ong, 1997; Yao, 1997). They suggest that the recent interest in and discourse on 'Chinese capitalism' as an alternative paradigm of development is little more than an essentialist invention of a new post-socialist and post-revolution discourse on *global capitalism*, where:

Chineseness is no longer, if it ever was, a property or essence of a person calculated by that person's having more or fewer 'Chinese' values or norms, but instead can be understood only in terms of the multiplicity of ways in which 'being Chinese' is an inscribed relation of persons and groups to forces and processes associated with global capitalism and its modernities. (Nonini and Ong, 1997: 3–4)

Dirlik (1997: 308), for example, argues that the characteristics of 'Chineseness' may be the *effect* of the development of global capitalism. On a related note, people like Greenhalgh (1994) suggest that the dominant discourse on Chinese capitalism suppresses the 'dark side' of Confucianism (e.g. authoritarianism and gender-bias).

Given the nature of the debates, there are no immediate solutions to what are fundamental epistemological differences in the conceptualization of 'Chineseness' and 'overseas Chinese' capitalism. Granting some validity to both sides of the arguments, I will support Alan Smart's (1997: 410) assertion (in response to Arif Dirlik's article) that:

If I can be old-fashioned enough to say that these hegemonic narratives are a mixture of truth and falsity, then we must attend to the truths as well as their deceptions. Chinese local officials and Hong Kong investors alike find elements of Confucian capitalism that work and which can be mobilized to resolve some of their problems.

Given this stance, I accept the interpretation that cultural practices and the precariousness of contextual forces (of a political and economic sense) engender networked relations of dependency (including 'loose affiliations' or 'strategic alliances') with financiers, suppliers, and market outlets (Redding, 1994, 1995). Even in large Hong Kong-based Chinese conglomerates, key activities are anchored in social relations which revolve around the family firm, and are held together, as noted above, by personal trust—the fundamental tenet of the system (Mitchell, 1993*b*: 241). These general points are most obvious in a more detailed examination of the primary vehicle of Chinese capitalism—the family firm.

Chinese capitalism is anchored around networks of family firms, and the male head of the household plays the key role in defining strategy from the smallest firm, to the largest transnational conglomerate (Hamilton, 1991*a*, 1992; Mackie, 1992; Redding, 1990; Goldberg, 1993; Yeung and Olds, 2000). Chinese capitalism clearly is patriarchal in nature; an assessment that emerges when one opens up the 'family' and examines internal decison-making dynamics, and the distribution of the benefits of the development process to individuals (Greenhalgh, 1994). The values and social networks noted above form, and are formed by, the family enterprise and the activities the enterprise becomes involved in (situated, of course, in a broader political economic context). In general ethnic Chinese firms tend to be small and medium-sized enterprises requiring low levels of capital investment and organizational coordination, with short-term financial risk, and situated within geographical and political territories where they have personal links and political protection (Redding, 1994: 101, 103; East Asia Analytical Unit, 1995). Typical industries associated with Chinese firms include property, textiles, electrical goods, furniture, toys, clothing, shoes, retailing, and finance (though this list is hardly inclusive). Smart and Smart (1991, 2000), Hsing (1998), and Yeung (1998) provide some fascinating analyses of the investment and production processes associated with such firms in southern China and Southeast Asia. Their research clearly highlights the role of complex yet organized social relations based upon social and institutional networks (primarily those of kinship) to activate the economic development process. These networks or relations are maintained through a variety of actions including gossip of support and discrimination, the issuance of credit, mutual investment, and gift exchange (material and non-material) (Hsing, 1998)—all with the implicit aim of trust-bonding and the maintenance of 'face' (Redding, 1994: 111)

Chinese firms are typically characterized as:

1) Small scale; relatively simple organizational structuring.

2) Normally focused on one product or market.

3) Centralized decision making, with heavy reliance on one dominant chief executive.

4) Family ownership and control.

5) A paternalistic organizational climate.

6) Linked via strong personal network to other key organizations such as suppliers, customers, sources of finance.

7) Normally very cost conscious and financially efficient.

8) Relatively weak in terms of creating large-scale market recognition for own brands, especially internationally.

9) Subject to limitations of growth and organizational complexity due to a discouraging context for the employment of professional managers. (There are now some exceptions to this).

10) A high degree of strategic adaptability, due to dominant decision maker.

(Redding, 1995: 64)

Large Chinese-controlled conglomerates based in Jakarta, Kuala Lumpur, Taiwan, Singapore, and Hong Kong (e.g. Cheung Kong (Holdings) Ltd., Hutchison Whampoa, Henderson Land Development Company Limited, Hang Lung Development Company Limited, New World Development Company Limited, Sun Hung Kai Properties, and The Wharf (Holdings)) also exhibit many characteristics from the list above, and they are playing a key role in the extension of Chinese capitalism throughout the Pacific Rim. These conglomerates, a complex mix of public and private companies, are directed by prominent families (the family heads are generally perceived to be 'heroes' in Asia), and supported by teams of Chinese and Western experts. Decision-making on 'core' issues is taken by the patriarch of the firm upon receipt of what he deems to be suitable levels of information, though local units are generally given a great deal of autonomy (Redding, 1991; Whitley, 1992*a*; Hamilton, 2000).

There is an extraordinarily complex relationship between the public and private firms within each conglomerate. The financial machinations of the corporate complex are closely guarded from publicity (a goal aided by relatively weak government regulations in settings like Hong Kong), and are only understood by key financial controllers working for the conglomerate, and the patriarch himself. The complexity of the relationships (again, hinged on social networks revolving around the patriarch) between public and private firms of one conglomerate, and the externalized networked relationship to other conglomerates and smaller firms, was highlighted recently in Hong Kong in a massive report, the result of a 1992 investigation under the Companies Ordinance of the laws of Hong Kong. The investigation of the Allied Group Limited (a medium-sized business organization by Hong Kong standards) and four related (listed) firms took thirty Coopers & Lybrand accountants 29,500 hours, and legal work of 4,700 hours to reach subterranean levels of analysis incorporating a web of 425 companies.

Two final points to note relate to internal and external conglomerate strategy. Internally, the patriarch of the firm usually involves his sons (assuming he has some) in the firm's activities from an early age, and he steadily increases the level of difficulty of the sons' responsibilities over time in the educational and socialization process. Inheritance tends to be evenly split between the sons and, if a conglomerate is divided any further upon the father's death, more networks of firms are established. Generally however, a network of firms exists before the father dies, and the sons carry on directing (with greater responsibility however) their separate yet linked firms (Hamilton, 2000). Again, it is abundantly clear that Chinese capitalism is patriarchal in nature.

Externally, in a standard investment project, the conglomerates position themselves economically and politically through the astute use of personal connections with:

(1) potential sources of current and future capital;

(2) potential partners in current and future investment projects;

(3) key regulators (political and bureaucratic) of current and future investment projects; and

(4) key sources of current and future productive outputs.

All positioning is highly strategic, reflexive, and maintained through the use of extended social networks which are valued *for themselves* as well as for the economic gains which flow from them (Yeung, 1998).

Extended social relations enable the transmission of information at a 'hypermobile' level in order to plan the *careful* flow of capital—in other words, capital flows tend to be activated by and through channels of embedded social relations that are imbued with trust. In the context of the contemporary world economy, these relations are increasingly extended across space, though they function in the same manner as do relations at the level of the locality. The main enabling technologies in this process are very simple—the basic telephone, and considerable amounts of air travel for important face to face contact.

Hong Kong-Based Chinese Property Developers, the International Financial System, and Global Cities

The headquarters of Chinese conglomerates are located in large Asian cities such as Hong Kong, Singapore, Jakarta, and Kuala Lumpur. These dense cities are nodes for historically unprecedented flows of people, capital, information, and goods in the region (Douglass, 1998*b*; Sassen, 1998). By being positioned in these cities, Chinese conglomerates have expanded at rapid rates through their connection to global financial flows, and their key role in exploiting urban restructuring processes that take place within these global cities.

Taking advantage of modern telecommunication and transportation facilities, the key personnel representing Chinese conglomerates are well placed to form contacts and maintain distant networks with other extraterritorial actors throughout the world. Frequent personal contact with ongoing and potential allies is encouraged in order to construct bonds of trust; a process enhanced in dense cities such as Hong Kong where swarms of firms and financial intermediaries are set up in the dense districts of Central and Wanchai. As the international financial system reshaped in the 1980s and 1990s, capital flows were directed towards East Asia, leading to the establishment of greater numbers of financial institutions (e.g. banks, finance houses, equity firms) and TNC regional headquarters in cities such as Hong Kong (Enright *et al.* 1997; Meyer, 1997; Wang and Wong, 1997). The growth of Hong Kong as a financial centre is evident in a number of indicators. For example, during the first half of the 1990s, an average of 317 of the world's 500 largest banks had Hong Kong offices. At the top of this hierarchy, nineteen out of the twenty world's largest banks had Hong Kong offices throughout this same time period (Hong Kong Monetary Authority, 1995: 88). Structural shifts within the formal labour force reflect the transformation of Hong Kong into a regional hub for service activities (see Table 4.1).

As Hong Kong becomes a major business hub in the Pacific Rim, knowledge levels about how ethnic Chinese firms operate rapidly improve (see e.g. the profile of family-controlled firms in *Euromoney*, Oct. 1994, or the Australian East Asia Analytical Unit's influential 1995 study *Overseas Chinese*

Table 4.1. Employment in Hong Kong's major sectors

Sector	1980	1994	1980–94 Annual growth (%)
Manufacturing	902,521 (46.5%)	440,179 (17.4%)	−5.0
Construction sites	88,682 (4.6%)	59,710 (2.4%)	−2.8
Services	938,390 (48.4%)	2,015,549 (79.7%)	5.6
Wholesale, retail, and import/export, restaurants and hotels	441,892 (22.8%)	1,026,201 (40.6%)	6.2
Transport, storage, and communication	74,109 (3.8%)	161,396 (6.4%)	5.7
Financing, insurance, real estate, and business services	123,883 (6.4%)	357,801 (14.1%)	7.9
Community, social, and personal services	298,506 (15.4%)	470,151 (18.6%)	3.3
Others	9,579 (0.5%)	12,313 (0.5%)	1.8
Total	1,939,172 (100%)	2,527,751 (100%)	1.9

Source: Hang Seng Bank (1995).

Business Networks in Asia). The twin processes of the internationalization of finance and credit, and the development of localized neo-Marshallian financial districts (Sassen, 1991, 1994, 1998; Amin and Thrift, 1992) are opening up mutually supportive opportunities for both international financial firms and Chinese firms through the provision/acquisition of direct and indirect capital flows.

The development and maintenance of social networks with key representatives of the conglomerates are nurtured by representatives of international financial institutions because of relative difficulties in defining a conglomerate's corporate strategy. These firms are viewed as opaque since government disclosure regulations in Asia-Pacific countries are not overly stringent, because of the complexity of the conglomerate's firms' relationships, because the conglomerates often invest in joint venture projects, and because, in the words of one financial analyst, 'too often the only person who knows how money is moving around the multitude of companies is the patriarch' (Nicoll, 1994: 28). This degree of opaqueness frays the nerves of financial analysts who have pressure on them to make judgements on investment strategy (i.e. should we sink capital into these firms?) and the obvious result is nurturing the formation of social networks with well-placed conglomerate personnel. This process is facilitated by the shifting of personnel (often from international finance firms to the conglomerates), or through share acquisitions (Olds and Yeung, 1999). For example, the Canadian Imperial Bank of Commerce (CIBC) founded a Restricted License Bank (Canadian Eastern Finance Limited) in Hong Kong in 1974. Out of this organization, Cheung Kong (Holdings) Ltd. (directed by Li Ka-shing), and CIBC (Li also holds approx. 10 per cent of CIBC) established the CEF Group in Hong Kong in 1986 with a fifty-fifty joint venture. The CEF Group acts as a merchant bank in the region providing financial services (corporate finance, capital markets, venture capital, investment management, merchant banking) to a diverse array of firms active in the Asia-Pacific region. In one sector for example (capital markets), CEF Holdings advised on or managed deals worth over US$32 billion in 1993 (Evans, 1994). The man (William Shurniak) responsible for setting up Canadian Eastern Finance Limited in 1974 was an executive director and group finance director for Li Ka-shing's Hutchison Whampoa when the Pacific Place project was launched.

Moving in the other direction, two former taipans (managing directors) of Hutchison Whampoa in the 1980s and 1990s have shifted to managing the Asia-Pacific affairs of international financial firms—John Richardson (chair 1980–4) to Barclays Bank and BZW, and Simon Murray (1984–94) to Deutsche Bank (Holberton, 1995: 10). These élites are desirable because of their level of expertise which is inseparable from, and owes a considerable debt to, thick social relations with key actors (including Chinese property tycoons) in global cities such as Hong Kong and Singapore. Business élites are strategically aware of their valuable 'power geometry', and their ability to manage flows of information and capital over space (Massey, 1993). Such élites have a significant influence over the nature of 'time-space compression' (Sklair, 1995, 1997). They are able to exercise their power by positioning themselves in the midst of a variety of social networks situated within a variety of systems (cultural/financial/political), effectively acting as bridges between Chinese conglomerates, and the international financial system; a system the conglomerates desperately need to tap into (Olds and Yeung, 1999). The extended social relations of such multiply situated actors enables *absence* to be rendered less significant through the trust mechanism. As John Richardson notes in Holberton (1995: 10), even global banks suffer from the 'tyranny of distance', and this holds them from making commitments in the region. Richardson's role is to alter perceptions of risk:

He cites his first deal as an example. In January [1995], Barclays was lead arranger for a $HK2.4bn syndicated loan (originally planned at $HK1.5bn) to Henderson Land, one of Hong Kong's leading property companies [and one of the investors in Pacific Place]. In London, however, management took some persuading.

'I have known Lee Shau Kee [Henderson's chairman] for 20 years,' says Richardson. 'London was cautious, but I told them: "If we can't do a deal with this guy then we can't do business in Asia." That's where I see my role: trying to steer us on a sensible course. Happily London supported us.'

Table 4.2. World stock market capitalization (as at April 1995)

Rank	Location	Market value (US$ billion)
1	New York	4,654.4
2	Tokyo	3,646.1
3	London	1,242.0
4	Germany	538.0
5	Paris	484.8
6	Toronto	332.5
7	Switzerland	324.2
8	Amsterdam	253.6
9	**Hong Kong**	**252.0**
10	Johannesburg	239.0
11	Australia	219.4
12	Taiwan	209.1
13	Kuala Lumpur	192.8
14	Korea	177.6
15	Italy	174.7
16	Madrid	166.8
17	Singapore	133.0
18	Thailand	124.8
19	Brussels	95.7
20	Mexico	90.1

Source: Data supplied by Nomura (HK).

Europe's fear is based on ignorance. Richardson is critical of banks which move staff around just as they have become more acclimatised and made business contacts.

Such personnel shifts thicken ties between Chinese conglomerates and international finance firms, building relations of trust and reciprocal economic advantage.

The economic growth of Chinese firms has been directly boosted by the growth of Hong Kong as an international financial centre, and the associated development of the colony's stock market (see Tables 4.2 and 4.3).

As noted above, the Chinese family firms such as the ones active in developing Vancouver's Pacific Place have both listed and unlisted arms. According to Gordon Redding of the University of Hong Kong Business School, the Hong Kong stock market is used (to use a 'crude analogy') by the listed firms as a gigantic vacuum cleaner, sucking up capital from around the world, for later use in the development initiatives of both listed and unlisted firms (interview, Apr. 1994). The listed firms in the property sector, the largest sector of the Hong Kong stock market (see Table 4.4), benefit from the flow of capital to Hong Kong from trust funds, pension funds, institutional and individual investors from around the world. Indirectly, the managers of these capital sources are providing assets for property development activities in both Hong Kong and abroad (Naughton, 1999). Such fund managers prefer to play in property markets indirectly because investment in listed firms is a relatively liquid option.

Table 4.3. Key indicators of the Stock Exchange of Hong Kong

Year	No. of listed companies	No. of listed securities	Equity funds raised[1] (HK$ m.)[2]	Total issued capital (HK$ m.)	Market capitalization (HK$ m.)
1976	295	319	n/a	23,257.50	56,674.94
1977	284	313	n/a	23,127.13	61,277.87
1978	265	298	n/a	24,915.61	65,938.58
1979	262	298	n/a	26,853.48	112,809.31
1980	262	309	n/a	33,080.48	209,752.50
1981	269	335	n/a	59,273.61	232,331.28
1982	273	342	n/a	63,560.69	131,639.82
1983	277	351	n/a	67,940.79	142,093.77
1984	278	348	n/a	69,944.56	184,641.57
1985	279	340	n/a	72,234.65	269,511.35
1986	253	335	14,707.16	73,106.35	419,281.38
1987	276	412	48,081.69	90,712.97	419,612.06
1988	304	479	18,506.40	106,213.58	580,378.02
1989	298	479	20,345.00	103,403.60	605,010.44
1990	299	520	21,152.78	108,808.32	650,409.78
1991	357	597	39,187.96	117,546.65	949,171.62
1992	413	749	104,828.13	136,111.21	1,332,184.10
1993	477	891	89,106.80	164,061.59	2,975,379.30
1994	529	1,006	51,640.16	177,567.72	2,085,182.06
1995	518	1,033	39,176.30	180,423.25	2,348,309.95
1996	542	1,272	99,984.89	202,861.28	3,475,965.40

Notes:
[1] Funds raised prior to 1990 do not include unit trusts/mutual funds, share option schemes, and funds raised in the six months prior to a contingent listing.
[2] US$1 = HK$7.8.
Source: The Stock Exchange of Hong Kong (1996, 1997).

Table 4.4. Turnover, market capitalization, and number of listed companies by industrial classification on the Hong Kong Stock Market, 1994

Classification	Turnover (HK$ m.)	% of total	Market capitalization (HK$ m.)	% of total	Listed companies Number	% of total
Finance	175,057.43	17.97	452,383.11	21.70	60	11.34
Utilities	103,988.05	10.67	321,724.78	15.43	11	2.08
Properties	332,151.19	34.09	533,318.52	25.58	85	16.07
Consolidated Enterprises	249,729.72	25.63	581,369.61	27.88	167	31.57
Industrials	87,180.31	8.95	128,723.88	6.17	183	34.59
Hotels	22,194.58	2.28	59,058.19	2.83	14	2.65
Miscellaneous	4,064.31	0.42	9,095.53	0.14	9	1.70

Source: The Stock Exchange of Hong Kong (1995).

In terms of capitalization levels, property has remained quite steady at around 25 per cent of total stock market capitalization (between the late 1980s and 1994), though turnover levels are very uneven. In Table 4.4 we can also see that the number of property companies listed on the Stock Exchange of Hong Kong is relatively low in comparison to property capitalization and annual turnover levels. This disproportion reflects the large size of Hong Kong-based property companies (such as the companies controlled by the property tycoons who invested in Vancouver).

Firms such as Cheung Kong, Hutchison Whampoa, Henderson Land, and New World also have high credit ratings from credit ratings agencies such as Standard and Poor's, and they are able to issue bonds in international capital markets to finance particular schemes (Olds and Yeung, 1999). This enables the family-controlled firms to retain control rather than diluting ownership levels (through the issuance of new shares). The securitization of debt is also more financially attractive to the firms in comparison to bank financing; a trend increasingly common in the Asia-Pacific region which banks term 'disintermediation' (Montagnon, 1994: 21).

As global capital flows of a private nature surge through Hong Kong, speculative bubbles are created in territorial property and stock markets. This condition is exacerbated in entrepôt city-states like Hong Kong where the state tightly controls land supply to raise indirect tax revenue (Yeh, 1992; Haila, 1999); developable land mass is limited; a small number of powerful property development companies control large proportions of annual property supply; FDI flows from China are directed into Hong Kong's property market;[3] the economy is rapidly expanding; the population is steadily increasing; and local and foreign credit for local property acquisition is quite easily available.

All of the tycoons who invested in Vancouver acquired the majority of their wealth via residential property development projects in Hong Kong (though they also develop commercial property). Inevitably starting off with individual properties, they benefited from a good sense of timing, in relation to all of the factors that I outlined above. Of course they had to be skilled in playing this market to their advantage. Their firm's main strategy is to control significant proportions of the Hong Kong property market by maintaining their development portfolios, and focus on a high cash flow via strong degrees of 'recurrent' income by using the pre-sale method (Holberton, 1993; Salomon Brothers, 1993). This approach substantially lowers the risk level (for the firms), and enables them to embark upon new projects.

The mainstay of the Chinese firms under examination continues to be property development in Hong Kong, and the sources of steady income from this

---

[3] Hong Kong's property market has been flooded with capital from China. In 1992, the Bank for International Settlements (BIS) estimated that US$10 billion of Chinese capital was invested in Hong Kong, mainly in the service sector (i.e. property) (BIS, 1992: 92). By 1994, the figure had reached $25 billion (BIS, 1995: 67).

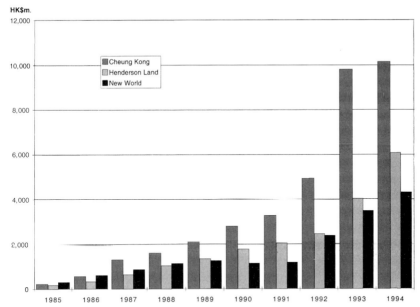

Fig. 4.1. Annual net profit rates of the three main property development firms of Li Ka-shing, Cheng Yu-Tung, and Lee Shau Kee

Source: Baring Securities.

sector fuels large profit levels (see Figure 4.1). With property income as a foundation, further growth is supported through: continuous take-overs (including a hong (Hutchison Whampoa) in 1979 for Li); investment in other firms; horizontal extension (ports, consumer goods, infrastructure, energy, and telecommunications) (Kraar, 1992*a*; Taylor, 1992); and, geographical extension (North America, Europe, and Asia). All of these ventures are built upon the formation of flexible social networks with key actors in relevant institutions (Olds and Yeung, 1999).

Section 2

The Historical Context

Vancouver, situated within the province of British Columbia (BC), is Canada's third largest city (see Fig. 4.2). Vancouver had a 1991 population of 476,378 and a metropolitan population of 1.59 million (Cleathero and Levens, 1993). By 1996, Vancouver's city and regional population had reached 514,000 and 1.83 million people respectively, with international immigration from Asia playing a key role in this growth trend (Greater Vancouver Regional District, 1999). Located on the west coast of North America, the city has been the western terminus of the cross-Canada railway since the turn of the twentieth century, and it is one of North America's largest ports (see Fig. 4.2).

The processes which underlie the development of Vancouver's UMP—the North Shore of False Creek (or 'Pacific Place' as the developer calls it)—have deep historical roots. Vancouver has long been influenced by global flows of capital, people, ideas, and images; flows which have impacted on the nature of the urbanization process. As King (1993: 89) remarks more generally, 'historical phases of the globalization process are inscribed in cities in many different ways, not only in the movements of international capital, but in the transplantation of ideas, institutions and cultural practices'.

Understanding the transformations at work in Vancouver today, particularly those related to Vancouver—Hong Kong linkages, must take place in the context of the formation of extended social relations between Asia, Canada, and Europe as early as the nineteenth century. The latest transformations under way in Vancouver are but a shift in the nature of these flows, as new people, capital, and ideas interact with local formations. While the shock of this transformation may be seen by some as yet another indicator of the 'space of flows' superseding the 'space of places' (e.g. Castells, 1989, 1996; Pred and Watts, 1992), I think more subtle insights can be derived from an analysis of the nature of these transformative flows, including the people and social relations behind them.

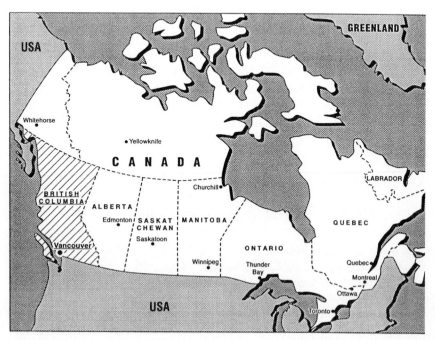

Fig. 4.2. Vancouver, British Columbia, Canada

Native people have lived in the Vancouver region for over 8,000 years. However, it was the arrival of European explorers, traders, settlers, and colonizers from the late 1700s on that initiated massive changes in this territory on the Pacific Ocean. As Harris (1992: 38) notes:

In a few years the area had passed through a remarkable transformation: from the local worlds of fishing, hunting and gathering peoples to a modern corner of the world economy within the British empire and an emerging federal nation-state, the Dominion of Canada. A transition that in Europe took a millennia, in the Lower Mainland took decades.

By the late 1880s, the European (predominantly British) diaspora dominated Vancouver in sheer number, and through the institution of a myriad of 'disciplinary forms of power' including an education system and codes of law. One of the most important legal imports from Britain was surely the commodified land system (ibid. 67). While only Europeans could gain leasehold title to land in the 1880s, this 'regime of property' laid the ground for the development of the city, and ultimately, the sale of land to Hong Kong-based Chinese investors over one hundred years later.[4]

Vancouver grew rapidly after its incorporation in 1886, acting as both a production centre and a service centre for British Columbia's growing resource economy (primarily logging, mining, and fishing). In the late 1880s and early 1900s the city was developed through the provision of housing, transport systems (roads, railways, streetcars), and industrial enterprises (sawmills, fish canneries). False Creek (where the Pacific Place site is now), to the south of Vancouver's original townsite, was 'changed in less than three decades from a quiet inlet with a marshy shoreline inhabited by thousands of waterfowl and surrounded by a dense forest, which the logging operations then in progress had not yet greatly changed, into a busy waterway serving the industrial centre of a large coastal city' (Burkinshaw, 1984: 13).

The future of this land was marked by an 1885 transaction in which the Canadian Pacific Railway (CPR) received rights to develop the north shore of False Creek (and much of the rest of Vancouver) in return for extending the mainline of the cross-Canada railway to Vancouver from Port Moody (now an eastern Vancouver suburb) (ibid.).

Between 1885 and the mid-1900s False Creek's transformation epitomized the overall development of Vancouver. The CPR cleared the land, transport infrastructure was established, and a variety of large lumber mills,

---

[4] As the British colonized Canada, they were also active in East Asia. The 1843 Treaty of Nanking confirmed the development of Hong Kong as a British colony, and ultimately laid the foundations for the development of this 'barren rock' into an economically dynamic entrepôt. And, as will become apparent in Chapter 5, the same Treaty opened Shanghai up to foreign traders and capital. While subsequent developments in Vancouver, Shanghai, and Hong Kong are related to numerous processes of change, these three port cities bear the historical marks, for better and for worse, of the colonizer's spirit. It is also somewhat ironic that much of the research for this book was funded by a Commonwealth Scholarship, and I presently work in a former British colony.

planing mills, lime kilns, brickyards, and wharves were established near the shoreline.

The industrial development of the North Shore of False Creek, typical of other North American cities, increased over time, reaching its apex in the 1930s. Interestingly, remnants of False Creek's industrial past were a key issue in the negotiations between Concord Pacific Developments Ltd. (the company which bought the North Shore of False Creek, hereafter called Concord Pacific) and the provincial government over the site in 1988. Figure 4.3 clearly identifies the industrial heritage of the central portion of the site.

After incorporation, Vancouver's population grew rapidly, from 3,000 in 1886 to 15,000 in 1891, and 27,000 in 1901, 120,000 in 1911 (in part due to annexations), 163,000 in 1921, and 250,000 in 1931 (Wynn, 1992: 69). Population growth was related to an expanding provincial and national economy based upon the exploitation of natural resources. The expanding economy attracted migrants from across Canada, though immigrant flows from overseas fuelled the majority of the city's population growth. As noted above, the vast majority of the immigrants to Vancouver (as to BC and Canada) were of British descent (e.g. 80 per cent of Vancouver's population claimed British origin in 1921) (Ley, 1995: 186). The immigrant flows which connected this colonial outpost to Britain funnelled mobile people who retained a strong British identity for the most part. In turn, these people constructed a functional and symbolic landscape which reflected their British identity, even though they were living in a territory on the other side of the world. As Ley (1995: 186) writes:

A colonial replica society was assembled, with a reproduction of the cultural memories of home. Consider the iconography of the provincial flag, incorporating both a crown and the Union Jack, eloquent testimony to loyalties that were freely rendered during the European War of 1914–18, when, despite its geographical isolation, British Columbia offered the highest share of volunteers of any province to the European front. Or consider the toponomy: British Columbia, marking a sharp geopolitical distinction with the American territories along the Columbia River to the south. The capital cities, first New Westminster, then Victoria, promoted an imperial fealty, while Vancouver, by 1901 the major city, was named after the British captain who charted the regional coastline. The southern suburbs of Richmond, Surrey and Langley maintained the family name of suburbs around central London. On the west side of Vancouver, in its middle-class Anglo-Canadian neighbourhoods, British military successes—Waterloo, Trafalgar, Alma, Balaclava and others—were celebrated in a parade of street names.

While the immigrants from Britain formed the majority in this period, immigrants from a variety of other countries in Europe and Asia travelled, lived, and worked in Vancouver and BC. Immigrants of Chinese descent first arrived in BC in 1858 via California. Two years later ships arrived directly from China with hundreds of immigrants. By 1863 4,000 Chinese people (mainly men) had followed the 'surge of eager gold-seekers north and east into the province with their gold-pans and shovels and weigh-scales' (Yee, 1988: 12). Chinese

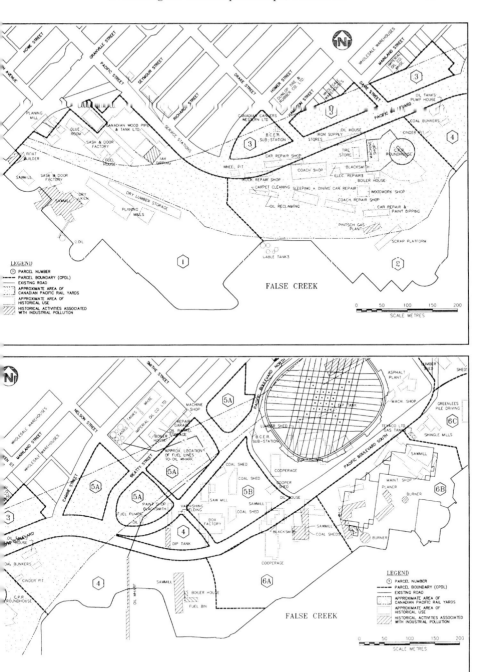

Fig. 4.3. Historical land uses on the North Shore of False Creek, Vancouver

Source: Pacific Place Remediation Project, n.d.

immigrants also worked in the canneries, as coalminers, and as general labourers. The immigrants in this early period, and for many decades more, were predominantly from the Canton Delta region of Guangdong Province in southern China, while a small minority had connections to trading houses in Hong Kong. As with all immigration flows, there were 'push factors'; in this case a series of economic crises, and the Taiping Rebellion, which led to the deaths of over 20 million Chinese people between 1850 and 1864 (ibid.). These migrants predominantly came from rural areas as well.

Flows of Chinese immigrants to BC waxed and waned in the period between the 1870s and the 1923 Chinese Immigration Act (which effectively barred all Chinese people from immigrating to Canada until it was gradually repealed starting in 1947). While over 17,000 Chinese immigrants were allowed in between 1881 and 1885 to build the dangerous BC leg of the Canadian Pacific Railway, at other periods only a few hundred immigrants were permitted in (Yee, 1988). This period was marked by the institutionalization of racial discrimination at all levels (including a head tax), anti-Chinese riots in Vancouver in 1887 and 1907, and the formation of a 'Chinatown' in the centre of Vancouver, on the far north-eastern corner of False Creek (Yee, 1988; Anderson, 1991; Ley, 1995). However, for the majority of BC's Chinese people (who were 'scattered throughout the province'), Vancouver was only a 'point of transhipment for goods from China' (Yee, 1988: 31). In Vancouver, the Chinese population was a small powerless minority, unable to vote, or work in many professions. Economically poor for the most part, they only numbered 3,500 in 1911 (out of approximately 120,000 people) and 6,500 in 1923 (out of approximately 163,000 people) (Yee, 1988).

Until the mid-1960s, Canada's immigration policies continued to favour European applicants, and the city's population reflected this policy with nearly two-thirds being of British or French ancestry, and another '28 per cent claiming European ancestry' (Ley *et al.*, 1992: 249). The city's Chinese people were primarily concentrated in Chinatown and the adjacent residential district of Strathcona. Even by 1961, only 15,000 Chinese people lived in Vancouver (the metropolitan population was 790,000) (Yee, 1988). However, this concentration of Chinese people, and their social relations linking them to a geographically distant Asia, laid a path that larger numbers of future Chinese immigrants would follow.

Vancouver from the mid-1960s to the mid-1990s: New Connections, New Outlooks

Vancouver's status as an industrial city, populated by residents of predominantly European ethnicity, began a three decade period of change in the mid-1960s. It is this transformation, built upon layers of historical economic and social formations, which provided the broad context which the Hong Kong-based financiers of Pacific Place found attractive. These changes created a *particular* Vancouver which the financiers and their agents felt confident about operating within. Moreover, key actors, including Stanley Kwok (Concord Pacific's first director and senior vice-president) and Victor Li (Concord's first chief executive officer and senior vice-president) also became Canadian passport holders during this period (in 1968 and 1983 respectively). Without these critical 'pull factors' capital flows from Hong Kong would not have been invested in the Pacific Place site, regardless of how wealthy they developers were, or how cheaply the site could have been acquired for.[5]

Further details on this broad context are outlined below. The three key interrelated processes of change are:

(1) increased immigration flows from Asia;

(2) the development of a Pacific Rim outlook and sensibility among key institutions; and

(3) the restructuring of Vancouver's central city.

Hooking up to New Flows of Immigrants, Money, and Knowledge

Flows of immigrants from Asia (including China and Hong Kong) to Canada only began to increase significantly from the 1960s on. This shift is directly related to the ending of federal government immigration regulations in 1967 which effectively permitted (and encouraged) government officials to discriminate on ethnic (racial) grounds.[6] Instead, a new immigration system was developed which treated all immigrants equally (in theory). This system utilized a 'points system', an immigration appeal board was established, and the 'sponsoring privileges' of all Canadian citizens were equalized (Anderson, 1991: 186). The altered immigration system also coincided with an increase in the maximum number of immigrants permitted into Canada. Since the mid-1960s immigrant flows have been in flux depending on targets set by the federal government (with input from the provinces). Historic figures of immigrant landings are clearly visible in Figure 4.4.

---

[5] These broad factors are rarely addressed in discussions of 'urban entrepreneurialism', the 'globalization of property capital', and 'property-led urban regeneration'. Property capital controlled by large Hong Kong-based developers is definitely not 'hyper-mobile'; rather, ethnic Chinese property capital is primarily directed to cities which satisfy a diverse array of social, cultural, political, and economic criteria. Of these criteria, it is critically important to have access to trustworthy and well-placed social networks which provide relevant and timely information. Obviously, this criterion implies the presence of a large ethnic Chinese population. However, few Western academics and government officials recognize this point.

[6] Jurisdiction over immigration matters is the joint responsibility of the federal and provincial governments in Canada. While the federal government sets broad immigration policy and landing targets, the provinces have greater input over the types of immigrants they admit (and market to).

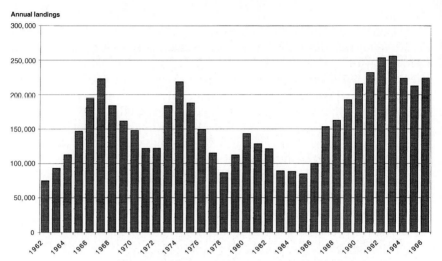

Fig. 4.4. Annual landings of immigrants in Canada, 1962–1996

Source: 1962–90 figures from Young (1991: appendix 1); 1991–3 figures from unpublished data supplied by Employment and Immigration Canada; 1994–6 figures from (<http://canada.metrop olis.net/research-policy/f&f/1a.html>, accessed 17 Nov. 1999).

It is important to note that these key shifts in immigration sensibility took place during the 1960s when 'liberalism triumphed as the ideology of public morality in Canada', demanding the rhetoric of equality match the reality of practice (Anderson, 1991: 186). While racial discrimination cannot be said to have stopped in Canada in 1967, these shifts in government policy did mark a significant dissolution of direct institutionalized discrimination. These shifts took place in the context of an increasingly educated Canadian populace, and the rise of a more liberal ideology in many Western nations. Other, less profiled factors, included the realization of senior government officials that they 'could not operate effectively in the United Nations, or in the multi-racial Commonwealth, with the millstone of a racially discriminatory immigration policy around her neck' (Hawkins, 1989, cited in Skeldon, 1994*a*: 26).

At the national level, these changes in immigration policy have led to a marked shift in the origins of immigrants to Canada (see Fig. 4.5).

This shift towards the admission of Asian immigrants is also related to the influx of Asian refugees from China and Vietnam; Asians fleeing Hong Kong (see below) during the Chinese cultural revolution (when Hong Kong was also in strife), the build-up to the 1997 return of Hong Kong to China, and the 1989 Tiananmen crisis; the greater tendency of Asian families to sponsor relatives; and the development of new forms of 'business' immigration categories—the 'self-employed' class in 1967 (which was revised in 1978), the 'entrepreneur' class in 1978, and the 'investor' class in 1986. The Canadian government devised the immigration points system, and developed

Per cent

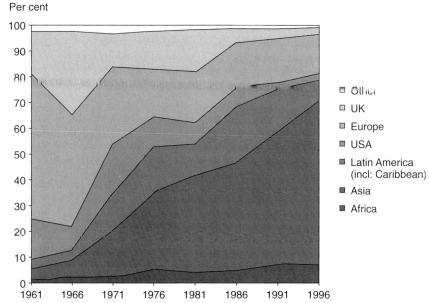

Fig. 4.5. Immigration by source area, Canada, 1961–1996

Source: Citizenship and Immigration Canada.

these new categories to 'foster the development of a strong and viable economy and the prosperity of all regions of Canada' (Young, 1991: 13). These schemes are meant to 'facilitate the entry of those with entrepreneurial skills and investment capital' (Hiebert, 1994: 256); a practice viewed as 'brain draining' by some critics within Asian nations (Segal, 1993; Skeldon, 1994*a*), while also leading to the formation of a two-tier immigration system in Canada (Ley 1999).

The 'entrepreneur' and 'investor' classification schemes allow high income people with proven business records and sufficient capital to buy Canadian visas if they invest capital in Canada. The entrepreneur programme requires immigrants to bring in a minimum of C$250,000 to establish or purchase a 'substantial interest' in a 'commercial enterprise' which would provide 'employment for one or more Canadians and make a significant contribution to the economy' (Hiebert, 1994: 256). The investor programme allows applicants with a 'net worth' of at least $500,000 to immigrate providing they invest between $150,000 and $500,000 (depending on province of destination) for between three and five years (Wong, 1993: 174). However, unlike the entrepreneur programme, 'investor' immigrants do not have to 'participate in the active management of a business' (Young, 1991: 15). In other words, they are free to live anywhere in the world (after meeting a three years' residency requirement), with the safety net of a Canadian visa (see

Nash, 1993; Wong, 1993; Segal, 1993; and Smart, 1994, on Canada's business immigration programme).

People from Hong Kong and other countries in the Asia-Pacific, who now make up the bulk of new entrepreneurial and investor immigrants, have been particularly attracted by these schemes (Nash, 1993; Smart, 1994; Citizenship and Immigration Canada, 1999, Ley, 1999). As noted in Section 1 of this chapter, income levels for many people in Hong Kong have risen rapidly from the 1970s to the 1990s, and they are able to afford the expenses entailed in acquiring a Canadian visa. Awareness of immigration opportunities in Canada are also enhanced by the thickening of social relations between families and friends living in Hong Kong and Canada; through the Hong Kong media which regularly covers changes in Canada's immigration policy, and the life of recent immigrants in major Canadian cities such as Toronto and Vancouver (the image-saturated mediascape in Appadurai's terms); and via the actions of the federal and provincial governments which have established immigration offices in Hong Kong (with highly visible marketing programmes). Suffice it to say, Canada's immigration policy is based upon a realization of the overlapping nature of flows of immigrants and flows of capital.

Annual immigrant landings from Hong Kong to Canada are evident in Figure 4.6. This also highlights the three main waves of Hong Kong immi-

Total landings from Hong Kong

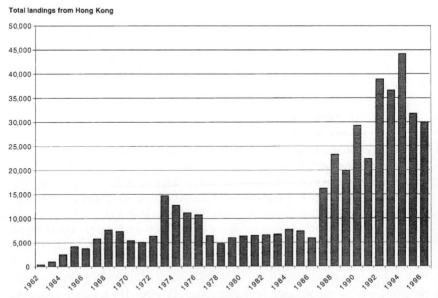

Fig. 4.6. Total landings in Canada from Hong Kong, 1962–1996

Sources: 1962–9 figures from Skeldon (1994*b*: 28); 1970–92 figures from data supplied by Immigration Section, Commission for Canada, Hong Kong; 1993–4 figures from data supplied by Employment and Immigration Canada; 1994–6 figures from Citizenship and Immigration Canada (1999).

Table 4.5. Immigrants to major destinations whose last place of previous residence was Hong Kong, 1980–1994

Year	Total no. of Hong Kong emigrants	No. of Hong Kong immigrants to Canada	No. of Hong Kong immigrants to Australia	No. of Hong Kong immigrants to the USA
1980	22,400	6,309	2,822	n/a
1981	18,300	6,451	1,960	n/a
1982	20,300	6,542	2,414	11,908
1983	19,800	6,710	2,756	12,525
1984	22,400	7,696	3,691	12,290
1985	22,300	7,380	5,136	10,975
1986	19,000	5,893	4,912	9,930
1987	30,000	16,170	5,140	8,785
1988	45,800	23,281	7,942	11,817
1989	42,000	19,994	9,998	12,236
1990	61,700	28,825	11,538	12,853
1991	69,700	22,340	16,747	15,564
1992	66,200	38,841	15,656	16,741
1993	53,400	36,510	8,111	14,010
1994	61,600	43,710	n/a	n/a

Source: Data supplied by Census and Statistics Department, Government of Hong Kong; Employment and Immigration Canada; Skeldon (1994*a*: 28).

grants to Canada—during the mid-1960s, the mid-1970s, and the late-1980s to early 1990s (when the North Shore of False Creek site was purchased and development was initiated).

The relative attraction of Canada to Hong Kong's immigrants cannot be overstated. Table 4.5 clearly highlights that Canada is the overwhelming destination of Hong Kong residents seeking a foreign visa during the 1980s and the first half of the 1990s.[7]

One of the attractions of the Canadian passport (unlike the American passport) is that the Canadian government permits immigrants to retain their original passport from their country of origin (if their original country permits them). With this status, Canadian immigrants have the option of making subsequent moves (after a three year period) to any other country (or return to Hong Kong in this case), while also paying no Canadian taxes on non-Canadian income sources (provided the person meets the criteria to be classified as 'non-resident'). The impact of this regulation is very significant, particularly in countries such as Hong Kong where income tax levels are relatively low (a flat 15 per cent), incomes can be relatively high, and

[7] This table, like all immigration data should only be viewed as an indicator of immigration trends. The processing of immigration applications is highly uneven with respect to time and by nation, 'official' figures are constantly being revised in the light of more accurate data, and large numbers of Hong Kongers moving to China are not included. The significance of student flows are also missing from this data set (e.g. over 70,000 people in Hong Kong have Canadian university degrees) (Nash, 1993; Skeldon, 1994*a*). These factors partially explain why the sums do not total up on an annual basis.

Hong Kong people (in general) are willing to be mobile across distant spaces (on the latter point see Pe-Pua *et al.*, 1996). For example, a July 1995 Hong Kong Trade Development Council 'Market Profile' fact sheet noted that over 40,000 Canadian citizens were working in Hong Kong during 1994 ('one of the most significant foreign presences in Hong Kong'), and the 1996 Canadian national election witnessed politicians flying to Hong Kong on electioneering trips. This form of 'flexible citizenship' is of particular benefit to Chinese business people. As Katharyne Mitchell (1997*b*: 551) notes: 'As capitalist networks articulate, Chinese businessmen who speak the language of the global economic subject, but are also imbricated in a Hong Kong Chinese discourse, are able to operate as the quintessential hybridized middlemen'. These mobile interlocutors of trans-Pacific capital flows are deemed to be model minorities in Canadian business and political spheres, a considerable change of opinion compared to the turn of the century. This is a topic that Mitchell (1995, 1997*a*, 1997*b*) and Aihwa Ong (1999) have explored in some detail.

The national immigration trends outlined above have distinct spatial implications. British Columbia, with approximately 10 per cent of Canada's population, has always attracted a disproportionate share of immigrants. Along with Ontario and Quebec, the province was perceived (until 1997 or so) to have a relatively strong economy, while large numbers of existing immigrant communities also prove attractive to new immigrants. Proportionate flows of immigrants to BC also increased from the mid-1980s to 1996 (see Table 4.6).

During the 1991–6 period, BC received more than a quarter of a million immigrants, a considerable number in a province with just over 3 million people. In the 1990s, net international migration became the most important contributor to the province's population growth (ibid.). This state of affairs is related to the weaker impact of the late 1980s/early 1990s national recession on BC (which made the province more appealing to immigrants), and the higher

Table 4.6. British Columbia's share of Canadian immigration flows, 1987–1996

Year	Planning Level (000's)	Actual (000's)	BC share (%)
1987	115–125	152	12.4
1988	125–135	162	14.3
1989	150–160	192	13.2
1990	200	214	13.4
1991	220	225	13.9
1992	250	253	14.3
1993	250	256	17.9
1994	250	224	22.0
1995	190–215	212	21.0
1996	195–220	224	22.6

Source: BC Stats (1999).

Per cent

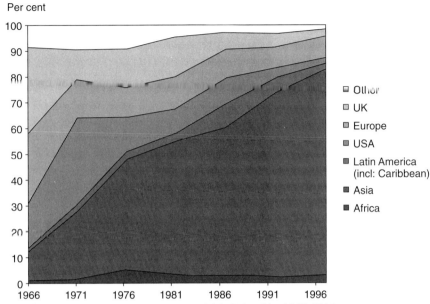

Fig. 4.7. Immigration by source area, British Columbia, 1966–1996

Source: BC Stats, Ministry of Government Services, Government of British Columbia.

proportion of Asian immigrants who choose to 'land' in BC.[8] While Asian immigrants only made up 22 per cent of the 1970 provincial total of 21,859 immigrants, this figure increased to 79 per cent by 1994 when 48,529 immigrants landed in BC (see Fig. 4.7). BC also attracts a disproportionate amount of Canada's business immigrants (Business Immigration Branch, Province of British Columbia, 1993; Citizenship and Immigration Canada, 1999; Ley, 1999).

Asian immigrants make up the largest proportion of BC's business immigrants. In 1993 for example, business immigrants from Hong Kong and Taiwan accounted for 83.5 per cent of BC's total business immigrants (Business Immigration Branch, Province of BC, 1993; Ley, 1999)

Asian immigrants to BC in the 1980s and first half of the 1990s primarily came from Hong Kong, India, China, Taiwan, the Philippines, and Vietnam. Hong Kong immigrants easily make up the majority of the Asian immigrant block; indeed Hong Kong has been the largest single source of BC immigrants since the late 1980s (with Taiwan coming a distant second). In 1994, for example, 33.3 per cent of all BC immigrants came from Hong Kong. Data on Hong Kong landings in BC is presented in Figure 4.8.

---

[8] While immigrants may 'land' in a province, and are reported in government statistics, they can move around the country freely. In the case of BC, a province deemed attractive to most immigrants, numbers are likely to be underestimated.

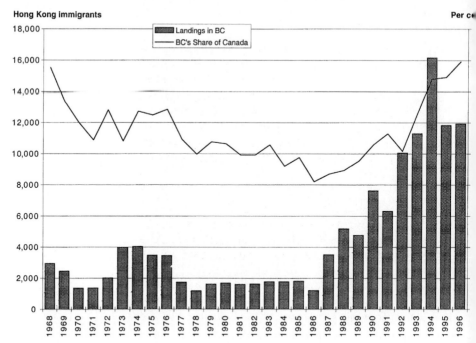

Fig. 4.8. Immigration to British Columbia from Hong Kong, 1968–1996

Source: BC STATS, Ministry of Government Services, Government of British Columbia; Citizenship and Immigration Canada (1997, 1999); BC Stats (1997).

Hong Kong immigrants are primarily attracted to Ontario, British Columbia, and Quebec. However, the national inequities are even more pronounced when taking into account the class of Hong Kong immigrant landing in Canada's provinces. Ontario and British Columbia in particular attract a large proportion (on a national basis) of business immigrants (Lary, 1994; Smart, 1994; Ley 1999). These immigrants have, on average, extremely high income, education, and training (workplace) levels—they are the 'best and the brightest' of Hong Kong's emigrants; a status which makes them *the* most highly prized immigrants on a global scale by North American, Australasian, Asian, and European governments (Ong *et al.*, 1992; Segal, 1993; Skeldon, 1994*a*; Ong, 1999). The instrumental nature of Canada's immigrant investor programme, and the focus on Hong Kong immigrants is no secret—indeed, the 1992 federal government Ministerial Task Force on the Immigrant Investor Program (IIP) could not state the aims of the programme any clearer:

IIP Fund promoters and sales agents have concentrated their marketing efforts in Hong Kong over the past several years exploiting the uncertainties surrounding the proposed changeover in governments in 1997. . . . Although Canada's focus on Hong Kong has paid dividends, that market now shows signs of returning stability. However, other markets such as Taiwan, the Middle East, Latin and South America are showing signs of potential growth. (Henders and Pittis, 1993: 14)

The Canadian and BC governments (regardless of ideology) perceive the influx of such business immigrants in overwhelmingly positive terms as the immigrants bring with them large volumes of capital, knowledge, experience, and connections. What all of the above discussion highlights is that Vancouver is feeling the direct and indirect impacts of an immigration policy that 'has harnessed the practice of labour migration to the principles of the free market and to the ideals of the enterprise culture. Immigration policy is thus economically selective, and more sensitive to the colour of money than to that of skin' (S. Smith, 1993: 61).

The federal and provincial governments have opened a selective regulatory window to entice in the types of immigrants who will (in theory) help Canada adapt and prosper in a globalizing economy. The global labour market is highly segmented, yet extremely fluid at this élite level. The fluid nature of this labour market is the product of state policy and programmes which were developed in the context of the global reign of neoliberalism (Sutcliffe, 1993). Hong Kong immigrants, in particular, have been enticed to acquire a Canadian visa, especially in the geopolitical context of uncertainties associated with the 1984 Sino-British Joint Declaration (Segal, 1993), and the economic context of a rapidly developing Asia-Pacific region.

The economic impacts of the business immigration programme in Canada are substantial though very difficult to track. The BC government estimates that 'since the investor program began in 1986, the program has received about $2.4 billion of which $290 million was invested in BC' (J. Gray, Province of BC, letter, 12 July 1995). Again though, these figures should be treated as rough indicators rather than as exact amounts. For example, immigrants under the investor programme can live in BC but invest in another province (where the minimum required capital level is lower). The monitoring of investment flows is difficult to track, and capital can easily flow out of Canada. Similarly, John Gray, Director of Business Immigration for the Province of BC, informed me that many of Canada's entrepreneur immigrants land in other Canadian provinces (particularly Quebec where less stringent regulations are in place) and then subsequently move to BC. However, the flow of immigrants from Asia is acknowledged by most observers as a key factor which helped BC weather a difficult national recession during the late 1980s and early 1990s.[9]

BC then has gone out of its way to attract business immigrants from Hong Kong, and flows of these élite immigrants have arrived in steadily increasing numbers. Figure 4.9 highlights the total number and proportion of business

---

[9] Readers interested in the Canadian business immigration programme should examine the following web site for relevant materials and sources: ⟨http://canada.metropolis.net/main_e.html⟩.

Hong Kong immigrants

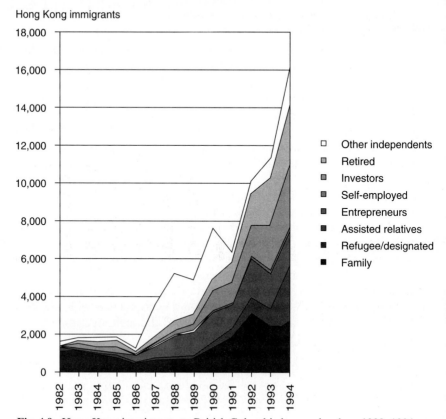

Fig. 4.9. Hong Kong immigrants to British Columbia by year by class, 1982–1994

Source: Data supplied by Central Statistics Branch, Treasury Board Secretariat, Ministry of Finance and Corporate Relations, Government of British Columbia.

immigrants (which includes the entrepreneur, investor, and self-employed classes) from Hong Kong who have moved to BC (though recall my caveat regarding data quality). I should also note that the Canadian government considers 'social and humanitarian immigrants' to be of the family, refugee and designated classes, while all other classes (other independents, retired, investors, self-employed, entrepreneurs, and assisted relatives) are 'economic immigrants'.

And finally, scaling down to the level of the city, Hong Kong immigrants to BC of all classes overwhelmingly flow to Vancouver (see Fig. 4.10) (Lary, 1994: 6; Citizenship and Immigration Canada, 1999; Hiebert, 1999; Ley, 1999). Even on a national scale, Vancouver has been attracting the largest share of Canada's business immigrants. For example, in 1993 Vancouver attracted 31.9 per cent of all of Canada's business immigrants: by comparison, Montreal and Toronto had 20.9 per cent and 19.3 per cent shares respectively ('Top sources of business immigration', 27 Jan. 1995). This movement should be expected for 'migrant

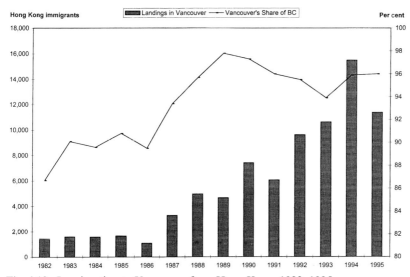

Fig. 4.10. Immigration to Vancouver from Hong Kong, 1982–1995

Source: Data supplied by Central Statistics Branch, Treasury Board Secretariat, Ministry of Finance and Corporate Relations, Government of British Columbia; BC Stats (1997).

streams' have historically been concentrated in Canadian cities (Olson and Kobayashi, 1993: 142). Moreover, contemporary immigrants from Hong Kong are highly urbane, and Vancouver offers them a greater quality of life that is inaccessible anywhere else in BC (see below). Figure 4.10 should also be seen in the light of discussions about the increasing level of interconnection between global/world cities in a period of world history marked by the deepening of globalization processes (e.g. Armstrong and McGee, 1985; King, 1990*a*; Sassen, 1991, 1994, 1998; Simon, 1992, 1993; Hamnett, 1994, 1995; Massey *et al.*, 1999). Vancouver is clearly hooked up to Hong Kong via flows of people (including mobile professionals), capital, information, images, and commodities.[10]

The steady influx of immigrants from Asia (particularly Hong Kong) is transforming Vancouver's social structure. A 422 per cent increase in metropolitan Vancouver's non-European population took place (as opposed to a 28 per cent overall growth rate) between 1971 and 1986 with the vast majority being of Asian ancestry (Ley *et al.*, 1992: 251–2). By 1991, 331,920 people (21 per cent) in the Vancouver Census Metropolitan Area claimed Asian ethnic origin. The growing significance of trans-Pacific migration is particularly marked in the early 1990s, the same time phase of the development of Pacific Place. As Hiebert (1999: 56) notes:

[10] Again, data on the scale of flows of Hong Kong immigrants to Vancouver should be viewed as a broad indicator of change rather than as an exact figure. Many Hong Kong immigrants land in other Canadian provinces and migrate to Vancouver. Hong Kong immigrants (like all Canadian citizens) are also free to travel and work overseas.

Greater Vancouver attracted the highest proportion of immigrants from Asian countries (80% of the landed immigrants to the CMA [census metropolitan area] in the 1990s have been from Asia). By 1996, nearly 365,000 residents of the metropolitan area were born in Asia (roughly equivalent to the *total* immigrant population just ten years earlier), and Hong Kong had replaced the United Kingdom as the single most important place of birth among immigrants living in Greater Vancouver. Over the decade, the number born in India, China and Vietnam doubled; the number born in Malaysia, the Philippines, and Pakistan tripled; the number born in Iran, Hong Kong, and Korea quadrupled; and the number born in Taiwan rose more than tenfold. (emphasis in original)

The city of Vancouver itself, with a population of 471,844, had 103,520 people (22 per cent) claiming Chinese origin in the 1991 census (Cleathero and Levens, 1994: 68), and 134,000 in the 1996 census (Hiebert, 1999: 69). Of the 1996 GVRD population, some 238,790 people claimed that Chinese is their 'mother tongue' (GVRD, 1999: 9). At a provincial scale, approximately 93 per cent of BC's Chinese population resides in the Vancouver area (Statistics Canada, 1999). The 1996 Canadian census figures, at a national scale (see Table 4.7), reinforce the significance of this trend, and highlight Vancouver's role as Canada's pre-eminent (in a relative sense) ethnic Chinese metropolis; a social formation being constituted by trans-Pacific flows of people out of places like Hong Kong, China, and Taiwan.

Obviously the 'Chinese' population in Vancouver is not homogeneous—it includes people of different genders, ages, religions, source countries (e.g. Hong Kong, mainland China, Vietnam, Taiwan), linguistic groups, incomes, professions, political beliefs, lengths of time in Vancouver, and so on (Ley, 1999; also see Ang, 1994 on this issue more generally). It is simply impossible to speak of *the* Chinese community. However, the steady increase in the total number and relative proportions of Asian (and especially Chinese) people who now live in Vancouver is undeniably altering the nature of what was overwhelmingly a city dominated by people of European (British in particular) descent.

As in the past, Vancouver's social transformation is also magnified by temporary flows of people between Vancouver and the origins of the city's immigrants (see one indicator in Table 4.8). This is an era of increased interaction of a temporary nature between places via air travel and the media. The 'non-places' of 'supermodernity' (Augé, 1995; Ibelings, 1998), such as Vancouver International Airport, connect Vancouver to the Norman Foster-designed new Hong Kong International Airport, enhancing the mediation of relations between people in these two cities. It is this conjunction of flows of more permanent immigrants, and temporary visitors, which alters the processes reconstituting place in a myriad of ways (Appadurai, 1996). Flows do not simply connect Vancouver to Hong Kong alone either, for Hong Kong is a key transactive hub in the Asia-Pacific region. The thickening of relations with people from Hong Kong guarantees the formation of a multiplicity of

Table 4.7. Population groups in three Canadian cities, with special reference to the Chinese, 1996

	Canada No.	%	Montreal No.	%	Toronto No.	%	Vancouver No.	%
Total—Population groups	28,528,125		3,287,645		4,232,905		1,813,935	
Single responses	27,251,880	95.5	3,203,785	97.4	4,052,315	95.7	1,733,105	95.0
White	24,156,215	84.7	2,812,235	85.5	2,751,650	65.0	1,196,320	66.0
Total non-White	3,095,665	10.9	391,550	11.9	1,300,665	30.7	536,785	29.6
Chinese	820,370	2.9	43,700	1.3	325,345	7.7	269,855	14.9
Multiple responses	496,455	1.7	74,420	2.3	165,030	3.9	50,755	2.8
All others	779,790	2.7	9,440	0.3	15,555	0.4	30,070	1.7

Source: Derived from Hiebert (1999, table 6).

Table 4.8. Cathay Pacific scheduled flights connecting
Vancouver and Hong Kong, 1988–1994

Year	Departures from Hong Kong to Vancouver	Arrivals to Hong Kong from Vancouver
1988–9	86,513	73,776
1989–90	91,649	77,977
1990–1	111,814	96,136
1991–2	122,192	110,598
1992–3	125,037	112,124
1993–4	135,604	124,934

Note: Yearly figures are from 1 April to 31 March.
Source: Unpublished data supplied by Cathay Pacific Airways Limited.

extended relations between Vancouver and the entire Asia-Pacific region. For example, this may take the form of an influx of consumption habits from Japan via Hong Kong (karaoke), or the incorporation of Taiwanese investors into a joint-venture property development project financed by Hong Kong developers.

The overall effects of the deepening of relations between Hong Kong and Vancouver are difficult to pinpoint. These effects must also be viewed in the broader context of deeper interlinkages between Vancouver and other Asia-Pacific countries such as China, Japan, Taiwan, and Vietnam. Among the changes evident in the city are the expansion of popular suburbs such as Richmond where residents of Chinese descent now make up approximately 37 per cent of the area's 129,500 residents (up from 7 per cent a decade previously) (Hiebert, 1999: 69). New consumption practices with a strong Hong Kong flavour have been developed in Vancouver including 'new shopping centres (the modern version of the conventional Chinatown), a new country club, new arrays of professional services (driving schools, financial and investment consultants), tailor-made condominiums . . . "Hong Kong" style restaurants' (Lee and Tse, 1994: 75), and 'deluxe Asian hotels' (Goldberg, 1991*b*). A variety of festivals and leisure events are popular such as the annual Dragon Boat races in False Creek. At the level of residential built form, recent immigrant flows from Hong Kong and the rest of Asia are associated (though not exclusively) with the development of relatively large houses for multiple generations (which detractors call 'monster houses'),[11] and the development of luxury high-rise condominiums—a familiar housing form for anyone who has lived in large Asian cities. Vancouver is also the site of the first ever full-scale Chinese classical garden (the Dr Sun Yat-Sen Classical Chinese Garden) to be built outside Asia. This garden is a Suzhou Ming dynasty (AD 1368–1644) scholars' garden,

---

[11] On the 'monster house' issue see Ley *et al.* (1992), Petit (1992), Majury (1994), Ley (1995), Mitchell (1993*a*, 1997*b*), and Smart and Smart (1996). I do not mean to imply every monster house is owned by Asians or Hong Kongers, for this is clearly not true.

coordinated by a Chinese-Canadian architect (Joe Wai), and built by Suzhou artisans in 1985 and 1986 (Keswick *et al.*, 1990). Well-known Hong Kong brand-name products and services are increasingly available in Vancouver. For example, the national headquarters of the Hong Kong Bank of Canada (a subsidiary of HSBC Holdings plc, which is headquartered in London, England) was established in 1981 with C\$140 million in capital. The Hong Kong Bank of Canada is now Canada's seventh largest bank (and largest foreign bank) with assets of C\$13 billion in 1993 (Bradbury, 1993), increasing to C\$25.6 billion in 1999 (<http://www.hsbc.ca/>).[12] Other well-known Hong Kong presences include Cathay Pacific (a regional office), Jardines, and World-Wide Shipping. Vancouver's small manufacturing industry has been expanding in contrast to the decline of manufacturing in most North American cities. In particular, Hong Kong capital and knowledge has propelled the development of the garment, electronics, and light consumers goods sectors (Hong Kong Trade Development Council, 1991; Johnson, 1994; Hutton, 1998). With respect to the mainstream media, there are two Chinese TV stations, two radio stations, three major daily newspapers, and a variety of magazines which cater to Vancouver's Hong Kong Canadians (Lee and Tse, 1994). Vancouver's education system is being transformed with an abundance of Asian language and culture programmes, as well as English as a Second Language (ESL) programmes. And, finally, a plethora of churches catering to Chinese clientele are operating across the city.

The immigration trends outlined above, along with the simple indicators of change that I just described, directly and indirectly enhanced the attractiveness of Vancouver for the Hong Kong-based financiers of Pacific Place. Vancouver is a *relatively* easy city to live and work in for people familiar with life in Hong Kong. There are channels of communication in Vancouver which can easily be accessed by people with the right connections in Hong Kong; channels which also stretch back to Hong Kong and beyond (as I noted above). 'Cultural tolerance', to use a phrase of the Hong Kong Trade Development Council (1991: 20), is considered to be working in the city's favour on a relative international basis. Flows of immigrants and visitors are prospective condominium purchasers; they generate the demand for a product which can be marketed in both Vancouver (where recent Hong Kong immigrants recognize the 'brand name' of Li Ka-shing in particular) *and* Hong Kong (through three of Hong Kong's (and Asia's) largest property development firms). On this point, it is worth noting that Victor Li and Terry Hui were aware of the prospective demand by Hong Kong immigrants as they were developing condominiums during the mid-1980s in Richmond (through a company called Grand Adex Developments). Finally, Vancouver is also a pleasurable place

---

[12] The Hong Kong Bank of Canada deepened its network in Vancouver and the rest of BC by acquiring the Bank of British Columbia in 1986. The decision to sell the Bank of British Columbia to 'foreign' interests was strongly debated at the time of the sale (a sale that was eventually approved by Premier Vander Zalm, under some duress).

for the Hong Kong Chinese to do business in. The financiers of Pacific Place can visit friends and family, enjoy superb Asian cuisine, and escape from the throbbing pace of life in Hong Kong—a veritable west coast holiday resort in an urban context.

New Sensibilities: Developing the Pacific Rim Metropolis

The history of Canadian cities is marked by swells of immigrants which are 'synchronized with boom periods of city-building' (Olson and Kobayashi, 1993: 139). As noted above, Pacific Place must be seen in this context. However, Pacific Place is a massive project, taking up a full sixth (80 hectares) of the downtown core. While trans-Pacific human flows linking Vancouver to Hong Kong are a critically important factor underlying the development of Pacific Place, there are several other intersecting factors that have created the *opportunity* for the developer to acquire this prominent site, and then develop it in a relatively supportive economic and political context. It is these factors which I turn to now, before I provide a subsequent overview of the more tangible urban restructuring process which also supports the development of Pacific Place.

The acquisition of the North Shore of False Creek in 1988 by the Li Ka-shing *et al.* is now seen as a key event in the history of Vancouver's urban development. Since 1988, as I will highlight below, this project (one of the largest in North America) has been developed roughly on schedule. While the acquisition and subsequent development of the site has certainly been controversial, the developers have managed to manoeuvre through Vancouver's local system with sophistication and subtle power. While this development process certainly attests to the skills of Concord officials in working the system to achieve their goals, they were (and are) strongly supported by a labarynthine 'infrastructure' of institutions, individuals, state policies, and restructuring processes which are constructing Vancouver into the archetypal 'Pacific Rim' metropolis. This broad constellation of support provides the local context in which the firm operates. By embedding itself in this context, Concord is able to operate with relative ease in what is still a parochial place by most global city (certainly Hong Kong or even Toronto) standards.

The origins of the Pacific Rim initiatives that have supported Concord Pacific in its acquisition and subsequent development of the site are related to the efforts of the state to diversify an economy that was (and still is) highly dependent (directly and indirectly) upon the natural resource sector (principally forestry, mining and petroleum, agriculture and fisheries). Even in 1990, one-quarter of the province's GDP (and jobs) was attributable to international exports (primary staple commodities) when C$16.6 billion was exported to foreign markets. The province's small population (approx. 3 million), and geographic position on the west coast of North America (far from the large eastern population base), has exacerbated the boom and bust nature of the provincial staples-dominated economy (Davis and Hutton, 1992; Hutton, 1994*b*).

From the 1960s on BC's export base began shifting away from more tradi-tional American and British markets towards Asia (Japan principally). This shift, in conjunction with rapid economic growth in the Asia-Pacific region, generated an increased level of awareness of the potential benefits of deepen-ing economic links across the Pacific. At the national level, the key impetus to the development of a Pacific Rim focus was the 1970 establishment of diplo-matic links with China. Since then the federal government has devoted increas-ing resources to hooking Canada up to the capital, immigrants, ideas, and technologies which flow out of Asian countries such as South Korea, Japan, Taiwan, Hong Kong, and Singapore (Evans, 1992: 516; also see Langdon, 1995, and Woods, 1994). Over time, Canada and BC have, along with many other states, adopted (and contributed to) the construction of the 'Pacific Rim' idea—a construct that emerged in the 1970s in association with 'revaluing' of East and Southeast Asia (see several excellent chapters in Dirlik, 1993, on this topic). Successive federal [provincial and municipal] governments have all demonstrated a 'multipartisan consensus' on the 'push into the Pacific' (Evans, 1992), though the late 1990s Asian economic troubles did generate some discussion in Canada about this push.

The development of a Pacific Rim focus at the federal, provincial, and municipal levels was strongly propelled by a severe recession during the first half of the 1980s. This recession crippled the national and provincial economies, unemployment rates rose dramatically, and government budgets were marked by huge deficits. At a global scale, however, economic problems in Canada (and BC) coincided with rapid economic growth in Asian territories such as Hong Kong. The divergence of economic growth rates between Canada and Asia lie at the base of the movement (in business and political circles) to hook Canada up to the dynamic Asian economies.

Since the early 1980s, a variety of state-directed initiatives in Canada have been developed to deepen bilateral relationships with the principal Asian powers (Evans, 1992). A host of other Pacific Rim initiatives (e.g. research cen-tres, trade organizations, educational programmes) have been developed with state assistance as well. Given the need for brevity, I will focus on state initia-tives which most directly impact on Vancouver and the direct context within which Concord Pacific operates. The private sector has also contributed signif-icant resources (financial and otherwise) to these state-directed initiatives, as well as forming a host of private business organizations focused on develop-ing links with the Asia-Pacific region. While many of these initiatives were ad hoc, and certainly not designed in a coherent manner, their broad thrust towards improving links with, and knowledge about, the Asia-Pacific region has altered the basic tenor of development policy at all levels—a process of change facilitated by significant cross-linkages between all levels of govern-ment and specific people working on these initiatives. In the context of increased immigration flows from Asia, the overall effect has been the recon-ceptualization (by political, business, and academic élites) of Vancouver into a

Pacific Rim/global/world-class city. From this perspective, Vancouver is now situated on the edge of a dynamic Pacific region. The future role of the city is not as a colonial outpost of Europe; rather, Vancouver is being fashioned into a node for global flows, strategically positioned mid-point between Asia and Europe where the time zone 'allows a normal working day to bridge working hours in London, New York and Asia' (Edgington and Goldberg, 1992: 7–15).[13] Fashioning Vancouver into a functioning way station for global flows is also linked to a vision of using the city as a route for Asian entrepreneurs into the larger North American market in the context of the North American Free Trade Agreement.

Key initiatives designed to strengthen the links between Vancouver and the Asia-Pacific region, especially during the 1980s and early 1990s, are high-lighted in Box 4.1.

The growth and interlinkages between institutions and actors involved in these initiatives (and other non-Pacific Rim focused institutions such as the Greater Vancouver Real Estate Board or the Vancouver Board of Trade) has enhanced the state of 'institutional thickness' (Amin and Thrift, 1994, 1995*a*, 1995*b*) in Vancouver.[14] More precisely, a plethora of public and private institutions have emerged which have 'high levels of interaction' among each other, 'patterns of coalition building', and 'mutual awareness that they are all involved in a common enterprise' (Amin and Thrift, 1994: 14–15). Since the early 1980s, these institutions in Vancouver have become increasingly powerful in defining the development trajectory of the city (and province)—namely, hooking Vancouver, BC, and Canada up to the people, capital, technologies, images, and ideas flowing to and from the Asia-Pacific region. As Edgington and Goldberg (1990: 40) summarize, 'the Pacific is one area where there is extraordinary consistency of vision among public and private sector organizations and individuals . . . this is doubtless one of the reasons for the great success that the city and the province have enjoyed *vis-à-vis* Asia Pacific trade during the past few years and augers well for the next century'. These institutions command considerable public and private resources that are used to structure the nature of the policies and processes which influence Vancouver's future. Taken together,

---

[13] The time zone issue is one that senior Cheung Kong executives are well aware of. In deputy chairman George Magnus's ideal world, he would sit in his yacht anchored off the shore of the Pacific Place project, enjoy a relaxed pace of life in a beautiful physical setting, and also finalize Li Ka-shing's bond deals in New York just prior to the opening of the Hong Kong office (G. Magnus, interview, Apr. 1994).

[14] I adopt Amin and Thrift's (1994: 14) definition of institutional thickness. For them, institutions include firms; financial institutions; local chambers of commerce; training agencies; trade associations; local authorities; development agencies; innovation centres; unions; government agencies; business service organizations; marketing boards, and so on. 'All or some' of these institutions 'can provide a basis for the growth of particular local practices and collective representations'.

Box 4.1 Initiatives that thicken links between Vancouver and the Asia-Pacific region

Federal and Provincial

- *Asia Pacific Initiative (API).* In December 1986 the federal and provincial governments signed an agreement to 'coordinate efforts to strengthen the evolution of Vancouver as Canada's Pacific Centre for trade, commerce and air travel' (Davis and Hutton, 1994: 23). Six million dollars was committed to setting up an Asia Pacific Centre Advisory Committee with significant private sector input. Initiative projects include: the formation of an Asia-Pacific Banking and Finance Institute (in 1989) to sponsor seminars on trans-Pacific finance; the sponsorship of 'multi-cultural activities' in schools (Edgington and Goldberg, 1992: 7–16); the formation of an International Maritime Centre (IMC) (in 1991) that will enable global shipping firms to operate out of Vancouver while not being taxed on worldwide business operations; the annual Dragon Boat Festival in False Creek; and the formation of a separate local airport authority (see below). On a related note, the APEC Leaders' meetings were held in Vancouver in November 1997, leading *TIME* magazine (17 Nov. 1997) to deem Vancouver 'Asia's New Capital'.

- *International Financial Centre Vancouver (IFC).* In 1987 Vancouver was designated as one of two international banking centres in Canada. Federal and provincial tax regulations were amended to enable member firms to earn tax-free income from their international operations. UBC urban land economics professor Michael Goldberg (author of *The Chinese Connection: Getting Plugged In To Pacific Rim Real Estate, Trade and Capital Markets*, 1985) was the IFC's first executive director. The IFC had approximately sixty member firms in 1993. See <http://www.ifcvancouver.com/>.

- *The Asia-Pacific Foundation of Canada (APFC).* The APFC was established by the federal government through an Act of Parliament in 1984. The Foundation's national headquarters are in Vancouver, with regional offices in Saskatchewan, Manitoba, Ontario, Quebec, Taiwan, and Japan. Funding for the APFC comes from the federal and provincial governments, the private sector, and Foundation programmes such as courses, cross-cultural training programmes, seminars, research, and conferences. Other APFC initiatives and responsibilities include: The Pacific Information Exchange (a computerized database); The Media Fellowship Program; and an electronic mail service and bulletin board; the Asia Pacific Economic Cooperation (APEC) Study Centre; the administration of Asian language and awareness programmes in schools, community colleges, and universities; and the management of the biennial series of GLOBE conferences on Business and the Environment. The main focus of all these initiatives is the building of links between Canada and the Asia-Pacific region. See <http://www.apfnet.org/>.

(cont.)

- *The BC Trade Development Corporation.* This provincial crown corporation was established in 1989 to work with the business sector and increase links with the Asia-Pacific region. A network of five regional trade offices in the Asia-Pacific region operates under the auspices of BC Trade to encourage inward investment, and BC exports. BC Trade subsequently became the BC Trade and Investment Office, under the Ministry of Employment and Investment.

- *International Commercial Arbitration Centre.* This centre was established under the International Commercial Arbitration Act (1986). The Centre is a neutral meeting ground for companies resolving international and domestic legal differences through a dispute-resolution mechanism (Model Arbitration Law).

- *Senior Appointees.* In 1988 the Canadian Prime Minister appointed David See-Chai Lam, a Hong Kong-born Chinese-Canadian philanthropist (who made his money in property) as BC's Lieutenant-Governor (the Queen's representative). This was a high profile appointment that is recognized in BC, Canada, and Hong Kong as a major symbol of the increasing influence and power of Chinese immigrants in Canada. Subsequent high profile appointments include Raymond Chan (as Canada's Secretary of State, Asia-Pacific), the highest ranking Asia-born politician in the Western world.

- *Education Initiatives.* A series of education-oriented initiatives have been established since the mid-1980s to enhance knowledge of issues regarding countries in the Asia-Pacific region. For example, in 1987 the provincial government initiated the Pacific Rim Education Initiatives Program. The main aim of the programme, which consists of a variety of initiatives (including student travel, language courses, Asia-Pacific study courses, and scholarships) is to 'prepare the province's students to compete in the marketplace of the 21st century by broadening their perspectives and focusing their studies on the cultures, histories, geography, and economies of the Pacific Rim nations' (Davis and Hutton, 1994: 24). The impact of this programme has been felt at all levels of the education system. At the tertiary level, Vancouver's two universities and many community colleges have developed a variety of programmes focused on Asian languages and cultures (particularly Chinese and Japanese). Major research and teaching initiatives have been developed in centres such as the Institute of Asian Research, and the David Lam Management Research Centre (at UBC), and the David Lam Centre for International Communication (at SFU). The universities also place considerable emphasis on maintaining ties with alumni who are based in Hong Kong (where the UBC Alumni association has some 300 members), Tokyo, and Singapore.

- *The Vancouver International Airport.* The Vancouver International Airport is now managed by a local authority (as opposed to the federal government). The airport is completing a $750 million expansion in the attempt to enhance its status as a 'gateway' from North America to the Asia-Pacific region.

(*cont.*)

The City of Vancouver

- *Economic Development Strategy.* Successive economic development strategies have been developed since 1981 to promote Vancouver as 'the key business communications centre linking North America and the Pacific Rim' (Vancouver Economic Advisory Commission, 1983; also see Magnusson, 1990, and P. Smith, 1992). Through this strategy, Vancouver is conceptualized as a 'strategic city' in the Pacific Rim. City officials realize they can never become a Hong Kong or Singapore so instead focus on developing Vancouver as a 'niche player' in key sectors such as finance, engineering, and law. These economic development strategies have informed the City's support for all of the above federal and provincial initiatives, and a considerable number of City-sponsored trade and economic missions to the Asia-Pacific region during the 1980s (under the leadership of Mayor Michael Harcourt, a social democratic mayor who became the province's Premier in 1992). These missions were linked to the formation and/or deepening of 'sister city' relationships with Asian cities including Hong Kong, Yokohama, Guangzhou, and Singapore (Davis and Hutton, 1994). See <http://www.city.vancouver.bc.ca/>.

- *The Hastings Institute.* The City established the Hastings Institute in 1991 to promote multi-culturalism and employment equity in the context of Asian immigration flows, racial tension, and cultural conflict. All levels of government, as well as the private sector, finance the Institute.

Private Sector

The private sector is involved in many of the above initiatives. Since the early 1980s, the business community has become increasingly non-provincial in outlook (Magnusson, 1990). Among the institutions to be established in Vancouver are:

- *The Hong Kong–Canada Business Association (HKCBA).* The HKCBA was formed in Toronto in 1984 and now has approximately 2,500 members (it is Canada's second largest group of business professionals, and Hong Kong's largest active overseas association). The Vancouver branch (which was formed in 1984) has over 800 members. Within the city of Vancouver, only the long-established Vancouver Board of Trade is larger (Goldberg, 1991*b*). See <http://www.hkcba.com/vancouver/>.

- *The Laurier Institute.* The Institute was officially established in 1989. The main goals of the Institute are to 'contribute to the effective integration of the many diverse cultural groups within Canadian society into our political, social and economic life by educating Canadian people of the positive features of diversity' (Mitchell, 1993*b*: 283). The Institute is funded and directed by people from the private sector—the vast majority of whom are 'directly or indirectly involved with Hong Kong business or investment' (ibid. 286). See <http://www.laurierinst.com/>.

the reach and influence of the Pacific Rim contingent is long, sinuous, and hegemonic.

In such a context, the potential involvement of Hong Kong's most famous tycoon—Li Ka-shing—in commanding the development of the largest, most high-profile property development project in Vancouver's history, was viewed with considerable delight by those with power. Since 1988 though, as the implications of the 'Midas touch' of Li (Mitchell, 1993*a*: 178) began to sink in, the pro-Li, pro-Asia-Pacific view has become even more dominant. Moreover, key actors, associates, friends, and family members linked to the Concord Pacific firm have become deeply embedded within this network of institutions. The overall effect of this push to the Pacific is that a network of institutions offers direct and indirect support for the smooth development of Pacific Place. Global flows of capital are facilitated by directing them to such a supportive context, particularly when the controller of these flows is an icon of *future* economic prosperity. The developers of Pacific Place were astute to recognize and reinforce, both publically and privately, that they had considerable influence over where the Pacific wave hit North America; a wave that Canada, BC, and Vancouver were desperately eager to dive into.

Urban Restructuring in Vancouver

The many initiatives outlined above are also linked to the restructuring of Vancouver's economy, and the city's changing social structure. This restructuring process underlies the development of Pacific Place in a number of ways.

The early 1980s recession in BC and Vancouver speeded up the decline of the primary and secondary sectors throughout the province. This period was marked by massive job shedding and rapid technological change (Barnes and Hayter, 1992). The recession also accentuated trends in a restructuring process that has transformed Vancouver into a city heavily dependent upon the services sector (Ley and Hutton, 1987; Ley, 1996; Hutton, 1998). This restructuring process, which picked up speed during the 1970s and 1980s, has altered the nature of Vancouver's labour market (and social structure) in a manner which ultimately supports the redevelopment of the North Shore of False Creek. Employment in the service sector now accounts for more than three-quarters of the metropolitan labour force—one of the highest ratios in Canada (Davis and Hutton, 1994: 19). The producer services component of the metropolitan economy grew by 90 per cent from 1971 to 1986, consumer services grew by 160 per cent (Barnes *et al.*, 1992: 187–8), and the proportion of downtown 'managerial' staff expanded from 4.5 per cent in 1971 to 11.7 per cent in 1986 (North and Hardwick, 1992: 219). Jobs in management, administration, the professions, and technological fields (the 'quaternary sector') have shown continual growth (in both total number and proportionate rate by sector) even through the severe 1980s recession (Ley, 1993*b*: 56; Hutton, 1998). This broad structural shift led to the decline of what little heavy industry there was in downtown Vancouver, and the opening up of large tracts of land for redevelopment (e.g. the South Shore of False Creek was redeveloped during the 1970s).

The growth of the producer services sector has had concentrated impacts in the city of Vancouver, where approximately 70 per cent of all producer services employment is based (Barnes *et al.*, 1992; Ley, 1996). Vancouver's CBD has expanded rapidly since the 1960s through the development of commercial and retail space. The North Shore of False Creek is located on the southern edge of the CBD—obviously, any developer of the site would realize the potential of treating the site as a commercial, retail, and residential extension of the downtown core. Indeed, previous proposals for the site have all sought to accentuate either a commercial or residential role for the site through a connection to the downtown core. The City of Vancouver also wanted to see the site redeveloped into residential uses for the most part—a goal which the developer clearly knew of. This policy is designed to generate a 'liveable' downtown core, complete with residents and the service establishments that cater to their needs. Equally important, downtown living is designed to reduce the scale of commuting in Vancouver, a low density metropolitan region facing increasing problems with respect to traffic congestion and atmospheric pollution.

The broad restructuring process outlined above has contributed to the 'embourgeoisement' of Vancouver's inner city. Vancouver's inner city is increasingly an economic, social, political, and ideological space dominated by the new middle class, and by planning policies that favour the new middle class (Ley, 1993*b*, 1996; Blomley, 1998). The consumption habits of the *ideati* (Beers, 1994) are closely bound up with life in the inner city. The impacts of this process in Vancouver have been profiled in considerable detail by Ley (1980, 1987, 1993*b*, 1996), Mills (1988, 1993), Ley *et al.* (1992), Hutton (1994*a*), and Lees and Demeritt (1998), and I do not need to belabour the point. However, what I do want to be clear about is that the Hong Kong-based financiers of the Pacific Place project are effectively riding this social transformation—taking advantage of the 'product' if you will, of the processes of change in Vancouver. What the developers were faced with in Vancouver during the late 1980s and early 1990s was a situation in which a potential source of local demand for residential (condominium) and commercial uses on the site was available. Furthermore, the whole inner city was (and is) being steadily transformed by a local culture driven by the 'liveable city' ideology (Ley, 1980, 1996; Magnusson, 1990). Vancouver is a model 'landscape of power' where the urban development principles of 'ecology', of 'leisure', and 'liveability', are expressive of the 'consumption preferences of professionals' working in the service economy (Zukin, 1991: 17). This local culture, so concerned with aesthetic form and 'quality of life', is ensuring that inner city residents have access to the *de rigeur* attractions of the post-industrial/post-modern city—the aesthetically pleasing waterfronts, the seawalls, the cafés, the quality restaurants, the boutiques, the theatres, the festival market-places, and so on. Vancouver is being transformed into a subtle if sleepy version of

Las Vegas—'an urban theme park . . . that lulls rather than jars' (Beers, 1994: 46). The developer of the North Shore of False Creek was able to claim a huge site smack in the centre of this consumption orgy under way in Vancouver. This veritable cornucopia of consumption opportunities is demanded by the new middle class who work in the downtown corporate complex. By acquiring this site, Concord Pacific is able to target their units to these relatively wealthy domestic consumers.

Equally important, Concord Pacific is seeking to link Vancouver more tightly to Hong Kong through the development of a trans-Pacific property market. Condominium units situated within a Vancouver that has been appropriated by the new middle class, developers, and a local state concerned with the visual and the consumptive, are much easier to market in Hong Kong. While there are many other factors which prospective purchasers of condominiums on the Pacific Place site take into account, the emphasis on leisure, the aesthetic, and consumption are key elements of Concord's marketing strategy in Hong Kong. On a relative basis, a residential unit on Pacific Place is considerably more appealing (and affordable) than anything available in Hong Kong to the entrepôt's *nouveaux riches*; a factor which improves the ability of Concord to sell overseas units. These factors were highlighted during one of my interviews with a senior Hong Kong Bank of Canada official when he mentioned that Hong Kong purchasers of Pacific Place condominiums often viewed them as the equivalent of both a 'cotton future' *and* a 'part-time holiday residence'—an urban version of the summer cottage on the Gulf Islands (off the west coast of Vancouver) that so many non-Chinese Vancouverites enjoy (M. Glynn, interview, Mar. 1994).

To briefly summarize then, the restructuring processes under way in Vancouver have enabled Concord Pacific to acquire and develop a large tract of downtown land in Vancouver for which the prospective demand is available in both Vancouver and Hong Kong. In turn, the liveable city ideology, which has broadly guided Vancouver's development since the late 1960s, supports the ability of Concord to link these two markets, and sell the same product in two very different contexts. It is this ability to identify and manage the opportunities for complementarity, double coding, and subtle differentiation, that marks the successful property globalizer.

By now it should be clear that this 'landing strip' for foreign capital, to use Harvey's (1994*b*) words, became available through the confluence of a series of restructuring processes which effectively opened the site up to new uses, while also providing the potential local and overseas demand for high-density residential and commercial uses. Local government planning policy was also supportive (in principle) of the redevelopment of the site, the provincial government was supportive of the redevelopment of the site, and a whole array of powerful institutions and people were eager to see Vancouver transformed into a Pacific Rim metropolis. And finally, as clearly detailed above, flows of immigrants connecting Vancouver to Hong Kong became more dense, acting as a key channel through which flows of information, capital, and knowledge passed between these two cities on the Pacific.

While this general discussion is useful in setting the broad context in which the developers of Pacific Place have operated, the next section of Chapter 4 will focus on providing a provisional account of how globalization processes are activated by trananational cultures—in this case Hong Kong's most powerful Chinese property developers. The future course of what some Vancouverites happily called 'a village on the edge of the rain forest' (Ley *et al.*, 1992: 235) has been changed forever: understanding how and why Vancouver is changing depends, in part, on understanding how the development of Pacific Place reflects the goals and method of operation of Hong Kong's most influential and powerful property developer—Li Ka-shing.

Redeveloping the North Shore of False Creek

The Early Years

False Creek is nothing more than a filthy ditch in the centre of the city

(Mayoralty candidate Jack Price, 1950, quoted in Burkinshaw, 1984: 45)

The industrial character of the land around False Creek had been in steady decline since the 1950s. Indeed, two mayoralty candidates in the 1950 election suggested filling False Creek in completely, and placing a symbol of modernity (the highway) straight down the middle of the reclamation area (Burkinshaw, 1984: 45). As Burkinshaw (1984: 51) described it, the state of False Creek's decline was so severe that False Creek was considered Vancouver's 'bad address'.

After a series of land exchanges in 1967, the CPR consolidated its land holdings on the north shore of False Creek. It was at this time that Marathon Realty (the real estate arm of CPR) first raised the issue of building residential towers on the declining industrial site. After a protracted debate on issues including leisure, aesthetics, and tax revenue generation (in which high density residential uses were demonstrated to generate greater tax revenue than industry), Vancouver City Council voted to remove False Creek's industrial designation. The origins of this important vote are related to the election of new members of The Electors Action Movement (TEAM)—a municipal 'reform' party primarily composed of the new middle class (Cybriwsky *et al.*, 1986). The vote was 'the most significant decision affecting the inlet since 1885', and it 'ushered in a period of transformation of the character of the Creek rivalling in scope and speed the original transformation from a forest-line waterway to an industrial harbour' (Burkinshaw, 1984: 59).

The 1970s were marked by conflict and indecision over the future of the North Shore of False Creek. During the height of the modernist era in North American city planning, a 1969 plan by Marathon Realty envisioned a C$250 million residential development project for 20,000 people (including a marina) spread out over 77 hectares. This plan was later scrapped after political conflict with the City of Vancouver (Beazley, 1994: 118; Gutstein, 1986; Lee, 1988). With the benefit of hindsight, residential development of this scale (and density) would not have worked in downtown Vancouver at this time in the city's history; for political, cultural, and economic reasons, there was not enough support for the site's redevelopment. Two subsequent (scaled down) proposals of Marathon's met with similar fates (Cybriwsky *et al.*, 1986: 111).

Lack of development on the North Shore began to contrast sharply with the mid-1970s emergence of a novel redevelopment project on the South Shore of False Creek. This project, coordinated by a tri-level alliance of liberal 'reform' governments, is the 'expressive landscape of liberal reform'; a landscape underpinned by an ideology representing the 'fusion of aesthetics, ecology and social justice'. (Ley, 1987: 47).

While Marathon Realty struggled with plans for their North Shore site, the City of Vancouver and the federal Ministry of State for Urban Affairs jointly sponsored a study on waterfront redevelopment opportunities in Vancouver. One of the proposals for redeveloping the waterfront land on the northern edge of the CBD incorporated a world's fair (recall that Expo '67 in Montreal was still in people's minds). However, it was not until February 1978 that the idea of sponsoring a fair was seriously raised again. Architect Randle Iredale prepared a 'concept study' for the redevelopment of the Marathon lands on the North Shore of False Creek (Olds, 1988, 1998*b*). After reading the Iredale 'concept study', the sponsor of the study, Provincial Recreation and Conservation Minister Sam Bawlf, proposed an 'international exposition to complement Vancouver's 1986 centenary'. Vancouver's centenary was simply a suitable excuse to hold a world's fair given that all fairs are linked to 'important' dates such as the centennial of the French Revolution (Expo 1889). This linkage is required in order to attract support from the community, all levels of government, and the Bureau of International Expositions (BIE) (ibid.).

While various potential sites were examined during the spring and summer of 1979, Premier William Bennett asked Paul Manning and Larry Bell (then Deputy Minister of Lands, Parks, and Housing) to recommend locations for a large domed sports stadium. In the autumn of 1979 Manning and Bell recommended that the world's fair under consideration be linked to the stadium and constructed on the False Creek lands held by Marathon Realty.

Mega-Projects Socred-Style: BC Place and Expo '86

In January 1980 Premier Bennett, suffering through a 'crisis in political support' (Ley, 1987: 50), announced his 'vision for the future, a vision to build a great meeting place for all our people that we would call British Columbia Place'. In Bennett's (1980) words:

British Columbia Place would bring together a package of land on the North Shore of False Creek for public use. It would provide us with the new amphitheatre we desire and need. It would be the hosting area for Transpo Exposition [Expo '86]. It would provide impetus to get on with transit improvements.

Our concept, preliminary as it is and wide open for suggestions, visualizes the possibility of parks, pavilions, shops, offices and restaurants and open public spaces, along with the new amphitheatre and other complexes where our industries and institutions can show the world how British Columbians work and play.

As Canada's gateway to the Pacific, as the front line of Canada's opportunities for trade and contact with that vast number of people and countries that are the Pacific Rim, this park of business and leisure will become for all British Columbians and our visitors the focal point of our great province . . .

This is a total and whole-hearted commitment by your provincial government
We will secure those lands needed on the North Shore of False Creek.
We will play our fair role in providing needed transit improvements.
We will proceed immediately to build a multi-purpose amphitheatre.
We will take the lead.

The announcement of BC Place, the subsequent development of BC Place Stadium, Transpo '86 (which later became known as Expo '86), and the rapid transit system (known as Skytrain) which cut through Vancouver's neighbourhoods, was reflective of a neo-conservative ideology that was sweeping the Western world. In BC the state, as in Britain, centralized power under a 'dominant executive' (Ley, 1987: 53), and then applied the 'megaproject development strategy, which it had used for decades in the interior [of BC], to the City itself' (Magnusson, 1990: 181).

In August 1980 a provincial crown corporation (BC Place Ltd.) was formed (through provincial legislation) to redevelop the North Shore of False Creek. As a crown corporation, BC Place had:

the powers of a private corporation, additional privileges and fewer legal restrictions. It represents the extension of the centralized administrative model advocated by Progressive reformers early in this century, and is a vivid illustration of the argument of Weber, Habermas and others concerning the range of social control exercised by the modern bureaucracy. The corporate model gives maximum discretion and minimum disturbance to technical specialists acting as the agents of a central executive. As one corporate planner observed, 'The Cabinet are our shareholders'. (Ley, 1987: 53)

BC Place's senior corporate officers and board of directors were many of Vancouver's most powerful business élites. Among the ten person board of directors in 1981 was Stanley Kwok, president, Pendero Development Co. As noted above, Stanley was a Hong Kong immigrant who landed in Canada in 1968 (recall the 'first wave' of Hong Kong immigrants that I noted in Fig. 4.6). Further details on Stanley Kwok are presented in Box 4.2.

After several months of negotiations, BC Place acquired 176 acres (a figure which later increased to 224 acres) on the North Shore of False Creek in November 1980 from Marathon Realty for $30 million in cash and $30 million

Box 4.2 Brief profile of Stanley Tun-li Kwok

Stanley Tun-li Kwok was born in China in 1928. Kwok was educated in architecture at St John's University in Shanghai, where he graduated in 1948 (one year before the Communists seized power in China). He fled to Hong Kong in 1949 where he began working for the well-known Hong Kong design firm Eric Cumine and Associates. Kwok lived in Hong Kong for nineteen years until 1968 when he reached the top of the Hong Kong architectural hierarchy (as director and president of the Hong Kong Institute of Architects). During this time he worked for many of Hong Kong's real estate tycoons including Stanley Ho, Run Run Shaw, Fok Ying Tung, and Kwok Tak Seng. He also met the three eventual main shareholders of Concord Pacific—Li Ka-shing, Cheng Yu Tung, and Lee Shau Kee.

One year after the Hong Kong riots of 1967 (which were related to the Chinese cultural revolution) Kwok migrated to Canada. As he commented, 'I saw 1997 written on the wall' and I was 'young enough [then 40] and daring enough' to start a new life in Canada (quoted in Williamson, 1992, p. B2). Skill and connections led Kwok to a series of senior positions with three property development firms:

1968–70   Vice-President, Grosvenor International

1970–9   Vice-President, Canadian Freehold Properties

1980–4   President, Pendero Development Company Ltd.

During this time he also served on various City of Vancouver committees which addressed issues related to the City's property development planning process.

Kwok was brought onto the Board of Directors of BC Place in 1981, where he was the only senior BC Place official of Chinese descent. Following the death of BC Place chairman Alvin Narod, and the resignation of the BC Place president Gil Hardman in 1984, he was appointed as president and chief executive officer. Kwok also served on the Expo '86 Board of Directors until 1986. Kwok remained as chairman of BC Place until April 1987 when the provincial government abandoned plans to redevelop the Expo '86 site and advertise the site internationally.

Kwok was 61 years old when he was recruited by Li Ka-shing, his son Victor, and George Magnus to become director and senior vice-president of Concord Pacific Developments Ltd. (see below for further details). Kwok served in this position from September 1987 to April 1993, when he stepped down to make way for Terry Hui, the 29 year old son of K. M. Hui (another Concord shareholder). Kwok is now president of Amara International Investment Corp., he practises architecture with Davidson Yuen Simpson (one of the firms that worked on the BC Place and Pacific Place projects), and he works as a consultant on numerous property development projects. Directorships include Cheung Kong (Holdings) Ltd. (he is an 'independent non-executive director'), the Bank of Montreal Asian Advisory Panel, the BC Business Council, the

(cont.)

Canadian Chamber of Commerce, the Downtown Vancouver Association, BC Hydro, the Pacific Rim Council on Urban Development, the Vancouver Urban Development Institute, the Vancouver Foundation, and KCTS-9 (Seattle public television).

Sources: Field notes; S. Kwok (interview, Feb. 1994); Edwards (1992); Williamson (1992); Shaw (1993).

in downtown building sites. The key negotiator for Marathon Realty over the North Shore lands was Gordon Campbell, a well-connected professional who later became a City of Vancouver councillor (from to 1984 to 1986), mayor (from 1986 to 1993), and provincial politician in 1994. Campbell had actually started his career as a bureaucrat within City Hall between 1972 and 1976; a time which included two years as Mayor Art Phillip's executive assistant (from 1974 to 1976) (Gutstein, 1986: 69).

The period between 1981 and 1984 was marked by considerable conflict between the City of Vancouver and BC Place over development plans for the site. While the crown corporation had power to override City planning controls, it was clear that political and market realities would not permit the corporation to do so. The distance between the City and BC Place touched upon virtually every aspect of the C$2 billion proposal—from process to density to social mix (Carline, 1986; Ley, 1987; Gutstein, 1986; Beazley, 1994). The 1982 plans for the site, summarized in Table 4.9, clearly demonstrate the differences between the two main parties.

Table 4.9. Development plans (and differences) between the City of Vancouver and BC Place in 1982

Uses	City of Vancouver Development Concept	BC Place Development Concept
Total housing units	7,500–8,000	12,000
Market units	4,400–4,900	8,500–9,500
Non-market units	3,100	1,500–2,500
Total commercial space	up to 3.0 m. sq. ft.	7.7 m. sq. ft.

Source: British Columbia Place and the City of Vancouver (16 June 1982: 2–3).

The first half of the 1980s in Vancouver (and BC) was an extremely bitter period (as expressed in Fig. 4.11) in BC's history. Battles over BC Place soured already poor relations between the provincial and city government (which was controlled by a left of centre coalition). Inner city community organizations began to feel the social impacts of BC Place and Expo '86, in part due to property speculation on the borders of the mega-project site (Olds, 1988, 1998*b*; Ley, 1994). The provincial government, under Premier Bennett, launched a

Fig. 4.11. Senior British Columbia politicians restructure Vancouver during Expo '86 era

Note: Premier Bennett is holding the 'Exploit 86' flag.
Source: Material distributed in the Downtown Eastside of Vancouver in 1985.

'restraint' (austerity) programme which brought the province to the brink of a general strike, the recession hit the city hard (as noted earlier), and labour conflict raged (particularly after the Expo site was declared a 'special economic zone' forcing union and non-union workers together on the same site) (Ley *et al.*, 1992). Planning for the site was also disrupted by the preparations for Expo '86.

BC Place Ltd. was restructured in 1984, and Stanley Kwok was appointed as the corporation's president and chief executive officer. Kwok slashed staffing levels at BC Place by more than 40 per cent, and he drew in (on contract) affable architects such as Barry Downs of Downs/Archambault & Partners who had useful experience masterplanning the South Shore of False Creek. BC Place adopted a new phased approach, and they concentrated on planning 'North Park'—a 75 acre sub-area of the larger site, close to the edge of Chinatown and Gastown. Kwok and the City's mayor (Michael Harcourt—who later became provincial premier in 1992) agreed to adopt Kwok's proposal for a consensual-style planning process where, according to City planner Johnny Carline (1986: 15):

City staff are in the same downtown office as the B.C. Place staff and consultants. Every idea is shared, every approach is explored together, everybody's concern gets equal time in the process. The confrontation of 1983 has been replaced by a desire to reach consensus—to make sure that the proposals are not their plans versus my plans, but *our plans*. (emphasis in original)

This approach to planning reflected dissatisfaction with the failures of the previous BC Place planning process. UMP sites are extraordinarily difficult to plan given their physical scale. The new planning process suited Stanley Kwok's non-confrontational personality and approach to property development (which is partly based upon years of experience in both Canada and Hong Kong). Kwok had also developed a trusting relationship with the City's mayor, Michael Harcourt, through work and through their frequent chance meetings on Sunday morning strolls along the South Shore of False Creek seawall. These random events allowed the pair to swap 'visions' for the North Shore while gathering knowledge about each other, and the institutions they represented (Williamson, 1992). It is this type of everyday action in 'concrete social situations' which highlights the codeterminative nature of structure and action (Boden, 1994: 4–7). These 'tiny local' moments of 'human intercourse' laid part of the foundation which would eventually transform Vancouver, and help connect the city to the powerful flows of capital being directed out of Hong Kong.[15]

Detailed plans for the North Park site were drawn up in 1985 and early 1986, and then put on hold for the duration of Expo '86 (from 2 May to 13 October 1986). Over 22 million visits were recorded to Expo '86 during this period, including most of the eventual developers of Pacific Place. Expo '86 played a number of different roles in Vancouver, and these are outlined in great detail by Anderson and Wachtel (1986), Ley and Olds (1988; 1992), and Olds (1998*b*). However, I should be explicitly clear that Expo '86 was used as the 'trigger for the development' (Bennett, 1980) of the North Shore of False Creek. Expo '86 provided the opportunity to use public funds to clear the site and prepare it for subsequent development. The fair was also used to spur on the redevelopment of a stable low-income community (the 'slums' according to Premier Bennett) which bordered the Expo site. This area, known as the Downtown Eastside by area residents, was traumatized by the forced eviction of between 500 and 850 elderly and handicapped residential hotel and rooming house residents; a process

---

[15] I also note this issue in some detail because Kwok's development (with City approval) of the 'cooperative' planning process, set the tone for the Pacific Place planning process between 1988 and the present date. As I will note later in this chapter, this approach blended well with the Hong Kong financiers of Pacific Place who prefer the technocratic planning approach of Hong Kong (where the 'public' is distanced from the actual decision-making process). On the Hong Kong planning system, see Ng (1999).

which drove several evictees to their premature death (Shayler, 1986; Olds, 1988, 1998*b*; Ley, 1994).

From the perspective of the provincial government, Expo '86 created a temporary sense of optimism, exuberance, and momentum which was associated with the site (and the city) for prospective investors (Ley and Olds, 1988; K. Murphy, interview, Mar. 1994). The spectacle of the fair attracted international attention to the North Shore of False Creek and the whole city of Vancouver (e.g. overseas tourism levels rose by 25 per cent in 1986 (in comparion to 1985) and they have risen progressively since 1988). There was a distinct Pacific Rim flavour to many of the event's attractions and Vancouver's role as Canada's 'gateway' to the Pacific Rim was reinforced time and again on the fair site, and through the media. As Magnusson (1990: 181) notes:

Expo was a key to the strategy: the focus for an effort to attract tourists and new investors. Both the tourists and the investors were supposed to come from the Pacific Rim, especially California, Japan and Hong Kong. This idea reflected the growing consensus in the business community that Vancouver's future depended on its development as a centre for Pacific Rim commerce and trade.

Even critics admit that Expo '86 did accomplish some of the provincial government's aims, albeit at a social cost (as outlined above), and a C$336 minimum deficit for the provincial taxpayers. With three years time to reflect, Bob Williams (a senior provincial politician with the democratic socialist New Democratic Party) remarked (Williams, 1990):

Expo 86, of course, gave us an international presence. As a result we were probably catapulted a decade or two ahead in terms of global economic interest. Our verandah is now crowded with suitors from Asia and Europe, changing the nature of our town irrevocably . . . Bill Bennett moved Vancouver along a decade earlier into Jane Jacob's city state.

However, it is important to reinforce the context that I laid above. Expo '86 took place at a time when immigration flows between Vancouver and Hong Kong were just about to increase at an historically unprecedented rate, primarily because of changes in federal government immigration regulations in association with strengthening fears about the 1997 transfer to China, and the 1989 Tiananmen massacre. While Expo '86 did manage to focus the attention of some investors on Vancouver for a period of time, broader processes of change were the primary factors underlying flows of capital and people from Hong Kong to the city.

Six days after Expo was closed, a provincial election was held and the neo-conservative Social Credit Party (hereafter known as the Socreds) was returned to power with a majority, though with a new premier—William Vander Zalm. Vander Zalm, a Dutch immigrant and long time member of the Socreds, is a highly conservative small businessman from the suburbs of Vancouver.

Privatization and the North Shore of False Creek

Within two months of the election (Dec. 1986), the provincial government announced a moratorium on the development of the BC Place site, including the North Park sub-area. In March 1987, the Minister of Economic Development, Grace McCarthy, notified the public and the City of Vancouver that the BC Enterprise Corporation (BCEC) would be created to take control over various provincial assets (including BC Place), and then sell them.

Much of the impetus to sell the land came from the new Premier. Vander Zalm was a dogmatic ideologue who believed the power of the state over the economy should be weakened (Leslie, 1991). In contrast to the corporatist conservatism of Bennett, this Socred government looked to Margaret Thatcher and Ronald Reagan for inspiration. Vander Zalm was particularly impressed with Thatcher's privatization initiatives under way in Britain during the mid-1980s, and the sale should be seen as part of the worldwide privatization movement that gathered speed at this time in history. Vander Zalm and McCarthy also wanted to capitalize on the sense of 'optimism' and momentum that the site still retained from its association with Expo '86. The two politicians felt that the site was 'the place to be' in 1986, and they had to act quickly to take advantage of this temporary lustre. If they didn't, the site would revert to a 'no man's land'—a situation they did not want to deal with in a province still suffering from the mid-1980s recesssion (K. Murphy, interview, Mar. 1994).

Following Grace McCarthy's April 1987 announcement that the North Park proposal was officially cancelled, BCEC staff worked at developing an approach to the sale of the land.[16] At this early stage in the process, McCarthy was in fact suggesting that the 204 acre (80 hectare) site could be broken up into 'a whole series of component sites, each with its own requirements, markets, and opportunities' (quoted in Palmer, 1990, p. A16). During the BCEC investigation, officials discovered a large number of potential issues to be dealt with including soil contamination, unresolved infrastructure agreements with the City of Vancouver, discrepancies with legal lot sizes, uncertainty about the land edge *vis-à-vis* the water edge, and so on. BCEC staff also worked through the practical development difficulties which would be faced if the site was broken up into smaller pieces. These practical concerns led BCEC towards the option of selling the site in one piece. This option was also favoured by the Socred cabinet, though for different political and ideological reasons. First, they were eager to capitalize on the waning euphoria associated with Expo '86; selling the site in one piece was viewed as a quick route to action. Secondly, Premier Vander Zalm's roots as a small

---

[16] The sale process was handled by the provincial government with no serious input from the City of Vancouver (even though the City is responsible for processing development proposals for the site).

businessman left him enormously frustrated with the length of time taken by the bureaucracy to handle such processes. Selling the site in one piece was a quicker route to satisfying Vander Zalm's desire for action (K. Murphy, interview, Mar. 1994). And thirdly,

the Socred cabinet was single-mindedly committed to getting the government out of the development process and to stemming the overwhelming flow of interest payments [that the BC Place was building up]. The public interest, which lay in maximizing the return on the government's land investment portfolio, was consequently subordinated to the cabinet's ideological principles. (Leslie, 1991: 257)

In this political context, BCEC recommended in August 1987 that the site be sold in one piece, and advertised worldwide (a decision endorsed by the Socred cabinet). This decision effectively excluded small-scale developers with low capitalization levels, and the field of prospective buyers was narrowed to consortiums and large-scale international property developers.[17] The scale of the site is evident in Fig. 4.12.

The actual sale of the North Shore of False Creek lands is a long and complex story—clearly detailed in Leslie (1991), Mason and Baldrey (1989), Matas (1989a, 1989b, 1989c), Matas and York (1989), Persky (1989), and a series of KPMG Peat Marwick Stevenson & Kellog/Peat Marwick Thorne reports released by the (New Democratic Party) provincial government in March 1992. Readers are directed to these sources should they wish to investigate the subject in any detail.

Suffice it to say, an official process was followed between April 1987 and May 1988 which resulted in the land being acquired by Concord Pacific Developments Ltd., a private Canadian company controlled by Li Ka-shing (the majority shareholder), Lee Shau Kee, and Cheng Yu-Tung (key secondary shareholders) and a variety of minority shareholders including the Canadian Imperial Bank of Commerce (CIBC). Concord's only serious competitor was the Vancouver Land Corporation, a consortium of local investors whose proposal came in at around C$30 to $40 million less than that offered by Concord (with the added disincentive of dependence on the volatile Vancouver stock market for a large proportion of development capital).

Concord Pacific was reported to have paid C$320 million, but after factoring in payment schedules, government offers to clean up the contaminated sections of the site, and so on, the actual cost is closer to $145 million (1988

---

[17] Kevin Murphy, the official in charge of the sale process for BCEC, informed me that they were well aware of the 'small club' of international property developers who had access to sufficient capital and organizational resources to acquire and develop the site. BCEC contacted all of these firms to inform them of the site's availability in August and September 1987. However, it is also important to keep in mind that the recession during the first half of the 1980s narrowed this club's size. Furthermore, the global stock market crash of 19 October 1987 forced some of the companies who expressed interest in the site to 'shelve' their investment plans (Leslie, 1991: 253).

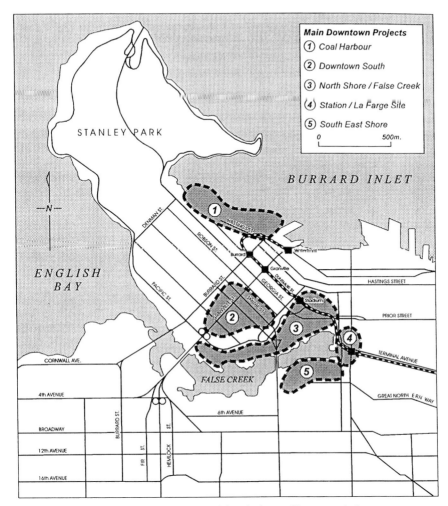

Fig. 4.12. The North Shore of False Creek in relation to Vancouver's downtown core

dollars) (Gutstein, 1990; Leslie, 1991). The payment schedule was $50 million cash in May 1988, $10 million on an annual basis between May 1995 and May 1999, and then $20 million in May 2000, $40 million in May 2001, $60 million in May 2002, and $100 million in May 2003. An additional bonus payment scheme, depending on the density of the project, was also arranged (which is worth a discounted value of $20 million maximum) (Leslie, 1991: 254–5). No interest is charged on deferred payment—in effect the provincial government shares in the cost of the mortgage. Concord company records from 1989 show a $50 million

---

[18] These are available on microfiche at the Vancouver Public Library, though only for 1989.

liability in the form of a bank loan—the likely source of the cash payment was the CIBC.[18] The provincial government also agreed to assume 'an open-ended unspecified liability . . . by agreeing to undertake site remediation at the Province's costs' (KPMG Peat Marwick Stevenson & Kellog/Peat Marwick Thorne, 1992, p. B-6).[19] The overall effect of this financial arrangement was that Concord Pacific tied up the future of one-sixth of downtown Vancouver for the cost of simply setting up the firm, and hiring staff to prepare a proposal. The provincial government, in contrast, arranged a deal in which the 'net loss' is 'unlikely to be less than $150 million' taking all factors into account (Leslie, 1991: 256). However, no alternative proposal came close to matching that put forward by the Hong Kong-based financiers of Concord Pacific. This is particularly true when BCEC took into account the large pools of development capital available to Concord Pacific—together, the three tycoons associated with Concord controlled five of Hong Kong's largest public firms (1994 figures are presented in Table 4.10), and many other public and private firms—a fact George Magnus made very clear to the provincial government. This simple indicator barely highlights the many other sources of public and private capital the tycoons can access (Olds and Yeung, 1999).

The enormous financial power of these three men also highlights the shift of global capital flows to the Asia-Pacific region, the importance of Hong Kong's stock market as a vehicle to access these capital flows, and the emergence of what are some of the largest property development firms in the world today.

The sale of the land, and the unveiling of Concord Pacific's plans for Pacific Place were announced at the BC Enterprise Centre on the former Expo '86 site on 27 April 1988. Headlines in the main local paper (*The Vancouver Sun*) suggested 'BREATHTAKING', 'Bouquets for $2 billion Pacific Place', and 'West Coast Venice'. The $2 billion proposal for the 82 hectare site included 10,000 dwelling units, 3 million sq. ft. (287,000 sq. m.) of commercial space (including an 'international financial centre'), 20 hectares of parkland, a 400 room hotel, and a 630-berth marina (see Fig. 4.13).

Massive local, provincial, and national media coverage resulted from this process over the next several weeks. In this coverage both the provincial government and the developer sought to emphasize, among other themes, how Vancouver was now 'on the Pacific Rim map'. Even critical academics such as Mitchell (1993*a*: 177, 178) have commented that 'the sale of the Expo lands to Li-Ka-shing can be seen as a deliberate move to increase the

---

[19] The final estimates of the soil remediation programme are in the region of $100 million. During negotiations with the BCEC, George Magnus informed the government they were 'not going to buy BC's problems' and refused to purchase the site for Concord Pacific unless this condition was met (G. Magnus, interview, Apr. 1994). The provincial government initially estimated (erroneously) that the remediation costs would total somewhere between $5–10 million (Blain, 1990; Matas, 1994).

Table 4.10. The twenty leading Hong Kong companies in market capitalization as at December 1994

Rank	Company	Market Capitalization (HK$ m.)	Percentage of market total
1	HSBC Holdings	222,684.53	10.68
2	Hong Kong Telecom	164,503.59	7.89
3	**Hutchison Whampoa***	**113,276.92**	**5.43**
4	Sun Hung Kai Properties*	107,393.76	5.15
5	Hang Seng Bank	107,198.33	5.14
6	Swire Pacific*	70,229.17	3.37
7	**Cheung Kong (Holdings)***	**69,223.02**	**3.32**
8	China Light	65,691.65	3.15
9	**Henderson Land***	**58,892.02**	**2.82**
10	Wharf (Holdings)*	56,581.31	2.71
11	**Hong Kong Electric**	**42,730.08**	**2.05**
12	Hong Kong Land Holdings*	40,657.49	1.95
13	Jardine Matheson Holdings	40,158.67	1.93
14	CITIC Pacific	37,591.32	1.80
15	**New World Development***	**32,902.53**	**1.58**
16	Cathay Pacific Airways	32,902.53	1.55
17	Hopewell Holdings*	27,934.54	1.34
18	Wheelock and Co.*	25,935.24	1.24
19	Hong Kong China and Gas	25,867.43	1.24
20	Jardine Strategic Holdings	23,989.72	1.15
	Total	1,365,667.10	65.49
	Market Total	2,085,182.06	100.00

Notes: * Denotes property company (or very significant property dealing).
  Bold emphasis denotes the companies controlled by the Li Ka-shing, Lee Shau Kee, and Cheng Yu-Tung.
Source: The Stock Exchange of Hong Kong, and Brooke Hillier Parker.

city's global integration by attracting capital from Pacific Rim investors'. However, as I noted above, the land was primarily sold for ideological reasons, to the highest bidder, in 'the shortest practical time period', as directed by the Socred cabinet (Palmer, 1990). In contrast to many officials and some ministers within the provincial government who knew of the 'Midas touch' of Li Ka-shing, Vander Zalm was a nationalist, and he preferred the idea of the site going to Canadian developers. As he himself said, 'All things equal, if there are two offers reasonably close, then I would prefer the Canadian one' (quoted in Mason and Baldrey, 1989: 204). My basic point here is that the push to the Pacific was still in its formative stages in 1987, and the Pacific Rim contingent had several more years of serious building to do before it could claim hegemonic status (as it has now). While the government clearly supported the interest demonstrated by Li Ka-shing in acquiring the site, they did not structure the whole process with him (or any other Asian investor) specifically in mind.

Since the site was sold to Concord Pacific, the provincial government has spent a considerable amount of effort 'justifying its actions as a means for

Fig. 4.13. The original Pacific Place proposal

Source: The Pacific Place Design Consortium.

cementing economic relations with Hong Kong, which was seen as the key source of new capital, new entrepreneurs, and new business connections' (Magnusson, 1990: 183). However, no amount of incentives, financial or otherwise, could have enticed powerful and wealthy Chinese tycoons like Li Ka-shing to Vancouver to acquire this site were there not a plethora of other goals which could be satisfied by acquiring the site. While the site was certainly undervalued (a factor Li searches for in all deals), these other less directly material goals were far more important, in my opinion, at encouraging Li to reach across the Pacific, acquire the site, and then devote the considerable human resources which have been required to initiate the development of this large project. Vancouver's planning and market context is exceedingly slow by Hong Kong standards, and capital returns are much higher in Hong Kong and the rest of the Asia-Pacific region than in Vancouver (on this point see any international chartered surveyor's annual international property market review report). At a Pacific Rim scale, the 'rent gap' associated the Expo site was a pittance. The materialist imperative, and the maximization of short-term financial returns, was clearly not the main aim of developing this project.

What I will do now is shift focus, and try to explain how this economic process—the acquisition and subsequent development of an UMP by global developers—is a social and cultural construct, reflective of the nature of Hong Kong-based ethnic Chinese capitalism, and of the dynamics associated with the Li family in particular.

Expanding the Network: Pacific Place and the Redevelopment of the North Shore of False Creek

> If I can't live there, my money cannot live there either.
>
> (Victor Tzar-kuoi Li, quoted in Stoffman, 1989: 124)

The acquisition of the North Shore of False Creek is the result of the decision of Li Ka-shing, Hong Kong's richest, most powerful, and well-connected property tycoon to deepen his family's linkages with Vancouver. A formal decision to move ahead with a bid for the site was taken during the summer of 1987 when Li Ka-shing, his son Victor, and their advisers (primarily George Magnus), were satisfied that the bid process had not been predetermined by the provincial government (the Premier in particular).

The decision to invest, and the subsequent development of the Pacific Place project on the False Creek site from 1988 until 1993, is the physical manifestation of Chinese capitalism integrating with Vancouver's property markets on an enlarged scale. The capital flows that link Vancouver with Hong Kong are interwoven with ethnic Chinese migrant flows, and the two flows are inseparable for the most part. Further, it is impossible to speak of a 'command and control' situation, where the global city of Hong Kong was simply used as a base to direct capital flows to Vancouver in a straightforward economic sense.[20] Rather, the development of Pacific Place is

---

[20] See Sassen's work (1991, 1994, 1998) on the global city as 'command point' in the organization of the world economy. As Thrift (1993a: 232) writes: 'it is at least debatable whether the world

the result of a more diffuse network connecting actors who are situated both within and external to the formal firms controlled by the Li family. In other words, this 'economic process'—the acquisition and redevelopment of 80 hectares (one-sixth) of Vancouver's downtown core—is a social construct strongly reflective of the nature of Hong Kong-based élite Chinese business culture. The tangible construction of buildings on the site is the result of the mobilization of a variety of resources (including knowledge, skills, and connections) to achieve a myriad of constantly changing goals; goals which reflect (for the most part) the aims of the Li family at a key stage in their development. Put simply, Pacific Place is an elegant marker of the intersection of a burgeoning trans-Pacific residential property market with trans-Pacific migration, and succession plans within one of the world's leading Chinese corporate groups (the Cheung Kong Group)—three factors which both constitute and are constitutive of the processes of globalization.

The following section examines some key phases and events in the development of Pacific Place in order to highlight the socially constructed nature of the property investment and development process:

- the decision to invest: who decides, and why invest now;
- locating a bridge; and
- establishing the institutional base.

While some effort is made to follow a chronological pattern, the need for brevity precludes much discussion of the actual development process (and in particular the role of City of Vancouver politicians and planners in this process).[21]

The Decision to Invest: Who Decides, and Why Invest Now

The rationale behind the decision of the Li family to deepen linkages with Vancouver has deep roots in both Hong Kong and Vancouver.

Li Ka-shing (see Box 4.3 for further details on Li) has two sons—Victor Tzar-kuoi Li (born in 1965), and Richard Tzar Kai Li (born in 1967). Like many from Chinese business families, the sons were groomed from an early age to take part in their family's firms, and it is impossible to separate 'work life' from 'home life'—the two are intertwined:

financial system in particular is "commanded" or "controlled" in any strong sense at all! More to the point, the new economic sociology has shown, rather convincingly, that command and control are concepts that need unpacking and that once that process begins then the meaning of these concepts begins to slip away, like sand, through the fingers'.

[21] Some issues related to the actual processing of the Pacific Place development project are covered in Folkes (1989) and Beazley (1994). The Beazley and Folkes theses address (in considerable detail) the controversial issue of citizen participation in the planning process. Unfortunately, a detailed account of the redevelopment of the North Shore of False Creek after 1980 has yet to be written.

Says Li: 'If my boys can learn from me, they will have more assets.'

The lessons started early. Richard recalls that he and his brother 'had little chairs in the corner of the board meetings since we were 8 or 9 years old.' Victor describes his dad as 'the best business professor,' especially for teaching how *not* to make money. Explains Victor: 'The most important thing I learned from him is how to be honorable and how to treat partners right,' Richard interprets the lesson this way: 'If a 10% share is reasonable and you can get 11%, take 9% because then a hundred more deals will come to you.' Another bit of wisdom that Richard says comes from his father: 'Use the expertise of others, whether your staff, your partner, or the government.' (Kraar, 1992*b*: 108)

In 1981, Victor left Hong Kong to attend Stanford University where he enrolled in the civil engineering programme. An overseas education at a respected institution is an increasingly common affair in Hong Kong; indeed there are 'strong links between prospective real estate investment and the location of family and friends, and where children and grandchildren were attending university' (Edgington and Goldberg, 1992: 7–9). As Goldberg (1985) and Mitchell (1993*b*) highlight, the education of children is a critically important factor in Chinese culture, and it reflects the fundamental role of the family in society.

Two years later (1983), when he was 18 years old, Victor became a naturalized Canadian citizen. That Canada was selected as the safe option for Victor's 'second home' is related to a number of factors:

- the variety of property investments Li Ka-shing has accumulated in Canadian cities (including Vancouver) since the late 1960s (Gutstein, 1990: 132);
- the holiday house the Li family vacationed at since the early 1970s on a street in Oakridge (a Vancouver neighbourhood) 'where many friends already lived' (Tierney, 1989);
- long-term linkages Li Ka-shing has formed with Canadian financial institutions in 1974 (as I noted in Section 1 of this chapter);
- the accessible nature of Canada's immigration system; and,
- the social and political climate of the country.

As Victor himself stated: 'One of the best things about Canada is the way it treats new people. The cultural diversity makes the investor feel comfortable. There's also political stability. Canada is one of the most comfortable places to do business compared to a lot of Western countries' (quoted in 'An inside Asian investor's view of Canada', 8). Similarly,

As a Chinese it is not easy living in a Western country. Sometimes we feel certain discrimination and, other times, are forced to give up our customs and our culture and join the melting pot.

Box 4.3 Brief profile of Li Ka-shing

During the main period under consideration (late 1980s to mid-1990s), Concord Pacific's main shareholder was Li Ka-shing, Hong Kong's richest billionaire. In 1994, Li's personal wealth was estimated to total US$7 billion (HK$45 billion), making him the world's sixteenth richest person. In 1994 he was the fourth richest person in Asia after the Sultan of Brunei and Japanese property tycoons Minoru Mori and Toichi Takenaka. Wealth levels have continued to rise, even through the Asia economic crisis. For example, by 1999 Li 'and family' had become the world's tenth richest person according to *Forbes Magazine*, worth approximately US$12.6 billion. Li Ka-shing's firms have a market value estimated to be at least US$22 billion, 15 per cent of total stock market capitalization in Hong Kong (Kraar, 1992b). The combined profits of Li's listed firms alone added up to more than US$1 billion in 1993. Known as *Chui Yan Li* (Superman Li) in Hong Kong, Li financially directs or is involved with a complex web of companies active in property, banking, oil and gas, telecommunications, infrastructure (especially ports and power), shipping, and retailing.

Property development in Hong Kong has been Li's main form of profit since the mid-1970s via two of his most powerful public companies—Cheung Kong (Holdings) Ltd. and Hutchison Whampoa. Cheung Kong is the main holding company for all of what is known as the 'Cheung Kong Group', including Hutchison Whampoa, Cheung Kong Infrastructure (which was established in 1996), and Hong Kong Electric.

While the vast majority of property development has taken place in Hong Kong, Li is increasingly diversifying his property portfolio with investments in China (where his firms are developing approximately 7.5 million sq. m. (80 million sq. ft.) of property), Toronto, New York, San Francisco, and London. The complexity of the Li conglomerate is significant. Few people, apart from Li and his two sons, chief executives, and senior financial controllers truly understand how the group's many public and private arms channel flows of capital around, and how the firms relate to the 'external' world. This level of complexity is all the more confusing given that Li invests capital from his considerable personal fortunes into projects throughout the world, including the Pacific Place project in Vancouver.

Key events in the growth of the Li empire are listed below:

1928   Born in Chaozhou, Guangdong Province. Li is a Teochew Chinese, the second largest dialect group in Hong Kong.

1940   Li's father sends him to study in Hong Kong during the middle of the Sino-Japanese war (1937–41) when the Japanese military prepare for an attack on China's coastal region. Li is one of over 740,000 refugees who flood into Hong Kong at this time.

1942   Li's father dies. As eldest son, he begins selling plastic belts and watchbands to support his family.

1950   Sets up own business (Cheung Kong) and factory (plastic combs, soapboxes, plastic flowers) with US$ 7,000 savings.

(cont.)

1958 Buys own factory and apartment building. Shifts into property development.

1965 First son (Victor Tzar-kuoi Li) born in Hong Kong.

1967 Second son (Richard Tzar Kai Li) born in Hong Kong.

1970 Scouted by Hong Kong & Shanghai Banking Corp., as suitable Chinese client. Beginning of long relationship with the bank's senior executives.

1971 Cheung Kong incorporated as a property owner and developer.

1972 Cheung Kong listed on the Stock Exchange of Hong Kong.

1974 Together with the Canadian Imperial Bank of Commerce, Cheung Kong forms CEF Holdings to carry out merchant banking activities.

1979 Hong Kong & Shanghai Banking Corp., sells Cheung Kong a controlling stake in the British hong Hutchison Whampoa.

1985 Hutchison Whampoa takes over Hong Kong Electric.

1987 Acquires 52 per cent of Husky Oil in Canada.

1988 Begins the redevelopment of the North Shore of False Creek in Vancouver.

1988 Begins the development of Suntec City in Singapore.

1990 Richard Li returns from Canada to work at Hutchison Whampoa.

1991 Li family control of Husky Oil increases to 95 per cent.

1993 Victor Li returns from Canada to work at Cheung Kong.

1994 Cellular service 'Orange' launched in Europe.

1996 Victor Li kidnapped and held ransom by Hong Kong gangster Cheung Tze-Keung ('Big Spender'). Freed after his father pays US$125 million ransom. Cheung later executed by Chinese government in Guangzhou.

1999 At 70 years of age, steps down as managing director of Cheung Kong; succeeded by Victor Li, now 34. Still actively involved in managing Cheung Kong Group.

Li Ka-shing is also a Beijing-appointed Hong Kong Affairs Adviser to Beijing; he sits on China's Preliminary Working Committee; he is a member of the Hong Kong Governor's Business Council; he is a business adviser to China International Trust & Investment Corp. (Citic), Beijing's main overseas investment arm; he acts as 'the chief western agent for the Chinese state arm's manufacturer Norinco';[22] he helped draft the Basic Law (Hong Kong's constitution after 1997); he was a former board member of the Hong Kong and Shanghai Bank; and he

(*cont.*)

---

[22] This information comes from Cahill *et al.* (1993: 43). Norinco, a child of the Fifth Ministry of Machine Building industry, is responsible for 'China's conventional weapons manufacture' (Holberton and Walker, 1994: 19). I have not seen this confirmed in any other publications, though the 1999 debate (e.g. see ⟨http://www.afpc.org/issues/panama.htm⟩) about Hutchison Whampoa's links to the Chinese government *vis-à-vis* their investment projects in the strategic Panama Canal makes reference to the weapons link.

is a major financial donor (including £1 million in the 1987 election year) to the British Conservative Party.[23] In Canada, Li has a variety of investments including just under ten per cent of the Canadian Imperial Bank of Commerce (the largest legal amount permitted to an individual shareholder; CIBC had assets in the range of C$132 billion in 1992 and C$240 billion in 1999), 95 per cent of Husky Oil, and property in Vancouver and Toronto.

Key characteristics associated with Li and his firms include:

- *Timing.* Li has an acute sense of timing, which is partially built upon his access to networks which provide accurate and rapid information. This sense of timing meshes well with the autocratic nature of the key decision-making process in ethnic Chinese firms, enabling Li to act very quickly, and in a decisive manner. This overall approach has assisted him in his aim of acquiring large scale undervalued assets (e.g. major property acquisitions in Hong Kong during the Chinese cultural revolution, and the 1973 oil-related recession).

- *Deal-making.* The sheer thrill of putting together a good 'deal' which satisfies all participants is a major source of Li's inspiration. Of course, the deals have to make a profit, but the process of their construction also matters to a great degree.

- *Relations with Finance.* Li has focused on the long-term formation of relations and joint ventures with financial institutions (including merchant banks). These include the Hong Kong and Shanghai Banking Corporation, the Canadian Imperial Bank of Commerce, CEF Holdings, and Peregrine Investment Holdings. Through restructuring and acquisitions, firms such as Cheung Kong can now act as merchant bankers themselves, participating in venture capital, fund management, securities trading, and corporate finance (UBS Global Research, 1994: 3). See Olds and Yeung (1999) and Yeung and Olds (2000) on this issue more generally.

- *Relations with Investors.* Li has made great efforts to develop long-term relations with global investors such as Paul Reichmann, Rupert Murdoch, George Soros, Robert Kuok, Cheng Yu-Tung, Lee Shau Kee, Gordon Wu, and the Bronfman family. This is accomplished through the sharing of important information and contacts, and the formation of joint ventures.

- *Relations with Politicians.* The formation of long-term relations with senior politicians (e.g. Margaret Thatcher, John Major, Li Peng (and family), Deng

(cont.)

---

[23] Margaret Thatcher is one of Li's personal friends. One symbolic expression of this friendship occurred on 16 March 1991 when Thatcher officially dedicated the David Lam park on the Pacific Place site while she was on her way to meet with the then Prime Minister Brian Mulroney (Farrow, 1991, p. B1). Also present at the meeting were BC Lt.-Gov. David Lam, Victor Li, George Magnus, and Stanley Kwok. Li's son Victor and George Magnus (from Hong Kong) acted as host for Li in this event. This form of symbolic inscription helps repay favours, honour friendships, and symbolizes the increasing power of the Hong Kong Chinese in Vancouver's development.

Xiaoping (and family)) is a key aspect of building networks of power. These relations often involve large-scale financial donations to political parties.

- *Information Flows.* The Li family businesses are renowned in Hong Kong for releasing low levels of information flow about their activities. The information that is released also tends to be quite opaque, and unimportant. Li exerts extremely tight control over information flows, and he has a distaste for the more critical Western media. Western business people are hired to deal with the Western press, and they are well known for their damage-control abilities.

- *Mega-projects.* Li's two main property development firms (Cheung Kong and Hutchison Whampoa) are Hong Kong's most experienced residential mega-project developers; a form of development which provides the firms with a major source of profit. The firms traditionally build up a large and inexpensive land bank, and then use their considerable expertise and resources to develop the projects quickly following highly effective pre-sale marketing campaigns (which are easier to conduct with large-scale property projects). The practice of using pre-sale keeps the firm's gearing levels (net debt to equity) at relatively low levels, and shifts risk from producer to consumer. This approach also leads the firms to focus on turnover (i.e. the commodity-production approach) rather than high profit margin. Li's mass residential projects tend to be located near major public transportation nodes. The firms have developed a strong track record over the years in Hong Kong, and this convinces landlords to cooperate with them. The Cheung Kong and Hutchison Whampoa brand names are well known in Hong Kong.

Note: the Cheung Kong web site is at <http://www.ckh.com.hk>, while Hutchison Whampoa is at <http://www.hutchison-whampoa.com/>.
Sources: Tierney (1987, 1989); Rafferty (1989); Kraar (1992*a*, 1992*b*, 1999); Taylor (1992); Cahill *et al.* (1993); Holberton (1993); *Euromoney* (Oct. 1994: 105); UBS Global Research (1994); Redding (1995); Seagrave (1995); Chan (1996); *Forbes Magazine* (<http://-www.forbes.com>, accessed 22 Nov. 1999); Baring Securities; Cheung Kong Holdings; Hutchison Whampoa; ING Barings.

Here in Canada, I feel very much at home. I can participate in the local community and at the same time feel proud of being a Chinese-Canadian. Canadians, by accepting people of different backgrounds, have created a cultural mosaic. (Li, 1992: 3)

By 1985, Victor had graduated from Stanford with an undergraduate degree in civil engineering, and a master's degree in structural engineering. He briefly worked for an architectural firm in Hong Kong before crossing the Pacific once again to set up a base in Vancouver at the age of 21. This move to Canada was sanctioned by his father; it was a chance for Victor, as one of Li's 'boys', to 'prove himself by gaining maturity and new experiences' (Kraar, 1992*a*: 108, 1992*b*: 62, 1999).[24]

As I noted above, Vancouver was a chosen as a suitable location for Victor's 'second home' (Kraar, 1992*b*: 63). Even though the city was experiencing an economic recession, steady immigrant flows from Hong Kong and other Asian countries had created a diverse ethno-cultural mix in the city (while also creating related market opportunities). These points were reinforced several years later when Victor suggested to a friend ('Mr Wong') that Vancouver was a good place to do business:

> Partly because of Canada's immigration policy, the city has experienced profound changes in recent years, becoming more active, international and, in particular, more oriented to the Pacific Rim. A population growth of three per cent annually—more than double Hong Kong's—means increasing demand for various services. And because certain industries are slow in responding to sudden change in demand and taste, there's a great opportunity for those who can fill the vacuum. (Li, 1992: 1)

Vancouver is also the closest Canadian city to Hong Kong, there are frequent direct flights between the two cities, the climate is relatively mild, the city is perceived by many to be relatively 'beautiful', and the physical setting is somewhat reminiscent of Hong Kong.

Victor's comments above, and his subsequent action in Vancouver highlight the important role of 'destination' socio-cultural factors in underlying the ultimate decision-making process of Hong Kong-based Chinese investors. Decisions over large-scale property development projects are taken (with

---

[24] Richard Li was also permitted to 'prove himself' in Canada, though in Toronto where the two young brothers would have enough space to express themselves. Richard attended high school in Hong Kong until the age of 14 (1982). He then moved to California where he completed high school, and then studied computer engineering and economics at Stanford University (the same university Victor attended). After graduating from Stanford, 'brief stints' were completed at Harvard University and London Business School before he moved to Toronto in 1986 (about the same time that Victor had moved to Vancouver). Connections enabled him to land a job as an investment banker for Gordon Investment Corp. (his father owned approximately 5 per cent of it at the time). At Gordon Investment he became 'the youngest ever executive director and then the youngest partner of any investment bank in Toronto' (Kraar, 1992*b*: 64; Matas, 1989*c*). Richard was pulled back to Hong Kong (at his father's request) in 1990, and he has worked at Hutchison Whampoa ever since. Richard became executive director in 1992 (at 25 years of age) and co-deputy chairman in 1993. He is also chief executive for the Pacific Century Group ⟨http://www.pacificcentury-grp.com/⟩, a services sector investment firm which was capitalized with US$400 million of profit from the $525 million sale of a 64 per cent stake in StarTV to Rupert Murdoch's News Corp in 1993. The sale was related to Li Ka-shing's growing concerns that his 'association' with satellite TV might create problems in Beijing (where he has connections to Li Peng and Deng Xiaping, and over $5 billion in investments) (*The Economist*, 31 July 1993: 59; *Euromoney*, Oct. 1994: 105). Richard's handling of the StarTV sale, which also resulted in the Li family gaining 2.7 per cent of News Corp, was his first highly visible step towards gaining 'credibility' with Hong Kong's élite business circle (*Far Eastern Economic Review*, 19 May 1994: 62). Richard also has good connections with property and political élites in Vancouver (Andrea Eng, a former student of Michael Goldberg's, is now a senior property investor for the Pacific Century Group; on Eng see McLaughlin (1993) and van Halm (1988)). Richard has been on Concord Pacific's board of directors.

professional assistance) by core family members, with the patriarch ultimately responsible (Redding, 1991, 1995; Hamilton, 2000). In this case both the son and the father had to feel comfortable with the socio-cultural 'atmosphere' in the location where the prospective property investment would be made. This factor helps explain why significant capital flows are directed to cities such as Shanghai (see Ch. 5), Singapore, Toronto, Vancouver, and San Francisco—all cities where extended social relations are built upon a social formation with a large proportion and number of Chinese people. The importance of a supportive socio-cultural atmosphere in making Chinese investors feel comfortable also helps explain why the public and private sectors in Vancouver have made such an effort during the 1980s and 1990s to build connections across the Pacific, and transform Vancouver into Canada's 'gateway' to the Pacific Rim. The élites who fashion public policy, and those who hold sway over private institutions such as the media, understand the critical role of extended social relations in guiding large-scale capital flows from Hong Kong (see e.g. Goldberg, 1985). These social relations are best nourished in cosmopolitan locales, where racial tensions are resolved and/or repressed from the public sphere (see Mitchell, 1993*b*, on the instrumental use of 'multi-culturalism' to enhance capital accumulation in Vancouver). Of course there are many other factors which 'pull' such investors over, but this factor is a relatively tangible one that local institutions could (and did) work at enhancing.

Just prior to Victor's move to Canada, Terry Hui arrived in Vancouver from Berkeley. Terry, who was 21 at the time, had just graduated from the University of California at Berkeley with a joint degree in electrical engineering and physics. Born in Hong Kong, though now a Canadian citizen, Terry came to join his father (Kau Mo Hui), a wealthy Hong Kong-based property developer who was working in Vancouver.[25] He quickly became his 'own general contractor' on his father's property development project in Vancouver (Fairview Heights). Says Terry, 'I was lucky to be here in 1986, just before the big housing boom . . . when I could just accumulate so much experience in such a short time. I had to write all the contracts, even though I had no background in construction, but I came in on budget and I had lots of fun' (quoted in Newman, 1993: 40).

With this base of experience, Terry set up a registered Canadian property development company with his friend, Victor Li, who had recently arrived in Vancouver. Victor and Terry knew each other through Tim Kwok, Terry's best friend (Kwok and Li were college room-mates at Stanford University, a few hours drive south of Berkeley). This company, which initially operated out of a 65 sq. m. office, grew quickly as the partners developed condominiums in Vancouver suburbs such as Richmond (where large numbers of Hong Kong immigrants were moving, as I noted earlier in this chapter) (Kraar, 1992*b*: 63). By the time the company, known as Grand Adex, had grown into a mid-sized

---

[25] As of 1995, Kao Mo Hui was chairman of Grand Adex Developments and Wing Hong Contractors.

firm, the pair were responsible for the construction of approximately 1,000 condominium units in metropolitan Vancouver. This modest experience gave the two young men an insight into the planning process associated with residential development projects in Vancouver, the potential market demand of new Hong Kong immigrants, and key design features which would make the residential projects and units more attractive to the immigrants. However, for Victor, the first heir to Hong Kong's largest corporate empire, this type of work was not of sufficient importance and scale to endow him with a local, let alone national or international reputation.

Victor was 21 years of age when Expo '86 was held. While Expo '86 was under way, there had been some public discussion about the future of the site following the Fair's closure. During the course of Expo '86, Premier Bennett organized a dinner party. One of the attendees was George Magnus, a close associate of Li Ka-shing's.[26] Magnus is one of Li Ka-shing's key interlocutors—Western managers with the responsibility for forming the interface between the Chinese and the Western management cultures of Li's firms, as well as handling negotiations with Western businesses and governments. Magnus also owns a 31 acre island in BC, 20 minutes by float plane from Vancouver, where he enjoys a 'recreation home, tennis court and heated saltwater pool' (Gutstein, 1990: 193–4).

After the Bennett dinner ended, Magnus had a brief conversation with the Premier about the future development of the BC Place site following Expo's closure. It was during this time that Magnus first registered his interest (on behalf of Victor Li and Li Ka-shing) in acquiring the site (G. Magnus, interview, Apr. 1994). Victor himself suggested that he 'had decided, even before the fair had closed, that he wanted to buy the site' (Matas, 1989*a*). This expression of interest, which I believe is sincere, was a sign of larger plans which the Expo site and Vancouver as a whole fit into.

As I noted above, it took over half a year before the provincial government, controlled by ideologues on a privatization drive, finally decided to sell the site (in the spring of 1987). The process for the sale of the site involved the submission of 'expressions of interest' by 15 October 1987, and a final proposal by 15 February 1988 (Matas, 1989*a*). This lengthy process was punctuated by much political bickering at the provincial level (see Mason and Baldrey, 1989; Persky, 1989; Leslie, 1991), and subsequent debate over the role of government ministers (Grace McCarthy in particular) in enticing Li Ka-shing to acquire the site (Gutstein, 1990).

However, from the perspective of the eventual developer, the site was much more than a devalued piece of property—a blank landing strip for over-accumulated capital that was rapidly piling up in Hong Kong. This large piece

---

[26] George Magnus's titles include deputy chairman of Cheung Kong (Holdings) Ltd., chairman of Hong Kong Electric Hldgs., and CEF Holdings Ltd., and executive director of Hutchison Whampoa Ltd., and Green Island Cement (Hldgs.). Magnus is British, and would have been in his late fifties when he was negotiating for the Li family in Vancouver.

of land offered the Li family the perfect opportunity to accomplish a number of interrelated goals (apart from making profit) during the first five years of the project's development phase (1988–93). It is also important to note that these goals have changed over time, as befits Li Ka-shing's agile approach to strategy. Indeed, since 1993, the Pacific Place project is being used to fulfil the ambitions of Terry Hui, while the Li family has steadily pulled back its level of involvement in the project. This is a significant point to note, for it reinforces the importance of conducting theoretically informed research that factors in *evolving* goals, objectives, agendas, and contexts.

First, the development of the Pacific Place project enabled the 23 year old (in 1988) Victor to 'prove' himself to his father, and to build up his *reputation* in both Vancouver (the city which effectively became the Li family's North American base) and Hong Kong.[27] The Grand Adex experience was the first level of an incremental climb upwards in the management of more difficult projects, while Pacific Place was widely perceived in Hong Kong to be Victor's first major business duty ('Tycoon Li grooms Victor as successor', 14 Jan. 1994; Chan, 1996; Kraar, 1999). This larger responsibility would have been demanded by his father for it permitted Victor to gain business confidence, and ensure that his reputation was deserved (in the view of élite Chinese and non-Chinese Hong Kongers), and not merely related to his family name. This point was hinted at when Victor commented that he sought to 'show the world that in Vancouver we can achieve something that we all feel proud of and that will be the cause for envy by the rest of the world' (Hamilton, 1988). On this point, it was important that the experience be related to a high-profile, large-scale property development project. An UMP, on the former Expo '86 site, in Vancouver, Canada (a city and country increasingly connected to Hong Kong) was the ideal type of project and location for Victor's 'baby', as George Magnus termed it when I interviewed him. Vancouver's social and geographic proximity to Hong Kong enabled information on Victor's achievements to be circulated across the Pacific on a continual basis. However, it is also worth noting that Vancouver was also the perfect place *outside* Hong Kong for this type of learning exercise to take place. Vancouver was viewed as being distant enough (especially from the glare of the Hong Kong media) for any potential problems to be quickly resolved and/or covered up (G. Redding, interview, Apr. 1994).

Secondly, it was preferable that Victor's reputation and business *experience* be enhanced through the vehicle of a large-scale residential property development project (recall that Concord originally proposed a project of 10,000

---

[27] Victor's age was widely reported to be 25 or 26 in the Canadian media in 1988 when he acquired the site. However, non-Canadian media sources (e.g. Kraar, 1992*a*, 1992*b*) note that Victor was 27 in 1992 and the 1994 Hutchison Whampoa annual report (which was produced in Mar. 1995) notes that he is 30. Given the frequency of the error, I can only speculate that Concord's public relations handlers provided inaccurate information, or chose not to correct erroneous figures.

dwelling units).[28] As noted above, Li-controlled firms such as Cheung Kong and Hutchison Whampoa are still viewed as 'traditional family-run' businesses by both the Li family, and the international financial firms which closely monitor their activities (see e.g. UBS Global Research, 1994: 4; Olds and Yeung, 1999). Therefore, Victor, as the eldest son, had to have the knowledge base and reputation to feasibly take over for his ageing father (who was 60 years old in 1988) in the control of Cheung Kong. Cheung Kong is one of Hong Kong's largest property development firms, and it has renowned experience and skill in developing mega-projects of a residential nature (Baring Securities, 1995c). While the transition from one generation to the next is gradual in Chinese family firms, and stability within Cheung Kong is maintained by a 'low turnover of senior staff' (UBS Global Research, 1994: 4), the opportunity for Victor to learn through the development of Pacific Place was *ideal* timing. The subsequent move of Victor back to Hong Kong to take up an appointment as managing director of Cheung Kong in January 1993, as deputy chairman for the same firm in January 1994 (a position he shares with George Magnus), clearly highlights the plans which were in place for Victor before the Expo site was acquired. Subsequent promotions and the overall succession process *vis-à-vis* the ageing of Li Ka-shing are displayed in Table 4.11.

Thirdly, the development of Pacific Place was used by Victor to 'build a strong base in Canada . . . both personally and financially' (Li, 1992). As I noted above, Li Ka-shing has made substantial investments in Canada since the late 1960s, and he also has major connections with Canadian financial institutions in Hong Kong. Victor also has a Canadian passport which guarantees him a safe base in the unstable geopolitical context of Hong Kong's transition to Chinese control. In effect, Canada now acts as the Li family's North American base. However, prior to the Pacific Place project, Victor was little known in Vancouver or Toronto, and he had few direct connections to Canadian élites. Pacific Place is a large urban redevelopment project by Canadian (and even North American) standards. The developers knew that acquiring a prominent UMP site would guarantee them a high profile in business, political, and social circles in both Vancouver, and Canada as a whole. A prominent profile (in association with an astute reputation) is important, for the Li family are treated as virtual royalty in Hong Kong; a status which brings with it access to timely and relevant information about the processes which may affect the health of the Li family empire. The long-term creation of a Vancouver base therefore demanded a suitable method to insert Victor (and therefore his core family members) into relevant networks; networks which were identified by contacts and advisers. Pacific Place, then, was effectively used as a vehicle to parachute Victor in to the top of Vancouver's social,

---

[28] What we have here is a case of the confluence of the goals of the Li family (who wanted a high density residential project for Victor's experience, and the enhanced financial returns), and the goals of the City of Vancouver (who wanted higher densities than those on South Shore of False Creek as the development was taking place in the context of a growing jobs–housing imbalance at the metropolitan scale, and the push for more ecologically friendly, high density housing).

Table 4.11. The succession path of Victor Li *vis-à-vis* Li Ka-shing, 1985–1999

Year	Victor Li's age	Victor Li's positions	Li Ka-shing's age
1985	20	Director, Cheung Kong	57
1988	23	Director and Senior Vice-President, Concord Pacific (based in Vancouver)	60
1993	28	Deputy Managing Director, Cheung Kong (based in Hong Kong)	65
1994	29	Deputy Chairman, Cheung Kong	66
1995	30	Deputy Chairman and Deputy Managing Director, Cheung Kong	67
1999	34	Managing Director, Cheung Kong	71

Source: Various company documents.

political, and business hierarchy. He (and his associates) were able to become 'players within the mainstream immediately' (M. Glynn, interview, Mar. 1994). Such a manoeuvre is possible because of the supportive base offered by Vancouver's public and private institutions (recall my comments about institutional thickness and the push to the Pacific), in association with Vancouver's 'very thin layer of Anglo political control' (Seagrave, 1995: 259). Vancouver's power hierarchy is relatively malleable in comparison to established old money, 'old boys network' cities such as Toronto or New York (M. Glynn, interview, Mar. 1994)—cities where the young, modest, and soft-spoken Victor would have had a tougher time fitting in. Here we see money being used a medium of 'emotional expression' as well as a 'medium of economic exchange'; a practice associated with the Chinese family firms where 'instrumental and expressive considerations are intermingled and undifferentiated' (Wong, 1991: 21).

The *fourth* main rationale is the diversification of the three tycoons' property portfolios. The 'fortunes and prospects' of the various firms controlled by Li, Cheng Yu-Tung, and Lee Shau Kee are 'inextricably linked' to Hong Kong's future prospects and success (UBS Global Research, 1994: 2). For example, in 1993 Cheung Kong, Hutchison Whampoa, and Henderson Land respectively generated 98 per cent, 88 per cent, and 95 per cent of their earnings in Hong Kong (Alexander, 1994). Overall, 80 per cent of Li's corporate assets were in Hong Kong in 1992 (Kraar, 1992a: 107). Investing in Vancouver on a more substantial scale (even if it is personal capital) allows the tycoons to diversify their portfolio in a geographic sense, and 'cushion' their holdings in Hong Kong and China in the context of political and economic uncertainties. While Canada 'does not offer a very high immediate return, it's an essential part of a healthy, balanced portfolio, providing good mid- to long-term asset growth' (Li, 1992: 3). This is particularly the case given that the land could be acquired so cheaply. In a related sense, Pacific Place also acted as a pilot project for the backers of Concord Pacific (and therefore their Hong Kong firms) in developing large-scale (in North American terms) property projects. It is worth noting, for example, that Cheng Yu-Tung became a financial backer of Donald Trump's 56 acre (US$2.5 billion) Riverside South project (also known as 'Trump City') on Manhattan's West Side in New York (Hutchinson, 1994).[29]

The actual decision to consider a serious bid for the site was made by Li Ka-shing and his son Victor. The decision-making process was facilitated by their ability to draw upon Victor's experience with Grand Adex, and a web of well-placed social networks in Vancouver and Victoria (where the provincial government is based)—networks which broadened in scope and depth during the course of dealing with this specific issue.[30] This network incorporated Chinese and non-Chinese contacts including senior property agents who had been handling Hong Kong investment flows into Vancouver's property market during the 1980s, powerful politicians (such as Grace McCarthy), powerful provincial officials (such as Kevin Murphy and Stanley Kwok), and financial institutions (such as CIBC and the Hong Kong Bank of Canada). These contacts, in association with the human resources of Li's firms in Hong Kong, enabled Li Ka-shing and Victor to access relevant, accurate, and timely information regarding issues such as: the City of Vancouver's expectations for the site; the future nature of the City of Vancouver's planning process for the site, and the broader downtown core; the history of the BC Place development proposals (including North Park); the political nature of key City politicians; the nature of the institutional milieu they would have to operate within; potential community resistance to the project; prospective

---

[29] It is worth noting that the gradual diversification of Li's corporate assets continues to the present day. For example, in June 1995, Li raised considerable speculation about Hong Kong's future by placing his 34.95 per cent controlling interest in Cheung Kong in a Cayman Islands trust (Sito and Fung, 1995). While his rationale was that he sought to avoid inheritance tax (for his sons' sake), the action was seen as embarrassing for Li given his excellent connections in Beijing (Holberton, 1993, 1995). The Li family has also invested heavily in telecommunications firms, especially in Europe (e.g. Orange plc, and Mannesmann AG), port facilities in Central America, and so on (Chan, 1996; Kraar, 1999).

[30] This is an obvious yet important issue regarding the formation of networks of social relations. *Specific events* enable these networks to be constructed, expanded, and imbued with trust. Highly active and respected people like Li Ka-shing are well positioned to form networks of social relations for they have access to the resources to initiate action. Moreover, Li is so well-known and capitalized now, that his firms receive thousands of offers to become involved in joint ventures around the world. These offers enable the Li family to participate in joint ventures of their choice (often with low levels of capital input on their part), while also building up trusting relations for subsequent ventures in the short- and long-term.

demand in local and Hong Kong markets; the likely net worth of the land; the possibilities of their bid achieving success in an uncertain political context (i.e. the erratic nature of Premier Vander Zalm); and the best approach to preparing a bid. Jon Markoulis also came up from Houston where he lived and managed the Li's North American real estate holdings. Markoulis used his analytical skills to perform a market analysis of the site in relation to expected development densities and various market trends (J. Markoulis, interview, Mar. 1994).

The collection of all of this information highlights the power of networks harnessed and structured in a specific way by these key élite actors. The global flows of capital that the Li family directed to Vancouver were the end result of a process in which relevant economic, political, and social information of both a local and trans-Pacific nature was accumulated. The power of the Li family to externalize meaning (through activating flows of capital) (Hannerz, 1992*c*), in a successful manner, was increased substantially by their access to, and skill in using and developing, networks of social relations built upon a foundation of trust. This process was clearly enhanced by having access to key actors who were deeply embedded in the Vancouver context, though who also understood the investor's logic. Conversely, this process was also enhanced by having key actors who were deeply embedded in the Hong Kong context, though who also understood the Vancouver context. Taken together, the investor was in an ideal position to make a decision about proceeding with a bid for the site. In short, money cannot be deployed without information and obtaining this information requires social networks which rely, to a greater or lesser extent, upon trust (Thrift and Olds, 1996).

Finding the Bridge

During the course of evaluating if a bid should proceed for the site, information on a suitable bid approach was also amassed. The key hinge of a successful proposal to the provincial government was the location of an organizer with the knowledge and skills to structure a successful process, while also meeting the needs of the financial backers of the project. Practically, this person had to be able to pull together the relevant professionals (e.g. architects), while also subtly manoeuvring through a highly charged local political milieu. As John Markoulis suggested to me, it was critical that this person also agree with, and implement, Li Ka-shing's 'trademark' process which is 'non-confrontational', while delivering 'benefits to all partners', while 'generating money', while producing a result which would build onto Li's reputation (interview, Mar. 1994).

Fortunately, for the Li family, Stanley Kwok (who I briefly profiled in Box 4.2) had publicly announced he was stepping down from the board of BCEC in April 1987 after the provincial government halted the North Park planning process. Following his April announcement (which he had been contemplating since the autumn of 1986), Kwok began preparing for a return to the architectural profession, and he made some arrangements to practise with the Vancouver firm Davidson Yuen. However, Kwok was unable officially to leave the board 'because it was not until' August 1987 'that a replacement had been found for him' (Hume, 1988). During this transition period Kwok also met Victor Li for the first time at a luncheon engagement (S. Kwok, interview, Feb. 1994). George Magnus then made arrangements for Kwok to be flown out to Hong Kong where he was taken on a yacht trip to discuss a variety of issues (with Li Ka-shing) and then was quickly offered the role of coordinating the Li proposal to the provincial government (G. Magnus, interview, Apr. 1994). Kwok was selected by Li (and Magnus) because he 'knew the site', he 'knew people', he 'was an architect', he 'was Chinese', and he knew 'our people' (ibid.; J. Markoulis, interview, Mar. 1994).

More specifically, Kwok had excellent connections with all of Vancouver's key political and business élites, as well as with the provincial cabinet and the BCEC board—the people who would ultimately decide which proposal would win the right to develop the Expo site. His prior development experience ensured that he understood the financial aspects of large-scale property redevelopment projects. As Kwok himself put it, 'I just happen to be an architect who understands money' (Williamson, 1992). Kwok also understood the fine details of the City of Vancouver's planning process for large-scale mixed-use redevelopment projects (through his involvement with the BC Place and North Park proposals), and he had built up close and trusting relations with the City Manager and several key city planners (the people who would eventually process the development proposal).

At a personal level, Kwok's excellent reputation in Vancouver played an important role in his being entrusted with a project which could quite significantly damage Victor's reputation were it not handled well. In business and political circles, Kwok was (and is) associated with the qualities of integrity and dependability. He is also a determined, self-effacing, soft-spoken man who was also old enough in 1987 (61) to be viewed as a 'wise' man, though young enough to command the full attention and confidence of the Hong Kong financiers (including Victor Li).

At the local level, Kwok knew how best to manage community opposition to the proposal. The Pacific Place site is adjacent to a highly organized low-income residential community. Organizations such as the Downtown Eastside Residents Association (DERA) were worried about Pacific Place's negative social impacts, particularly in the aftermath of the Expo '86 mass evictions (Olds, 1988, 1998*b*; Sarti, 1988; Hulchanski, 1989; Mitchell, 1993*a*; Beazley, 1994; Ley, 1994; Blomley 1998). Equally important, Kwok had an astute sense of how to manage local media coverage of property development issues. These were skills that Kwok had fine-tuned during his time guiding the development of the North Park proposal, and Expo '86. This deep level of local knowledge and connections was particularly important at the initial stages of the development process because the City had not yet confirmed what its policies for the site were. Civil society in Canada (and Vancouver) is more developed than in Hong Kong. The nature of civil society is reflected in Vancouver's planning system, which is much more community-based in comparison to the technocratic Hong Kong system (on the Hong Kong planning system see Ng, 1999). Local citizens' groups, critical politicians (on the City Council), and the local media can force issues into the public sphere, and push for changes which the developers must sometimes agree to. This is a form of civil society which Hong Kong-based Chinese developers absolutely detest. Rather, their experience (and preference) is to operate in a society characterized by deference to authority, the strong admiration of wealthy people, an unopen legal system, and opaque information flows (G. Redding, interview, Apr. 1994). Given the importance of this project to the Li family, Stanley Kwok was the perfect person for the job. Kwok could (better than anyone else) massage the process to ensure that the developers achieved their goals, while also structuring a process (and a public relations approach) that would quell the concerns of the majority of the interested public.

The mesh between global and local is dependent upon cultural hybrids like Kwok who use their expert knowledge to interpret local conditions and negotiate difference for the more culturally and geographically distant financiers. He is one of the true transnational 'cosmopolitans', a person who is able to manage meaning strategically in ever-shifting and diverse circumstances. Hannerz (1990: 246) writes of this group: 'Their decontextualized knowledge can be quickly and shiftingly recontextualized in a series of different settings . . . What they carry, however, is not just special knowledge, but also that overall orientation toward structures of meaning to which the notion of the "culture of critical discourse" refers'. Cosmopolitans, ever savvy to the world of intercultural negotiation, occupy an important niche in the contemporary global economy. They are particularly significant players in the global property industry for the sector is associated with the production of built form within particular locales (see Mitchell, 1995, 1997*b*; Mitchell and Olds, 2000). As Kwok himself stated:

Sometimes there are insights into certain situations that maybe someone who has been living in both worlds can understand. We have very basic cultural differences. Although it is the same problem and the same issue, you can approach it from a different way. And it's useful for each side to see how the other would have approached it. That's how you bridge things. (quoted in Edwards, 1992)

Former Socred cabinet minister Grace McCarthy also made the same point: Stanley is a terrific bridge between the Chinese and Canadian business communities. He bridges it well and he brings them together, and that's very important' (quoted in Williamson, 1992, p. B2).

The opportunity to get involved in this project was also enticing from Kwok's perspective, for it allowed him to 'fulfil his dream of planning and designing a major portion of a city' (quoted in Shaw, 1993, p. C6). Obviously, Kwok was honoured to have Hong Kong's most powerful family put 'their trust' in him to play such a prominent role in this project, particularly given its role as Victor's educational tool.

Kwok began working for the Li family in 'about July 1987', even though he did not officially begin working for them until September 1987.[31] In fact, Kwok was their first Vancouver employee. He would have come to them just after working for BCEC in designing the process for marketing the site. While Kwok never broke any conflict of interest regulations in BC, such a shift in roles highlights the relative laxity of the provincial government's regulations on an international scale. If a more stringent regulatory regime had been in place, the whole complexion of the subsequent bid and development process would have changed quite significantly (assuming the Li family had proceeded with a bid).

I have devoted considerable space to the events by which the Hong Kong financiers came to be aware of the site, the complex rationale behind their decision to invest, and the logic of using Stanley Kwok as both local coordinator, and human bridge between Hong Kong and Vancouver. This is because all subsequent events in Vancouver after September 1987 (including the preparation of the bid, the formation and structure of the institutional base (Concord Pacific), and the specific actions of Concord in proceeding through the various phases of developing the site) reflected this rationale, and the search for complementarity (between Hong Kong and Vancouver).

Obviously, I cannot review the complete Pacific Place development process. However, what I will do now is highlight how the Hong Kong-based Chinese financiers established a more substantial permanent base in Vancouver in order to reach across space and implement their initial objectives until Victor Li returned to Hong Kong in 1993.

Establishing the Institutional Base

While the Li family began pulling together key actors to make a bid for the site during the summer of 1987, a specific firm to sponsor the bid had not yet been established. On 21 October 1987, Concord Pacific Developments Ltd., a 'private Canadian company', was established 'for the purpose of purchasing and developing the former Expo '86 lands on the North Shore of False Creek in downtown Vancouver' (company materials).[32] The practice of setting up a

---

[31] There is some discrepancy about when Stanley Kwok started working for Concord. Jon Markoulis suggested it was 'about July' (interview, Mar. 1994) while Stanley noted it was in September (interview, Feb. 1994). I have not had an opportunity to confirm the correct date. Kwok did inform me that he was very careful about a potential conflict of interest, and his action was 'cleared' in accordance with provincial government regulations. Like many global property developers, Li Ka-shing has previously attempted to hire well-placed government officials with important knowledge and contacts (Gutstein, 1990: 139). This practice occurs at a local scale as well, as evidenced when the first senior planner for the North Shore of False Creek (Craig Rowland) left the City of Vancouver to join a private property development firm which owned land adjacent to the Expo site.

[32] The name Concord Pacific is the inverse of the name of a Hong Kong firm which Cheung Kong has shares in (the Pacific Concord Group). Some individual buildings on the site (e.g. the

private firm is very common in Hong Kong, for private firms allow greater flexibility in business practice, and they are not forced to release information to the public. As Craig Aspinall, the first Concord spokesperson noted (when the sale of the site was announced), 'this is a private Canadian company and they tend to be private. We're not going to comment on business deals or the internal workings of the company or its finances' (quoted in Constantineau and Power, 1988).[33]

Li Ka-shing makes heavy use of private firms, and even his public firms such as Cheung Kong are operated with a relatively low public profile. The practice of operating with a low profile makes it 'difficult to assess . . . structure and decision-making processes' (UBS Global Research, 1994: 4; Nicoll, 1994), and his firms are regularly ranked at the bottom level of broker's surveys in Hong Kong for the 'quality of information flow' (see e.g. Hewett, 1994). Suffice it to say, this philosophy of practice has been incorporated into Concord's method of operating in Vancouver, though tempered by the need to engage in a relatively public planning process. Since 1988, the firm's handlers have developed a range of skills at being able to engage in public discourse, while also releasing very little information on the rationale behind their actions, or other information which could be used by the firm's local critics.

As noted above, Concord Pacific was originally formed by the Li family. However, once the site was secured, shares in the private firm were divided between Li Ka-shing, Cheng Yu-Tung (chairman of New World Development Co.), and Lee Shau Kee (chairman of Henderson Land Development Co.). Li was the controlling shareholder with a 50 to 60 per cent stake in Concord until the mid-1990s. Cheng and Lee held about 15 to 20 per cent each during the first several years of the development phase. Minor stakes in the firm have been held since 1988 by a number of investors including CIBC and the Hui family of Hong Kong (recall Terry's instrumental role in helping Victor get established in Vancouver). Share proportions have changed over time in keeping with personal commitment to the project (G. Magnus, interview, Apr. 1994). While Li Ka-shing retained control of Concord Pacific until the mid-1990s, the Lee and Cheng shares have been gradually transferred to the Hui family from Hong Kong (primarily in 1993 and early 1994) and 'Mrs. Lin Shieh Han-Chien, chairman of Taiwan's Hung Kuo property group' (Newman, 1993: 38; Kraar,

---

Concordia) are also names used by Cheung Kong in Hong Kong (Concordia Plaza in this case). Relatedly, the inscription of corporate names into Vancouver's landscape is increasingly common. For example, while Concord originally called their project Pacific Place, they now use the term Concord Pacific Place. GM Place (a large indoor stadium for ice hockey, basketball, and music concerts), and the smaller Ford Centre for the Performing Arts were also built in the early 1990s.

[33] Craig Aspinall was a senior Socred media relations adviser. He also worked for BCEC and had connections to business organizations in Vancouver such as the Vancouver Board of Trade. As manager of media relations during the 1983 and 1986 provincial elections (Gutstein, 1990: 139), he obviously had close relations with William Bennett, William Vander Zalm, Grace McCarthy, and Stanley Kwok. Aspinall is also a neo-conservative ideologue, and he was eventually replaced by Blair Hagkull, a much younger, smoother PR spokesperson.

1992*b*: 63). The increase in the Hui share proportion reflects Terry Hui's May 1993 appointment as president and chief executive officer of Concord Pacific.[34] Since then Concord Pacific has become a publicly traded Canadian company (now called Concord Pacific Group Inc.). A complex series of financial trans-actions has seen Li Ka-shing's Hutchison Whampoa, along with a network of other Chinese tycoons and Vancouver-based realtors, create a linked web of firms (including Burcon, Oxford Properties, and Concord Pacific). These firms now control a large portfolio of property within Canadian cities (including the Pacific Place site, and the former railway lands site in central Toronto). This stage of the development process (from the mid-1990s on) is, however, beyond the scope of this book.

The practice of sharing the benefits of a development project follows the classic ethnic Chinese business approach (Redding, 1990, 1994; Hamilton, 2000). Joint ventures such as Concord are usually arranged by a lead investor, who subsequently invites several of his trusted friends to take part in the pro-ject. All of the original investors in Concord Pacific are friends of Li Ka-shing, and they have a common 'understanding' about how business is conducted (Newman, 1993: 38). This process is described in Matas (1989*c*):

Victor Li said he could not recall exactly when partners joined him for the Expo deal, but spoke about friends forming business partnerships. 'A son talks to me and says, you know I'm doing a project in Vancouver. I say, well, if you allow me, I'd like to partici-pate, and he says, let me think about it . . .

'It's a gradual event. If you like it, we include you. They say fine. Hands are shaken. Whenever you need the money, just bill me. That's the way we do business.'

Mr. Li said his family could handle the Expo lands project alone. 'No problem from a money standpoint,' he said. 'But if you got a successful project and if you want a cele-bration party, you better bring in enough shareholders to have a party. Its no fun cele-brating by yourself'. . . .

'When we drew up the original thing, after we got the site, there was no formal agreement more than two pages between all the shareholders,' Mr. Li said. 'With all these shareholders, their word is their bond. That's why I want them to be my shareholders.'

By 'repaying some favours' (G. Magnus, interview, 1994), and inviting all of these other shareholders to share in the development of the Pacific Place project, the Li family further builds up and extends their networks of trust. At the same time, Cheng Yu-Tung and Lee Shau Kee were able to play in

---

[34] Terry Hui was appointed at a key stage in the evolution of the firm and project. First, Victor Li had been called back to Hong Kong to work at Cheung Kong. Secondly, the development process was shifting from re-zoning to actual construction. There was less need for Stanley Kwok now that the critical (more public) phase had been successfully passed through. It was now time for the 29 year old Terry, a person more committed to staying in Vancouver, to use the firm and project as a vehicle to improve his reputation and business skills. While there were rumours in Vancouver that Kwok had fallen out with the Li family, it is clear this transition took place for the sake of Terry Hui, one of Victor's friends.

the Vancouver property market for the first time on a large-scale basis. In return, these 'uncles' of Victor (Ouston, 1989: 26; also see Mitchell, 1993*a*) helped support a key stage of Victor's grooming process in which their 'nephew' was prepared to take over control of Cheung Kong.

Pacific Place is one of many such joint ventures between these tycoons. For example, Singapore's largest ever private mixed use commercial project (Suntec City, <http://www.suntec.com.sg/>) was financed by a consortium of Hong Kong investors including Li Ka-shing, Run Run Shaw, Tan Sri Frank Tsao, Cheng Yu-Tung, Lee Shau Kee, Chou Wen-Hsien, Chow Chung Kai, King Sieh Ting, Li Dak-Sum, Robert Wang Wei-Han, and Anthony Yeh Yuan-Chang (Suntec Investment Pte. Ltd. materials). This US$2 billion project (known as Suntec City) was also initiated in mid-1988, at the same time as Pacific Place was being launched.

The formation and operation of these consortiums helps build up and expand élite Chinese business networks across space, and into new sectors of the economy (Redding, 1990; Yeung and Olds, 2000). The formation of Concord Pacific and the subsequent development of Pacific Place must be seen in the context of the operation and spread of Chinese capitalism. Concord Pacific (and its offshoots) is the creation of a new breed of corporation that is not tightly bounded, nor a pure legal entity in the formal sense. This new type of corporation is 'not organized hierarchically or coordinated by bureaucratic control mechanisms. It is instead a looser web organized horizontally, and leaving a great deal of autonomy in the local units' (Redding, 1995: 67). The desire for this form of consortium approach stems from operating in an Asian context where 'personalism' enables economic activity to proceed. As Redding (1995: 63) writes: '*Personalism* does in Asia what law does in the West. It stands behind exchange processes and serves to guarantee their reliability. In societies where individual or corporate rights are only weakly protected by a legal infrastructure, other means must be developed if the transactions needed in a normal economy are to flow smoothly' (emphasis in original).

Familism in Chinese business firms also facilitates the operation of loose coalitions of firms in various locales; coalitions that are reshaped in an ever-changing manner. In effect, Concord Pacific can be said to have roots within Asia-based Chinese business culture, though manipulated to best fit the Canadian regulatory, political, and socio-cultural context.

Once established, Concord, like many of Li's firms, also branched out to connect up with Western firms. In Asia, Cheung Kong and Hutchison Whampoa have formed alliances with non-Chinese partners such as Procter & Gamble, Motorola, AT&T, Cable and Wireless, Lockheed and Telstra (Oram, 1994; Redding, 1995). In Vancouver, Concord formed a strategic alliance with the British Columbia Telephone Group of Companies (the second largest telecommunications company in Canada). A 'state of the art' communication and electronic monitoring system is being developed on the site, and Pacific

Place will be North America's first fully operable optical fibre residential community. The initial cost of C$20 million is being shared by Concord Pacific and BC Tel. It is worth noting that one of Li Ka-shing's flagship firms (Hutchison Whampoa) has considerable telecommunications experience through its firms Hutchison Telephone, Hutchison Telecommunications, and Hutchison Paging.

Concord also recouped costs and strengthened and extended social networks by parcelling off and selling development sections of the site (e.g. International Village near the old Chinatown; a leisure complex; a site for an ice hockey stadium) to Asian-based (predominantly Chinese) and North American investors. This practice also permits Concord to focus on pure property development, their specialty.

Considering the size of the redevelopment project, Concord's office is very small. In 1988, less than six people worked for the firm on a permanent basis, and even in 1995, in the construction management phase, the project employed fewer than 30 staff (excluding construction workers). As I noted above, key actors for Concord Pacific until 1995 have included Li Ka-shing's son Victor, Stanley Kwok, and Terry Hui. Jon Markoulis moved to Vancouver from Houston once Concord acquired the site, and he has remained with Concord to this date. As with Stanley Kwok, Victor and Terry are part of the 'transnational élite . . . professionals and business people living and working in several global sites and involved in the control of capital and information between these sites' (Mitchell, 1993*b*: 268). As Victor Li put it, 'I tell people that my home is Cathay Pacific Airlines, seat 1A' (*Vista*, Oct. 1989: 40). Terry Hui sees 'himself as "operator and deal maker," at once part of East Asian and Canadian cultures and time zones' (Williamson, 1994), which explains why his Vancouver office hours often begin around noon (enabling him to spend half a working day on Vancouver time, and half a working day on Hong Kong time). In the mid-1990s, Hui spent two or three hours on the telephone to Hong Kong per day. However, this frequency of connection does not mean Hong Kong directs Concord's strategy. All of the people I interviewed (including George Magnus in Hong Kong) noted that Concord Pacific is basically managed in Vancouver. As Hui notes:

It's all done among friends, so we keep each other informed on all the operational stuff, but no one has time to deal with details. It's never an issue of who has the power to decide, but all major issues are discussed as a matter of courtesy. I always consult to make sure everyone agrees. Since I have a vested interest in the company, my decisions are very much in line with those of the other shareholders. (quoted in Newman, 1993: 38)

The only time Hong Kong is directly involved in decision-making is when significant costs or liabilities are considered. Such discussions have often centred on demands that the City of Vancouver makes regarding the provision of services of some form (which involve expenditures or long-term liabilities), or a proposed change to the development plan for the site. Consensus within the firm is not problematic because the shareholders, board members, and firm employees are a relatively small and tightly knit group of friends with a shared vision of how they see the project (and the firm) developing.

While Concord has had a plethora of human and financial resources to draw upon, the development process associated with an UMP is a lengthy one, particularly in comparison to Hong Kong where larger projects are approved and constructed within five years' time. In Vancouver, the development pace is much slower due to the nature of the planning system and civil society. The local state has complete power over the development process provided the land is privately owned; a situation that significantly impacts on the pace and scale of financial returns. Obviously, the financiers of Concord realized this when they decided to acquire the site from the provincial government. While this project was not viewed as a maximum capital return outlet on a global scale for the financiers, they clearly wanted to maximize their financial returns, and at the same time build a long-term base for future projects in Canada.

The implementation of goals for the Pacific Place project began taking place as soon as Stanley Kwok started working for the firm (before the site was acquired). Concord, like all of the bidders for the site, had 'secret' access to a variety of senior officials representing the City of Vancouver (Krangle, 1988) to help them understand what would likely be acceptable to the City in a final development plan. Kwok also began the long process of working to ensure that the City's mayor understood and supported Concord's ultimate goals for the site. Fortunately (for Concord), Vancouver City Council changed complexion in 1986 when Gordon Campbell of the centre/right NPA party was elected as mayor.[35] Campbell, 'a 1970s liberal who had become a 1980s conservative' is a 'developer and businessman, young, personable, well-educated, and well-travelled'—in short, the epitome of 'the free market internationalization' of Vancouver (Ley *et al.*, 1992: 265). The 1986 municipal election, in which Campbell was accompanied by seven NPA councillors (out of ten in total), fundamentally influenced the nature of the City's dealings with Concord at key formative stages of the approval process. Indeed, the NPA (under Campbell) retained control of Vancouver City Council until 1993 (when Campbell left to enter the provincial political scene), ensuring that political support for Concord's project was consistent at critical points.

This favourable political context at the local level was used by Concord as much as possible from 1988 on. Soon after acquiring the site, Li Ka-shing led a large entourage to City Hall to explain the global significance of his investment

---

[35] The previous City Council was led by Michael Harcourt, and it was controlled by a centre-left coalition which was considerably more critical of property developers.

activities, and how 'serious' and committed they were to implementing their plans for the site (K. Dobell, interview, Feb. 1994). Since then Concord staff have built up close relations with various politicians and key City officials through formal and informal functions, including regular private meetings with the Mayor, the City Manager, and the Director of Planning. For example, Concord Pacific, Grand Adex, and Interville (a subsidiary of Henderson Land) contributed more than $12,000 to assist the NPA in a municipal election race during 1993 (Lee, 1994). Concord also contributed to the federal election campaigns of conservative politicians.

The formation of linkages with political élites in Vancouver is one of many methods by which the firm has deeply embedded itself in the local scene. This approach to business stems from Li Ka-shing's philosophy that all of his firms (local and overseas) become 'part of the local community' (J. Markoulis, interview, Mar. 1994). The actual process of embedding began from the first day the Li family decided to invest in Vancouver— through the hiring of a respected local representative who was already connected (Kwok). These enactors of change then used their knowledge to identify windows of opportunity to advance the firm's interest in the short and long term.

This approach is reflected at a basic level in the firm's sponsorship of numerous public events and institutions in Vancouver such as the Dragon Boat Festival, an annual Indy car race, the Laurier Institute, a waterside walkway through the site, and a 1996 festival to highlight the perceived role of Expo '86 in transforming the city. The vast majority of these events revolve around the False Creek basin where the site is located, while supported institutions tend to address issues related to racial discrimination, multiculturalism, and the enhancement of both Pacific Rim linkages and a Pacific Rim mentality.

At the level of design, this approach meant recognizing the 'parochial' and 'provincial' nature of Vancouver despite pretensions to global city/world class status (G. Magnus, interview, Apr. 1994; J. Markoulis, interview, Mar. 1994). The original idea of using 'exciting' international architects such as IM Pei (who was considered for the project) was quickly discarded after Kwok notified Li and Magnus that they would be resented in Vancouver (particularly in association with Hong Kong financiers). Instead, Kwok recommended a team of experienced Vancouver-based architects who understood the City of Vancouver's development approval process, and the local vernacular. While some had international experience (particularly the California-born Rick Hulbert), none would be considered influential on a national or global basis (particularly in comparison with the élite architects who were involved in Shanghai's UMP). The Vancouver architects were 'solid basic' professionals who would 'get the job done', to the extent that creativity (as a factor) was a relatively unimportant criterion when hiring them. In other words, 'they knew where to put the doorknobs' (G. Magnus, interview, Apr. 1994).

More important was their ability to reach some consensus between the demands of the firm, and the demands of the City politicians and officials.[36] The end result is a mix of modern and postmodern styles—strong West Coast vernacular in some parts of the site (see Fig. 4.14), while other areas and structures are more reflective of the neo-modern Pacific Rim condo-style that is increasingly being developed along the waterfronts of Sydney, Auckland, and Vancouver (see Fig. 4.15). It is this latter form of housing which is frequently marketed in Hong Kong newspapers, and at open houses in Hong Kong hotels, for the design, amenities, and financial packages are subtly differentiated enough to appeal to both the burgeoning Asian markets and domestic consumers in these cities.

At an institutional level, Concord officials have become active participants at enhancing the state of 'institutional thickness' that I described earlier in the chapter. Their network now runs through most of Vancouver's key economic, political, and social institutions such as the Asia-Pacific Foundation of Canada, the Vancouver Board of Trade, the Downtown Vancouver Association, the Hong Kong Bank of Canada,[37] the University of British Columbia, the Hong Kong–Canada Business Association, and so on. After being set up for over a decade now, the firm has become a symbol (in many business, political, and media circles) of the ideal 'Pacific Rim firm' (e.g. see *TIME*, 17 Nov. 1997). This layer of support enables the firm to acquire relevant and timely information, and they are able to act quickly on opportunities given their local autonomy.

To date this project has been controversial, yet Concord Pacific has managed to manoeuvre through Vancouver's cultural, political, and economic system in a sophisticated manner (especially considering the scale of the UMP). The project is being built roughly according to schedule. The first condominium tower, with units priced between C$224,000 and $748,000 was pre-sold in 1992, half going to Canadian residents in a two week period, and half to Hong Kong residents in two days. Concord promised, after a previous conflict over another Vancouver project which sold out before being offered to Canadians, to allow Canadians two weeks to invest in their buildings before they are advertised overseas (mainly in Hong Kong). Ironically, this 'penalty' merely heightened the rush of local people (or foreign buyers using local agents) to

[36] The key architects who worked for Concord Pacific in the phase under examination (1988 to mid-1990s) are John Davidson, Barry Downs, Rick Hulbert, and Graham McGarva. The landscape architect Don Vaughn and Stanley Kwok have also had a significant role in the design process. Of course, the final results are strongly reflective of City of Vancouver regulations, and the influence of key planners such as Larry Beasley, Ian Smith, and Pat Wotherspoon. City design guidelines are very detailed, and the process of reaching a final result requires hundreds of hours of work and negotiation.

[37] For example, Victor Li is a board member of the Hong Kong Bank of Canada. Recall that Li Ka-shing's Hong Kong portfolio includes major holdings of the Hong Kong and Shanghai Bank, the bank that owns the Hong Kong Bank of Canada. Both banks are major suppliers of mortgages for the purchasers of condominium units at the Pacific Place on both sides of the Pacific. The Hong Kong Bank of Canada also financed the construction of the first condominium tower on the Pacific Place site. The Hong Kong Bank of Canada's web site is ⟨http://www.hsbc.ca/⟩.

DESIGN CONTEXT

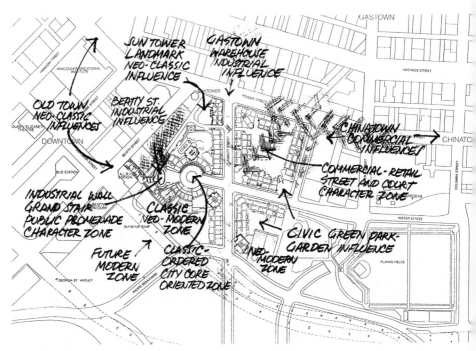

Fig. 4.14. Incorporating local references into the design of the International Village sub-area of Pacific Place

Source: Pacific Place Design Consortium.

purchase condominium units on the site. In total, approximately 2,100 units (21 per cent of the 9,100 maximum) have been sold by 1998, mainly to people from Vancouver and Hong Kong (via agents, in hotel exhibitions, and at the Hong Kong-based Cheung Kong office). And as implied in the Introduction to this book, the vast majority of units have been sold via the pre-sale (off-the-plan) process.[38]

Concord Pacific's success in implementing *their* goals (leaving aside the issue of the positive and negative impacts that the project creates in neighbouring

---

[38] The pre-sale process has been perfected in Hong Kong by Cheung Kong. The knowledge gained in Hong Kong has been applied to Vancouver, finely altered to take into account local preferences with respect to issues such as the design of the presentation centre, mortgage arrangements, 'selling' style, and so on. However, the presentation centre is more than simply a market-place for property. A variety of educational materials including maps and globes are on display, with Vancouver clearly identified. The Vancouver in this presentation centre is situated on the edge of the Pacific Rim, part of a network of global cities through which flows of capital, goods, people, images, and ideas are funnelled. Place has been reconstituted once again, as it was when the colonialists came to the rainforest. This time though, the processes of change were encouraged for the most part by local decision-makers.

Fig. 4.15. Hong Kong advertisement for a Pacific Place condominium

communities, and the city as a whole) is, in my assessment, due to the ability of the firm's many representatives (in both Hong Kong and Vancouver) to embed themselves within and exploit relevant networks and institutions on both sides of the Pacific, binding together diverse knowledges in the pursuit of power. Access to the site at a 'fire-sale' price was facilitated by a provincial government controlled by ideologues, and representatives of the Cheung Kong Group were more than willing to take advantage of the opportunity. This was particularly true in the context of (and their awareness of) unprecedented flows of migrants from Asia to Vancouver (generating some of the demand needed to sell units on the site), urban restructuring processes that supported the aims and objectives of the developers, and the establishment of a state of institutional thickness (with respect to a Pacific Rim outlook) within local, provincial, and national political-economic spheres.

5

Liquid Images. Producing the Global Finanscape in Shanghai, China

Section 1

Situating the Actors: The Global Intelligence Corps, Architecture, and Property Development

This analysis of the role of élite architects and the production of global flows of images is decidedly non-representational (on non-representational theory, see Thrift, 1996, 1997, 1999b). Rather than providing an interpretation of the meaning and significance of the seductive images and design aspects of the plans for a new international financial centre in Shanghai, attention is directed to the economic, social, and intellectual underpinnings of the production of global flows of images and property development expertise. This approach enables a detailed yet situated exploration to be undertaken on the key role of the Global Intelligence Corps (GIC) in the production of these gleaming new urban spaces—the 'citadels' (Soja, 1994; Marcuse, 1997b) of the late twentieth century city.

Architecture, as Larson (1993) so forcefully reminds us, is a 'heteronomous' profession. While the rhetoric and discourses[1] associated with the profession hark back to the days (idealized of course) of independent artistry, architects today are *dependent* upon numerous other processes, institutions, and actors to enable them to engage in work. The GIC in particular, as architectural professionals who provide services to prestigious clients, must be aware of their situated position with respect to relational networks, institutions, and key material outlets (i.e. texts) for their ideas. This is because they often attempt to implement a myriad of internal (professional) and external (societal) goals during

---

[1] By 'discourse' I mean, following Gregory (1994: 11), 'all the ways in which we communicate with one another, to that vast network of signs, symbols and practices through which we make our world(s) meaningful to ourselves and to others'. Similarly, Larson (1993: 5), who also draws on Michel Foucault in formulating her definition, suggests discourse is 'all that a particular category of agents say (or write) in a specific capacity and in a definable thematic area. Discourse commonly invites dialogue. However, in architecture (as in all professions), discourse is not open to everyone but based on social appropriation and a principle of exclusion. Lay persons are not entitled to participate in the production of the profession as a discipline'.

the processes of formulating the images that they hope to see inscribed in the landscape.

In Section 1 of this chapter, I begin with a description of some basic features of contemporary GIC firms, including their position within the professional hierarchy, and their heavily masculine nature. I then move on to provide an overview of the structural underpinnings of the architectural profession that the GIC effectively mirror, and that the GIC play an important role in renewing (Cuff, 1989*a*, 1999). Indeed it is the GIC, above any other segment within the 'built environment profession', that services the dominant private and public actors who have power in both defining and profiting from the processes driving broad systemic change. This section also includes a discussion of the GIC's intellectual roots in modernism, and their continued support for this form of development planning. Following this subsection, I provide a discussion of the various roles and techniques that the GIC adopt to engage in the business of architectural practice, while also engaging in internal professional discourse over the nature of the profession. Many of these roles and techniques relate to the use of social networks, and the production of a high profile 'celebrity' reputation that effectively masks the architect's relative loss of power over the actual building process. Relatively autonomous professional discourses are flourishing however, especially within texts, and they play a key role in structuring the nature of the global flows of images that the GIC firms create. The last subsection of Section 1 consists of a brief discussion of the role of the global city as the social, economic, and political milieu within which the GIC operates. The nature of the GIC cannot be understood without clarifying how they are situated within networks and institutions based in cities such as London and Paris. The manipulation of these networks and institutions enables the GIC to locate opportunities for work, and to forcefully engage in the discursive fields that constitute Architecture.

The Nature of the GIC

As the architectural critic Martin Pawley (1992: 31) points out,

Expertise is an international commodity. That is why architects were among the pioneers of the global economy: the world without frontiers where governments, financiers and consultants coalesce on any continent to provide the technological know-how that produces bridges, dams, airports, new cities and great buildings.

The GIC are playing an integral role in this transnational creation of global flows of expertise, ideas, images, technology, and development models (King, 1990*b*; Rimmer, 1991*a*; Ford, 1998; Pawley, 1998). By the GIC I mean: the very small number of élite architectural and planning firms that aspire for prestigious commissions in cities around the world. These firms tend to be synonymous with high-profile charismatic men for whom architecture and city building is both a professional and personal pursuit; a pursuit that fully consumes them throughout their lengthy careers. On this latter point French architect Jean Nouvel expresses himself in characteristic style: 'For me architecture is more than life itself. I would not only die for architecture, I would kill for it. Kill. Kill. Kill for architecture' (*World Architecture*, No. 31: 26). The Swiss-born Parisian Charles Eduard Jeanneret, alias Le Corbusier (1887–1965) and the Germans Walter Gropius (1883–1969) and Ludwig Mies van der Rohe (1886–1969) are historical exemplars of the GIC. Modern exemplars include the Italian Renzo Piano, the Italy-born but British Richard Rogers, the England-born Norman Foster, the France-born Jean Nouvel, and the Netherlands-born Rem Koolhaus.

The GIC are a product of the uneven bifurcation of the architectural profession 'between a minority of firms known for design excellence and the majority, oriented to more mundane forms of service' (Larson: 1994: 470; also see Zukin, 1991; and Crilley, 1993*a*, 1993*b*). Yet, even within this smaller segment, there are divisions for this is not a homogeneous group. I would therefore split this segment into two further divisions. The first division consists of large firms such as Skidmore Owings & Merril (SOM), RTKL Associates Inc., and Kohn Pedersen Fox Associates (KPF) that are active around the world, including in Shanghai (Tan and Low, 1999). The second division consists of smaller firms associated with 'signature architects' such as the men outlined above along with other 'names' like Michael Graves, Cesar Pelli, Richard Mier, Charles Venturi, Frank Gehry, and Philip Johnson (this is not an exclusive list) (Larson, 1993). The firms headed by these men are not necessarily large in size, but they often have a small number of offices in major world cities. It is these 'signature architects', and more specifically the GIC architects with *European* offices and strong links to French institutions, that were drawn into the Luji-azui International Consultation Process (LICP).[2]

The GIC segment of the architectural profession amplifies the patriarchal hegemony of the profession. 'Big build' is a heavily masculine business as the all male line-up above implies. Professionally, this situation has arisen in part because of the gendered nature of architectural education—the selective ' "great monuments great men" approach, one that isolates and objectifies the designer and the work' (Ahrentzen and Anthony, 1993: 15; also see Agrest *et al.*, 1996; Rendell *et al.*, 2000).[3] Professional schools continue to train students to worship the 'masters'; the all male 'geniuses' covered *ad nauseum* in architectural history books. These texts, virtually all written by male architectural

---

[2] This book focuses on the European-based GIC. Larson (1993) provides an extremely insightful analysis of American-based élite architectural firms and the mechanics of fame (also see Wiliamson, 1991; Barna, 1992; and Cuff, 1999, on the American scene).

[3] Also see Carranza (1994) on Le Corbusier's 'objectified' and superior view of women which plays itself out in his modernist sketchings or Larson (1993). At a more general level, the writings of Beatriz Colomina (e.g. *Sexuality and Space*, 1992) are relevant with respect to the issue of gender and the production of space by designers.

critics, construct Architectural history in a manner that renders females as spectators, or else excludes their achievements as producers. In the business arena, architecture and property development at the mega-scale is managed by some of the most powerful members of society (regardless of which nation you focus on) and power over property capital and urban development processes is primarily held by men. Indeed, the construction of masculine identity for some of these men is associated with their power to produce urban space that other people take notice of. Fainstein (1994: 4) only touches upon this matter in her book *The City Builders*, but it could be read as a subtext throughout her analysis. As she notes:

To a greater extent than I initially anticipated when starting this research, I found that not just economic and political pressures but personality and gender factors affect the development industry, and particular enterprises strongly reflect the aspirations of men who run them. Although women now constitute a significant proportion of real-estate brokers, men continue almost totally to dominate the major development firms. As I have studied the large projects that have changed the faces of London and New York, I have been struck by the extent to which they have been driven by male egos that find self-expression in building tall buildings and imprinting their personae on the landscape.

Since architects must deal with these powerful actors, the clients who afford them the opportunity to work, the GIC's male nature facilitates the process of acquiring and conducting prestigious work. As one relatively well-known woman architect (Joan Goody) interviewed by Larson (1993: 119–20) in the 1980s stated:

The Frank Lloyd Wrights in their capes and broad rimmed hats . . . came across as being the Magus. And these strong men (and their clients were men) would allow themselves to be beguiled by men, although this was somehow a female role which represented the artistic 'other world.' . . . When I come to the 10 per cent leap of faith and I say 'Trust me, this is the way it will look better, I have done many buildings of this size' . . . they can't quite do it.

This is also the impression I acquired during the course of interviewing actors involved with the two UMPs in Vancouver and Shanghai. It is difficult for me to imagine the Shanghai authorities respecting a female architect as seriously as they did the four 'foreign' men—Perrault, Fuksas, Ito, and Rogers—who were involved in the LICP. Charismatic male bonding is a supremely facilitative method of enabling firms to acquire architectural work.[4]

---

[4] This situation is not helped by the patriarchal nature of Chinese society. Also see Pepchinski (1993) who discusses how the high proportion of female urbanists from the former East German nation are locked out of the large redevelopment projects in Berlin—their double status as *Easterner* and *woman* cannot compete with the élite Western male architects who appeal to the former West German officials who guide the transformation of Berlin. On the redevelopment of Berlin and the Potsdamer Platz UMP, see Strom (1996) and Cochrane and Jonas (1999).

The Structural Underpinnings of the GIC Firms

GIC firms ultimately depend upon the processes of economic development, structural change, and sympathetic clients to supply them with the *opportunity* to work. Like the colonial urbanists (cf. Wright, 1991), the nature of the modern GIC, and the specific actors involved in the Shanghai case study, are related to broad structural shifts affecting the world economy over the last several decades (Cuff, 1999). Anthony King (1990*a*: 131–9; 1990*b*) closely links the internationalization of producer services industries such as architecture and planning to the internationalization of the economy, the growth of foreign direct investment flows into the built environment, and the changing nature of the 'new international division of labour' (NIDL) that concentrates service sector agglomerations in world cities (Cohen, 1981; Friedmann and Wolff, 1982; Friedmann, 1986; Sassen, 1991, 1994; Dicken, 1998).

The expansion and restructuring of the world economy over the last two decades has led to demand for vast systems of infrastructure, mass housing, commercial and industrial space, and public facilities in cities and regions where the accumulation process is occurring (Armstrong and McGee, 1985). This has enabled architectural, planning, and engineering firms specializing in these systems to acquire work outside of the global cities and grow in size. Much of the growth of 'global' contracts for such firms took place in the 1970s related to the OPEC boom, though by the 1980s these links were spread more evenly around the world on a relative basis (Baden-Powell, 1993; King, 1993). Concurrently, the growth of the global city as the key node through which global flows pass (Sassen, 1991) has created demand for architectural and planning services *within* these cities (King, 1990*a*; Sassen, 1991). This process was clearly evident in the global cities of London, Tokyo, Hong Kong, and Frankfurt where many European-based GIC firms were awarded large projects (Moore, 1999). The clients of the GIC are virtually all large multinational corporations and the national, regional, or local state in economically strong regions.

Demand for the architectural and planning services of the European-based GIC in the 1980s and early 1990s is also related to geo-political change—in particular, the demise of the 'Iron Curtain' and the fall of the Berlin Wall. These political shifts encouraged various levels of the state in Germany to 'do city planning on a massive scale and provide the necessary conditions to ensure an effective and competitive market-place' (Hassemer, 1993). Private investors such as Sony and Daimler-Benz AG hired firms including the Rogers Partnership to work on several plans for the restructuring of large sections of Berlin with the aim of: attracting foreign investment in property; revalorizing a formerly moribund (or non-existent in the case of Eastern Germany) property market; encouraging the development of the producer services sector; enabling the city to act as a 'gateway between East and West'; putting together a bid for the 2000 Olympic Games (that went to Sydney); and transforming the city's symbolic and functional landscape in a manner expressive of its new role as an 'important' capital city (Hassemer, 1993; also see Krätke, 1992; the *Architectural Review*, Jan. 1993; Balfour, 1993; Lash, 1993; Pepchinski, 1993; Häubermann and Strom, 1994; Strom, 1996; Cochrane and Jonas, 1999).[5] If firms such as Rogers's weren't participating directly through consultancies, they were often participating indirectly by acting on international juries for other Berlin projects.[6] The state- and private-sector-propelled restructuring of Berlin, which the GIC are actively involved in, has been 'railroaded through' with little opportunity for effective public participation, and it has also effectively locked out any former East German architects (their architects, including many women, fail to possess the necessary symbolic capital to participate in competitions).[7]

More recently, the GIC firms have been attempting, along with many other Western architectural and planning firms, to acquire work in the Asia-Pacific region (Langdon, 1995; Sudjic, 1993*b*; Baker, 1997; Pawley, 1998; Cuff, 1999; Tan and Low, 1999). This recent phase of the internationalization of architectural services is related to the late 1980s recession in the West, the collapse of the 'bubble economy' in Japan, and the economic boom in East and Southeast Asia (until the late-1990s Asian economic crisis hit). The expanding economies of the Asia-Pacific region during the 1980s and first half of the 1990s generated the demand for monumental transformations of infrastructure systems, many of which interlink through the city. The Asian city is being restructured to act as 'switch gears in a global exchange system, logistical centres for managing flows between distant points' (Harris, 1993: 3; also see Rimmer, 1993, 1994).

---

[5] I spent considerable time at the International Urban Development Association INTA 17— New Town Experience Joint Conference and the World Property Market Exhibition in Hong Kong (26–30 Sept. 1993) discussing these changes with representatives of the Berlin government. Dr Volker Hassener, Berlin Minister of Urban Development and Environmental Protection gave a speech at the conference which outlined his vision for the city. Later, at a wine and cheese reception, Hassener's conversation (which I only listened to) was peppered with comments about how they were using the 'best architects in the world' and how the celebrated architect Richard Meier (from the USA) spent 'over two weeks' with him reviewing proposals for the city's various redevelopment projects. Hassener clearly felt that he was accumulating symbolic capital through his association with Meier, and he also enjoyed speaking of his own major role in guiding the massive transformations under way in Berlin. However, as Pepchinski (1993: 84) notes, the Berlin authorities only associate with famous architects who do *not* engage in critical public discourse regarding their plans (e.g. Rem Koolhaus is banned from participating in any further architectural competitions after publicly criticizing the first Potsdamer Platz competition).

[6] For example, the jury for the competition to convert the Reichstag building to house the Bundestag included Richard Rogers, and the final winner was Rogers's friend and former partner Norman Foster.

[7] Smaller yet still significant plans were under way in Vienna in the early 1990s and various members of the GIC (including Rogers) were drawn in to design buildings at the US$1.4 billion Donau City project on the Danube River. The private development company behind Donau City (WED Wiener Entwicklungsgesellschaft für den Donauraum AG) was formed by the City of Vienna along with Nomura, Japan's largest investment house, and the initial feasibility study was conducted by Jones Lang Wootton Consulting and Research (company materials).

For example, total infrastructure expenditure between 1995 and 2004 in the region (excluding Japan) is expected to reach US$1.47 trillion, with annual expenditure ranging from $100 billion in 1995 to $210 billion in 2004 (Thornton, 1995: 42; also see *Euromoney*, Feb. 1995: 72–75, or the *Asian Infrastructure Monthly* that was started up by the *Financial Times* in Mar. 1995). The associated development of commercial and residential space in the region is occurring at a similar scale and in China alone 'clients are planning at least $500 billion in massive commercial complexes, hotels, office towers, and, most urgently, infrastructure' (*Architecture*, Sept. 1994: 106).

It is within this broad structural context that the contemporary GIC became closely associated with the proposed (and sometimes realized) development of spectacular built structures and massive spatial transformations taking place in cities around the world. Interestingly most of these projects are associated with the infrastructure through which global flows pass. This is not a coincidence either for the GIC architects express an astute business sense in realizing that built structures associated with flows will be increasingly developed in a globalizing world. At a more theoretical level, the GIC have a finely toned ontology of movement, and an intellectual curiosity about the role of architects and architecture in expressing the changing nature and impact of global flows. As three prominent GIC architects note:

Our strategy equips Lille [France] for its role as headquarters of the theoretical community generated by the new infrastructure. What is important about this place is not where it is, but where it leads and how quickly. (Rem Koolhaus (*Architecture*, Jan. 1995: 68))

Architects adore reducing the city down to a project, and drawing it out and tracing it with crosses on the map. All that is now over. You can't draw the city anymore, because the city is only the result of a logistical interlaced network of services and transport, energy flows, economic activity and political action. (Jean Nouvel (*World Architecture*, 31: 27))

I am searching for an architecture that will express and celebrate the ever-quickening speed of social, technical, political, and economic change; an architecture of permanence and transformation where urban vitality and economic dynamics can take place, reflecting the changing and overlapping of functions. (Richard Rogers, 1991: 45)

In the 1980s and early 1990s, for example, the following selective list of projects were designed by the European-headquartered GIC, all acting as the physical nodes through which global flows pass:

• Massive airports as components of regional development schemes associated with human and capital flows. For example, Sir Norman Foster and Partners designed the new Chek Lap Kok airport (Hong Kong), and the new Stansted Airport (London); the Renzo Piano Building Workshop designed the new Kansai airport (Osaka); the Richard Rogers Partnership designed the new Heathrow Terminal Five under current review (London), and the new terminal at Marseille Airport.

- Major telecommunications structures associated with flows of images, ideas, and capital. For example, the Richard Rogers Partnership designed the Reuters Data Centre and the Channel Four headquarters building (London); Jean Nouvel designed the Media Park (Cologne); Sir Norman Foster and Associates designed the Torre de Collserola (Barcelona Telecommunications Tower), and the ITN headquarters (London).

- Major office towers and headquarters of TNCs, many of which are associated with flows of capital, images, and ideas. For example, the Richard Rogers Partnership designed the Lloyd's of London Headquarters (London), Twin Towers for the new Donau City project (Vienna); Sir Norman Foster and Associates designed the Hong Kong and Shanghai Banking Corporation headquarters (Hong Kong), the Commerzbank Zentrale (Frankfurt), Century Tower (Hong Kong), and the Millenium Tower (Tokyo); Jean Nouvel designed the *Tours sans Fins*, La Défense (Paris).

- Master planning for mega-project sites at waterfront sites or nodes of transportation infrastructure associated with flows of capital, images, ideas, and humans. For example, Sir Norman Foster and Associates planned the Wilhelminapier pier in the Kop van Zuid project (Rotterdam), the King's Cross project (London), the central area of Berlin following the fall of the Wall; the Richard Rogers Partnership masterplanned Potsdamer/Leipziger Platz (Berlin), King's Dock (Liverpool), Lujiazui (Shanghai), Royal Albert Docks (London); Rem Koolhaus's Office for Metropolitan Architecture (OMA) planned Euralille and Lille Grand Palais—the hub of the new cross-Channel high speed rail network and centre of the London/Brussels/Paris triangle; the Renzo Piano Building Workshop masterplanned Potsdamer Platz (Berlin).

- New state institutional facilities associated with flows of ideas. For example, Sir Norman Foster and Associates are designing the new German Parliament, Reichstag (Berlin); the Richard Rogers Partnership designed the new European Court of Human Rights (Strasbourg); Jean Nouvel played a major role in designing the Institut du Monde Arabe (Paris); Dominique Perrault designed the new Bibliothèque Nationale de France (Paris).

The vast majority of these powerful icons of late modernity were awarded via juried international architectural competitions. Moreover, the lead architectural firms for these projects consistently drew upon the services of the Ove Arup Partnership, a transnational engineering firm that is headquartered in London (see Sommer *et al.* (1994) for further details on Ove Arup Partnership).

The Intellectual Foundations of the GIC's
Involvement in Mega-Projects

Clients require firms with the skills and interest in working on large-scale 'spectacular' buildings and massive urban (re)development projects. It is only actors educated in, and supportive of, modernist approaches to city building who would be interested in supporting these types of projects. The contemporary GIC are rooted in the tradition of technocratic planning propagated by the Congrès Internationaux d'Architecture Moderne (CIAM) between 1928 and the mid-1950s, particularly through *The Athens Charter* (Le Corbusier, 1957/1941). CIAM members and supporters, heavily influenced by the nineteenth-century 'Haussmannization of European capitals' (Holston, 1989: 48) worked on many mega-planning exercises in the first half of the twentieth century. Some of the most prominent architects (and their projects) include Le Corbusier (Chandigarh, Ville Radieuse, A Contemporary City for Three Million Inhabitants, The Radiant City, Plan Voisin), Frank Lloyd Wright (Broadacre City), Ernst May (Magnitogorsk), and Lúcio Costa and Oscar Niemeyer (Brasília).

Neo- or late-modern GIC architects, contemporary versions of their historic idols, have adapted modernist architectural and planning approaches in planning the 'switching centres' of our globalizing world. Modernists are philosophically supportive of the 'rational' and 'objective' ordering of the built environment; a disposition that blends exceedingly well with the goals of the 'developmental state' in East Asia (on the developmental state see Douglass, 1994, or Woo-Cumings, 1999) and global property developers. Under modernism, the uses of space are defined by detached and 'heroic' state-sponsored technocrats (including architects and planners) who are educated to rationally plan for *the* public good. Space itself is 'seen as isotropic, homogeneous in every direction. . . . abstract, limited by boundaries or edges, and rational or logically transferable from part to whole, or whole to part' (Charles Jencks cited in Ley, 1989*a*: 60).

For modernists such as Gropius or Le Corbusier an abstract uniform approach to design applies equally well in all of the world's cities and regions. This approach emphasizes the ideologically derived aesthetic qualities of order, unity, purity, simplicity, functionalism, and utilitarianism where 'form follows function'. Modernist plans are decontextualized and dehistoricized. Festering cities (see Holston, 1989, on the physical metaphors used by CIAM) are *flushed* clean with the 'shock of the new'. The *tabula rasa* approach to planning leads architects to conceptualize of place as space: open and available for restructuring in accordance with the abstract theories of the 'experts'. To be inscribed is to be saved from the inevitable processes of slow death according to this logic. The modernist approach to architecture and planning treats the complete city as a 'machine', where planners break the city down into its essential functions, to be 'taylorized, standardized, rationalized, and assembled as a totality' (Holston, 1989: 51; Jencks, 1991). In this process modernists celebrate the development, application, and innovative use of technology and materials in their city building work (Davies, 1988).

The rhetoric of some contemporary GIC discourse (see Rogers, 1991 or his 1995 Reith Lectures on BBC Radio) implies a continuation of the socially transformative vision of the modernist project. The weaknesses of modernism (as critiqued by Jacobs, 1961) arose because modernism was not fully achieved; our world, and modernist potential, shaken by the 'exploitative economic system' (Rogers, 1991: 62). Such talk exhibits elements of the ideology of the early- to mid-twentieth century avant-garde modernists including the Soviet Constructionists and Le Corbusier (1967/1933). The avant-garde modernists viewed architecture and planning as an instrument of social change enabling the development of a more egalitarian society, a 'consciously subversive' challenge to the excesses of bourgeois capitalist society and its institutions (e.g. private property) (Gottdiener, 1995: 133; also see Berman, 1982; Harvey, 1989*a*; Holston, 1989; Ley, 1989*a*; Jencks, 1991; Larson, 1993). As such, their designs for buildings, larger (re)development projects, and complete cities were driven by the modernist utopian ideology of progress that asserted 'collective action and collective rights over private interests both in ordering the city and in managing the forces of industrial development' (Holston, 1989: 41). In the context of late twentieth-century development trends however, ecological objectives are now highly positioned in the GIC's broader social objectives.

In keeping with the modernist approach to planning and design, GIC architects such as Rogers, Perrault, Piano, and Foster will accept work in cities and nations where they have little understanding of the social, cultural, political, and economic context. They are firms that offer 'universal' solutions to universal problems—a pure modernist design ethos underlying monumental self-referential architecture. 'Jetting around the world and doing buildings [and larger projects] every time the plane lands', in the critical words of the famous Indian architect Charles Correa, is a perfectly defensible approach to the GIC architects (*World Architecture*, 27: 76). Global clients, or local clients with global ambitions, find such firms and their modernist approach highly attractive: the GIC firms are perceived to be the 'expert systems' laden with appropriate knowledge that will enable the client to connect their project to a non-local world system. This is particularly true in China, where the state and quasi-state entrepreneurs associate Western firms with the development of the modern city. The GIC are the harbingers of modernization, and they use this role in a professional attempt to restore a 'fully achieved' modernism as the dominant approach to city building.

Building Mega-projects, Building a Profession

As Crawford (1991: 27) notes:

modern professions, rather than simply existing as the sum of the professional interests of the individual members, instead are complex social constructs that structure their autonomous identities in relation to the specific configuration of the economy and society in which they operate. Successful professional identities depend as much upon devising convincing ideological representations of professional practices as on the actual practices themselves.

Crawford's interrogation of the profession's attempt to practise architecture *and* 'fashion a successful identity' (ibid.) is closely aligned with the recent analysis of Magali Sarfatti Larson in her brilliant 1993 book *Behind the Postmodern Facade*. Both analysts point to the need to address not only how architects acquire work, and the images they create for their projects, but also how they concurrently engage in autonomous professional discourse (also see Colomina, 1994).

What Larson suggests is that élite architects are constituted through professional discourses that exist independently of the actual client-related practice of architecture. Architectural élites become famous through the collective and publicized judgements of other professionals and associated 'cognoscenti' who are attached to the profession (e.g. architectural critics). Architects engage in professional discourse by disseminating their knowledge (in the form of images, and written and spoken words) through appropriate channels including competitions, exhibitions, consultations, professional organizations, universities, books, and professional journals, and selective forms of the general press. The content of discourse may range from pure aesthetics to broader social and philosophical issues, while the discourse itself, 'almost by definition, transcends locale' (1993: 103). The knowledge of élite architects must be received, honoured, and reproduced by the professionally designated gatekeepers. In other words, their work needs to be situated within a portfolio rather than a particular place (Cuff, 1999: 86; Deutsche, 1996). Honour may take many forms including invitations to participate in or jury international competitions, favourable critical reviews, the creation of significant levels of professional debate, knightings (in England), and awards. Within the profession, the greatest honour of all is the establishment of a form of hegemony like that held by the Modern Movement in the first half of the twentieth century. Ultimately, 'it is the recognition granted within the profession that gives architects elite status and lifts them above the level of a small or purely local practice' (1993: 100). 'All architectural elites', including the GIC, 'exist by and within the profession's autonomous discourse' (1993: 135–6).

The 'frame' (Hannerz, 1992*a*) through which the global flows of images are created is heavily dependent upon the discursive field of architecture as it is perceived by the architect(s) publicly responsible for the drawings (Larson, 1993: 14). The client's will (via the 'terms of reference') certainly defines the basic criteria that the architect's images must satisfy (e.g. 'design for 4 million sq. metres of high rise floor space'), and the client disseminates flows of images along a myriad of paths to satisfy their own particular goal(s) for the development project. However, the nature of the images, and the many paths through which the flows of images proceed after the point of creation also depend upon autonomous professional discourse that élite architects must always engage in. In adopting this conceptualization of the nature of the GIC we should expect to discern dual (sometimes overlapping) paths for the global flows of concepts and images—each driven by a separate logic—that of the professional architects, and that of the client.

Hooking into the World of the Client and the World of the Profession

The importance of autonomous professional discourse to élite architects leads them to strategically build up networks of relations with the profession's gatekeepers. This practice involves the constant maintenance and extension of social networks through private channels and professional service (such as defending the profession from the criticism of people such as Prince Charles).

However, as alluded to above, architecture is a *heteronomous* profession—it is structurally dependent upon broader processes and actors that architects do not control to *enable* them to acquire and conduct work (Larson, 1993: 64; Cuff, 1999). Since architectural firms are businesses, they depend upon clients to provide architects with the opportunity to develop and disseminate their ideas and therefore improve their capacity to build an élite reputation. As such, they must also engage in the practice of architecture, and build networks of relations with powerful actors and institutions who may become paying clients.

The tensions and contradictions between the 'autonomous pursuit of architecture and the heteronomous conditions of its making' (Larson, 1993: 14) are addressed through the development and/or support of techniques that enable élite architects to engage in both professional practice and professional discourse. The basic theme running through each of these techniques is the production of an élite reputation that enables the firms to form networks of interpersonal relations on a global scale. GIC firms attempt to achieve this goal through seven interrelated techniques.

First, senior GIC architects continually maintain private contacts with potential clients and other powerful actors (e.g. chartered surveyors) who may direct work to their firm. Relationships with sub-consultants such as engineering firms are maintained for the purposes of conducting work, and acquiring future recommendations.

Secondly, senior GIC architects attend and speak at numerous conferences and business events such as the annual international property market fair (MIPIM) in Cannes, and the World Development Council's annual Global Superprojects Conference and Exhibition. This generates business leads and develops their reputation as authoritative experts.

Thirdly, as with other producer services firms such as accounting, a steady turnover of GIC staff is encouraged to form 'networks of acquaintances and reservoirs of good will' that may assist them in 'getting recommended to clients' at a later date (Larson, 1993: 10).

Fourthly, the GIC deliberately construct media images of themselves (Larson, 1993); a technique first associated with the modernist Le Corbusier (Colomina, 1994). The GIC are extremely knowledgeable about the role of the media in engendering support for their firms, their products, their ideas, and their profession. Skilful manipulation of the media is conducted by facilitating coverage of their projects and activities regardless of where the projects are located. The GIC (and their supporters) disseminate global flows of ideas and images through the discursive spaces of books, exhibitions, catalogues, architectural magazines, corporate magazines, photographs, world's fairs, museums, art galleries, conferences, public lectures, television and radio presentations, direct consultations, and internet web pages (Larson, 1993; Cuff, 1999). Contacts and close relationships are formed and maintained with key media producers and other members of the cognoscenti who have important links to the media. The GIC realize, in Si Newhouse's words (the owner of Conde Nast empire) that 'power is writing about power' (cited in Jencks, n.d.: 22). Specific graphic materials are always prepared for the professional and popular presses, and digitized CADD images are developed for use on television and video media. These images are disseminated by the GIC firms themselves, though the clients also use the images for their own goals.

Fifthly, GIC firms position themselves, through past practices and ongoing relations, to participate in international architectural competitions and international consultations (such as the LICP). These mythic, highly mediated, and discursive events boost the international profile of the firm's representatives and their 'product'. Competitions and consultations provide an opportunity for architects to attempt to change 'authorized notions of what architecture is, for those who listen to the specialized discourse of architecture' (Larson, 1994: 472). Élite GIC actors also seek to act as jurors in international architectural competitions that are sponsored by powerful state and private sector clients; a practice that enables them to further the careers of colleagues while building up a range of contacts that could lead to future work opportunities for their own firms.

Sixthly, the élite architects heading GIC firms are advertising tools (Huxtable, 1984; Zukin, 1991; Crilley, 1993*a*, 1993*b*; Knox, 1993*a*; Larson, 1993). As Lash and Urry (1994: 200) note:

the social composition of the producers, or at least those who are in the first line, is often part of what is 'sold' to the customers. In other words, the 'service' consists of a process of production which is infused with particular social characteristics, of gender, age, race, educational background and so on. When the individual [client] buys a given service, what is purchased is a certain social composition of the service-producers. . . . This is particularly the case where the service is wholly or in part semiotic.

Because of the nature of professional discourse, GIC architects are soaked in 'symbolic capital'. Clients recognize and contribute to the formation of this status in order to heighten their status as architectural 'patrons' while also legitimating their development projects. Visually striking property projects 'branded' by the GIC can create 'recognition factor on the skyline', that then translates into a 'designer label' product (Huxtable, 1984: 68–9). The client—

'corporations, developers, even city governments—try to use for profit, publicity, or both the designer's name in symbiosis with their designs' (Larson, 1993: 139). By means of architectural patronage both the client and their project(s) have improved potential to gain greater favour with the discerning public, the media, and potential investors. Élite architects are deemed to have the capacity to conceptually reorient actors that the client is dependent upon (Zukin, 1991; Crilley, 1993*b*). As Donald Trump clearly stated: 'I like to get somebody with a big reputation because I think the reputation pays for itself' (quoted in Hutchinson, 1994: p. x). Reputation can pay for itself because the GIC are well connected to, and well covered by, the business, professional, and popular media. And, for UMP developers such as Trump, Petronas, or an Olympia and York, it is 'the media' that generates 'the interest in the designs that we develop' (a senior O&Y spokesperson cited in Larson, 1993: 132). While the association of names such as Pelli, Rogers, Johnson, Perrault, or Nouvel with a client's project guarantees a certain degree of international media coverage for the client, this coverage also benefits the GIC firm. Architects use the coverage to attract further business, and to enhance their power in defining professional discourse. This latter aim is achieved by 'double coding' design projects so that the form and underlying theory of the project appeals to the client and the professional cognoscenti (ibid.: 147).

And seventhly, most GIC architects teach at architectural schools in prestigious Western universities. This enables them to propagate their images and ideas, 'cherry pick' bright and devoted students to become junior employees, and attract 'cultural capital' that appeals to professional gatekeepers and sophisticated clients (Larson, 1993).

The above techniques enable the GIC to situate themselves in advantageous positions with respect to the acquisition of flows of information that they deem important. In turn, they process this information and use their extended social relations to disseminate flows of information, including ideas and images. On this point, however, it is important to recognize that, unlike ethnic Chinese property developers, the investment of architectural resources is not as spatially fixed (see Harvey, 1982 on the spatial fixity associated with property investment). As a consequence, the GIC pay greater attention to forming relational networks with *global* actors such as representatives of professional associations, media producers, transnational property developers, or senior state representatives. Their dependence upon, and understanding of, *local* actors (e.g. local politicians, community groups, the local media) is relatively less important and detailed than that of the Chinese developers active in cities like Vancouver or Sydney.

The GIC and Global Cities

The GIC inhabit the 'neo-worlds' of late capitalism. They easily negotiate the stretched out social spaces tied to both the *business* networks of architecture (the moneyed white-collar property developers and senior state officials) and the *professional* networks of architecture (the intelligentsia-managed institutions that help define the discourse of Architecture). The workland of the GIC has no physical boundaries for they can afford to travel constantly; their workland merely has social boundaries that they are well equipped to pass through it afforded the opportunity (Cuff, 1999). GIC elites tend to excel at intercul tural communication, they are knowledgeable about current affairs around the world, they have the appropriate social graces to blend in with diverse crowds at champagne receptions and ribbon-cutting ceremonies, and they can engage in animated and stimulating conversations with little prompting. These social skills are the result of years of experience and, more importantly, an internal and sincere desire to be considered part of the transnational intellectual scene—a coterie of cosmopolitan professionals who 'keep in touch via global cultural flows and who are not only at home in other cultures, but seek out and adopt a reflexive, metacultural or aesthetic stance to divergent cultural experiences' (Featherstone, 1990*a*: 8; also see Lash and Urry, 1994: 309; Cuff, 1999).

While the GIC are extremely mobile in social and geographical senses, they are ultimately dependent upon one socio-spatial formation for their life force— the global city. Like the ethnic Chinese tycoons analysed in Chapter 4, the nature of the GIC is related to the capacity of these firms to situate themselves advantageously at nodes through which global flows of people, images, technology, capital, and ideas pass. This enables the GIC firms to engage in both the business and the profession of architecture by directly and indirectly exploiting these flows to their advantage.

In the *business arena*, for example, the headquarters of TNCs and other large corporations tend to be based in global cities. These businesses require architectural services for their own buildings and the GIC have a 'suitable' reputation for corporate clients. Moreover, the overall agglomeration of corporations in global cities generates an aggregate demand for services related to urban design and planning. While the local state tends to be responsible for this task, they often hire large architectural and planning firms such as the GIC as consultants.

Global cities provide GIC firms with an abundant source of highly skilled professional labour. Appropriate educational institutions are located in global cities and these provide a steady stream of new talent. Labour shifts between architectural firms are also relatively simple in one large city. Overall, a suitable labour force is available for GIC firms because architects, by and large, prefer to live in the gentrified inner city districts of global cities—districts where these reflexive educated élites can satisfy their aestheticized consumption needs (Zukin, 1991).

On a practical business level, GIC firms need to have efficient access to transportation infrastructure, and airports in particular. Increasingly their services are provided worldwide and rapid access to airports for flights overseas enables them to negotiate contracts, to conduct on-site work in as easy a manner as possible.

Large state institutions (e.g. museums, libraries, exhibition centres, convention centres) are also based in global cities; cities that commonly double as national capitals. This double role of global/capital city leads political regimes to devote considerable resources to the development and maintenance of state institutions in the city.[8] State largesse then translates into the demand for architectural services and the GIC benefits from this demand. GIC firms are considered desirable by the state for two main reasons. First, they provide consistent and creative design skills that are innovative within the conceptual boundaries of state representatives. GIC firms also have the necessary semiotic skills including knowledge of global referents to design expressive structures in accordance with state goals. Secondly, GIC firms are willing 'signs' in processes (e.g. design competitions) that are symbolic expressions of state power. The successful management of both these roles is enhanced if GIC firms understand the social, cultural, economic, and political milieu that the state representatives are operating in, and if the GIC's élite architects are well connected to these state representatives. It is only the urbane well-connected cosmopolitans who revel in this milieu and slide through élite networks to work the milieu to their advantage. These types of cosmopolitans are formed, reside, work, and draw inspiration from the dynamic context of the global city.

In the *professional arena*, as noted above, GIC élites become élite through their engagement in architectural discourse via the production of portfolios (Deutsche, 1996). Élite architects primarily engage in discourse through professional organizations, the specialist design press, and architectural training institutions. Larson (1993: 11–12) summarizes this point:

the institutional bridges that connect different segments of this profession are also centres for the production and reproduction of discourse. Schools, professional societies, foundations, institutes, editorial boards, specialized publishers, and (because architecture is an art) museums and art galleries all concur in reinforcing the special place of the elite form-givers creating, through this elite, a measure of ideological and practical unity in this divided profession.

---

[8] The importance of state largesse to the European-based GIC cannot be overstated, and the French case is a perfect example. Over the last several hundred years monumental transformations of Paris's urban structure have been planned and often executed in accordance with the goals of various French and Parisian politicians and officials (see Harvey, 1985: 62–220; Wright, 1991; Sutcliffe, 1993; Winterbourne, n.d.). Throughout this long period 'architect-urbanists' (Wright, 1991) were involved in and benefited from these state-sponsored transformations. The GIC are merely the contemporary beneficiaries of a Parisian devotion to urbanism, and a conception of Paris as 'cultural centre of world status' (Winterbourne, n.d.: 25). Since the late 1960s for example, virtually all of the contemporary European-based GIC have been involved in designing or acting as jurors for large projects in Paris (including the *Grands Projets*). This has enabled the careers of GIC architects such as Rogers (under Pompidou) and Perrault (under Mitterand) to 'take off'. The development and renovation of institutional structures not only generates demand for GIC services, but it also plays a critical 'breakthrough' role in the formation of an élite international reputation (Larson, 1993).

However, what Larson fails to specify in her otherwise excellent book is that all of these institutions are spatially concentrated in the global city. Architects who wish to become members of the élite segment of the profession must deeply embed themselves in networks and institutions associated with the global city. The autonomous discourse of the profession is managed by élites within these institutions, and they have the capacity to enable or disable the efforts of architects who wish to alter the nature of this discourse. This task is made much simpler by working in global cities where proximity enhances the formation of direct and indirect networks of relation with the institutional gatekeepers. Project development for the GIC firms also favours initiatives in existing global cities (e.g. Paris) or in emerging global cities (e.g. Shanghai) where institutional attention is enhanced. Greater coverage of the activities of the GIC élite is possible in cities where 'institutional thickness' (Amin and Thrift, 1994) exists, or in cities that institutional élites find exotic.

Section 2

The Historical Context

Shanghai (*Hu*) has a long and well-known history of interaction with the rest of the world: indeed, a 'Superintendancy of Foreign Trade' had been established on the banks of the Whangpoo River in this coastal city as early as 1267 (Wei, 1993; Pan, 1993), and textiles and trade dominated the regional economy. The city had developed as a mature urban centre by the sixteenth century, through a continued dependence upon cotton, silk, porcelain, and transportation, and reached its pre-colonial apex in the late seventeenth century when it 'had become one of the world's greatest ports, with a forest of masts and a volume of shipping equal to or greater than London's' (Pan, 1993, introd.).

It was the 1843 Treaty of Nanking that forced the city open to international finance, trade, and residence in extraterritorial enclaves for just over one hundred years. The Treaty of Nanking, an agreement ending the British-initiated Opium War (1840–2), effectively prised open Shanghai transforming it into an entrepôt of three cities—the Chinese city, the International Settlement, and the French Concession (with separate legal, administrative, and police systems) (Murphey, 1980; Wei, 1990; Pan, 1993; Perry, 1993). The Treaty transformed Shanghai into one of the most cosmopolitan and divided cities in the world with the British, French, German, Russian, American, and Japanese forming the bulk of overseas residents (each with a separate national post office).[9] Also

---

[9] Deyan Sudjic suggested to me that colonial era Shanghai could be considered the 'first post-modern city' given its highly fragmented and divided nature, and its intermediation of global flows of images, capital, and people (interview, July 1995). For empirical evidence of social cleavages in Shanghai, particularly among 'the Chinese' residents, see Perry's (1993) excellent book *Shanghai on Strike: The Politics of Chinese Labour*. This book is also a powerful antidote to the universalizing tendencies of the Fordist-Postfordist binary (as it is applied to labour forces and cities).

present were millions of Chinese refugees from different ethnic groups (who settled in ethnic enclaves), Canadians, Indians, Dutch, White Russians (fleeing the Bolshevik victory), and diaspora cultures of overseas Chinese, Ashkenazim, and Shephardim Jews, symbolized by the Sassoon family, originally from Baghdad, later Bombay (where trading enterprises were set up, though they were incorporated in London), Hong Kong, and finally Shanghai (Murphy, 1980; Wei, 1990; Clifford, 1991; Pan, 1993; Perry, 1993; Wei, 1993; Hook, 1998; Lee, 1999). As a local gazetteer noted in 1930:

> Exploring a corner of Shanghai is really like finding the whole world in a grain of millet. Disney Road, Peng Road, and Wusong Road in Hongkou are full of Japanese residents, just like in Japan. North Sichuan Road, Wuchang Road, Chongming Road and Tiantong Road are full of Cantonese, just like in Guangdong. The western section of Avenue Joffre is full of shops run by Frenchmen just like in France. The foreign goods stores outside Little East Gate are mostly operated by Fujianese, just like in Fujian. Salty Melon Street in Nanshi is full of shops run by Ningbo people, just like in Ningbo. Foreign residents and Chinese from every province all congregate here. So it is no exaggeration to describe Shanghai as a miniature world. (cited in Perry, 1993: 17)

While grim testaments to the level of exploitation in Shanghai are numerous, there was a positive side as well, demonstrated by the influx of deterritorialized European (German, Austrian, and Polish) Jews escaping Nazism, who enriched an already vibrant literary, musical, cinematic, and artistic scene (Kahn, 1994*a*; Lee, 1999). Shanghai was the cosmopolitan node in which streams of mobile people came together for a variety of purposes including, most importantly, the making of money.

'Foreign' financial institutions were set up in Shanghai immediately after the Opium War. Between 1847 and 1865, for example, ten British banks and one French bank were set up. By the 1890s, banks from Germany, Japan, Russia, and the Netherlands opened representative offices in Shanghai. The most prosperous financial era of Shanghai was from World War I to the early 1930s, when banks from other countries including the USA and the Philippines were set up. Thirty foreign banks and eighty domestic banks were located in Shanghai, and the city acted as a national and regional (Asia-Pacific) financial centre (Shanghai Municipal People's Government, 1991). The city was an economic powerhouse, accounting for nearly 50 per cent of China's gross industrial value, and attracting over 40 per cent of China's foreign direct investment in the first half of the 1930s (Zhao, 1993: 218). Related financial institutions were highly active at this time. In 1934, for example, annual transactions in bonds on the Shanghai Stock Exchange (which was set up in 1905) reached 4.77 billion yuan, and the gold market ranked number three behind London and New York (Shanghai Municipal People's Government, 1991: 13–18). Insurance, banking, and securities markets were formed, with strong links to markets in other world cities such as London and Paris. Thus Shanghai has been a node through which local, national, regional, and global capital flows have intersected for nearly a hundred years.

Urbanization in this node of global flows was rapid and distinctive, fuelled by pulses of enormous wealth flowing through the city, the three regulatory systems that divided the city, and multiple cultures, each imposing their own mark on the landscape (Hemiot, 1993). In keeping with the function of this city as Asia-Pacific's most powerful financial centre, landscapes of power were constructed, centring on the Bund, next to the Huangpu River (Zhang, 1993). Much of the wealth was used to support the development of large European-style structures along the Bund in the 1920s, reminiscent of cities such as Liverpool. As Zhang (1993: 93) notes, these structures, that were designed to be landmarks, were the result of several conditions:

1) Politics—architecture as a symbol of imperialism; 2) Economics—the display of family or corporate wealth; 3) Culture—the reminiscence of European international metropolises; 4) Landscape—as a sign of entrance to Shanghai; 5) Technology—comprehensive performance in design, construction standards, the use of new materials and facilities. Essentially, the 'landmarks' of the Band [Bund] were not just easily visible objects to assist travellers with their route, but rather an historic record of the colonial rule in China and the architectural interaction between the Eastern and Western cultures.

A wide variety of architectural styles was inscribed in the landscape including European Classic Style and Eclectic Style (during the late 1890s to 1920s) and European Modernism (from the 1920s on). For example, in keeping with the ideology of capitalism, the British-controlled Victorian classical Hong Kong and Shanghai Bank building (1923) sought to express seemingly timeless financial, commercial, and industrial power. Designed by British architectural firm Palmer and Turner, a brief suggesting 'Spare no expense but dominate the Bund', led them to incorporate 'eight columns of Sienna marble supporting the dome of Venetian mosaic', and a '300-foot long marble counter in the banking hall' (Pan, 1993: 62). While some of the fifty or so Western architectural firms set up in Shanghai in the late 1920s attempted to incorporate Chinese design principles in their plans, the overarching role of the architect, and of architecture, was to reinforce and symbolize the inflow of 'modern' Western (Euro-American to be more precise) culture to the 'backwards' East (Murphy, 1980; Wu, 1993; Zhang, 1993). In colonial-era Shanghai, market and state-framed images were formulated in the global cities of the West, or in Eastern cities by agents of the West. These flows of images helped constitute the flows of capital, ideas, and technologies that linked East and West in a relationship of imperialism.

Shanghai played a prominent economic and cultural role in China until the creation of the People's Republic of China (PRC) in 1949. Exploitative treatment of the Chinese in Shanghai and other treaty port cities instilled deep-rooted hatred of the functional and symbolic consumer city (Murphy,

1980). This decadent bourgeois and 'Satanic' city of the West, the 'bitch-goddess who gnawed at the souls' of the Chinese left a bitter legacy of anti-urbanism that influenced communist policy towards settlement after the revolution of 1949 (Murphy, 1980: 29). Shanghai's future was about to change, and it soon felt the imprint of a vigorous communist ideology. As Rhoads Murphy (1980: 33) notes in his classic book *The Fading of the Maoist Vision*, 'the chief need was seen as changing these cities inherited from colonialism to serve the nation as a whole instead of their foreign owners, and to change their character accordingly'. Murphy continues with a revolutionary poem:

> So many deeds cry out to be done,
>
> And always urgently.
>
> The world rolls on,
>
> Time passes.
>
> Ten thousand years are too long;
>
> Seize the day, seize the hour,
>
> Our force is irresistible.

Direct foreign influence was ended, and the city entered a twenty-five year period of restructuring in keeping with a Maoist version of communist ideology—anti-urbanism, anti-treaty port, heavy industrialization, low population growth, firm state control, and the elimination of all signs of bourgeois identity. Between 1949 and 1976, while the Shanghai's economy continued to contribute significantly to the national economy, little effort and capital was reinvested in the city, and this was indicated in declining relative growth figures (Kirkby, 1985; Hyslop, 1990; Fung *et al.*, 1992; Zhao, 1993; Jacobs and Hong, 1994; Yusuf and Wu, 1997). The city's tertiary (service) sector also started a three decade long decline (it had stood at 41.7 per cent of Shanghai's GNP in 1952) (Zhao, 1993). While there were efforts at developing satellite towns around Shanghai, this programme met with mixed success (Kirkby, 1985; Atash and Wang, 1990; Fun *et al.*, 1992). In the city proper, Shanghai's treaty port past was rooted out wherever possible, either to be eradicated, or simply transformed in both function and symbolism (Murphy, 1980). The Shanghai and Hong Kong Bank building described above, for example, became City Hall for the Shanghai Municipal Government. However, the historical legacy of Shanghai's status as a 'window to the world', as an international financial centre, as a cosmopolitan centre, as a city of global architectural styles—as a basic emblem of modernity—continues to leave its mark on the contemporary restructuring of Shanghai. Indeed, *all* of the Shanghainese people I interviewed suggested that it is Shanghai's former status as a global city that inspires them in their contemporary drive to modernize the city, albeit firmly under Chinese control this time.

The Reform Era: Connecting China to Global Flows of Capital and Technology

Contemporary developments in Shanghai are directly related to the end of Maoism in the late 1970s, and the establishment of a new order by the Chinese Communist Party at the third plenum in December 1978 through the implementation of the New Open Door Policy.

The main goals of post-1978 reform policies are to restructure the Chinese economy:

- away from collective forms of ownership and control of the means of production and away from the associated socially-directed allocation of the surplus product;

- towards a growth of individual and private ownership and control, with increasing allocation of surplus according to 'efficiency' criteria in the state sector, and to owners/controllers of the means of production in the new private sector and old (transformed) collective sector;

- towards an increasing role for markets in the circulation of goods, services, capital and wage labour. (Cannon, 1995: 4)

The goals of greater economic efficiency and rapid economic growth clearly imply an openness to 'foreign' flows of capital, technology, ideas, and people provided they directly relate to *economic* development and the transformation of China into a 'modern' nation. In other words, there are narrow criteria in place on which flows are 'welcome', as evidenced by the ongoing debates about flows of ideas about human rights, or internet access (Lucas, 1995).

The above reform goals have resulted in the implementation of a wide variety of initiatives in all sectors of the economy. For the sake of brevity, I will concentrate on the initiatives that are most relevant for understanding the structural processes that underlie the development of Pudong and the Lujiazui Central Finance District until 1995 or so. While I endeavour to limit the detail in this discussion, it is important to highlight these state-led initiatives for they *underpinned* the LICP that took place in 1992. Understanding these factors helps us understand the rationale of the SMG in inviting the GIC to play a role in planning Shanghai's new international financial centre. The GIC were invited to participate in Shanghai's restructuring at a key point in post-Mao Chinese history: the timing of this invitation is an insightful indicator of the nature of the reform process in the early 1990s, and changing conceptions about the role of the city in regional and national development strategies.

Please note that this overview of national reform initiatives and their impacts is also part of my attempt to provide a provisional discussion of the LICP, and of the role of transnational cultures in globalization processes. I begin the discussion at the national scale, then work down to the regional/municipal scale (Shanghai), then down to a specific development zone (Pudong), then finally down to Lujiazui Central Finance District (one zone in Pudong) where I discuss the LICP and the GIC. Unlike the shorter Vancouver case study, a more detailed multi-level context must be provided because of the greater complexity of the situation in China; a situation related to the strong role of the state in the development of the case study UMP, and the complex and extremely influential interlinkages between central government action and local change in the Chinese urban context (Kirkby, 1985; Tang, 1989; Naughton, 1995; Ng and Tang, 1999; Yeh and Wu, 1999).

The post-Mao economic reforms in China were 'kicked off' with the Open Door Policy and the Four Modernizations scheme, which then led to a series of incremental and ad hoc reforms since 1978 (see Box 5.1).

Box 5.1 Chronology of key national reforms in the People's Republic of China, 1978–1995

1978   Start of economic reforms and Open Door Policy.

1979   Passage of joint-venture law.

1980   Creation of four special economic zones in the southwestern provinces, Guangdong and Fujian (Shenzen, Zhuhai, Shantou, and Xiamen).

1981   Beginning of land reform.

1984   Start of corporate reform.
       Opening of another fourteen coastal cities (including Shanghai).
       Hainan Island becomes a special economic zone.

1985   Creation of foreign exchange swap centres in Shanghai and Shenzen.
       Pearl, Xiamen, and Yangtze River Delta opened to foreign investment.

1987   Passage of bankruptcy law/start of price reform.

1988   Hainan special economic zone upgraded to provincial status.
       The coastal development strategy extended to all coastal provinces, including the Shandong and Liaoning peninsulas.
       Pudong in Shanghai is 'launched'.

1990   Stock exchanges in Shanghai and Shenzen established.
       Pudong in Shanghai officially designated as a special economic zone.

1992   Five ports along the Yangtze River and thirteen cities along the Chinese national border are declared 'open cities'.
       The service sector opened to foreign investment.

1993   Socialist market economy included in the constitution.

1994   Tax reform and introduction of single exchange rate.
       Beginning of banking reform.

1995   New regulations to guide direction of FDI (including further opening up of service sector).
       Further overhaul of tax system for foreign invested enterprises.

Sources: Adapted from a table in Dresdner Bank (1994), and supplemented by information from Chen (1993), World Bank (1997*b*), and Li and Li (1999).

More specifically, the interrelated reforms that structure the processes driving the development of Lujiazui, and enabled the GIC to participate in the planning of Shanghai's new international financial centre, are noted below.

Attracting Foreign Direct Investment Flows

The most important reform initiatives that underlie the development of Lujiazui are related to the active encouragement of FDI.[10] FDI is strongly desired by the Chinese state in order to facilitate the economic development process, maximize foreign exchange earnings, 'relieve domestic capital supply bottlenecks', transfer technology and skills to Chinese enterprises and workers, promote employment, and increase interaction between the domestic economy and the outside world (Kueh, 1992: 637; World Bank, 1997b; Li and Li, 1999). Since 1979 China has constantly developed new policies and regulations to attract FDI flows. While the majority of policies and regulations originate with the central government (via the State Council), regional and local levels of government have also developed new policies and regulations with respect to FDI.

The scale of capital flowing into China since the Open Door Policy was initiated in 1978 has been enormous.[11] US$467.734 billion in (FDI) flows were pledged by foreign investors in China between 1979 and 1996 (US$111 billion in 1993 alone, during the middle of the LICP), while actual (utilized) FDI flows during the same period totalled $174.885 billion (Sun, 1998a: 18; see Fig. 5.1 for annual figures).

The main interrelated factors that have been posited for China's success in attracting FDI flows include:

- The rapid expansion of the domestic market, driven by a strong economic performance;
- The gradual opening of the domestic market to FDI, inducing a large number of market-seeking investments. In 1992, some service industries, such as transportation,

[10] Disproportionate attention is devoted to the issue of FDI because it is the fundamental process which enables Lujiazui Central Finance District to be developed so quickly. Correspondingly, a key rationale for inviting the GIC to be involved in the LICP was the perceived impact the 'famous' architects would have in improving the attractiveness of Pudong as a site for foreign investment.

[11] The statistics which are used to represent FDI flows should be used as indicators, rather than as precise figures, particularly in relation to property investment. There are three main problems with Chinese FDI statistics. First, the regional reliability of FDI statistics is variable (Leman, 1994a). Secondly, a considerable portion of FDI flows into China are 'roundtripped'—that is, Chinese investors (including various arms of the state) set up shell companies in Hong Kong, transfer capital to banks in Hong Kong, and then reinvest in China (Hornick, 1994, Li and Li, 1999). Thirdly, all FDI figures represent 'direct' foreign investment into a territory or sector: however, it is clear that many fund managers for financial institutions (including pension funds) prefer to invest in China's property markets in an indirect manner. Fund managers lessen risk by investing capital in listed firms which are active in China's property market.

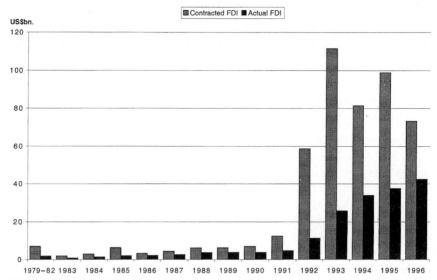

Fig. 5.1. FDI flows into China, 1979–1996

Source: Hang Seng Bank (1994); Lardy (1994); BIS (1995); Baring Securities (1995*a*); ING Barings (1997).

banking, real estate and retail trade, and 52 cities and areas became open to foreign investors;

- Low-cost production and rich natural resources, attracting a large number of TNCs;
- The restructuring of the economy towards market-based mechanisms and other economic reforms, significantly improving the overall enabling framework for foreign (and domestic) investors;
- High economic growth in neighbouring countries and the improvement of relations with the Republic of Korea and Taiwan Province of China. These economies used to have negligible investment outflows to China in the 1980s; they now have become major sources of investment in China, ranking third and sixth respectively. (UNCTAD, 1994: 68, 71)

Capital flows into China have been predominantly *sourced* from the Asia-Pacific region (see Table 5.1). There are two main reasons for this pattern. First, China's development is linked to the global shift of capital flows to the Asia-Pacific region since the early 1980s with the aim of taking advantage of skilled and unskilled low wage labour, natural resource supplies, and burgeoning domestic and regional markets. The restructuring of the Chinese economy both contributes to and is impacted by this broad structural shift. Secondly, China is explicitly capitalizing on the 'Greater China' factor (Jones *et al.*, 1993; Sung, 1993; *The China Quarterly*, Dec. 1993; Tsang, 1994; Hsing, 1998; Sun, 1998*a*). In keeping with the pragmatic nature of Dengism, links with the ethnic Chinese living in East and Southeast Asia have been encouraged, and many former

Table 5.1. Foreign direct investment into China by source country/region, 1983–1996

Country/region	No. of projects	Pledged FDI value (US$ bn.)	Share (%)	Actual FDI value	Share (%)
Hong Kong	156,818	237.75	60.86	101.31	57.84
Taiwan	31,473	29.98	7.67	14.92	8.50
USA	19,708	28.00	7.17	14.17	8.09
Japan	13,252	20.43	5.23	13.97	7.98
Singapore	5,888	17.27	4.42	6.17	3.52
S. Korea	6,222	6.78	1.74	3.76	2.15
Britain	1,469	9.08	2.32	2.66	1.52
Canada	2,738	3.93	1.01	1.08	0.62
Germany	1,243	4.25	1.08	1.78	1.02
Other	19,453	36.34	9.30	5.33	8.75
Total	258,264	390.66	100.00	175.15	100.00

Source: Derived from Sun (1998*b*: 692).

'enemies' of the state have received a warm welcome in Chinese cities, towns, and villages. Cultural, linguistic, and familial ties have been extremely facilitative in guiding capital flows to China from Hong Kong and Taiwan (the two largest 'foreign' investors) (Smart and Smart, 1991; Hsing, 1993, 1994, 1998). In contemporary China, flows of humans (especially emigrants) are tightly interwoven with the flows of capital that propel the restructuring of cities such as Shanghai.

The sourcing of FDI flows into China (and Shanghai) plays a key role in defining the sector that capital flows into given the tendency of Hong Kong and Taiwanese investors to focus on manufacturing and property (Hsing, 1993; Walker *et al.*, 1995). This pattern suggests that it is important for architects (who wish to design for property developers active in China) to embed themselves in the networks that guide property capital flows. However, the capital flows that connect China to other nations are relatively disengaged from the European bases of the GIC (witness the low levels of FDI from European countries in Table 5.1). This disjuncture, as we shall see, has implications for the subsequent development of Lujiazui, and the failure of the GIC to carry on working in Shanghai once the LICP was completed.

Sectorally, most foreign investment is in manufacturing, although other industrial sectors are increasingly capturing shares of the FDI pie (especially the automobile industry and metal processing sectors). The main aim of encouraging FDI in manufacturing sectors is to 'link the domestic economy to the world economy in order to foster industrialization' (Lardy, 1992: 5). In 1992, the State Council announced the formation of new policies to encourage the development of China's tertiary sector, and to link this process with the encouragement of FDI flows. The Communist Party Central and State Council stated 'areas allowed to make direct use of foreign capital will include finance, trade, commerce, transport, and tourism' (cited in Yabuki, 1995: 107).

Table 5.2. Contracted foreign direct investment flows into China by sector, 1987–1993 (per cent)

Sector	1987	1989	1991	1993
Agriculture	3.4	2.2	1.8	1.1
Industry	47.9	83.3	80.3	45.9
Building	1.5	1.2	1.1	3.6
Telecommunications	0.4	0.9	0.8	1.3
Commerce and catering	0.8	1.2	1.5	4.1
Real estate and public utilities and service	39.7	9.4	12.6	39.3
Others	6.3	1.8	1.9	4.7
Total	100.0	100.0	100.0	100.0
(US$ bn.)	(3.7)	(5.6)	(12.0)	(111.4)

Source: Hang Seng Bank (1994).

This policy is spatially related, and open coastal cities such as Shanghai have benefited most. With this announcement, and further reforms, FDI flows have shifted to the 'tertiary' (service) sector (UNCTAD, 1994; Yabuki, 1995; Zhang, n.d.; Sun, 1998a). The rationale for encouraging FDI into the tertiary sector includes diversification of the economy, skill transfer, the development of a 'business culture', enhanced access to international markets (including capital and commodity markets), the amelioration of inadequate housing conditions, and the facilitation of industrialization processes (UNCTAD, 1994: 107–9). Key tertiary sector industries include telecommunications, retailing, transportation, banking, insurance, business consulting, and real estate (see Table 5.2). Obviously, any reforms that encourage FDI in banking, insurance, property, and tourism will directly propel the development of the Lujiazui Central Finance District, and generate the rapid development context that makes it difficult for architects to operate within with foresight.

Regionally, FDI flows are primarily focused on the special economic zones (SEZs) (e.g. Shenzen), the Open Coastal Cities (e.g. Shanghai), and the Open Economic Zones (e.g. Pudong) (see Table 5.3). These 'preferential areas' for FDI are administered by relatively autonomous regional and local levels of government. A wide range of incentives are offered to 'foreign' investors to set up export-oriented projects (e.g. factories to manufacture commodities) or invest in infrastructure and property development projects. The inducements include a wide variety of tax incentives (holidays, reductions, exemptions), exemptions from the direct provision of subsidies to workers (e.g. housing), priority status to infrastructure provision, special land-use rights, reduced tariff rates). As Potter (1995: 173) notes, these inducements must be applied for, and this enhances the 'monitoring' and control capabilities of the state over foreign investment projects.

Table 5.3. Utilized foreign direct investment flows into China by region, 1987–1993 (per cent)

Region	1987	1989	1991	1993
Guangdong	27.8	35.1	41.6	27.2
Shanghai	8.1	11.2	3.1	11.4
Fujian	2.1	9.2	10.1	10.4
Jiangsu	3.3	3.4	4.7	10.2
Shangdong	2.5	4.3	4.6	6.7
Liaoning	3.4	3.3	7.8	4.6
Beijing	4.0	8.5	5.2	2.4
Others	48.8	25.0	22.9	27.1
Total	100.0	100.0	100.0	100.0
(US$ bn.)	(2.6)	(3.8)	(4.7)	(27.8)

Source: Hang Seng Bank (1994).

The 'differential incorporation of a large socialist state into the capitalist world economy' is possible through the application of territorially defined regulations that are unevenly applied (Chen, 1993: 112; Hayter and Sun, 1998; Sun, 1998*a*, 1998*b*). The rationale for treating specific regions as regulatory windows through which global flows of capital and technologies are accessed includes 'the advantages of surplus labour, raw material supplies, easy transport facilities', 'existing conglomerate economies', early successes in Southern China in attracting investment (Kueh, 1992: 642–3; also see Yeung and Hu, 1992*a*), and the historical role of the coastal cities as 'windows on the world' (Yeung and Hu, 1992*a*). By 1994, '80 percent of China's exports came from eleven coastal provinces that account for 40 percent of China's total population' (World Bank, 1994*a*: 22). In theory, regional inequalities will diminish over time as the 'fruits' of the economic development process spread inland and as coastal cities develop to a sufficient level so that they can act as efficient service centres for regional economies (Phillips and Yeh, 1990; Yeung and Hu, 1992*a*; Tang *et al.*, 1993; Goodman and Segal, 1994). A case in point is Shanghai and the Pudong project. This open coastal city is designated by the central government to act as the 'dragon head' for the Yangtze Delta Region (the dragon) (Hook, 1998; Marton, 2000). As President and General Secretary Jiang Zemin stated in 1992:

We must take the development and opening of Pudong in Shanghai as the dragon head, advance another step to open cities on the banks of the Yangzi River and establish Shanghai as an international economic, financial and trading centre as soon as possible, in order to induce a new economic leap in the Yangzi River Delta and the entire Yangzi River Valley. (cited in Jacobs and Hong, 1994: 239)

While Shanghai's population is in the range of 13 million, over 193 million people live and work in Zhejiang, Anhui, Jiangsu provinces (which together is deemed the Yangtze Delta Urban System (YDUS)) (Leman, 1995*a*, 1995*b*).

The scale of this economic region is huge in Asian terms: the YDER is '4% smaller than Indonesia in terms of GDP (at current market prices, US$), 11% larger than Thailand, and 132% larger than Malaysia' (Leman, 1995a: 22). The Pudong project (and Lujiazui) are explicitly designed to service the YDUS (Yang, 1993; EIU, 1994; Jacobs and Hong, 1994; Leman, 1995a, 1995b; Olds, 1997). However, preliminary analyses point out that the rhetoric of regional development is not being matched by the decline of regional inequities; a factor leading to regional conflict and rising migration to the coastal regions (Goodman and Segal, 1994; Cannon and Zhang, 1996; Hayter and Sun, 1998).

Accessing Global Capital Markets

The above reforms are associated with a series of 'strategic' initiatives to link China's economy to the international financial system. These reforms have been developed and implemented incrementally on an ad hoc and experimental basis. The lessons that these reforms generate are being used to guide the ongoing overhaul of China's complete financial system so that it can achieve the ambition 'to integrate itself with the international financial system' (Walker, 1994b; World Bank, 1997b).

Equity markets were formally established in Shanghai (Dec. 1990) and Shenzen (July 1991), and capitalization levels have fluctuated wildly since then. The markets consist of A shares (for Chinese nationals only),[12] B shares (for foreign investors only), and H shares (for foreigners only) that are listed on the Hong Kong, New York, and Sydney stock exchanges (Lindorff, 1993; Zhang and Yu, 1994). In China, both the central government and local government decide which enterprises will be allowed to issue A and B shares, while the central government alone chooses H share allocations. This practice ensures the gradual development of the exchanges. The exchanges can also be used as precise development tools through the strategic allocation of the right to issue. Furthermore, it is important to understand that the state is the majority owner of most of the 'limited stock companies' listed on the stock exchanges (Karmel, 1994: 1119). For example, most of the development zones in Pudong (including Lujiazui) have listed firms on the Shanghai Stock Exchange, and the Shanghai Municipal Government is the majority shareholder. This fact is important to keep in mind, for it helps explain why the property development process was not halted while the GIC architects were developing conceptual plans for the Lujiazui site.

The formation of stock markets is designed to enable Chinese firms to access international capital markets (partly to limit exposure to debt markets that are subject to interest rate changes), raise foreign exchange (B shares must

---

[12] The division between A and B is somewhat arbitrary in reality. Hong Kong and Taiwanese investors have been using their 'connections' to sink over US$1 billion in the A share market (*The Economist*, 22 Oct. 1994: 130).

be paid for in US dollars), further foreign investment flows into the Chinese economy, facilitate the 'revitalization' of Chinese enterprises, generate revenue for both local and central governments through direct and indirect taxes on turnover and operations, attract the savings of Chinese citizens to finance capital investment projects (rather than personal consumption), and generate private profits for key state officials (Hu, 1995; Sze, 1993, Glen and Pinto, 1994; Karmel, 1994). The stock markets are rapidly attracting European, American, Australasian and Asian financial houses (e.g. Barings, Credit Lyonnais, Salomon Brothers, Goldman Sachs & Co., Peregrine, Jardine Fleming, Sanwa, Nomura) who generate demand for Grade A office space in Shanghai's emerging business districts. The stock markets also reshape social dynamics in Chinese cities such as Shanghai, reinvigorating speculative impulses long repressed by the pre-reform era government (Hertz, 1998).

A variety of markets for futures, debt, bonds, swaps, and foreign exchange have also been set up in coastal cities such as Shanghai. Many of the markets have been strategically located in Luziazui Central Financial District to generate critical mass and agglomeration tendencies (Yusuf and Wu, 1997: 70–4).

Accessing Knowledge to Access the International Financial System

Another key trend underlying the drive to plan a new international financial centre in Lujiazui is the permission given to foreign-funded producer service firms to gradually expand services in China, particularly in designated coastal cities. These include brokers (see above), investment banks (e.g. Merrill Lynch), chartered accountancy firms (e.g. KPMG), engineering firms, and legal firms. Many serve the TNCs that are investing in China, and a growing number of Chinese enterprises.

The first foreign banks were permitted in the Chinese SEZs in 1982. The gradual reform of regulations is permitting foreign banks to move from representative office status to 'branch' status. At the end of 1993, there were 302 representative offices of foreign financial institutions from more than 30 countries and regions established in 18 cities. While Beijing has the largest number of representative office in China, Shanghai had the largest number of branches of foreign banks. By 1996, 123 branches were set up in 23 Chinese cities (Walker *et al.*, 1995). Foreign banks are currently allowed to engage in a range of activities such as: accepting foreign exchange/currency deposits; lending to foreign and Chinese enterprises in foreign exchange; providing financial advice (e.g. on major infrastructure projects); operating joint venture banks, WFOE and JV [JVE] finance companies; and making overseas acquisitions (particularly in Hong Kong) for Chinese financial institutions (Potter, 1995). Banks also offer international settlement services, and underwrite B share issues. However, all activities must be conducted in foreign exchange (in order to protect the national banking industry) although some minor 'experiments' with the handling of renminbi accounts are being sanctioned by the central government.

The main impact of this reform on urban structure is to encourage the agglomeration of producer service firms in 'open cities' such as Shanghai. Given the 'closed' nature of the pre-1978 Chinese economy, there were very few Class A office buildings to house firms. In the rush to China, there was a rapid explosion of demand for what little office space existed, and for four and five star hotels that could be converted into office space. This has encouraged the speculative development of office buildings in districts such as Lujiazui (Tan and Low, 1999). Moreover, the Chinese state feels the need to develop the symbolic space that they feel producer services firms should be housed in, thereby symbolizing China's modernity.

A Decentralized and Entrepreneurial State System

Reforms in administrative structure and responsibility have been wide-ranging. The main impact of the reforms 'has been to significantly decentralize economic power to lower-level governments' (Bowles and Dong, 1994: 68). Administrative and financial power has been decentralized from central planners to provincial authorities, cities under central government control (Shanghai, Beijing, and Tianjin), and county and municipal governments (*China News Analysis*, 15 Apr. 1994; Duckett, 1998; Yeh and Wu, 1999; Wu, 2000). These processes have led to the development of subsequent forces that continue the steady decline of central government control and the emergence of 'local autonomy' and bureaucratic entrepreneurialism (Hsing, 1993, 1994, 1998; Goodman and Segal, 1994; Potter, 1995; Smart, 1998).

Within cities such as Shanghai, power has been decentralized to individual districts, or special administrative zones such as Pudong New Area. The decentralization of power has enabled regional and local levels of government to generate funds through a wide variety of specified techniques (e.g. land leasing, business activities, the issuance of bonds, stock exchanges). Extra budgetary fund-raising by local governments is steadily increasing in an overall budgetary sense due to successes (in raising funds) and losses (of central government transfer payments) (Bowles and Dong, 1994: 55; Hsing, 1994; Yabuki, 1995; Smart, 1998; Leaf, 1998). In cities like Shanghai, which have long been forced to transfer funds to the central government, extra budgetary funds offer enhanced flexibility to achieve development plans. This factor helps explain why the development process in Lujiazui could not be halted while the LICP was under way (as we will see later in this chapter). The local state has also been permitted to encourage foreign direct investment flows and approve cooperation agreements and foreign investment projects up to a certain value (e.g. US$30 million in Shanghai).

Overall, the dominance of state-owned enterprises in the Chinese economy has significantly decreased since the 1978 reforms were initiated. The 1980 state share of gross industrial output value was 76 per cent with the remaining shares held by collectives (23.5 per cent), private firms (with less than eight employees) at 0.02 per cent and 'other' (private firms employing more than eight people, joint ventures and wholly owned foreign firms) at 0.48 per cent. By 1992 the respective figures were 48.1 per cent, 38 per cent, 6.76 per cent, and 7.11 per cent (Bowles and Dong, 1994: 55). These shifts are even more complex, however, as the division between 'state' and 'non-state' is 'misleading' as 'the local state often owns enterprises in the non-state sector' (ibid. 50).

In this context, the local state has increasingly become involved in business activities, including property development (Duckett, 1998). This trend is possible because state-owned enterprises have been delegated much more power to manage their own affairs. Managers are afforded greater flexibility in allocating resources and generating profits through investment practices such as forming joint ventures to develop commercial, residential, or retail property projects. Investment flows are not necessarily localized, and some Chinese enterprises have invested in non-Chinese stock and property markets. Other state funds have been used to form companies that are then listed on the Shanghai, Shenzen, or Hong Kong stock markets. A perfect example is the Shanghai Lujiazui Development Company that is listed on the Shanghai Stock Exchange through the B share scheme (for foreign investors). The Shanghai Municipal Government set up this firm in 1990 to develop the Lujiazui Finance and Trade Zone. Entrepreneurial enterprises have also been able to access capital to invest in speculative property ventures (including many projects in Lujiazui); a development that generates significant contradictions between the need to halt the property development process to plan effectively (the GIC's ideal), versus the need to maximize financial returns in both the short and long term (the enterprise ideal).

Expanding Money Supply in China

The combined impacts of all of the above reforms have contributed to a rapid increase in money supply, particularly since 1990 (see Fig. 5.2). The two major components of money supply growth in China are: (1) expansion of domestic credits; and (2) change in net foreign assets of the banking system (due to favourable balance of payments levels) (Jardine Fleming, May 1995: 2).

The surge of money supply in the early 1990s, in combination with a 'virtually non-existent regulatory and supervisory framework where banking and finance are concerned' (Shale, 1993: 32) fuelled the speculative activities of quasi-state enterprises who then played in both the Chinese and Hong Kong property markets (CY Leung, interview, May 1994; Walker *et al.*, 1995). While credit tightened up in 1994 (the continuation of an austerity programme initiated in 1993), money supply increases are relatively high by most national standards. This factor is a critical force in the development of office districts such as Lujiazui (and the associated inflation problems that are plaguing

Year on year percentage change

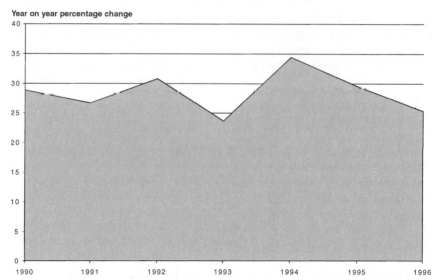

Fig. 5.2. Annual percentage increase in money supply (M2) in China, 1990–1996

Source: Baring Securities (1995*a*); ING Barings (1997).

China and compounding speculation in property markets). The instrumental management of money supply has explicitly been used by the state to guide the property development process, and ensure the continuation of what some have called a 'dangerously inflated bubble economy' (Hornik, 1994: 29; Lardy, 1998: 195–7).

Land Reform, the Restructuring of the Economy, and the Restructuring of the City

As with all of the above reforms, land reforms have encouraged the development of market relations, the influx of foreign capital, and the decentralization of power over land to lower levels of government. This process of reform is constant, incremental, and ad hoc in nature.

The collectivization movement in the 1950s abolished private land ownership in China and replaced it with two forms of 'socialist public ownership': 'ownership by the whole people' (state owned) and 'ownership by the working masses' (collective owned) (Jones Lang Wootton, 1993*a*). Under this Soviet-inspired land use system, land could not be sold, mortgaged, leased, or inherited (although many of these transactions informally took place). In short, land was not treated as a commodity.

In the early years of the Open Door Policy, governments in Guangzhou, Shenzen, and Fushan began collecting 'levies' for the use of land. It was not until April 1988 that China's constitution was amended to permit the transfer of land use rights from the state for a designated period of time. The primary rationale behind this and subsequent reforms in 1990, and more recent reforms, is to attract foreign investment into property and restructure the land supply and land allocation system to enhance 'economic' efficiency (Walker, 1991; Sun, 1994). From the perspective of the state, the specific occupiers of the land (e.g. residents, enterprises) in the pre-reform period benefitted to the detriment of the masses (Walker, 1991). Through the reform lens, flows of foreign investment generated through the land leasing system are used to finance large-scale urban restructuring initiatives such as the provision of infrastructure, and the development of new housing. Indirectly, capital raised through land leasing (and associated taxes) enables state enterprises to shed welfare responsibilities, and thereby become more competitive in an increasingly open economy.

While the Chinese state wishes to encourage elements of a marketized system, it does not mean to create a Western-style land market (with full ownership rights). Rather, land-*use* rights are simply being commercialized; state ownership of land remains a key priority; and, 'the market mechanism is not to be brought to fullest play, but is to be qualified' (Wang Xianjin, director of the PRC State Land Administration and chairman of the China Land Society, cited in Walker, 1991: 40). The key theme running though Wang's comments, and the ideological justification of the reforms, is the separation of 'use and management' from 'ownership'.

As with the reforms noted above, land leasing is only permitted in territories that the central government wishes to have directly connected to global flows of capital. Power over the legally sanctioned land leasing process has also been decentralized to lower levels of government. Land is leased in specified zones throughout Chinese cities for anywhere between forty and seventy years, primarily to companies set up to develop property projects. The companies are often joint ventures between various arms of the state, or between state enterprises and foreign investors. Foreign investors also set up WFOE to develop property projects. Land use rights may be acquired directly from the state, or from the holder of the transferred land use rights. Land is leased through direct negotiation, through bidding, and through auctions.

In general, the land in Chinese cities is changing in use from residential and industrial uses to commercial and retail uses in accordance with policies inscribed in masterplans. The majority of these zones are located along transport arterials, at transport nodes, and in government-designated development zones. The decision-making process behind the specification of these zones remains under technocratic state control (i.e. in the hands of planners and engineers subject to political approval), though the urban planning process is best characterized as 'grossly ineffective' (Leaf, 1998: 151). This is because the reform era has generated a multitude of institutional shifts, processes of change, and global scale linkages that have undermined the 'effectiveness of the state as an instigator of change' (ibid.; also see Yeh *et al.*, 1997). In other words, the capacity of the state to plan cities is weak; certainly weaker than the GIC ever expected it to be when they accepted the invitation to participate in the LICP.

In the context of land use reforms, and reshaped planning mechanisms, the scale of the land leasing process in China has expanded quickly in the 1990s. Various arms of the state (fuelled with credit from state banks) have speculated in property development projects throughout southern China, and in central cities such as Shanghai. As noted above, FDI flows have also flooded into property development projects throughout Chinese cities and towns. The combination of state credit with FDI flows has generated a frenzy of property development throughout China that began (for the most part) in 1991 and continued with vigour through the first half of 1993—the exact period in which the LICP was held. For example, in a 25 March 1995 *South China Morning Post International Weekly* article, the Ministry of Construction 'conceded it had more than four trillion yuan (about HK$3.64 trillion) of unsold property on its hands as a result of the speculative building boom over the last four years' ('China stuck with huge glut', p. 12). Such trends have also led to the mass displacement of residents in Chinese cities as the local state redefines land use patterns. However, the social impacts of displacement are mediated as property developers must contribute (financially and/or 'in kind') to replacement housing for the displaced residents (Dowall, 1993a, 1993b; World Bank, 1993b; Leaf, 1995).

To summarize, the LICP took place at the absolute height of the speculative frenzy associated with land use reforms (see the *China News Analysis*, 1 Feb. 1994, on property speculation in China in 1992). Consequently, all aspects of the LICP process must be viewed within the context of rapid land reform, the dependency of the state on revenue generated from FDI flows into property, and the dependency of the state on foreign investors to build the functional and symbolic spaces that will transform China into a 'modern' nation. From the perspective of all arms of the Chinese government, global flows of images exist for one main purpose—to enhance global flows of capital into designated Chinese territories and sectors.

The Development of Shanghai in the Context of National Reforms

> Shanghai used to be a financial centre where people exchanged currency freely, and it should continue to serve as the centre. To attain an international seat in banking, China has to rely on Shanghai first.
>
> (Deng Xiaoping in 1992, quoted in Kennedy, 1995)

> Between 2000 and 2010 we want to turn Shanghai into a financial and trading centre of the Asian and Pacific region. Our objective is to achieve complementarity with other regional financial centres.
>
> (Mayor Huang Ju in 1993, quoted in Walker and Cooke, 1993)

Shanghai's long-term objective in the year 2010, proposed by the last session of the People's Congress, is to make Shanghai one of the international centres of economy, finance and trade; and to make Pudong an international standard, export-oriented, multi-purpose, modern new area. On the basis of the objective, aiming at Shanghai's development in the 21st century, the overall planning of the city has to embody both 'international standard' and 'modernization'.

(Geng Yixiu, Chief Planner, Shanghai Urban Planning Administration Bureau, conference presentation, 11 Oct. 1993)

The Political Context

Urbanization processes in Shanghai since 1978 are directly linked to the implementation of the nationally sanctioned reforms outlined above.

In the early 1980s state and foreign investment was directed to the booming cities and towns in and near the SEZs of South China, and to other coastal port cities, as well as Hainan Island (Cannon and Jenkins, 1990; Kueh, 1992; Yeung and Hu, 1992*a*). Population and industry in Shanghai, China's largest city, continued to concentrate in the very dense inner city. Transport and communications facilities were severely lacking, housing shortages existed, and environmental pollution was at a near crisis state (Hyslop, 1990).

This situation continued until the early to mid-1980s when initiatives were developed and launched by a new group of 'developmentally oriented technocrats' in Shanghai's leadership (Arnold, 1992: 243; Jacobs and Hong, 1994) with increasing support from the national Chinese government. In 1983, the Shanghai Economic Region was established to facilitate economic integration between Shanghai and the broader region the city is situated in (Tang, 1989). From 1984 on, China's State Council approved of linking Shanghai's regeneration to the Open Door Policy by designating it as an open coastal city (see Fig. 5.3).

Under this nationally designated status the Shanghai Municipal Government was enabled to set up economic and technological development zones, and offer tax incentives, special land use rights, and attractive tariffs to foreign investors. In 1985, the central government began reducing Shanghai's very high (on a relative basis to other Chinese cities) revenue remittance rate (Fung *et al.*, 1992: 148), and the Shanghai Economic Development Strategy Report (that was initiated in 1983) was approved (ibid.; Tang, 1989). The SMG's General Development Plan—'the blueprint to develop the metropolis into a major multifunctional city and one of the largest economic and trading centres in the western Pacific Region'—was endorsed by State Council in 1986 (Fung *et al.*, 1992: 142). In the same year, the central government designated the Changjiang (Yangtze River) Delta as an open coastal region.

There are two main reasons why Shanghai only received gradually increased levels of support from the central government in the first half of the 1980s. First, when reforms were initiated in the late 1970s, the central government

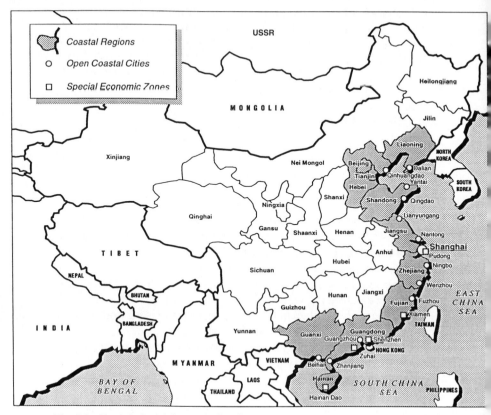

Fig. 5.3. Shanghai and the coastal regions

realized that it could not damage Shanghai's economic base with the types of experiments under way in southern China. Shanghai was the largest contributor of gross tax revenue to the central government (approximately 82 per cent in 1981 according to Jacobs and Hong, 1994: 229) while net figures were also high given the low levels of national expenditure on the city. Secondly, a variety of politicians with strong Shanghai links only began concentrating in the CCP hierarchy in the mid-1980s.

The level of central government support for Shanghai increased substantially in the late 1980s and early 1990s. Former mayor Jiang Zemin (1985–7) began amassing a variety of titles in Beijing in 1987, and he is now China's president and CCP general secretary. After shifting to Beijing, his support for Shanghai (and Pudong) has been consistent for he sees the city playing a vital role in contributing to national economic development processes. For example, in May 1995 Jiang made a trip to Shanghai pronouncing 'The central government places great hopes on Shanghai, that is the economic centre of the country and sees the largest concentration of the working class' (Zheng, 26 May

1995). During this visit he announced that '100 major Shanghai enterprises will receive central government aid to transform them into national MNCs'; a move that will certainly 'help bolster office space demand' in commercial districts such as Lujiazui (Daewoo Securities, 1995: 10).

Central government support for Shanghai was enhanced after the success of Mayor Zhu Rongji (1988–91) in handling the June 1989 pro-democracy demonstrations without any public bloodshed (Walker, 1994a). Some of my interviewees also suggested that the strength of the central government's support for Shanghai was magnified because of the Tiananmen Square massacre, and the pro-student rallies in Hong Kong. In the aftermath of Tiananmen, Beijing realized that they needed an international financial centre in firm Chinese territory. Hong Kong's role as an intermediary of trade and capital flows is critical to China's economic development: developing Shanghai into a complementary intermediary would enhance stability should problems arise with Hong Kong's population in the transition to Chinese control. The Tiananmen crackdown also resulted in the removal of 'disgraced former general secretary Zhao Ziyang', who had previously pushed for national support of the southern provinces versus the Shanghai region (Cheng, 1990: 57).

The 1991 promotion of Zhu Rongji to vice-premier in Beijing certainly helped gain important national support for the city. With a particular interest in economic affairs, Zhu has maintained a strong interest in Shanghai's urban development affairs since moving to Beijing. During the middle of the LICP (in 1992), Zhu consolidated his power by entering the Chinese Communist Party (CCP) Politburo. By 1997, the party congress designated Zhu the third-ranking figure in the CCP, behind president Jiang Zemin and Li Peng. Zhu eventually replaced Li as prime minister in March 1998, solidifying a political context favourable to Shanghai's long-term economic development.

Huang Ju replaced Zhu Rongji in 1991 as mayor of Shanghai. He was a strong supporter of the Pudong project, and also participated in some of the meetings where the GIC discussed their plans for Lujiazui Central Finance District. He was promoted to the CCP Politburo in September 1994. Similarly, Shanghai party leader Wu Bangguo was appointed to the CCP Secretariat of the Party Central Committee. Both have important contacts in both conservative and reformist factions of the communist élite. The current mayor is Xu Kuangdi.

Finally, Deng Xiaoping made regular personal and business trips to Shanghai for Chinese New Year, until his death in February 1997. After a famous February 1992 visit to the rapidly growing region of southern China (which he praised), he urged Shanghai to do more for the country. Deng suggested to government officials that it was important to bring about 'a change each year and great changes every three years' (Stine, 1993; Zheng, 17 Feb. 1995). Deng also stated:

Shanghai now entirely has the conditions [to develop] a bit more quickly. In areas of talented personnel, technology and administration, Shanghai has obvious superiority, which radiates over a wide area. Looking backwards, my one major mistake was not to include Shanghai when we set up the four special economic zones [in 1980]. Otherwise, the situation of reform and opening to the outside in the Yangzi River Delta, the entire Yangzi River Valley and even the entire nation would be different. (quoted in Jacobs and Hong, 1994: 224)

As the above discussion implies, the development of Lujiazui Central Finance District is critically dependent upon support from the central government.[13] Power has also been steadily decentralized from Beijing to the Shanghai Municipal Government, and from the SMG to district level governments throughout the city. Key officials in Beijing have structured a regulatory regime that enables local government to entice the controllers of global flows of capital, technology, and images to focus in on the city, all with the aim of turning Shanghai, once again, 'into a financial and trading centre of the Asian and Pacific region' (Walker and Cooke, 1993; Olds, 1997; Yusuf and Wu, 1997). The global flows of images and development expertise that the GIC were brought in to provide were sought within this multi-layered political context.

Reform-Related Change in Shanghai

The national reforms outlined above, and increasing levels of political support for Shanghai from Beijing, have led to a process of 'creative destruction' that may be unmatched for sheer scale in recent urban history. State officials have recognized that Shanghai must take on three principal economic roles by the turn of the century (Leman, 1994*b*):

- as China's major transactional city providing access to what is expected to become the tenth largest trading nation by the end of this decade;

- as the principal economic powerhouse, or 'dragon's head', of the country's largest integrated economic basin now emerging in the Yangtze River Basin (in which one-third of the national population produces more than 50% of the country's industrial and agricultural outputs);

- as the major economic anchor in the Yangtze Delta Region in which 160 million people (13% of the national population) account for more than 27% of China's industrial output.

---

[13] It is worth noting the staggering material implications of the thoughts and words of powerful elderly men in Beijing. The Three Gorges dam scheme, which is displacing 1.2 million people in Hubei and Sichuan provinces, has its origins in an eight line poem ('Swimming') that Mao Zedong wrote in 1956 after he swam the Yangzi for the first time (Gittings, 1993). The comments of Deng Xiaoping have had similar impacts throughout China since 1978. While mega-projects throughout the world are dependent upon the support of key politicians who are personally attached to the projects (witness Mahathir's KLCC in Malaysia), the scale of the mega-project tends to be much larger in authoritarian countries.

A wide variety of initiatives have been launched in this city in the attempt to achieve these goals (see summary below). These initiatives were developed by various arms of the SMG, and the myriad of state-supported institutes (some of which are based at universities) that assist the relevant bureaux and commissions of the SMG. The primary policy vehicles for these initiatives is a twenty year programme in three phases (1991–5; 1996–2000; 2000–10), a host of specific plans that are produced more regularly (e.g. the SMG is required (by statute) to produce an urban masterplan every five years), and the annual Government Work Report which is submitted and approved at the Shanghai Municipal People's Congress.

A variety of 'foreign' institutions and firms are also assisting the SMG in its efforts to plan strategically the city's restructuring. The World Bank[14] and the Asian Development Bank (ADB) have funded both tangible projects (e.g. bridges, road systems) and strategic planning initiatives to guide Shanghai's territorial and sectoral restructuring. For example, in 1991–2, the ADB hired Chreod Ltd., of Ottawa Canada (in association with PPK Consultants and Kinhill Engineers of Australia) to complete a strategic plan for Pudong (see McLemore, 1995), and the ADB recently completed another study on the development of Shanghai's tertiary sector. The SMG also hires consultants itself (such as the Paris-based Institut d'Aménagement et d'Urbanisme de la Région Ile de France (IAURIF)) to assist in the development of metropolitan planning strategy.

Restructuring the City into the Space of Flows

The development of Lujiazui is a key component of the central and local government's strategy to develop Shanghai's tertiary sector (that includes both financial services, retail services, education, and high-technology industries), and turn the city into what vice-mayor Xu Kuangdi terms a 'golden highway' between 'China and the rest of the world' (quoted in Walker, 1994a).[15] According to the SMG's 'General Concept for the Stepping Up of Development of the Tertiary Industry' (the overall blueprint to 'guide the development of the city into an international economic, financial and trade centre in the early years of next century'), all arms of the government need to enhance the GDP proportion of tertiary trade from '30.8% in 1990 to 45% in 2000' (*China Economic News*, 1993). When reforms were initiated in China in 1978 the city's GDP

---

[14] The World Bank has lent US$1.37 billion to Shanghai in the past fifteen years (out of a total of $20.4 billion which has been lent to China) (Zheng, 21 Feb. 1995). The money has been primarily directed to infrastructure projects and the agricultural sector. These projects fit within the Bank's overall policy on urban development and economic development which is outlined in World Bank (1991). Bank officials are very keen to stop Shanghai from turning into a Chinese version of the congested city of Bangkok.

[15] SMG officials and advisers are all aware of the strong contribution of the tertiary sector to the economies of Hong Kong, Singapore, and Tokyo, and they use these cities as development models to emulate.

Table 5.4. Changes in the structure of employment in Shanghai versus China, 1978–1995

Year	Share of each sector of total employment (per cent)					
	Primary		Secondary		Tertiary	
	China	Shanghai	China	Shanghai	China	Shanghai
1978	70.5	34.5	17.4	44.1	12.1	21.4
1980	68.7	29.2	18.3	48.7	13.0	22.1
1985	62.4	16.6	20.9	57.9	16.7	25.5
1990	60.0	11.4	21.4	60.2	18.6	28.4
1995	52.9	9.8	23.0	54.5	24.1	25.7

Source: Derived from Ash and Qi (1998: 156).

proportion of tertiary trade was only 18 per cent. By the end of 1990 it had jumped to 30.8 per cent, 31.8 per cent in 1991, 33.2 per cent in 1992, 37.8 per cent in 1993, and 39.6 per cent in 1994 (Farouk, 1995; Shanghai Municipal Government, 1993; Walker, 1994*a*). In a comparative sense, there are signs that the government is making some progress in achieving this goal, as highlighted in Table 5.4.

The financial services sector itself contributed nearly 24 per cent of total GDP in 1993 (Xiao, 1994). Clearly, all vestiges of the Maoist anti-service sector ideology have disappeared.

The government is attempting to achieve this goal through a mix of policies to relocate industrial development out of the central city, reduce population density in the central city, attract FDI and other forms of overseas capital (e.g. debt), attract foreign technology, and attract management skills and knowledge about development strategies. The implementation of all of these policies, in association with central government reform initiatives, will theoretically enable Shanghai's economy to be restructured.

The physical base of this plan is the implementation of a major infrastructure scheme that is funded, to a large degree, by foreign capital flows (direct and indirect). Between 1991 and 1996, US$ 10 billion was invested in infrastructure (Wu, 1999: 209; also see Walker and Cooke, 1993), gradually increasing in the mid-1990s (post-LICP) to US$22.1 billion between 1994 and 2000 (FPD Savills Research, 1999: 2). The projects include: the construction of the Nanpu and Yangpu bridges over the Huangpu River; the construction of inner and outer ring roads (with some lengthy elevated stretches); the construction of two subway lines (one was completed in April 1995); the construction of tunnels under the Huangpu River; a major upgrading of Shanghai's port at Waigaoqiao,[16] and preparation work for a new airport in Pudong (see Fig. 5.4).

---

[16] The Waigaoqiao Port is being redeveloped by Li Ka-shing's Hutchison International Terminals (HIT), an arm of Hutchison Whampoa. HIT formed a fifty-fifty joint venture with the Shanghai Port Authority to upgrade existing terminals (where only 28 per cent of traffic was

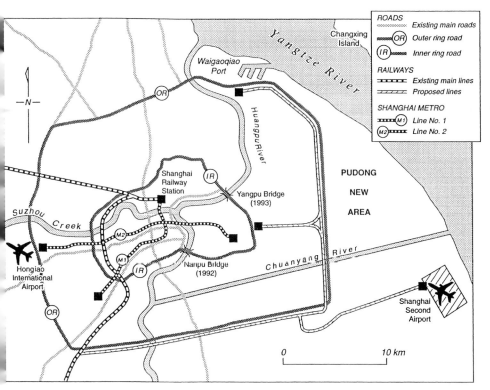

Fig. 5.4. Infrastructure plan of Shanghai

Source: Adapted from material supplied by JLW Research and Consultancy.

Infrastructure improvements are certainly not limited to these schemes. The city's telecommunications infrastructure is being improved and connected to a new national fibre-optic cable network while China's first city-scale digital cellular network is now operating in Shanghai. Approximately 750 roads were being worked on when I was in Shanghai, and the whole city seemed like one large construction site (perhaps a bombed out city would be a better analogy). Walker (1993), for example, notes that approximately 5,000 construction projects were undertaken in Shanghai in 1992, and by the late 1990s this number had increased to 22,000 (FPD Savills Research, 1999: 5). Massive urban renewal schemes are under way, and approximately 6 million sq. m. of new

containerized in 1992) and they have options on all future terminals (Marriage and Militante, 1992). The World Bank is also loaning capital to restructure Shanghai's port facilities. Shanghai's port is China's largest port, and the fourth largest in the world (Timewell, 1994). The Shanghai port had a throughput of 163 million tons in 1992 (Economist Intelligence Unit, 1994). Again, here we see Li Ka-shing strategically positioning one of his firms at a node of movement and flow, in a city where he has excellent *guanxi*.

housing is being built per year (primarily in the suburbs and in Pudong) (Walker, 1993).

The development of Shanghai's infrastructure, in association with other initiatives (see below), is focused on strengthening the city's tertiary sector. This strategy leads directly into municipal government expenditure where the SMG targets a large proportion (55 per cent in 1992 and 1993) of its annual 'fixed investment' into the development of the services sector (Leman, 1994*b*: 23).

The infrastructural base outlined above is interrelated with three other reform-oriented initiatives that are also designed to support the growth of the tertiary sector:

(1) the opening up of Shanghai's financial markets;

(2) land reform; and

(3) the formation of development zones.

Lujiazui Central Finance District is a creature of the intersection of these initiatives.

Opening Shanghai's Financial Markets to Hook into Global Flows of Capital

The main method of developing Shanghai's tertiary sector is through the opening up of Shanghai's financial markets, and the development of the financial services sector. Numerous Chinese financial institutions have set up or expanded their Shanghai offices, in part following political direction to contribute to Shanghai's development. For example, in 1992, over 300 Chinese financial institutions set up offices in Shanghai, bringing the 1992 total to 1,762 (*China Economic News*, 22 Feb. 1993). By February 1995, there were '2,510 licensed financial institutions and outlets in the city' (*Shanghai Star*, 14 Feb. 1995: 6). The People's Bank of China was ordered by Beijing to shift its headquarters to Lujiazui Central Finance District from Beijing, as were many other of China's largest banks. The growth of domestic enterprises is related to the strategy of developing a number of national markets in the city. As noted above, China's largest markets in securities, bonds, commodities' futures, and China's first interbank currency market all began operating in Shanghai within the last three years (though the markets are expanding in a highly uneven manner). Insurance services are also increasingly available. The continued growth of the securities market is particularly important to the Shanghai Municipal Government. While the stock exchange has suffered from a variety of problems, primarily related to an ineffective and opaque regulatory framework (Montagnon and Walker, 1995; Walker, 1994*a*), volatile growth patterns are expected to continue over the next decade (Baring Securities, 1995*b*). The SSE (Shanghai Stock Exchange), which up to a million Shanghainese trade in, was relocated into a purpose-built building in Lujiazui Central Finance District in 1996. This twenty-seven storey structure is fitted out with the most advanced telecommunications infrastructure, 10,000 IDD lines, an uninterrupted power supply, and club house (with pool and workout facilities). The design of the structure is virtually identical to the Tokyo Teleport Telecom Centre Building, or the Communications Centre of the Yokohama MM21 Teleport.

As noted above, China has gradually allowed foreign banks and brokerages to set up in key coastal cities, SEZs, and the interior of the country. In 1991, seven foreign banks opened branches in Shanghai. This was the first time since 1949 that foreign funded banks could operate without limits on their territorial activities (*China Trade Report*, Mar. 1992: 5). By late 1992, there were '13 foreign bank branches, two joint Chinese foreign finance companies, one wholly foreign owned finance company, and one joint venture merchant bank' (Boreham, 1993). In April 1993, there were '20 branches and 35 agencies' (representative offices) set up in Shanghai (Wu and Xu, 1993: 14). Two months later in June 1993 Sender (1994: 56) notes that there are 'at least two dozen foreign brokerages in the city'. In February 1994, Crothall (1994) counts 21 foreign bank branches with another 20 applications in review. One month later (Mar. 1994) there were 26 foreign brokerages in Shanghai (Walker, 1994*a*), and by November 1994, there were 31 foreign-funded branch offices and 86 representative offices set up, along with '30 foreign brokerages' (*The Economist*, 24 Dec. 1994–6 Jan. 1995: 83). And by May 1995, 35 foreign funded bank branches and 95 representative offices were licensed in Shanghai (Xiao, 1995; also see Yusuf and Wu, 1997: 72). Japanese institutions have the largest presence in Shanghai (nine out of 31 branch offices and 24 out of 86 representative offices) (Kennedy, 1995: 49). Some foreign banks have also started to shift their 'China headquarters' to Shanghai from Hong Kong (e.g. Citibank in 1994). If Shanghai's financial markets continue to open up to foreign involvement (there are a wide variety of restrictions on access to futures, currency, and equity markets, as well as banking services) the growth of international financial institutions will occur, many located within the confines of Lujiazui Central Finance District. Shanghai officials are cognizant of the number and proportion of foreign banks in Hong Kong; a situation they are seeking to emulate. Moreover, given that China is desperately trying to join the WTO, and FDI flows into the service sector of 'developing' countries are steadily increasing (UNCTAD, 1994), liberalization trends will likely continue.

Opening Shanghai's Property Markets to Hook into Global Flows of Capital

As with the south of China, Shanghai experimented with land reform in the mid to late 1980s. At that time, foreign investors had to pay a land use fee, and there was no secondary land market. A result of this type of early land use experiment is the US$200 million Shanghai Centre which was financed by The Portman Companies, American International Group (AIG), Kajima Corporation, and Shangri-la Asia Limited.[17]

---

[17] The Shanghai Centre project is a classic 'city within a city' project. The designer (and co-developer) is John Portman from Atlanta. The complex includes 25,000 sq. m. of Class A office space, an advanced telecommunications system which is operated by BellSouth of the USA, three

Table 5.5. Land use rights granted in Shanghai, 1988–1995

Year	Number of leases	Total site area (million sq.m.)*
1988–91	12	9.803
1992	192	19.788
1993	244	49.326
1994	452	15.942
1995	258	6.403

Note: * Figure refers to land area leased.
Source: Unpublished data provided by CY Leung & Company Ltd.

The first formal shift towards city-wide land reform took place on 29 November 1987 when the SMG drafted 'Regulations For The Transfer of Land Use Rights For Valuable Consideration in Shanghai City'. These regulations came into effect on 1 January 1988. Two years later, in the context of national land reform initiatives, Shanghai further reformed its land lease regulations. Since then, Shanghai has made heavy use of land leasing (see Table 5.5) to attract FDI flows, restructure the city, generate capital for infrastructure projects, and fund new housing for residents (primarily in suburban locations).

In accordance with government regulations, land is leased for a period of forty to seventy years through direct negotiation, the tendering process, or via auction. The vast majority of leases (approximately 90 per cent according to my contacts) are conducted through the negotiation method. Power has been decentralized to such a level that all projects valued under US$10 million do not require municipal (SMG) level approval. This regulation permits local districts in Shanghai to exercise considerable discretion, and it also encourages competition between districts—a feature common in 'open' Chinese cities (Hsing, 1993, 1994; Leaf, 1994, 1998).

The emergence of marketized property relations in which land can be leased by the state through district-level government offices (theoretically following a strategic plan set by the SMG) has led to the transformation of land uses, particularly along transportation corridors, and throughout the centre of the city.

levels of retail and personal service outlets, a 700 room five star hotel (with associated 24 hour business centre), a 1,000 seat theatre, 472 fully furnished apartments, a 4,000 sq. m. exhibition hall (in association with 24 separate function rooms), several bars, restaurants and nightclubs, a healthclub, and a preschool and playgroup. Several of my interviews took place in the Shanghai Centre. While the critique levelled against such fortress developments (e.g. Jameson, 1984; Davis, 1992; Sorkin, 1992) has many relevant points, this form of development is inevitable in a city like Shanghai where there is little office space, hotel space, or available housing for 'foreigners' who the Chinese government are inviting in as quickly as possible.

Again, specific zones for land leasing activities are designated by the SMG in accordance with a city-wide master plan.

There are virtually no attempts made to preserve historical structures in the city unless money can be made from them. Even *The Economist* (24 Dec. 1994–6 Jan. 1995), hardly an anti-development magazine, notes with awe the lack of concern for 'history', as the 'wrecking balls' come in to wage 'wide-scale destruction' throughout Shanghai.

The leasing of land and the encouragement of foreign investment into property is one of the main sources of local government revenue, and this has spurred on the land leasing process. Sender (1993: 73), for example, notes that US\$2 billion was raised by the SMG in 1992 (the year the LICP was held) through land leasing. Wu and Xu (1993: 17) note that \$2.65 billion and Rmb 1.53 billion was raised from land leasing in 1992. The 1993 figures were approximately the same according to my contact in the Shanghai Foreign Investment Commission (Xia Zhongguang, interview, Nov. 1993). Land leasing has been estimated to provide 25 to 50 per cent of all local government revenue; a potential source of revenue unlikely to be shut off to facilitate an 'ideal' planning context for the European-based GIC.

With economic reforms and increasing linkages with the rest of the world, foreign businesses and banks have moved to Shanghai in search of office space. However, there was very little suitable office space in the city when foreign and domestic service firms began this geographic shift. One Jones Lang Wootton (1994) publication noted that by November 1994 Shanghai had only 194,000 sq. m. of Grade A office space. In comparison, Bangkok's stock was 1,100,000 sq. m. (five times as much), Jakarta's was 1,800,000 sq. m. (eight times), Kuala Lumpur's was 2,400,000 sq. m. (11 times), Singapore's was 3,200,000 sq. m. (15 times), and Hong Kong's was 5,000,000 sq. m. (23 times). Given this state of affairs, many firms were operating out of four and five star hotels while they awaited the construction of new office space. Strong demand for commercial space, in combination with FDI flows, bureaucratic entrepreneurial behaviour, increased money supply (that fuels the quasi-state partners in joint ventures), the power to forcibly relocate *hundreds of thousands* of residents living on desired property,[18] and a huge cheap labour force of formal and

---

[18] In Chinese cities, the local state has the power to forcibly relocate residents from their housing and community. While the vast majority of residents are provided with replacement housing, they have no formal power in defining when the relocation process will take place, how much information is available about the process, what type of housing they will receive (size, services available, and so on), and where the housing is located. They are also not necessarily relocated along with their neighbours to ensure the continuity of local community. In Shanghai, hundreds of thousands of residents have been relocated. During my field work phase I heard a wide variety of estimates on total numbers (from 200,000 to 2 million people). Two 1995 newspaper articles (based on SMG statistics) suggest that '200,000 households' (approximately 620,000 people) have been relocated in the 'past three years' while an additional 620,000 people will be moved in the near future ('Fire hits controversial Shanghai area', 1995; Chan, 1995; also see Kahn, 1993, 1994b, 1997). In such a

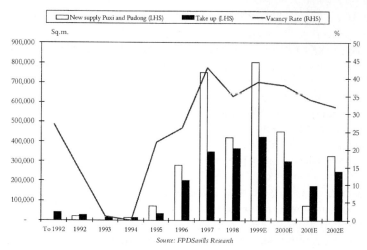

Fig. 5.5. Shanghai Grade 'A' office supply, take up, and vacancy rate

Source: FPD Savills Research.

informal construction workers (Wu, 1994; Rush, 1995; Leaf, 1998), has led to the initiation of a large number of office construction projects in Shanghai, propelling office supply levels up at a staggering rate (see Fig. 5.5).

Severe competition for the existing office space in the early 1990s drove rent levels up quickly. Demand for leased commercial space is also accentuated by the very short-term speculative nature of the development process (Hillier Parker, 1995). Many developers only wanted to sell whole buildings, or sell individual floors, and this effectively held space out of the leasing market. By the mid-1990s though, the Shanghai property market bubble burst, highlighting the speculative nature of property market relations in reform era China (Lardy, 1998: 195–7; Ramo, 1998).

In summary, some 'market' principles have been applied to land reform practices in Chinese cities such as Shanghai. They are being used to guide the reform of urban land markets and the introduction of market mechanisms that theoretically 'improve' the 'allocative efficiency' of Chinese institutions

developmental context, the SMG will not tolerate any serious delays in the relocation of residents, in part because 'time is money', and in part because 'Shanghai wants to be Deng Xiaoping's model city . . . There can't be much dissent here. That would mean the officials didn't do their work well' (a former SMG official quoted in Kahn, 1994*b*). In some ways, the process of displacement should be expected, for, as Deutsche (1996) and Leckie (1995) note, large-scale urban growth *requires* the deterritorialization of entire groups of residents. At a global scale, over 10 million people are being displaced annually in the developing world, while the 'vast majority'—82 per cent of all displaced people—are concentrated in South and East Asia, according to the World Bank (which are undoubtedly conservative figures) (Cernea, 1994: 47). Readers interested in displacement issues in China and Asia are directed to Cernea (1993, 1994), the *Ecologist* (1994), Huus (1994), Leckie (1994*a*, 1994*b*, 1995), World Bank (1994*b*), and Cernea and McDowell (2000).

(Dowall, 1993*a*, 1993*b*, 1994). However, the complex reforms urged by multi-lateral institutions such as the World Bank (1993*b*) and consultants (such as Dowall) advising the SMG in the early 1990s are being implemented slowly, in an ad hoc fashion, and meshed with the rise of bureaucratic entrepreneurial-ism. Shanghai's property markets will likely continue to exhibit a risky mixture of *capitalisme sauvage* and decentralized and proactive (as opposed to a more benign regulatory role) state involvement for some time (see Smart, 1998, on this point more generally).

Development Zones: Territorial Windows into Global Flows of Capital and Technology

The third (related) method of hooking Shanghai into the shifting structure of global capital and technology flows is the creation of regulatory windows that focus investment into specific spaces throughout the city. As noted above, development zones have been set up to attract FDI, and encourage the development of Shanghai's tertiary sector. The main zones in Shanghai include (also see Fig. 5.6):

- *The Minhang Economic and Technological Development Zone* which is 3.5 sq. km. in size. Minhang is focused on technologically advanced export-oriented light industry (EIU, 1994). Minhang is located in a satellite town 30 km. south south-west of the central city that was founded in 1957 (though the zone was only created in 1986).

- *The Hongqiao Economic and Technological Development Zone* which is 65 hectares in size. Hongqiao is focused on financial services firms, hotels, for-eign residences, and retail services.[19] This was one of the first districts in China to develop design guidelines that encouraged 'Western-style high rise buildings' (Wu, 1993). Hongqiao is located near the airport on the western side of Shanghai, and was initiated in 1982.

- *The Caohejing New Technology Zone* which is 5 sq. km. in size. Caohejing is aimed at 'high-tech and newly emerging technology (e.g. electronics, optical fibre communication, bio-chemicals and computer software)' (Jones Lang Wootton, 1993*c*: 7). It is located about 11 km. to the south-west of the city centre (7 km. from the airport). Caohejing was created in 1988.

- *Pudong New Area* was originally 350 sq. km. in size, though its boundary has expanded to incorporate 522 sq. km. Pudong is composed of a number of sub-zones, that are aimed at services, high-tech industry, port facilities, and free trade. The Lujiazui Finance and Trade Zone is located in Pudong, across

---

[19] The chief Shanghainese organizer of the LICP was the original chief planner for the Hongqiao Economic and Technological Development Zone. His experience in this zone was instrumental in helping him guide the development of the LICP, and form the final master plan for Lujiazui Central Finance District.

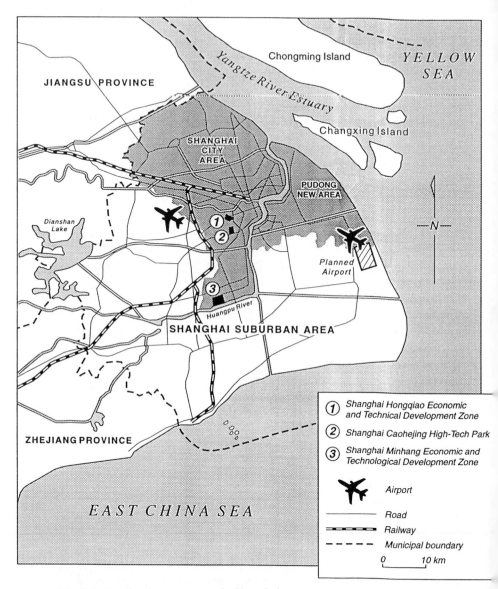

Fig. 5.6. Key development zones in Shanghai

the Huangpu River to the east of the central part of Shanghai. Pudong was formed in 1990. Further details are available below.

The Initial Impacts of these Initiatives

The impacts of the reforms in Shanghai are substantial. Once Shanghai was designated as an Open Coastal City in 1984, FDI began flowing into the city.

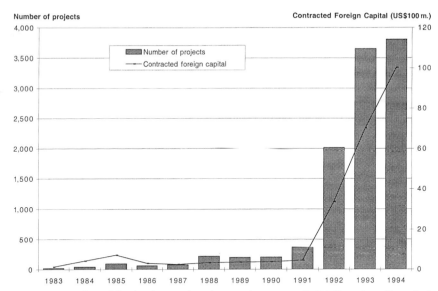

Fig. 5.7. Number of foreign invested projects and contracted FDI flows into Shanghai, 1983–1994

Source: Shanghai Foreign Investment Commission (1995).

However, it was not until the announcement of key preferential policies in 1990 and 1992 that these flows began to match those of southern China (see Fig. 5.7).

Between 1983 and 1994 $23.7 billion of FDI was contracted in Shanghai (Shanghai Foreign Investment Commission, Mar. 1995), and the total number of foreign invested projects rapidly increased. A large proportion of this total FDI was directed into real estate (for specific details see below). Needless to say, these FDI flows, in conjunction with state initiatives, are creating a myriad of impacts throughout the city.

As is the case in all of China, most FDI flows tangibly into Shanghai through the legal entities of the EJV, the CJV, or WFOE. The vast majority of foreign investors form relationships with various arms of national, provincial, or municipal government to minimize delays in the approval of project applications, and ease the implementation of the project development phase (Shanghai Foreign Investment Commission, 1995; Walker, 1994*a*).

While the total number of projects has rapidly increased since 1992, the number of foreign invested enterprises with a total investment of $US10 million or more has increased at an even steeper level (Shanghai Foreign Investment Commission, 1995). This steeper growth rate is a sign that recent investors have begun sinking higher volumes of capital into Shanghai per project (as the investors become more confident of Shanghai's future development path, and expected return rates are realized).

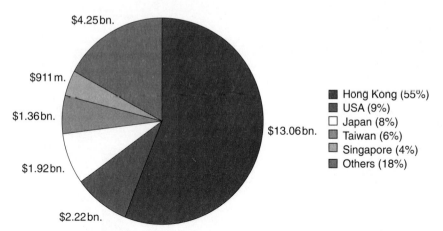

Fig. 5.8. Cumulative contracted FDI flows into Shanghai by source, 1983–1994 (US$)

Source: Shanghai Foreign Investment Commission (1995).

As Chen (1993: 109) notes, the capitalization levels of FDI ventures are relatively high in Shanghai, in comparison to the rest of China. The city's prominence on a global scale has enabled it to access the 'third wave' of foreign investors (large TNCs) into China (UNCTAD, 1994: 68). Shanghai has attracted approximately 120 of the world's 500 largest TNCs (ibid. 70). Large investors include 3M, AT&T, BASF, Cheung Kong, Coca Cola, Du Pont, Henderson Land, Hutchison Whampoa, ICI, Johnson & Johnson, Mitsubishi, New World Development, Philips, Pilkington, Unilever, Volkswagen, Xerox, and Yaohan.

The flow of foreign capital into Shanghai is primarily embedded in extended social relations that connect ethnic Chinese people throughout the Asia-Pacific region (Fig. 5.8). Hong Kong investors were the quickest to focus on Shanghai once the government began offering incentives to attract 'foreign' capital, and their interest in the city has been maintained throughout the first half of the 1990s.

Given that Shanghai developed preferential policies that favour the tertiary sector, it is not surprising that FDI flows reflect this bias (see Table 5.6). This table also highlights the massive flow of foreign capital into property. $10.7 billion of FDI was pledged into Shanghai's real estate sector between 1983 and 1994 (54 per cent of total contracted FDI into Shanghai; 9 per cent of total foreign invested projects). In terms of average real estate value, there were 981 projects out of a total of 10,741 projects in this time period (which averages out to $109 million per project). While this figure is 'contracted' FDI versus 'actual', it does highlight the relative importance of land leasing and property development to Shanghai's overall economy, especially during the early 1990s when the LICP was under way (Yusuf and Wu, 1997: 79–80; Wu, 2000). In such a context, the importance of attracting FDI flows into Pudong, and the Lujiazui Central Finance District, cannot be understated.

Table 5.6. Cumulative pledged FDI flows into Shanghai by sector, 1983–1994

Sector	Pledged FDI ($100 m; %)	Number of Projects
Primary industry	0.32 (0.13%)	58 (0.55%)
Secondary industry		
Manufacturing component	93.20	7,584
Total	106.8 (45%)	8,109 (75.5%)
Tertiary industry		
Real estate	107.24	981
Catering*	11.79	512
Total	130 (54.9%)	2,574 (23.9%)

Note: * Catering is primarily composed of the tourism sector including hotels.
Source: Shanghai Foreign Investment Commission, 1995.

Marching to the World: The Pudong New Area Project

'Revitalizing Shanghai, Developing Pudong, Serving the Country, and Marching to the World' (Shanghai government slogan)

This final stage of 'scaling down' before I focus on the specifics of the GIC and the LICP recognizes the position of Lujiazui Central Finance District as the *key* component of a much larger project—Pudong New Area (see Fig. 5.9).

Pudong New Area is a 522 sq. km. area (1.5 times the size of urban Shanghai) to the east of the Huangpu River composed of farm land, low density industry, and associated residential districts. Pudong is China's largest development project to date, 'amidst a plethora of Special Economic Zones, districts and regions that have characterized China's search for an "outward-oriented" economic viability' (MacPherson, 1994: 62). While many people think of Pudong purely as a modern creation, MacPherson's article outlines Pudong's long history (that includes a 1921 scheme of Dr Sun Yatsen's to use the 'Great Port of Pudong' as a tool in the 'national reconstruction' of China).

The development of Pudong in reform-era Shanghai was first incorporated in Shanghai's 1984 'Outline of Report on Shanghai's Economic Development Strategy'. Two years later Pudong (as a development concept) was noted in the 1986 Shanghai master plan (Tang, 1989). However, it was not until May 1988 that the Pudong New Area (*Pudong Xinchu*) was 'launched' at an international conference, and a specific division within the SMG began consistently working on the area's development strategy. In October of 1989, the Shanghai Pudong New Area Development Office released a draft plan entitled 'The Projects of Shanghai Pu-Dong New Area' with an English-language version. In April 1990, the CCP Central Committee and the State Council officially designated Pudong as a national development project. As Premier Li Peng stated 'The development of Pudong and the opening of Pudong to the outside is a matter having important strategic significance for Shanghai and the entire nation' (quoted in Jacobs and Hong, 1994: 233). This new status enabled the Shanghai

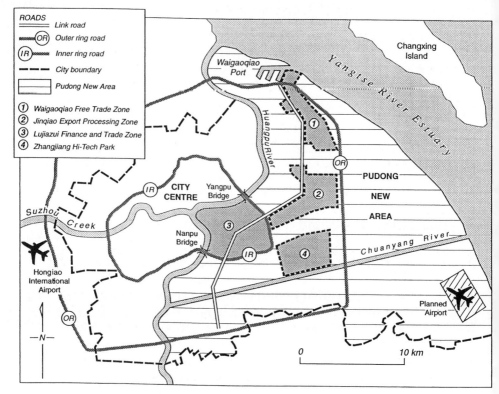

Fig. 5.9. The Pudong New Area project

government to offer a comprehensive range of ten preferential policies (incentives) to attract domestic and foreign capital sources, and to draw upon central government resources. Two years later, in March 1992, as part of Beijing's enhanced support for Shanghai, the State Council reinforced its wishes to see the Pudong project play an important role in facilitating the development of the Yangtze River Delta, and the entire Yangtze River Region. Five additional 'preferential policies' were obtained from Beijing (Jacobs and Hong, 1994: 234). One month later, in April 1992, the Three Gorges Dam project was approved. Later that same month, SMG's advisers recognized that this was their 'last chance' to 'create a modernized Shanghai'—the opening up of Pudong had to be quickened (MacPherson, 1994: 80; also see V. Wu, 1998).

By 1 January 1993, the Pudong New Area Administration was set up to administer and implement the development of the project. This organization has greater power than any district-level government in Shanghai, though it is subordinate to the SMG.

The Rationale for Pudong

While other development zones around China have received central government support, these zones are components of what are primarily *regional* development strategies. Pudong, in contrast, is both a regional *and* a national development zone; a status that is constantly reaffirmed when Beijing politicians visit Shanghai (and vice versa). Pudong is designed to 'promote the regeneration and development of west Shanghai, restore Shanghai's function as a national economic centre, and lay the foundation for Shanghai to become one of the economic, financial and trade centres in the Far East' (Shanghai Pudong New Area Administration, 1993: 5). The project also plays a number of complementary roles. First, at a national level, it is designed to shift the central government policy focus away from the 'favoured south to the central and northern parts of China' (Chen, 1993: 112). Secondly, Pudong is designed to act as a 'laboratory',—a

testing ground for a host of new government policies for the 1990s, aimed at the reform of systems of business ownership, enterprise management, investment, employment, housing, social security, land tenure, taxation, accounting, business and market-place law, and of the government's role in market intervention. Successful government policies, designed to help the country [move] towards a market-led economy with certain planning controls, will then be applied to other parts of the Shanghai region or elsewhere in China. (Zhao, 1993: 234)

Pudong's development on newly accessible land (due to infrastructure improvements) enables it to be used in this experimental sense. As Zhao also notes, it was a 'precondition' that revenue flows from 'old' Shanghai to Beijing be maintained while the SMG attempts innovations on what is effectively conceived to be empty space.

The Plan

The SMG has developed a vague three stage plan for Pudong that they are attempting to follow:

The first stage is the starting stage (1991–1995). The focus is on planning, improving environment and completing river-crossing and avenue building projects to pave the way for foreign investors while starting the initial construction of the Waigaoqiao, Jinqiao, Lujiazui and Zhangjiang zones so as to attract both domestic and foreign investment and to exploit the functions and the advantage of the policies as much and as early as possible.

The second step is the development stage (1996–2000) with a focus on urban infrastructure projects concerning avenues and public utilities to form a fundamentally complete structure in Pudong New Area. And the initial construction of the zones is expected to lead to a healthy circle. Efforts will be focused on some zones to promote development and attract foreign investment.

The third stage is the full scale stage (the first two or three or more decades of the next century). Full-scale construction will make Pudong a modern symbol of the 21st century export-oriented international metropolitan Shanghai. (Shanghai Pudong New Area Administration, 1993: 5)

The overall area master plan for Pudong was completed in 1991 and revised in 1994 (in association with the revisions of the Shanghai master plan). The initial plan was partially financed by the Asian Development Bank, and many of the ideas for the sub-areas were acquired from visits to North America (including Silicon Valley), Europe, and Asia. While many international ideas have been incorporated in the overall plan, it is clear that Pudong is basically designed to replicate many aspects of Hong Kong or Singapore's economic structure.

The main thrust of the master plan is the close integration of Pudong with the rest of Shanghai. This aim is being addressed through infrastructure development schemes and numerous other sectoral planning initiatives. As noted above, at least ten major infrastructure projects including two Asian Development Bank-funded bridges, inner and outer ring roads, subway lines, rail lines, and tunnels are in various stages of construction and more are planned in order to increase accessibility to the area. As the site is across the Huangpu River deep sea ships must be able to pass under bridges and this requires minimum clearance of 50 metres (Pudong Development Office of Shanghai, Municipal People's Government, The People's Construction Bank of China, 1991). By 1995, the government had invested 'more than US$3.0 bln in Pudong's infrastructure and another US$12.0 bln is planned over the next 15 years' (Daewoo Securities, 1995: 10).

Four key sub-districts were delineated within Pudong's boundary in the first half of the 1990s (see Fig. 5.9):

Lujiazui Finance and Trade Zone is 28 sq. km in size. Lujiazui is an extension of the Shanghai's administrative, financial, commercial, trading, and information centre, which is situated across the Huangpu River in Puxi. This will be the city's new business, trade, and financial centre by the year 2000. The core area, Lujiazui Central Finance District (sometimes called 'Little Lujiazui'), is the subject of the LICP that I am examining in this book.

Jingqiao Export Processing Zone is 18 sq. km. in size. Jingqiao is being developed for high tech, export-oriented, non-polluting industries, and the tertiary sector (e.g. transportation, higher education).

Beicai-Zhangjiang Zone is 17 sq. km in size. Beicai-Zhangjiang is designed to encourage the development of high technology industries, science parks, and an educational centre.

Waigaoqiao Free Trade Zone is 62 sq. km. in size. Waigaoqiao is a port area, export processing zone, free trade zone, transport and storage centre, and foreign enterprise zone. As well as factories and bonded warehouses, projects include a 1.2 million kw. power plant, an oil and natural gas exploration base, and a port with four wharves and a deepwater harbour.

(Sources: Asian Development Bank, 1993; Jones Lang Wootton, 1993c; EIU, 1994; V. Wu, 1998)

The Development Corporations

While the Pudong New Area Administration is in charge of the overall planning of Pudong (and the separate zones), four development corporations were set up in Pudong in the early 1990s to coordinate 'infrastructure and land development, real estate and project investment, and the development and operation of services' (Zhao, 1993: 236). These four companies—the Shanghai Jinqiao Export Processing Development Company, the Shanghai Lujiazui Finance and Trade Zone Development Company, the Shanghai Waigaoqiao Free Trade Zone Development Company, and the Shanghai Zhangjiang Hi-Tech Park Development Company—were all capitalized and allocated land by the SMG in 1990 and 1991. Three of them (Lujiazui, Waigaoqiao, and Jinqiao) formed subsidiaries that were listed on the SSE in May 1992, and all three have subsequently issued B shares as well. While their status as listed firms enables them to access external capital flows, it also drives the firms to achieve maximum profit in the short term. There have been numerous complaints from foreign investors and journalists about the process of land pricing, the uneven application of regulations, and the tendency of some (Jinqiao in particular) to renege on land leasing agreements (see e.g. EIU, 1994). This is an issue that is dealt with in further detail below.

Financing Pudong

Needless to say, the financing of Pudong New Area is extremely expensive. The first stage during the eighth five year plan was estimated in 1990 to cost at least US$10 billion (Cheng, 1990: 57), and a minimum of US$70 to 80 billion by the time stage three is complete in thirty to forty years (Gold, 1991). Money to date has been raised from Beijing, the SMG, the Asian Development Bank and World Bank, the loans and bond issues, land leasing, development companies listed on the SSE, and via FDI (Cooke, 1993; also see Cheng, 1992; Zhao, 1993; V. Wu, 1998). The SMG is hoping that 'at least half' of the total cost of developing Pudong will be covered by foreign investment flows (Sender, 1994: 56). This strategy was outlined in a metaphorical sense by Ye Longfei, executive vice-chairman of the Shanghai Foreign Investment Commission:

we will not only adopt the method employed in Shenzhen of, 'building nests to attract birds' (meaning building infrastructure facilities and standard factory buildings ourselves), but also try the method of Yangpu of Hainan Province of 'alluring birds to build nests', (meaning let foreign businessmen invest in the development of whole lots of land), and also the stratagem being used in Xiamen of 'having birds come and bring nests with them', (meaning inviting foreign businessmen to invest in the development of land and bring with them their investment partners). (quoted in MacPherson, 1994: 78)

The importance of state largesse to the development of Pudong, particularly during the first five years after its 1990 'kick-off', cannot be neglected. While I would not go as far as the arch neo-conservative Milton Friedman, who called Pudong a 'Potemkin village for a reigning emperor . . . a subsidized monument to Deng' that is best likened to the Pharaoh's pyramids (*Far Eastern Economic Review*, 11 Nov. 1993: 5), Pudong's rapid development is a sign of the continuation of direct and indirect state control in China over economic matters in the reform era.

Incentives to attract foreign investment flows include:

* Income tax is at a reduced rate of 15 per cent. Enterprises due to operate for ten years or more are exempted from tax in the first two profit-making years and allowed a 50 per cent reduction over the following three years.
* Imports of equipment, raw materials, and vehicles for offices and homes and exports of products are exempt of duties and taxes.
* Production should be export-oriented. Goods sold locally will be subject to duties and taxes.
* Investment in the construction of infrastructure projects such as airports, ports, railways, roads, and power stations will be given further tax relief.
* Tertiary enterprises, including banks, are open to foreigners.
* Land leasing will be for fifty to seventy years.

(Source: Asian Development Bank, 1993)

The Development of Pudong in the First Half of the 1990s

The regulatory transformation of this area from three traditional counties (Minhang, Jiading, and Baoshan) into a unified project of national importance has brought about a massive transformation within the space of five years as succinctly illustrated in Fig. 5.10 and Table 5.7 (also see Arnold, 1992; Asian Development Bank, 1993; Hong Kong Trade Development Council, 1993; EIU, 1994; Walker, 1994*a*; Brooke Hillier Parker, 1995; V. Wu, 1998).

By the end of 1996, Pudong's population had reached 1.5 million, with total population expected to increase to 2.5 million by 2005. GDP also continues to climb, reaching Rmb 42 billion in 1996 (this represents 18 per cent of Shanghai's total GDP) (First Pacific Davies, 1997: 3), while some 800 foreign-invested projects were established in 1996 alone. In total over US$27 billion has been invested into Pudong from overseas to October 1998, spurring on the development of 5,405 'foreign invested projects' (⟨http://pudong.shanghaichina.org/pudong/economic/index.html⟩, accessed 6 Dec. 1999). Some of the early foreign investors include Volkswagen, Hewlett-Packard, Li Ka-shing's Hutchison Whampoa, Hitachi, BASF, Sharp, Mitsubishi, and Johnson. The Pudong New

Annual percentage change

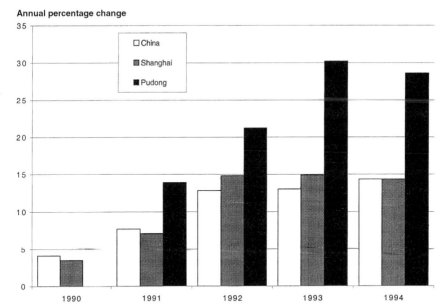

Fig. 5.10. GDP annual growth rates of China, Shanghai, and Pudong, 1990–1994

Source: Shanghai Foreign Investment Commission (1995), and Brooke Hillier Parker (1995).

Table 5.7. Selected economic indicators for Pudong, 1990–1995

	1990	1995	Growth (%)
Total GDP	6,024	41,465	588
Primary sector	222	422	90
Secondary sector	4,589	28,392	518
Tertiary sector	1,213	12,651	942
Total population (m.)	1.33	1.49	12
Workers (m.)	0.40	0.80	100
GDP per capita (yuan)	4,529	27,829	515
Exports (US$ m.)	—	2,475	n/a
FDI (pledged) (US$ m.)	34	3,256	949
Total consumer retail sales	1,428	11,000	670

Note: All figures in million yuan, unless otherwise indicated.
Source: Derived from Ash and Qi (1998, table 5.8).

Area authorities estimate that 'about 87 world-famous multinational corporations' have settled down in the development zone, bring with them approximately US$10.97 billion in development capital' (ibid.). Domestic investors from other parts of China (including the central and provincial governments) have also invested in Pudong to a significant degree (Zhang, 28 Apr., 1995).

In the context of such 'creative destruction', the historical landscape in the main zones of Pudong has been obliterated within the space of a few years,

replaced by construction sites, high rise buildings, multi-storey housing, warehouses, factories, and infrastructure systems. Agricultural land between the
zones has also disappeared at a rapid rate (Foster *et al.,* 1998). Pudong's landscape bears the mark of a developmental state eager to 'catch up' with the rest
of the Asian NICs, while also expressing state power and legitimating the CCP.
At another level, the development of Pudong represents a reconfiguration of
state logic on the role of the city in the economic development process. As
MacPherson (1994: 80) notes:

The Pudong project shares with its predecessors, a recognition (suspended during the
1950–78 period) that national economic development and urbanisation are inextricably
linked, and that great cities (now termed *zhongdian chengshi* or 'key-point' cities) are the
arenas where the expansion of economic life takes place.

The 'bourgeois poison' associated with urbanity (Murphy, 1980) is no longer a
concern in 1990s China. The Maoist dream of rural-based development and
'self-reliant' cities has evaporated, replaced by a vision of shimmering skyscrapers and high-tech factories working to propel regional and national
economic growth (Leaf, 1998: 146). The future path to a prosperous China is
obvious, as their friends in Hong Kong, Singapore, and Tokyo have so clearly
demonstrated.

This is perhaps the most appropriate point at which to scale down in a
geographic sense once again, and begin the analysis of the development of
Lujiazui Central Finance District, Pudong. As should be clear by now, the GIC
were drawn into a process fundamental to the building of an 'international
standard' Shanghai, a phrase I heard again and again during field work
throughout Asia. The global flows of images and expertise that the GIC provided were part of this nationally sanctioned process.

Manhattan in Twenty-First Century Shanghai?
Planning for Global Finance in Lujiazui, Pudong

Background

The Lujiazui Finance and Trade Zone (originally known as the Lujiazui-
Huamu Complex District) is *the* most important sub-area within the entire
522 sq. km. Pudong project. While the whole zone is 28 sq. km. in size, initial
development is being concentrated within three sub-zones (see Fig. 5.11) that
total up to 3.02 sq. km.

This low density commercial, light industrial, and residential zone is in the
midst of a massive restructuring process. As I write, industrial enterprises,
small commercial shops, government facilities, and thousands of residents are
being relocated to make way for Shanghai's new business, trade, and financial
centre. Like London Docklands, the historical layers of built form and social

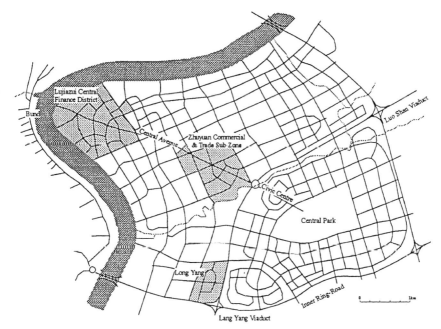

Fig. 5.11. Lujiazui Finance and Trade Zone
Source: Morgan Stanley (1994).

formation are being devalorized, to be replaced by an international standard 'landing strip' to 'lure in' unregulated 'foreign finance capital to build the office space that would lure major financial institutions to set up' (Harvey, 1994*a*: 426).

Lujiazui Finance and Trade Zone is planned as Shanghai's new tertiary (service) sector centre, with emphasis on financial services, 'trade and commerce' (retail, real estate, business consulting, etc.), and 'municipal administration' (government services) (Shanghai Pudong New Area Administration, 1993; First Pacific Davies, 1997). The site is across the Huang Pu River from the Bund and Puxi district, the historic business area for foreign companies before the revolution. As such, Lujiazui is viewed as a modern extension of the colonial-era Bund, a 'twenty-first century Bund' if you will (see Fig. 5.12).

Both the Shanghai city government and the national government are hoping that Lujiazui will become a 'city of the twenty-first century'—a futuristic financial hub for China and the whole Asia-Pacific Region (Pudong Development Office of Shanghai, Municipal People's Government, The People's Construction Bank of China, 1991; Wilson, 1993).

While there is undoubtedly an element of boosterist rhetoric in the above comments, there are clear signs that the city of Shanghai will become one of Asia's largest and most powerful financial centres within a decade or two, a key

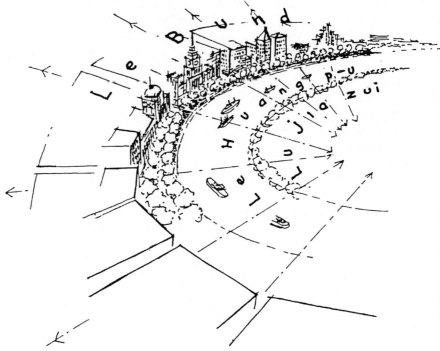

Fig. 5.12. The Bund and Lujiazui Central Finance District

Source: Shanghai Lujiazui Central Area International Planning and Urban Design Consultation Committee (1992*b*: 17).

node through which the world's most populous nation interacts with the international financial system. In part the emerging status of China as an economic power is due to some of the factors outlined earlier—the expansion and restructuring of the Chinese economy in relation to a global economic shift towards the Asia-Pacific region (Castells, 1992, 1993*a*; Bowles and Dong, 1994; IMF, 1994*b*; World Bank, 1997*b*; Lardy, 1998), Hong Kong's catalytic role in China, and the critical role of Shanghai in the Chinese economy. As Sassen (1991, 1994) has pointed out so clearly, such processes both create, and are dependent upon, the formation of localized agglomerations of producer services in key global cities.

In the effort to connect Shanghai into the space of flows, and encourage the development of the producer services sector in Lujiazui Central Finance District, the SMG drew upon the services of the GIC in an international consultation planning process (what I have been calling the LICP) that formally lasted from May to November 1992. This *opportunity* (for the GIC) arose because of the structural shifts outlined above in this chapter, and in Chapter 2. It should be clearly evident by now that the global flows of images and expertise that the GIC provide for UMPs are underpinned by waves of capital that are shifting throughout the world, often in response to state policies, and primarily through networks that link together a skein of global cities. Regardless of the rhetoric of these supposedly independent and 'critical'[20] élites who produce 'art' (Larson, 1993), their existence ultimately depends upon the grinding turbulence and 'creative destruction' produced by global capitalism.

In this heteronomous context the GIC provided the client (the SMG) with images and associated concepts that were then used by the client for a variety of purposes. The specifics of this situation are outlined below when I analyse the origins of the LICP that the GIC were hired to take part in, the role of the GIC in this process, and the subsequent representations of the process that were used to enhance the client's goals. However, the nature of the global flows of images and expertise that were formulated for the LICP are also related to the autonomous professional discourse that these transnational cultures are engaged in. In short, there are other circuits or paths that these images are routed through; a process facilitated by the double coding techniques outlined in Section 1 of this chapter. The specifics of this situation are also outlined below when I describe why the GIC wanted to take part in this project, how their images were created, and how these images were subsequently used to enhance their professional status.

These two themes—the LICP from the perspective of the client, and the LICP from the perspective of the GIC firms—are intertwined in what is principally a chronological narrative. However, in order to ground the discussion in specific events and ideas, I focus on the role of one of the four 'foreign' firms— the Richard Rogers Partnership—in formulating global flows of images and expertise in relation to Shanghai's new international financial centre. Of all of the GIC firms who were involved in the LICP, the London-headquartered Richard Rogers Partnership (in conjunction with the Ove Arup Partnership, the Bartlett School of Architecture Unit for Architectural Research, and Cambridge Architectural Research) received the most support from the Chinese clients, and the most media coverage following the consultation process.

My subsequent discussion about the role of the LICP and the GIC in the development of Lujiazui Central Finance District is necessarily broad in scope. Key events are identified that have impacted on the eventual process, though they may not have taken place during the specific time frame of the LICP itself.

The Lujiazui International Consultation Process

The first formal discussions on developing a modern central business district took place between 1979 and 1984. After the Open Door Policy was passed by Beijing, planners within the Shanghai Urban Planning and Design

---

[20] For example, Richard Rogers situates his work in 'opposition to our present exploitative economic system' where architecture is 'sacrificed to the private interests of the market and short-sighted economies of public officials' (Rogers, 1991). However, it is this same economic system that affords him (and his staff) the opportunity to work on large-scale development projects around the world.

Institute[21] developed two proposals—'Planning proposal for The Bund, Lujiazui and Shiliupu areas' and 'Detail planning for Lujiazui Area'—to encourage the redevelopment of this area of the city, and the broader transformation of Shanghai's social and economic systems. These plans drew upon some of the principles that Le Corbusier articulated for CIAM in the Athens Charter of 1933 (Huang, 1993). In the opinion of most of the participants in the LICP, these and all subsequent plans for Lujiazui reflected the influence of a key SUPDI planner (and part-time Tongji University professor), Mr Huang Fuxiang. Huang Fuxiang was born in 1932 and received a relatively cosmopolitan upbringing. Such a background, in association with English-language training, left him with an interest in international architectural debates, and the ability to communicate easily with foreigners. As Pye (1991) notes, a large number of the technocrats throughout China today have a pre-revolutionary Shanghai background. Famous US immigrants such as An Wang (the computer entrepreneur), Yo-yo Man, and I. M. Pei, came from the Shanghai area (also see Pan, 1990: 281–2), as did most of Hong Kong's entrepreneurial industrialist class—the class that is acknowledged as propelling Hong Kong's economic development in the key transition period of the 1950s and 1960s (Wong, 1988, 2000; Haggard, 1990; Skeldon, 1994a).

In the two year build-up phase for the 1986 Shanghai Master Plan, Lujiazui was identified by Huang and the SUPDI as a future extension of the historic downtown district across the Huangpu River, and as the hinge for a future east–west axis. This change of perception was partially related to the influence of officials from the Institut d'Aménagement et d'Urbanisme de la Région Ile de France (IAURIF) (the Paris-Region Institute for Management and Urban Planning).[22] In September 1985, IAURIF signed cooperative agreements with the SMG and Beijing Municipal Government to provide technical assistance on metropolitan planning issues. The formation of professional and social relations between Parisian and Shanghainese politicians and officials at this time laid the ground for the eventual involvement of the GIC in Shanghai. The key French official guiding the formation of this

---

[21] The Shanghai Urban Planning and Design Institute (SUPDI) is an arm of the Shanghai Municipal Government. The Institute prepares plans for various parts of the city, and it conducts policy research. Staff members include urban planners, architects, and engineers. Officials from this organization coordinated the LICP, and developed the final master plan for LCFD.

[22] IAURIF is a uniquely French institution. It is a 'para-public organization' in that it is a public foundation, though staffed by 'private sector' personnel. IAURIF was established in 1960. The Chair of IAURIF is the same Chair of the Regional (Paris) Council, and regional councillors have the majority within IAURIF's board of directors. The Regional Council provides approximately 60 per cent of IAURIF's budget. The remaining board members are made up of the founding members of IAURIF (including the National Bank of France, and the Ministry of Construction). IAURIF staff members generate the remaining portion of their budget through consultancies, both in France and overseas. Clients include private French firms, the Asian Development Bank, and the World Bank. Their work focuses on metropolitan planning issues, including strategic planning, and infrastructure planning (G. Antier, interview, Oct. 1994).

relationship was Gilles Antier, Géographe-urbaniste, and Director, International Affairs, IAURIF.

In 1986, a detailed plan ('Lujiazui District Plan') was prepared that emphasized the need to concentrate the tertiary sector (particularly financial services) in a 1.7 sq. km. central business district. The plan suggested that between 1.8 and 2.4 million sq. m. of built space should be provided for tertiary sector uses. Of this total, only 500,000 to 700,000 sq. m. of grade A office space was planned, while a slightly larger proportion (800,000 sq. m.) was planned for housing (apartments). Skyscrapers were viewed as the preferred form of built structure in keeping with the planner's ideas about what a central business district (CBD) skyline should look like. Their model CBDs were Manhattan in New York, Central in Hong Kong, Shinjuku in Tokyo, and La Défense in Paris. The desire to encourage the skyscraper form was based upon the association of towers with modernization, and a recognition that Shanghai is the most 'international' of all Chinese cities, particularly with respect to built form. A large telecommunications tower with facilities for viewing was included in the plan (an icon of development that has been included in all subsequent plans for the site, and was finally opened in May 1995).

One year later IAURIF assisted the SUPDI to firm up Lujiazui's design principles and layout patterns. However, in 1987, the underlying processes were not in place to drive the development of such a central finance district, and the SMG could not fund the development of the zone itself. While some districts in Shanghai (e.g. Hongqiao) were being developed, Lujiazui did not exist in an appropriate regulatory sense. First, it was not a 'window to the world' as the Chinese government is so fond of saying: foreign and domestic capital flows are only directed to Chinese territories that have an identity as defined by central government policy. And secondly, key national and local government land reforms had not yet been developed.

In 1988 and 1989, IAURIF was again called upon to help formulate mid-term revisions to the 1986 Shanghai master plan. Gilles Antier worked with key SUPDI officials to push for the development of Pudong. Prior to this date, senior SMG politicians' opinions were decidedly mixed on the concept of Pudong. Antier suggested to Mayor Zhu Rongji, who was in the midst of efforts to 'open' Shanghai up to foreign flows of capital and technology, that a developed Pudong would help achieve Zhu's aim. Moreover, Antier stressed that Shanghai's future development pattern should be multi-nodal, with the east side of the Huangpu River taking the bulk of new industry and people. Eventually, Shanghai would resemble a Chinese version of Paris with the Seine cutting through it, or London and the Thames; an urban vision Zhu was particularly smitten with.

Following the central government's 1990 announcement to 'open Pudong' as an economic zone, the SUPDI and the East China Architecture and Design Institute (ECADI) prepared revised plans for Lujiazui that reflected the new pressures on the SMG—to develop Pudong as quickly as possible, and in a visually striking manner. The SUPDI's plan was endorsed for implementation by the SMG in 1991. In total, 3.7 million sq. m. of floor space was planned for (1.3 million sq. m. more than the 1986 plan maximum). This large increase was related to the growing awareness by Shanghai's planners of the size and economic impact of central business districts in Western and Asian nations; an awareness that was developed through further work with IAURIF, correspondence with foreign city planners in cities such as Yokohama (where they were developing the MM21 project), and literature reviews. SUPDI also realized that the CBD needed to act as 'an important symbol and image of the results of reform' and the 'successes' of the Open Door Policy (Huang, 1993). The most appropriate method to express the reform era, in their minds, was through the emergence of gleaming skyscrapers that thrust upwards. Obviously, this was also the favoured model of key SMG politicians. However, it is important to note that the planners were not unadorned lovers of free-wheeling American CBDs such as Houston. They favoured the spatial organization of skyscrapers in a coherent manner; one expressing 'strong urban form'. These ideas came from images of European cities, and the La Défense project in particular. While they did incorporate some American ideas about zoning and the subdivision of land into specific planned plots, the planners and politicians felt a strong affinity with urban form that is symbolic in a monumental manner. The hand of the powerful state is more obvious to the Shanghainese in Paris, than in cities like New York, Houston, or Hong Kong, where development seems relatively haphazard in form.

In September 1990, the SMG set up the Shanghai Lujiazui Finance and Trade Zone Development Company to coordinate the physical development of the site, particularly the development of property, and the leasing of land. The government capitalized the development company, and sold it 1.51 sq. km of land in the 28 sq. km. Lujiazui Finance and Trade Zone for the discounted rate of Rmb 100 per sq. m. Of this total, the company only controlled 0.56 sq. km. of land in the 1.7 sq. km. Lujiazui Central Finance District.

In late 1990 and early 1991, officials in SUPDI realized that Lujiazui needed to have a stronger international profile, and that some form of foreign involvement would be useful for this purpose. Mayor Zhu Rongji also put pressure on government officials to revise and improve the Lujiazui master plan as he was unhappy with the state of urban planning expertise in Shanghai. Zhu has a tendency to ask for non-Chinese advice, as evidenced by his summer 1993 request for the 'foreign monks' (his words) of the World Bank to formulate measures to slow China's rapidly growing economy, since he believes that 'outsiders sometimes have greater wisdom because they can look at things from the outside' (Nicoll, 1993: 3). The ability of Zhu and Huang Fuxiang to perceive the involvement of international planning assistance with sympathy and interest (rooted as it is in their historical and contemporary interaction with non-Chinese systems) was a crucial support factor for the LICP.

SUPDI staff members discussed various methods to attract international attention to the site that would both draw in foreign capital flows, improve the Master Plan, and engender domestic political support for Lujiazui at the local and national level. Gilles Antier from IAURIF was in Shanghai in January 1991 working on the Pudong project when SUPDI staff broached the subject of an international competition for Lujiazui. Antier returned to Paris and set up a meeting with key officials representing the Etablissement Public d'Aménagement de la région de La Défense (the Public Development Corporation of La Defense (EPAD)), and the Ministère Français de l'Équipment (the French Minister responsible for public engineering). Key personalities including Joseph Belmont, Jacques Guaran, and Rémi Masson came to the meeting. Mr Guaran (who was in charge of the China and Taiwan desk of the Department of Economic and International Affairs in the same ministry), and Mr Masson (of EPAD) had experience in China during the late 1980s, and they were familiar with the key aspects of the Chinese planning system. Mr Belmont is Président de la Mission Interministérielle pour la Qualité des Constructions Publiques. He has been in this influential post since 1985 (from 1978 to 1985 he was Directeur de l'Architecture for the French Government). Mr Belmont is the key French official who helped President François Mitterand and Émile Biasini (French Minister for Major Governmental Projects) set up the system of international competitions for important national and local public projects. In this role he managed most of the international competitions associated with the Parisian *Grands Projets* including the Opéra de la Bastille, the Bibliothèque Nationale de France, the Institut du Monde Arabe, the Parc de la Villette, the Grand Arche de la Défense, and the (non-competitive) Pyramide du Louvre. In this important role Belmont worked with 'most of the world's famous architects and planners' (interview, Oct. 1994) including all of the GIC architects who would eventually take part in the LICP.

After some discussion between these officials, and subsequent consultation with SUPDI staff, a decision was made to begin the process of organizing some form of international consultancy process for Lujiazui. Mr Guarran organized an invitation that was sent to Mayor Zhu Rongji on behalf of Mr Besson, the Minister of Public Engineering. In April 1991 Mayor Zhu Rongji travelled to Paris where the two politicians signed an agreement that Shanghai 'intended to held [hold] an international consultation of urban design and planning [and] was looking forward to technical and financial aid from the France [French] side [in] order that the international consultation could be carried out' (Shanghai Lujiazui Central Area International Planning and Urban Design Consultation Committee, 1992*a*: 4). Zhu Rongji and several senior Chinese officials also visited the La Défense project and were very impressed with the physical and symbolic nature of the project.

Apart from interest on behalf of the Shanghai officials, the key force driving the LICP process to this stage was undoubtedly energetic French officials who were deeply committed to improving the quality of Shanghai's planning process given the rapid changes under way in the city. These officials also real-ized that this was the first time in post-1949 Chinese history that the govern-ment was opening up a high-profile large-scale project to foreign involvement. The international consultation process was a large symbolic step that the French officials felt genuinely honoured to take part in. Moreover, some of the officials (particularly those from the Ministry of Public Engineering) viewed this exercise as an opportunity to generate subsequent business for French firms. Interestingly, those French officials with the least experience in China held the latter view.

The consultation process and the role of Parisian actors highlights the role of Paris as a global city where Parisian actors mediate flows of images and expertise, and where Parisian urbanity becomes a global reference point. These contemporary global flows have their origins in the long history of French interest in urbanism in Paris and elsewhere (Harvey, 1989a; Wright, 1991), and in the largesse of the French and Parisian state with respect to urban develop-ment initiatives of both a material and symbolic nature (Savitch, 1988; Kearns, 1993; Shurmer-Smith and Hannam, 1994; Sudjic, 1995a; Winterbourne, n.d.). The French, experienced with international competitions, the *Grands Projets*, and the development of a modern business district from 'scratch' (the 750 ha. La Défense project), felt that they had much to contribute in Shanghai. The impetus to be involved was also related to their understanding (and support for) a strong state role in planning urban space, and the historic role of France in treaty port Shanghai. On this latter point, the romance associated with France's colonial past is a significant (though unquantifiable) factor in explain-ing the increasing flow of French business people and tourists to Shanghai, and Indo-China.

Following Zhu's Paris trip, the 'Groupe Français d'appui au développement de Shanghai-Pudong' (French Back-Up Group for the Development of Shanghai-Pudong) was set up. Mr Belmont led a team from this group (Mr Guaran, Mr Masson, and Mr Abadie) to Shanghai in June and October 1991 to discuss options for technical assistance. After some deliberation, the French and Chinese officials decided to organize an international *consultation* process versus an international *competition* process. The main reasons for this decision are related to the pace of change under way in Shanghai (consultations can be run more quickly), the Chinese preference to remain in control of the develop-ment process, the GIC firm's unease with putting their name to a proposal in which so little background information was available (see below), and the desire of the organizers for unconstrained creative options that would stretch the conceptual thinking of Shanghainese politicians and planners. On this lat-ter point, senior politicians (particularly Zhu Rongji) and senior SMG advisers realized that Chinese urban planners were following standardized and inflexi-ble patterns that resulted in a mediocre product. These patterns, with their roots in the pre-reform era where urban planning and innovative thinking were debased, needed to be shaken up according to the Shanghainese officials I interviewed. In their view, the LICP had the potential to work as a social learning process where creative thinking was demonstrated by foreign experts in a relatively free-wheeling planning exercise. Most importantly, however, this process was viewed by the SMG as a mediatized publicity show, a discursive event that would raise the international profile of Lujiazui and Pudong. The LICP was the 'final touch' to the package of reform initiatives that were being used to hook Shanghai up to the flows of capital and technologies shifting around the world.

Following Zhu Rongji's Paris trip, ten diverse architects with 'international reputations' were contacted by Joseph Belmont for consideration by the Shanghai officials: from Britain, Richard Rogers and Norman Foster; from Italy, Renzo Piano and Massimiliano Fuksas; from Japan, Toyo Ito and Sinohara; and from France, Jean Nouvel and Dominique Perrault. Other famous architects such as I M Pei were considered, but Pei declined to become involved because of previous procedural difficulties when working in China. The Shanghai organizers ended up choosing Rogers, Fuksas, Ito, and Perrault as the four 'foreign experts' while one 'local' Shanghai team was composed of officials from the SUPDI, ECADI, the Shanghai Municipal Institute of Civil Architectural Design, and Tongji University (my host institution during field work).

The selection of these four particular élite architects (note that all the firms incorporate the full names of the lead architect) to take part in the LICP is an indicator of the deep knowledge of Joseph Belmont of the interrelation between architecture, politics, and the media. 'Only a French bureaucrat' would understand how to choose a mix of élite architects of different ages, styles, and unique skills in a manner that appealed to both the Chinese decision-makers and the architectural cognoscenti who subsequently profiled the LICP (D. Sudjic, interview, July 1994). And, as noted above, Belmont had the contacts and reputation to quickly pull these élites into the process for consideration.[23]

All of the firms invited to take part in the LICP have worked in Paris, other European cities, North America, and Japan, though none had previously worked in China. For example, Richard Rogers's international profile owes its greatest debt to Paris. His 'breakthrough' project in Larson's (1993) terms, was the Pompidou Centre, that he and Renzo Piano (with partners) designed after winning an international competition between 681 entrants in 1971 (Silver,

---

[23] The remaining part of this chapter focuses on the Richard Rogers Partnership, and Rogers in particular. Information on Massimiliano Fuksas is contained in Rambert (1997), the Aug. 1996 issue of *A&U*, and on the web site 〈http://art.dada.it/fuksas/home.htm〉; information on Dominique Perrault is contained in Perrault (1996, 1999) and *Arca plus*, (6/1, 1999); information on Toyo Ito is contained in *Croquis*, 14/1, 1995, *Architectural monographs*, No. 41, 1995, and *JA library*, No. 1, summer 1993.

1994; Sudjic, 1994*b*).[24] Like the Lujiazui project, the development of the Pompidou Centre was closely linked to the support of senior government politicians (President Georges Pompidou) and officials, and an élite jury (including Philip Johnson, Oscar Niemeyer, and Jean Prouvé). Since then, Rogers has been involved in these types of planning exercises in 'some ten French cities' (Rogers, 1991: 28), the firm has received over twenty commissions in France (Pawley, 1992), and he has acted as juror on a number of other international competitions in Paris (including the competition to design the 7.2 billion franc Bibliothèque Nationale de France that Dominique Perrault's firm won). France, then, 'has just the sort of political and cultural environment in which a high profile architect like Rogers thrives' (Davies, 1992: 35). Box 5.2 summarizes some key background features of Rogers's professional life.

This lack of expertise in China was deemed irrelevant by the organizers since the teams were supposed to supply the 'shock of the new' associated with modernism. The SMG wanted architects who would symbolize the *new* China, the China that is opening up (albeit selectively) to global flows of technology, capital, and ideas. The last thing they wanted was a postmodern architect who would attempt to incorporate vernacular tradition in designs for an *international* financial centre. In turn, the GIC firms were perfectly willing to participate in this process even though they lacked local knowledge. They could offer potential solutions because they felt knowledgeable about the nature of the processes and problems affecting *all* modern cities. In Rogers's words, Shanghai 'is a modern city, and they are shaped by the same kind of pressures all over the world' (Rogers, quoted in Sudjic, 1992*b*). From this modernist perspective, 'experts' are those who understand the nature of the interconnection between global flows and urban development processes, rather than the specificities of local systems. The GIC firms were dealing with Shanghai, a city transforming itself into an intersection point for global flows, much like the cities of Tokyo, London, Paris, and Rome that these firms had worked in for many years.

The Paris-based organizers realized that these 'internationally renowned groups' would be intrigued by the opportunity to take part in such a monumental project—the design of a new financial centre in the world's fastest growing economy in the world's fastest growing region of the 1990s. Rogers, for example, viewed the LICP as a 'fantastic opportunity to learn from past mistakes, and to communicate from those mistakes' (Rogers, 1994: 3). The reform era in Shanghai was perceived to be an exciting turning point, a *window of opportunity* in which environmental and political priorities (in relation to city

---

[24] The influence of the Pompidou Centre is seminal both in France and the rest of the world. It is the 'godfather of the *Grands Projets* of President Mitterand' (Sudjic, 1994*b*: 66), influencing a generation of designers to break down the division between 'popular' and 'high' culture, to encourage indeterminacy and flexibility in the built structure, and to combine high-tech modern styles with anti-authoritarian impulses (Frampton, 1992). The influence of the Pompidou Centre is also evident in the work of Dominique Perrault and Jean Nouvel, the two French architects who were considered for the LICP.

Box 5.2 Brief profile of Richard Rogers and the Richard Rogers Partnership

The Richard Rogers Partnership has offices in London, Berlin, and Tokyo. The Partnership was founded in 1977 with John Young, Marco Goldschmied, and Mike Davies. The London office employed approximately sixty architects, including eight directors and fifteen project architects in 1994. By 1999, the office had grown to include 130 people including ten directors, seven associate directors, project architects, model-makers, administration, and a computer support team. The firm's specialties (as they define it) include master-planning, airports and transportation, retail sports and leisure, industry and research, innovation and ecology, housing, conservation, offices, headquarters, and public buildings.

Prior to 1977, Rogers practised in Team 4 with Su Rogers and Norman and Wendy Foster (1963–7), in Richard and Su Rogers (1967–70), and in Piano + Rogers with Renzo Piano (1971–7). Rogers is also chairman of The Architectural Foundation, the Building Experiences Trust, and the National Tenants Centre, and vice-chairman of the British Arts Council. He has taught at a variety of architectural institutions including the Architectural Association (London), Cambridge, Yale, Princeton, Harvard, Cornell, UCLA, Berkeley, McGill, and Aachen, and has given hundreds of lectures to professional and public audiences in Europe and North America. He is also an Honorary Doctor, Royal College of Art, London; Honorary Fellow, American Institute of Architects; Honorary Fellow, Royal Academy of Art, The Hague; Member, United Nations Architects' Committee; Member, RIBA Council and Policy Committees; Honorary Member, Bund Deuthscher Architekten; Membre de l'Académie d'Architecture. He was also appointed a Life Peer in England in 1996, and chose the title 'Lord Rogers of Riverside'. The projects associated with Rogers have won numerous national and international awards. Exhibitions have been staged at the Museum of Modern Art, New York; Louvre Museum of Decorative Arts, Paris; Grand Palais, Paris; Museum of Modern Art, Warsaw; Institute of Contemporary Arts, London; Graham Foundation, Chicago; Pompidou Centre, Paris; and Deutsches Architekturmuseum, Frankfurt. Rogers is regularly called upon to act as a juror for international architectural competitions (e.g. the Kansai International Airport, Kansai, Japan which Renzo Piano won (in conjunction with the Ove Arup Partnership)). Most recently he was appointed as head of the British government's Urban Task Force (which produced an influential 1999 report titled *Towards an Urban Renaissance*).

Selective List of Events, Projects, and Honoraria

1933   Born in Florence, Italy.

1959   Architectural Association, London, AA Diploma.

1962   Yale University, M. Arch.

1971   Wins competition (with Piano and Arup) for Pompidou Centre, Paris (1971–7).

(*cont.*)

1978 Wins competition for Lloyd's of London Headquarters, London (1978–86). Royal Academician.

1982 Inmos Microprocessor Factory, South Wales.

1984 Masterplan for Royal Docks, Docklands, London.

1985 The Royal Gold Medal for Architecture.
Eero Saarinen Professor of Architecture, Yale.
Richard Rogers + Architects by Richard Rogers published.

1986 Chevalier, l'Ordre National de la Légion d'Honneur.
London as it Could Be, Exhibition, Royal Academy of Arts, London.
Richard Rogers: A Biography by Bryan Appleyard published.
Norman Foster, Richard Rogers, James Stirling: New Directions in British Architecture by Deyan Sudjic published.

1987 Kabuki-cho Building, Tokyo (1987–93).

1989 Winner of competition for European Court of Human Rights, Strasbourg (1989–95).
Winner of competition for Terminal 5, Heathrow Airport.
Reuters Data Centre, Docklands, London (1989–91).
New Terminal, Marseille Airport (1989–92).

1990 Walter Neurath Memorial Lecture.
Master plan for King's Dock, Liverpool.
Master plan for Docklands in Dunkirk.
Winner of competition for Channel 4 headquarters, London (1990–4).
Tokyo Forum Competition.

1991 Knighthood.
Master plan for Bussy St George, Marne La Vallée, France.
Master plan for Nice, La Plaine 2, Nice.
Master plan for Potsdamer/Leipziger Platz, Berlin.
Architecture: A Modern View published.

1992 *A New London* published (with Mark Fisher, Labour MP).
Daimler Benz Competition, Potsdamer Platz, Berlin.
Master plan for Lujiazui Central Finance District, Pudong, Shanghai.
Master plan for Val d'Oise, Roissy, Paris.

1993 Daimler Benz Offices, Berlin.
Twin Towers, Donau City, Vienna.
Master plan for Dortmund.
Master plan for Treptow, Berlin.

1994 *The Architecture of Richard Rogers* by Deyan Sudjic published.

1995 The Reith Lectures, BBC Radio.
Daiwa Bank European Headquarters, London.

(*cont.*)

1996   Appointed Life Peer ('Lord Rogers of Riverside').
Richard Rogers Partnership: Works and Projects by Richard Burdett published.
Seoul Broadcasting Centre, Seoul.
Master plan for Greenwich Peninsula, London.

1997   *Cities for a Small Planet* published.

1998   Chair of UK Urban Task Force.

Source: The Richard Rogers Partnership, unpublished materials; 'Sir Richard Rogers, global architect', 1992; Sudjic (1994*b*); Burdett (1996); Urban Task Force (1999); (<http://www.richardrogers.co.uk/>, accessed 7 Dec. 1999).

building) were in transition. The Rogers firm felt that they had a real chance to participate in moulding this transition process through innovative example. I think that this perception is also related to Rogers's openly expressed frustration with the British government and British culture in the 1980s and early 1990s under Conservative rule (see e.g. Rogers, 1991, 1995*e*; Rogers and Fisher, 1992; Sudjic, 1994*b*). In contrast to Britain—a country ruled by short-sighted conservative politicians where the market guides urban development processes (e.g. London Docklands)—this was an opportunity to work in a context where the state plays a much stronger role in defining the nature of urbanism. As Rogers (1991: 20) notes:

Good architecture, in this age as in any other, is born of an enlightened client, generous financing and a public-minded brief. It is the absence of precisely this sense of public pride and patronage rather than the alleged inhumanity of Modernism that has been the most pernicious factor at work in British architecture.

So, the LICP represented an opportunity for Rogers to escape the overly conservative and historicist base of Britain to the arms of a public (state) client, ostensibly concerned with charting a long-term future course in a truly visionary manner. Moreover, given that Rogers's friends from Paris had a strong role in guiding the process, the opportunity was even more enticing. This approach to architecture is that of the classic teleological modernist. As Holston (1989: 9) remarks,

the only kind of agency modernism considers in the making of history is the intervention of the prince (state head) and the genius (architect-planner) within the structural constraints of existing technology. Moreover, this intervention is really an overcoming of history, for it attributes to the prince and the genius the power of negating the past by reference to a new future.

Apart from the timing of the project, the *monumental scale* of Lujiazui, in association with its location in an emerging global city, also attracted the GIC firms. What modernist architect could resist the opportunity to guide the transformation of 170 ha. of critically important urban space in China's largest city? Certainly not élite architects from a profession that continues to slavishly honour the grandiose visions of Le Corbusier in Paris and Chandigarh, or Frank Lloyd Wright in Broadacre City—the future city of the twentieth century. Their involvement reveals much about the role of global architects as perceived arbiters of twenty-first century urbanism who are able to fashion a visionary utopia in action where architecture is restored to its ultimate position as an expression of a 'timeless, continuous and universal culture' (Larson, 1994: 474; on contemporary and colonial modernism see Ley, 1989*a*, King, 1990*a*, Rogers, 1991, or Wright, 1991, 1996). Rogers (1994: 3) himself suggested, with reference to Lujiazui, 'In the late 20th century there is a possibility of an *ideal city* absorbing the new political economic and social knowledge of the day' (emphasis added). His remarks are very reminiscent of the rationalizations offered for 1960s style urban renewal in North America, where large projects were identified with 'progress': these projects were *architecturally* superior in that they 'seem almost always to be more rational . . . One of the reasons . . . is because large projects involve more people and bring in other disciplines as a total team' (Skidmore, Owings, and Merrill Engineer Fazlur Kahn quoted in Larson, 1993: 195). While modernism on this scale had received a critical death blow in North America by the 1970s, it is alive and well in the Asia-Pacific region today (see e.g. Koolhaus and Mau, 1995: 1008–89). Modernism, the 'imposition of a rationalist abstraction upon historical reality' in which people are 'compressed into the matchstick figures that a corporate society models and its social engineers plan for' (Ley, 1989*b*: 239, 241), is writ large and fast in the Shanghai of the 1990s. Superior architectural logic has meshed with superior developmental state logic in the aim of transforming Shanghai into a twenty-first-century node for international finance.

Finally, Shanghai is a *glamorous city* still linked to the exotic colonial past of the international treaty port. Apart from the undeniable personal excitement of working in such a city (a feeling that also attracted me to this case study), high-profile projects in exotic cities attract the attention of both the popular and the professional media, and the professional cognoscenti. All of the GIC firms received 'kudos' for working in China, and in Shanghai in particular. As noted in Section 1 of this chapter, this is an important factor in enhancing the status of élite architects in the professional world. For example, Deyan Sudjic, editor (in 1993) of *Blueprint,* and one of Richard Rogers's main boosters, is fascinated with Asia's 'exploding cities' and the opportunities they present for architectural innovation (see e.g. Sudjic, 1993*b*). His profiles of Rogers's proposals for Lujiazui (Sudjic, 1992*b*, 1994*b*) are all the more exuberant because they take place in Shanghai, a city undergoing such rapid changes that 'they demand the boldness represented by the Shanghai project' (Rogers's version) (Sudjic, 1994*b*: 130).

Following some financial problems in late 1991 and early 1992, the French support group finally located enough capital to sponsor the LICP. The organizers, with the assistance of Tao Ho (a prominent Hong Kong architect), used their networks to convince France's largest state bank (la Caisse des Dépôts et Consignations) and a Hong Kong firm (Chi Cheung Investment controlled by Paul Kwong Cheung) to quickly back the LICP. In total, the LICP is estimated to have cost 5 million francs, a sum split evenly between the SMG and various arms of the French government (with Chi Cheung Investment). However, this sum does not account for the considerable time resources used up by the many French officials who assisted in the organization of the LICP.

In February 1992 the French support group sent a package to the new mayor of Shanghai, Huang Ju. The material in this package laid out the procedures for the LICP, as it had been drafted by both Shanghainese and French officials (who were known as the Shanghai Lujiazui Central Area International Planning and Urban Design Consultation Committee). Once the mayor and other senior SMG politicians agreed with the nature of the LICP, SUPDI staff prepared the background documentation.

The LICP formally began in early May 1992 when the five teams were sent a formal invitation to take part in the LICP. For their efforts, each team was paid 300,000 francs. The teams received background documentation on the site and the consultation process that helped them prepare for a visit to Shanghai in late May. From 27 to 29 May 1992, all of the key actors involved in the LICP met in Shanghai. The LICP was officially initiated by the secretary-general of the SMG, Xia Keqiang.[25] On 28 May Xia, who later became vice-mayor during the course of the LICP, addressed the visiting 'experts' and summarized the SMG's main goals for the LICP:

The Chinese Government has made 'developing and opening up Pudong' a focal point in the nation's affairs. Speeding up the development of Pudong, Shanghai will stride into the 21st century and will become economic, financial and trade centre of the Far East. Being the core of Shanghai CBD and the centre of Pudong, the planning and development of Lujiazui central area has been put on the agenda, and close attention has been paid to it by the professional planners, and investment circles at home and abroad. We warmly welcome sistercities, international organizations, far-seeing investors and businessmen showing good concern with China's economic reform and Shanghai's development and revitalization, to involve in the development of Pudong New Area. We are also heartily grateful to French Government Ministry of Public Engineering, and the relevant enterprises and experts inviting sensible and creative planners and architects with world fame, to participate in this creative activity of consultation with profound significance and grand scale, to provide us with Lujiazui central area land use plan (zoning) and urban design scenarios to help us to finalize better both the plan and the urban design and their implementing strategy. Then the world will know more and show more interest on the development of Lujiazui

---

[25] Apart from Xia (also an engineer), Vice-Mayor Zhao Qizheng took the most interest in the planning processes associated with Pudong and Lujiazui in particular. Zhao managed the senior political manoeuvrings to ensure that the LICP proceeded in line with its original plan. While Mayor Huang Ju was supportive, he did not demonstrate the same interest in urban planning issues as Zhu Rongji. Zhao Qizheng is chairman of the Shanghai Pudong New Area Administration.

Fig. 5.13. Joseph Belmont (left), Massimiliano Fuksas (centre) and Jean Nouvel (right) on a Shanghai skyscraper, May 1992

Source: Shanghai Lujiazui Central Area International Planning and Urban Design Consultation Committee.

central area and Pudong new Area, and the intention of development will come as true as possible.

Your achievements will surely be recorded in the history of Shanghai urban development and people of Shanghai will bear your friendship and contribution in mind. (Shanghai Lujiazui Central Area International Planning and Urban Design Consultation Committee, 1992*a*: 1)

The terms of the proposal, and subsequent interaction with SMG officials, made it clear that this international financial centre should 'provide Shanghai with the means for a new economic boom, making it one of Asia's major money and trade markets. The new district is a symbol of this ambition and, at the same time, represents an urban experiment of international importance'. They go on to add 'In a programme of this scope, the coming together of internationally renowned groups onto one site could well lead to a profound re-evaluation of town-planning, dealing not only with Shanghai but the town of the future' (Shanghai Lujiazui Central Area International Planning and Urban Design Consultation Committee, 1992*b*: 1).

In Shanghai the teams met with the French and Chinese organizers to discuss the goals of the process, they received a briefing on the nature of Shanghai's urban planning system and urban development trends, short trips were taken through the site by bus, and a number of high-rise rooftops were used as viewing sites (see Fig. 5.13). At this time, Rogers's lead architect on the project, Laurie Abbott, acquired as much data as possible that was not included in the brief and other background documentation. Other advisers joined the Shanghai meeting as well, including Jean Nouvel from Paris.

Following this four day trip to Shanghai, the teams returned to their offices to prepare their conceptual plans for Lujiazui Central Finance District. The conceptual plans of the four foreign teams were created in their Paris, Rome, Tokyo, and London offices. Indeed some, like the Ito proposal, were faxed back and forth between Tokyo and Paris offices.

Contextual information on Shanghai and Lujiazui consisted of aerial photographs, master plans for Pudong and Lujiazui, land use maps, infrastructure maps, geological maps and statistical data (e.g. demography, housing, employment). Apart from the four day inaugural meeting (which the organizers paid for), no additional funds were available for travel expenses to Shanghai. When queries did arise, they were addressed through correspondence with the Shanghai organizers, or informal meetings with the French back-up group.

Over the next four months staff members from all five teams worked in their offices to create concepts and images for the future development of Lujiazui Central Finance District. The foreign firms drew upon their considerable base of experience in global cities, rapid access to sources of information on international financial centres, and high-tech design facilities to create their product. Obviously, given their lack of Chinese experience, their creative references were not drawn from Chinese cities. For example, the Ito proposal drew heavily on a 1992 master plan they had submitted for the redevelopment of a large site in Antwerp (that is profiled in *Architectural Monographs*, No. 41, 1995). Perrault's plan was devised through references to New York, Venice, and Paris (see Fig. 5.14) while also reflecting a *Grands Projets* emphasis on simple geometric forms boosted up to monumental scale.

The Rogers proposal was coordinated by the Richard Rogers Partnership in conjunction with the Ove Arup Partnership, the Bartlett School of Architecture Unit for Architectural Research, and Cambridge Architectural Research. As noted above, Laurie Abbott was the project architect, and he was responsible for coordinating all key stages of their submission. Abbott has been working with Richard Rogers since the late 1960s. He is well known in architectural circles for his 'remarkable gift for deftly conjuring up ideas in graphic form' (Sudjic, 1994b: 30), his ability to understand and design complex structures, and his fine attention to detail (Silver, 1994). For example, Abbott was responsible for the superstructure and mechanical services in the highly detailed Pompidou Centre. Many of Abbott's graphic images are used in books on Richard Rogers (see e.g. Sudjic, 1986).[26] Apart from Rogers and Abbott, Hal Curry, Mike Davies, Marco Goldschmied, Simon Smithson, John Young, and Andrew Wright from the Rogers Partnership worked on the Lujiazui plans.

---

[26] While Richard Rogers has input into most designs, he is primarily responsible for developing concepts, putting them down in writing, verbalizing the concepts, making connections, and inspiring staff members. Rogers is a true 'signature architect'.

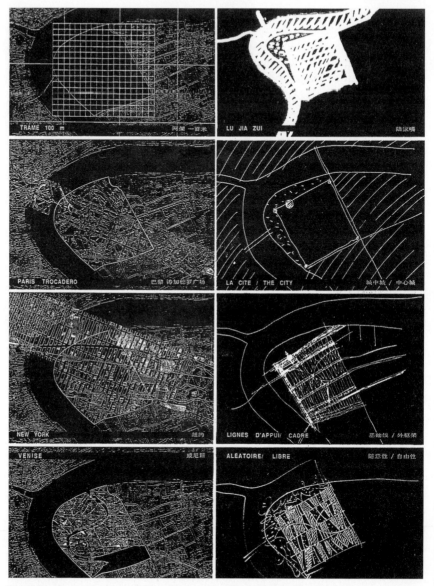

Fig. 5.14. Paris, Venice, and New York as a reference for Lujiazui

Source: Shanghai Lujiazui Central Area International Planning and Urban Design Consultation Committee.

Engineers from the Ove Arup Partnership contributed many ideas regarding transport infrastructure and energy use for the Rogers submission. The key Arup representatives were Guy Battle, Alan Mason, and Susan Freed. Ove Arup & Partners, with fifty-three established offices in twenty-three countries, have worked on hundreds of the world's landmark buildings, infrastructure systems, and master plans. Projects (developed and proposed) include London Docklands, the Lloyd's of London building, King's Cross, the Manchester Olympic site bid, the Sydney Opera House, the Barcelona telecommunications tower, the Pompidou Centre, the Hong Kong and Shanghai Bank Building, Stansted Airport, Century Tower in Tokyo, the Frankfurt Commerzbank building, the Torre de Collserola (Barcelona Telecommunications Tower), the Second Severn Crossing, the Kansai Airport Terminal, and the canopy structure within the Grande Arche, La Défense (Rimmer, 1991*a*; Sommer *et al.*, 1994). These projects are often carried out in conjunction with GIC firms including the Rogers Partnership, Norman Foster and Associates, Renzo Piano, Dominique Perrault, Jean Nouvel, James Stirling, and others ('Secrets of the Arup Archipelago', 1992). All of these firms make astute use of the media to radically displace traditional senses of place with neo-modernist built structures—that is, 'modern architecture as mass media' (Colomina, 1994).

One of the key factors behind Arup's success is the formation of 'long-term relationships' with architects (Secrets of the Arup Archipelago', 1992: 77); relationships that often begin with 'joint participation in architectural competitions' (Sommer *et al.*, 1994: 87). The origins of the Rogers–Arup relationship go back to the 1960s, and it was cemented with the joint development of the Pompidou Centre in the early 1970s. Since then, the Rogers–Arup team has worked very closely together on numerous projects around the world, and Arup engineers have an open invitation to sit in on the weekly Monday conferences between the Rogers partners. Both firms are linked by professional and personal friendships between architects and engineers that is rooted in mutual respect, a shared liberal philosophy, and a shared belief in the creative, intuitive, and some would say poetic application of technology to communal problems (ibid.; Sudjic, 1994*b*). The importance of the personal relationship factor highlights the need for GIC firms (architects and engineers) to be jointly located in global cities where these relationships can be maintained.

The Rogers Partnership also drew upon the Bartlett School of Architecture Unit for Architectural Research, and Cambridge Architectural Research for specific services such as space usage and use mixes. Many of the ideas that the academic partners contributed were drawn from previous exercises in planning UMPs such as King's Cross in London (see e.g. Hillier and Penn, 1992; Hillier *et al.*, 1993). The input of academics such as Alan Penn was heavily based upon the application of quantitative computer models to the relationship between pedestrian and vehicular movement and urban form; an approach that is propagated by the University of London's influential Space Syntax Laboratory (⟨http://www.spacesyntax.com/⟩). These applications incorporate universal assumptions regarding space usage, and are ill-equipped to factor in cultural specificity.

In Hannerz's (1992*a*) terms, the images developed by GIC firms such as Rogers express considerable power to define the future of space and place. The GIC generated centralized flows of images and expertise. With their access to design technology, expert knowledge systems, and the media, the GIC were able to formulate and externalize powerful representations of an idealized twenty-first century Shanghai.

The firms were told to organize 4 million sq. m. of floor space into

Offices	2,650,000 sq. m.
Housing (luxury)	300,000 sq. m.
Hotels and similar accommodation for foreign and domestic residents	500,000 sq. m.
Conference and exhibition centre	250,000 sq. m.
Shopping centre	120,000 sq. m.
Cultural centre	100,000 sq. m.
Miscellaneous services	30,000 sq. m.

while taking into account, and making recommendations on: urban form (including links with the Bund, links with the rest of Pudong, the relationship to the Huangpu River, the creation of an entrance, use mixes), infrastructure systems (including transportation services, flood protection), and urban design (including height limits, view corridors, open space, streetscape).

While the GIC firms had considerable freedom in the LICP to incorporate the above components in whatever form they wished, the firms were operating in the pressured context of extremely rapid urban development processes. In contrast to the slower pace of mega-project developments in cities like Paris (where La Défense took some thirty years to complete), the SMG wanted the maximum amount of development on the site, in as short a period as possible. As alluded to above, this planning exercise took place at the exact same time that China was starting to experience its most frenzied period of property speculation ever. On the Lujiazui site itself, contracts to build approximately 40 per cent of the floor space (1.6 million sq.m.) were 'in process' (twenty office towers over thirty storeys high), while a number of building sites were under construction. Plans for one eighty-eight storey building (that is financed by the Ministry of Foreign Trade) suddenly appeared on the maps the GIC firms were being sent while other developers refused to consider moving their plot of land (to fit with future master-plan alterations) because of suspicion and fear of attracting bad luck (the Hong Kong investors in particular).

Further pressure to enhance the leasing of land came from the Lujiazui Finance and Trade Zone Development Company. In May 1992 (when the LICP was initiated) the company created a listed arm (the Shanghai Lujiazui Development Company) on the Shanghai Stock Exchange. As with all Chinese firms on the SSE, only A shares were traded at first. Clearly, a development moratorium in Lujiazui was out of the question. As noted previously in this chapter, the status of the company as a listed firm generates contradictory goals: the satisfaction of shareholders who are concerned with short-term returns, and the long-term planning of an important development zone.

By 30 October 1992 the five conceptual proposals for Lujiazui were submitted to Mr Belmont in Paris. A 'Franco-Chinese Technical Board' (*comité technique franco-chinois*) composed of six people (three French and three Chinese 'experts') produced an analysis of the five plans and submitted it to the 'Senior Consultants Committee' (*Commission de Sages*) This committee was composed of eight 'Chinese leading cadres' and five foreigners including Xia Keqiang, vice-mayor of Shanghai (who was president) and Joseph Belmont (who was vice-president). Other members of the senior committee included architects from Hong Kong, Chinese and foreign academics, officials from the Pudong New Area Administration, and representatives of the Lujiazui Finance and Trade Zone Development Company. In turn this committee relayed information to a senior SMG committee (*Comité d'Organisation*) that mayor Huang Ju chaired.

All of the people associated with the LICP met again in Shanghai from 20 to 22 November 1992 to review the five submitted conceptual master plans, and the evaluation reports prepared by the technical committee. For the sake of brevity, Figures 5.15–5.19 contain a one paragraph summary (and an associated image) of each of the five conceptual master plans as defined by the French Support Group for the Development of Shanghai-Pudong. The summary thus begins:

The proposals submitted for the development of the Lu Jia Zui business district presented five possible approaches for a contemporary city.

They have a certain number of aspects in common, in particular concern for having a global vision for the project to be created. The development of such a district cannot be reduced to simply placing edifices on isolated pieces of land.

Such a development must be based upon a certain 'concept' of a city in the 21st century. The parts of the city must be examined in relation to this concept: infrastructure, networks, public services, business districts, residential areas, etc.

As noted above, this book is not focused on the specific ideas contained within the plans that were submitted to the SMG. Indeed, each of the plans contained enough information to mandate lengthy analyses. However, before I move on to discuss the post-LICP stage, I will highlight several highlights of the Rogers plans that are effective 'markers' to the nature of the firm, the principles underlying the images, and the inspiration driving the Rogers team to become involved in Shanghai.

The images that the Rogers team formulated during the LICP need to be seen in the context of Richard Rogers's ongoing attempts to disseminate his ideas about the interrelated issues of urbanism, modernism, and the future of the city. Drawing upon experiences in cities and towns from England, France, Germany, and Japan, the Rogers group developed a plan for Lujiazui that

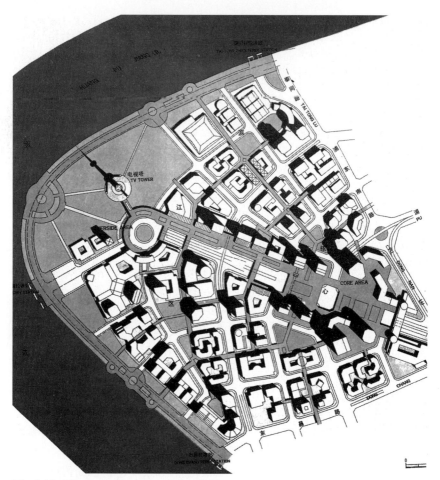

Fig. 5.15. The Shanghai team proposal

Notes: The Shanghai team is very familiar with the site, the programme, the means to implement the proposal and, more generally, with Shanghai. Its proposal provides the image of a city ambitiously conceived along a central axis which feeds the district while ensuring a large amount of flexibility for future construction.

reflects their deep-rooted belief in a renewed avant-garde modernism before it was 'coopted' by property developers, the cost-cutting state, and 'uncritical' architects (Rogers, 1991, 1997).

The necessary social principles (as the architects define them) that are embedded in this plan are *sustainability* and *public value*. The application of these principles, in association with the continuation of an unapologetic international style, and the full engagement of advanced technology, structured the nature of each of the Rogers images.

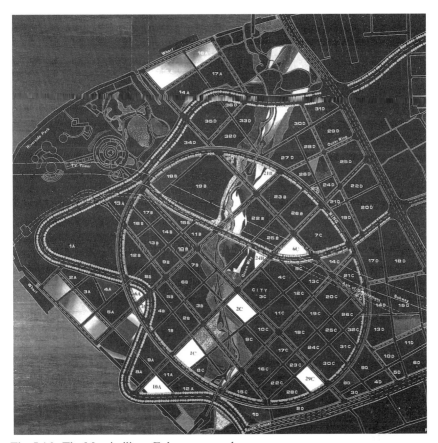

Fig. 5.16. The Massimiliano Fuksas proposal

Notes: The Massimiliano Fuksas proposal suggests placing a traditional city on the site of the city of the future. It has kept this form, but has reversed the respective heights. The old, low city has been transformed into a group of skyscrapers dominating everything in the area.

The key features of the Rogers plan are:

- A series of radiating Boulevards that describe the principal connections to the Shanghai Central Business District (CBD) to the west and the new development centres and Pu Dong to the east.
- A grand circular park, the focus of [a]new commercial centre and a park of an appropriate scale.
- A ring of buildings around the park clustered on either side of the main spine of the development; a light rail loop.
- Six sub-centres or 'neighbourhoods' along this ring defining the location of the most intense development.
- A vehicular loop road emanating from the mouth of the tunnel and giving access to six collective parking structures located along the spine.

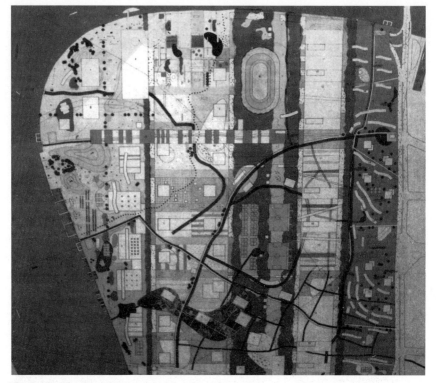

Fig. 5.17. The Toyo Ito proposal

Notes: The Toyo Ito proposal brings a completely new vision to the city based on an idea of flux more than an idea of space. This concept relies on the idea of urban function juxtaposed and super-imposed, but treats it differently. Toyo Ito invents a village which is simultaneously ordered and random and which is progressively defined as it is built.

- Secondary sub-centres of less intensive development along the river frontage. (Source: Richard Rogers Partnership, 1992: 4)

These six key features are underlain by the most important aspect of the plan—the transport infrastructure system (see Fig. 5.20). This approach to guiding property development reflects the team's awareness of the disastrous nature of the *laissez-faire* London Docklands planning process where the construction of infrastructure was left until after property was developed (Brownill, 1990; Sudjic, 1992*b*; Rogers, 1994, 1997). A series of separate yet interrelated transport systems was planned for, with a heavy emphasis on public transportation systems, the bicycle, and foot. This initiative, which is rooted in the team's concern for the failing state of the world's ecosystem, met with some resistance from Shanghai's politicians who see the automobile as a symbol of modernization (L. Abbott, interview, Mar. 1993; Rogers, 1994, 1997).

Fig. 5.18. The Dominique Perrault proposal

Notes: Dominique Perrault believes that a city cannot exist without a 'founding act'. In this case, Perrault has conceived of this act as a large wall of skyscrapers rising adjacent to the river and the old city. It constitutes a vast filter between the city of the future and the old city, between the urban substance and a large park bordering the river.

This infrastructure system then guides the overall form of the site. In what is surely their most striking and circulated image of all, an uneven circle of skyscrapers rises from this infrastructure base and thrusts high into the sky creating a *Blade Runneresque* city that satisfies the SMG's desire for a 'distinctive skyline' and a symbol of the reform era (see Fig. 5.21). The complementarity between modernist architects who are excited by 'innovative and indeed revolutionary' (Rogers, 1991: 36) buildings, and a developmental state should not be unexpected. China, like the Brazil of Brasilia, is a country where there is a 'number of affinities between modernism as an aesthetic of erasure and reinscription and modernization as an ideology of development in which governments, regardless of persuasion, seek to rewrite national

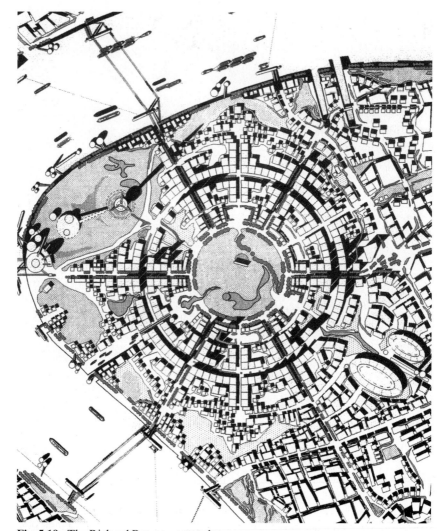

Fig. 5.19. The Richard Rogers proposal

Notes: The Richard Rogers proposal is the result of a very rigorous process which integrates all of the data which might influence the future district. It has organized the district in a large circular urban structure which is harmoniously constructed inside a loop in the river to better integrate with the Bund.

histories' (Holston, 1989: 5; also see Simon, 1992, in the case of Africa, or Armstrong and McGee, 1985, and McGee, 1976, in the case of Asia and Latin America).

While the historic Bund 'gave Shanghai a world famous skyline . . . it is on a 19th century scale. Lujiazui will relate to it, but it will be larger, on a scale *appro-*

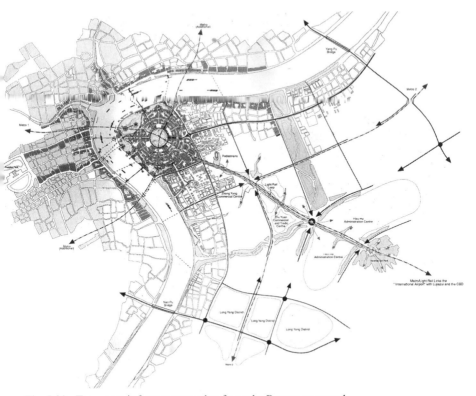

Fig. 5.20. Transport infrastructure plan from the Rogers proposal

Source: Shanghai Lujiazui Central Area International Planning and Urban Design Consultation Committee.

priate to a city of the 21st century ' (Rogers quoted in Sudjic, 1992*b*: 2; emphasis added).

The massing of the skyscrapers is designed to fluctuate upwards from the edge of the site peaking at a circle of buildings up to 120 m. high (a figure much lower than any of the other proposals). In a baroque vision of the future city, a series of radiating boulevards cuts through the circle to enable the formation of view corridors from the site to the Bund (and vice versa), and maximize daylight and natural ventilation across the site (Rogers, 1994: 2). Many elements of this image reflect the partnership's master-planning exercises in a series of provincial cities and towns in France during the late 1980s and early 1990s. These plans, for Bussy St George, Aix en Provence, Dunkerque, Strasbourg, and Nice reflect a typically French vision of urbanity 'with monumental public spaces, formal vistas and high buildings at focal points', in association with the added 'ingredient of symmetry and axiality' (Davies, 1992: 36).

The 'content' beneath the image-conscious skyline is representative of

Fig. 5.21. The Lujiazui Central Finance District skyline as proposed by the Rogers team

Source: Shanghai Lujiazui Central Area International Planning and Urban Design Consultation Committee.

a vision of urbanism that values (1) a mixture of uses to encourage social diversity and the more efficient use of infrastructure, (2) the reduced consumption of natural resources (within the site), and (3) a built form that is both modern in function and symbolism.

In contrast to the early modernists who 'undervalued urban intensity and complexity' (Rogers, 1991: 12),

> our approach was to create not a financial ghetto separated from the life of the city but a vibrant, mixed, commercial and residential quarter capable of acting as a focus for the whole of Pudong, and of driving its economy. This approach also avoids vulnerability to the boom and bust cycle of the international office market, which bankrupted single-function developments such as Canary Wharf. (Rogers, 1995*b*)

In their plan, commercial, residential, retail, and leisure uses were mixed together in a highly dense district. Indeed, the Rogers proposal attempts to achieve this mix while satisfying the SMG's requirement of planning for 2.65 million sq. m. of commercial space by raising the volume of housing in the plan (from 300,000 to 750,000 sq. m.). Rogers believes that 'high-rise architecture can have a place' in encouraging the 'messy diversity' where 'many functions overlap' (Sudjic, 1994*b*: 121). Alan Penn of the Rogers team suggested to me in a casual conversation that this emphasis on mixed uses reflects the application of Jane Jacobs's (1961) ideas. In theory, this mixture of uses, in conjunction with a well-developed public transport system, will encourage an active and vibrant street life, and a more efficient use of natural resources (Rogers, 1997). For example, electrical/heating and parking infrastructure could be 'balanced out' so residents use the infrastructure while workers are away from the offices, or a higher proportion of residential units would enable people to live close to work. However, as Jencks (1991: 177) notes in relation to other 'urbane [*sic*] mega-build' projects, the plan generates a rather 'oxymoronic result' with the emphasis on mixture and pluralism in a *master plan* for a huge site, thereby neglecting Jacobs's main point of 'piecemeal growth'.

This attempt at achieving a better balance and mix of uses is also linked to the proposed development of a 'coordinated energy strategy' and a linked computer software system that is designed to enable SMG planners to perform analytical appraisals of system change. For example, the computer programs will theoretically allow planners to model the impacts of population increase on the sizing of roads and services, or the energy consumption impacts of the designs of proposed buildings. This feature is rooted in Rogers's love of technology, and his belief that: 'design based on linear reasoning must be superseded by an open-ended architecture of overlapping systems. This "systems" approach allows us to appreciate the world as an indivisible whole; we are, in architecture, as in other fields, approaching a holistic ecological view of the globe and the way we live on it' (Rogers, 1991: 58).

Many of the lessons for the energy reduction aspects of the Lujiazui master plan were developed in the Rogers Partnership's 1992 master plan for Val d'Oise, a new town on the outskirts of Paris (Sudjic, 1994*b*: 139); a fact that helps explains the team's poor understanding of the possibilities of such technology-intensive schemes being instituted under the current Shanghai planning regime. The inclusion of 'solid environmental principles' in the Lujiazui plan reflects the partnership's belief that the architect's role is 'crucial in developing a policy of sustainable development for society' (Sudjic, 1994*b*: 138). Moreover, for Rogers, China represents a potential threat to the global ecosystem if the nation's politicians and planners mimic the contemporary Western city. As Rogers (1994: 2) notes:

we discussed at length with our Chinese counterparts the issues of energy use and the global energy crisis. China, with one quarter of the world's population has not yet developed its full technological power, and the environmental implications of continuing rapid economic development are a serious issue in regional and global terms. America's annual oil consumption ranks the highest in the world, at 9.1 tons per person. If China developed consumption to that extent, the ecological implications would be such that we really would have no future. However, Switzerland and Sweden, both better off economically than America, tend to have a lower energy use average, demonstrating that, with appropriate regulations and tax encouragements, a high standard of living is achievable with lower energy use.

For Rogers then, Lujiazui (on paper) was the ideal 'compact city'; a lively energy-conscious development that would consume fewer natural resources than an equivalent city in the West, while also acting as a demonstration project for other cities in China and the rest of the developing world.

All of the above principles for Lujiazui were implemented in the classic *tabula rasa* approach associated with modernists. While they did attempt to integrate the planned district of Lujiazui with the rest of the city, and account for city-wide infrastructure systems and the television tower on the site, Lujiazui was effectively treated as a blank slate where their global ideas could take root. While the plan's images are the potential result of a 'robust framework which can be remoulded provided the principles remain in place' (Rogers, 1994: 2), the framework contains no acknowledgement of the complex national and local economic and political processes at work which I outlined earlier in this chapter. Even at the local scale, this plan does not recognize the nature of the planning process in Shanghai and Pudong, nor the dependence of the local state on foreign capital flows, nor the nature of the property investors active in Shanghai,[27] nor the political pressures leading Lujiazui to be developed as quickly as possible. Finally, at the micro scale (on the site itself) the Rogers plan, informed by such distanced thinking, fails to address the future existence of the 51,000 people (primarily industrial workers) who lived (until the early 1990s) within the 1.7 sq. km. site, or the 169,000 people who lived within a broader 'adjacent area' of 4 sq. km. (the statistics are from the official invitation that the Shanghai Lujiazui Central Area International Planning and Urban Design Consultation Committee (1992*a*) sent to each of the teams).

The 'disengaged voyeurs' (Ghirardo, 1991: 9) approach to mega-project planning becomes internalized in architectural speak, and situated within a 'thick cocoon of self-referential discourse'. The Rogers team, as with all of the teams (foreign and domestic), were virtually oblivious to the people who lived on the ground. The vast majority of these people were and are being forcibly relocated from Lujiazui to nearby or distant blocks of poorly designed flats—reminiscent of the 'prison-estates of tower blocks and housing projects of the 1960s' that are associated with the 'haunting' double of an initially emancipatory modern movement (Lash, 1994: 112). There are no resisters in Lujiazui though, no movement seeking to use new frameworks of knowledge that 'can be used as rational critique upon the "system" itself', 'in heterodox opposition

---

[27] Hong Kong and mainland Chinese investors, in particular, have no time for the rational application of environmental criteria to their property development projects. Short- and medium-term returns are the key criteria. Given that they are the main investors on Pudong property markets (First Pacific Davies, 1997), it would have been useful for the Rogers team to factor in this issue.

to the dystopic consequences of modernization' (Lash, 1994: 113). In Chinese cities, the 'nails [stubborn residents] get hammered down' by the state (or 'roof eaters' as government housing officials are also known), and in the process their displaced lives facilitate the urban land development process (Huus, 1994: 73; Kahn, 1993, 1994*b*, 1997).[28]

In short, the Rogers contribution was pure paper architecture; an ideal city expressive of the modernist ecotopia that the Rogers team would love to see inscribed in material form. The images contained in the plan are the graphic representations of élitist utopian thinking. They were formulated by transnational cultures active at a global scale, yet embedded in networks and institutions more closely associated with Europe. That no master plan of such complexity and technological sophistication could ever be implemented in the messy and frenzied context of Shanghai was an insignificant issue; rather, Lujiazui Rogers was pure theory.[29]

The Post-LICP Phase

Revising the Lujiazui Master Plan

The five conceptual plans, which averaged approximately twenty pages each, were used to prepare a number of recommendations for the revision of the Lujiazui Central Finance District master plan. These recommendations dealt with transportation issues, green space, urban form, the feasibility of phased

[28] I spent one full day (11 Nov. 1993) interviewing residents about the relocation issue in six different areas of Lujiazui (with the assistance of an interpreter). To summarize, many residents knew they were going to be relocated though they had no idea when they would find out the specific relocation details (including where they would be relocated to). The residents had mixed feelings about the relocation. If the residents had strong links to community facilities and amenities, and/or had housing units they were satisfied with, then they were generally unhappy about the future move. Nearly all residents were unhappy about the uncertainty associated with their low levels of knowledge regarding the specific details of the relocation process. However, if the residents had poor quality housing (many units had no gas for cooking, running water, or toilet facilities) they expressed a desire to move regardless of the uncertainties involved in the relocation process. All residents expressed an understanding that they must move if the SMG desired them to do so. Few understood what the exact plans were for Lujiazui, though approximately one-quarter (of thirty-four people I met with) understood that the changes were linked to a plan sanctioned by senior levels of government (in Shanghai and Beijing). Given this, they felt that the project must be developed, and that people are thought to be moving for the sake of the masses.

[29] While there were obvious expectations on the team to prepare creative plans, and there were no additional travel resources available from the Shanghai or French organizers of the LICP, the Rogers Partnership could have created a plan which better reflected the processes at work in Shanghai. However, the team's resources were put into creating a model 'compact city' on the basis of the limited background documentation which the organizers provided, in association with the input of technocrats with virtually no experience in China or Shanghai. As their plan stated, 'preparation of these proposals has involved a wide range of disciplines: Traffic engineers, Transportation, Ecologists, Specialists in the design of public spaces, Computer Programmers, Geographers Environmental, Wind Specialists and Service Engineers' (Richard Rogers Partnership, 1992: 9). This completely decontextualized plan reflects the narrow focus of these specialists on matters technical while disregarding issues related to politics, economics, and culture—the fundamental determining forces of the actual 'window of opportunity' Rogers was searching for.

implementation, urban vitality, the historical context, future changes in information and technology, links with other districts, programme planning, administration of the zone, and recommendations for the next stage.

For all intents and purposes the LICP was effectively finished. In early 1993, a small team of planners from the SUPDI, the Lujiazui Finance and Trade Zone Development Corporation, ECADI, and Tongji University worked for two weeks to develop three options for the future development of Lujiazui.[30] The first option incorporated many of the Rogers' proposals; the second option mainly utilized ideas from the Shanghai team's proposals; and the third option reflected slight alterations to the existing 1991 plan (that the SUPDI had developed) through the incorporation of some ideas from all of the proposals. The first two options involved a considerable amount of change to the existing infrastructure, and the shifting of leased sites to satisfy the design criteria.

In this same period, several meetings were held by the senior consultants commission and the technical committee to review progress. As expected by many Shanghainese officials and French experts (those with previous experience in China), the third option was selected. This pragmatic option required the fewest changes to existing infrastructure, virtually all of the leased sites were left in their original location, and overall urban form was made more distinctive through the reorganization of building massing. A large international seminar composed of Chinese and foreign 'experts' was held in Shanghai from 5 to 7 March 1993 in which this decision was confirmed. Figure 5.22 clearly demonstrates the minor changes to the urban structure in Lujiazui Central Finance District, even in comparison to the oldest plan for the site (from 1986). Several further revisions were also recommended to Lujiazui's overall urban form to create a distinctive skyline including the development of three extremely tall skyscrapers in close proximity to create a 'tri-tower landmark' (one of Joseph Belmont's ideas), a curved sweep of skyscrapers facing onto an enlarged central park, and the enhanced provision of infrastructure.

By May 1993 the revised master plan was approved in principle by Vice-Mayor Xia Keqiang with formal approval coming from the SMG in early 1994. The revised master plan for LCFD will permit sixty-nine buildings, with a total buildable area of 4.18 million sq. m. (45.2 million sq. ft.). Seventy-five per cent of total buildable area is devoted to finance, business and trade, office and hotel buildings, 16 per cent to shopping malls, 6.6 per cent to residential and 2.4 per cent to 'culture and entertainment'. Thirty-four per cent of the total land area is devoted to open space (including a 100,000 sq. m. central park).

---

[30] The revisions were coordinated by Huang Fuxiang. The team consisted of Huang Fuxiang, Ni Bing, and Wang Bing from SUPDI; Cheng Bo-Qing, Zhou Weiming, and Gao Qi from the Lujiazui Finance and Trade Zone Development Corporation; Li DongJung from ECADI, and Li Zhihong from Tongji University. This team was primarily composed of people who prepared the Shanghai team's conceptual proposal for the LICP.

1986-Plan-Lujiazui Central Financial District

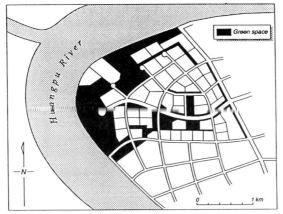

1991 Plan

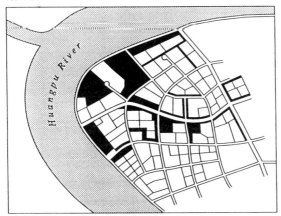

1994 Plan

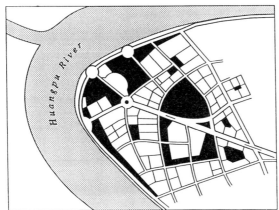

Fig. 5.22. Comparative urban structure, 1986 Plan, 1991 Plan, and 1994 Plan

Source: Compiled from various Shanghai Muncipal Government documents, and material supplied by Jones Lang Wootton.

Circuits of Images

Following the completion of the formal LICP process (May–Nov. 1992), the images that were created for Lujiazui have been directed along two main circuits.

The Money Circuit: Enhancing Confidence in Shanghai

The LICP has been used by the SMG to enhance the confidence of potential investors, and central government politicians who are supporting Pudong. There are three main methods in which the SMG has attempted to do this.

First, the SMG used the LICP to generate a considerable amount of local, national, and international *media* attention. Local Chinese media followed the November 1992 meetings closely, while international media outlets began covering the LICP within a week of the November 1992 meetings. Images from the well-produced plans were transmitted to foreign media outlets such as the *South China Morning Post* to accompany articles on the LICP (e.g. Besher, 1993; Kohut, 1993; Wilson, 1993). As with all international architectural competitions, the consultation process helped 'turn the desired building [district] into a monument before the fact: Publicity and publicness, the fact of being public, become an integral part of the project's extraordinary symbolic essence' (Larson, 1994: 478). The identity of the district was transformed immediately from a former industrial and residential zone, into a 'high tech city set to rise out of Shanghai's shadow' (Wilson, 1993). This was a critically important action for Lujiazui is, as noted above, designed to be China's most important functional and symbolic tertiary sector zone. Even though the pace of building in China is staggeringly quick by Western standards, it still takes several years for buildings to be financed and constructed. These images immediately suggested that Lujiazui was at the beginning of a monumental restructuring process that was clearly charted out. In a political economic context where Shanghai needs the long-term support of both Beijing and foreign investors, these striking images served useful symbolic and legitimation functions.

Secondly, the models and graphics that the teams developed have been heavily used since November 1992 by various arms of the SMG to impress foreign fund managers, foreign and domestic (direct) investors, and foreign and domestic politicians. These models are viewed by visitors when they tour Shanghai and make what is now a mandatory stop at the Shanghai Pudong New Area Administration and Shanghai Lujiazui Finance and Trade Zone Development Corporation offices. Through these models it appears as if the GIC firms constructed a modern high-tech Shanghai; a twenty-first century 'international standard metropolis' that matches the CBDs in global cities such as New York, Hong Kong, Singapore, and Tokyo. This practice is not insignificant, for the presentation of aesthetically pleasing images in association with the names of prominent international architects implies serious concern with the long-term planning of Lujiazui Central Finance District. It is no secret that the high-density business districts in most Chinese cities are dismal failures with respect to design and environmental conditions. These models, however, suggest the Shanghai government has (with expert assistance) an understanding of what a *serious* international financial centre should look and function like. Such statements enhance the confidence of foreign investors in particular. For example, in late October 1994 Morgan Stanley Asia Limited (Hong Kong) organized a visit to a series of cities in China for a group of international fund managers.[31] Following the visit, the organizer (Peter Churchouse) wrote:

Almost equally impressive has been progress in the development of the Lujiazui financial heart of the Pudong adventure (Figure 1). The planning of this area is impressive. Visitors to Shanghai Lujiazui Finance & Trade Zone Development Company, the developer of this 28-square-kilometre area, are greeted with a huge model of the core business district as it will look on completion of the 90 or so blocks. Light shows illustrate the buildings already under construction, under negotiation, or still awaiting sale; the roads, mass transit, and pedestrian links that are on the way; and the environmental pleasantries in store for users and occupiers . . . This plan shows a degree of urban design sophistication unusual in China. (Morgan Stanley, 1994: 4)

These representations of urban space embody a 'particular way of understanding, a particular interpretation of the place it is depicting' and their design—'for instance, what they include and what they omit—reflects different experiences, priorities and interpretations' (Massey, 1995: 20). The Lujiazui of the models is sleek, clean, and striking, designed to hit the right chords with a foreign and domestic élite who guide powerful financial flows. In other words, the imagescape underlies the financscape, helping to facilitate (though not generate) urban restructuring processes in Shanghai's Pudong project.

And thirdly, the images have been used in a series of publications that the Shanghai Pudong New Area Administration and the Lujiazui Finance and Trade Zone Development Corporation have published, and web sites that were set up from 1998 on. The handbooks and brochures are published in Chinese and English and contain numerous images of the models the GIC firms prepared during the LICP process. In these publications, and in the web sites, text often suggests that the 'Central Area of Lujiazui Finance Zone' was 'designed by world-famous experts' (Shanghai Pudong New Area Administration, 1993: n.p.). One English language publication was prepared in 1994 that was solely devoted to the LICP. The eight page brochure

---

[31] The amount of capital controlled by such fund managers can have a huge impact on a city, region, and nation. While I do not know how much these particular fund managers controlled, a similar Morgan Stanley/China trip was taken in 1993 by fund managers controlling US$400–$500 billion (*Far Eastern Economic Review*, 14 Oct. 1993: 74).

emphasizes that the final plan for Lujiazui was based on the 'advantages of the five projects as well as comments from specialists from home and abroad'. As late as December 1999, the Shanghai Lujiazui Development (Group) Co., Ltd. continues to advertise the link to 'world-renowned experts and domestic architects':

Trans-century deeds require trans-century planning. A great undertaking depends on keen insight. In order to build Lujiazui into a first-rate city of the world as well as a central business district of Shanghai, the internationally well-known architectural designers were invited to Shanghai and worked with their local colleagues. They finally presented the master-plan for consultation by adopting the world's latest urban planning methods. You can see the ingenuity in each individual building. The whole concept of plan is reflected perfectly in a best combination of the underground, the ground-level and air design. Three 100-floor skyscrapers are surrounded by nearly one hundred 30-to-40-storey super-high buildings, just like the stars twinkling around the bright moon. The 100-thousand-sq.m Central Green Land is sheltered by trees and flowers with a carpet of green grass. The 100-meter-wide Central Avenue is running across the whole region. All these give expression to the harmony between romanticism and realism, the accord of passion with reason. At this peak of development in human civilization, the embryo of a modern metropolis is smiling to the new century. (⟨http://www.shld.com/ljz03/ljz005.htm⟩, accessed 8 Dec. 1999; grammatical errors in original)

Here we see the LICP being used by the SMG as a technique to accumulate symbolic capital as patrons of architecture by associating themselves, and their new international financial centre, with these élite professionals. That the foreign plans had few impacts on the actual master plan is an insignificant fact in this form of promotional material. Lujiazui was simply branded by the world's design élites, and the SMG made full use of their 'signatures' to achieve broader goals than the practical development of 170 ha. of space.[32]

The Professional Circuit: Enhancing Professional Status and
Rebuilding the Modernist Tradition

Since the completion of the LICP, none of the GIC firms has acquired subsequent projects in Shanghai or China. Given the hopes of some of the French organizers and many of the architects, this could be viewed as a somewhat surprising state of affairs. However, as I noted at the start of this chapter, these architectural firms were primarily enticed in to act as advertising tools for Lujiazui Central Finance District, Pudong, and Shanghai. Moreover, these

---

[32] My thanks to Nigel Thrift for the 'branding' term, that Lash and Urry (1994) also use. In a related sense, 'designer label' architectural production is used by the Disney corporation when they commission celebrities such as Michael Graves (Crawford, 1991) to design hotels. Larson (1993, 1994) uses the term 'signature architects' and Ghirardo (1991) uses 'big name "art" architects'. As I noted in Chapter 4, the Li family name performs a similar function for the Pacific Place site. World property markets are facilitated by the use of the branding function.

architects' thickest professional networks revolve around European cities, and Paris in particular. Given that the principal flows of capital that fuel property development projects in Shanghai are intertwined with ethnic Chinese net-works connecting Shanghai to Hong Kong, Macao, and Taiwan, the lack of new work is even less surprising (none of the lead architects has offices in these territories).

While the firms may not have directly gained from taking part in the consul-tation process, they have made heavy use of the LICP to further their élite pro-fessional status by disseminating images and concepts developed during the process. Richard Rogers in particular has used the LICP because it, like all architectural competitions, has the 'potential of changing (more indirectly than directly) authorized notions of what architecture is, for those who listen to the serialized discourse of architecture' (Larson, 1994: 472). Moreover, the potential for changing such notions was enhanced because the international consultation process took place in the exotic and highly profiled city of Shang-hai. As Larson (1993: 135–6) notes: '*All* architectural elites exist by and within the profession's autonomous discourse. In addition, the level of highest visibil-ity is *a media event*, architectural discourse seized upon and amplified by the general press' (emphasis in original).

The LICP afforded Rogers the opportunity to insert his development con-cept and images into debates over the nature of the profession, and the role of architecture (and architects) in addressing issues beyond the aesthetic. This approach implies considerable effort to externalize flows of meaning based on the Shanghai proposals. However, as Pawley (1992*b*: 32) remarks, for Rogers 'no effort expended on an unexecuted project will ever be wasted, so long as cultural continuity ensures that future generations can still recognize it for what it is'.

Within days of the November 1992 meetings in Shanghai, Deyan Sudjic, an influential London-based architecture correspondent for the *Guardian*, then editor of *Blueprint*, and book writer (e.g. *The 100 Mile City*) provided a full two page article ('Birth of the brave new city ' in the *Guardian* (2 Dec. 1992). Sudjic, like Rogers, has been an active critic of the British government's lack of sup-port for architecture, preferring instead the grand city-building exercises con-ducted in cities such as Paris, Barcelona, and Singapore (see e.g. Sudjic, 1992*a*, 1992*b*, 1995; Boyle *et al.*, 1999).

This article, like many others written on the LICP over the subsequent years, explicitly suggested that 'the Chinese *selected* the Rogers' masterplan . . . as the basis for a masterplan to shape the development' of Lujiazui. However, as I have noted above, this was a consultation process, and while the Rogers proposal was favoured by the Chinese officials (of all the foreign proposals) it was not selected (J. Belmont and J. Guaran, interview, Oct. 1994) for implementation.

Sudjic and Rogers use the media here and in other publications (Sudjic,

1994*a*, 1994*b*) as a vehicle to disseminate Rogers's ideas about a renewed high-tech modernist approach to city building. This is a modernism associated with a powerful state role in planning cities, strong ecological principles,[33] mixed use districts, and enhanced public transportation systems. Sudjic (1992*b*: 3) balances the tone of this first article between a subtle criticism of British urban policy, while also suggesting that Rogers offers a future model for Asia, where 'there is no conceptual underpinning on offer, other than unplanned Houston-style chaos or third world shanty-town squalor' (a rather Eurocentric comment). In Sudjic's mind: 'Rogers's plan, a reminder that there are more serious alternatives to the stage sets of those who believe that the urban model of Renaissance Europe still has some relevance to the post-industrial city, goes a long way to filling the gap' (ibid.).

The images in this article, as in Sudjic's (1994*b*) book *The Architecture of Richard Rogers*, are used to illustrate Rogers's concepts, and suggest that Rogers has the knowledge that can help Britain develop modern cities that symbolize a *future* course of development, rather relying on historical tradition and heritage conservation. To a degree, this argument is also linked to the long-running battle between adherents of Prince Charles's 'Vision of Britain', and modernist architects (and their supporters). At last, imply the modernists, the potential exists (through Shanghai) to prove the utility and social value of our method, and in the process repair the damaged legacy of modernism.

Apart from the articles by Sudjic, Rogers's role in Shanghai has been profiled in the professional and popular press (e.g. *Architectural Design*, 63(7–8), 1993; *l'ARCA*, 75, Oct. 1993; Kohut, 1993; Wilson, 1993; Chiow, 1994; Burdett, 1996; Rogers, 1997: 44–53; Ho, 1998; Moore, 1999). All of these articles are amply illustrated with images from the Rogers plan, or photographs of their model. The professional press is used as 'the discourse of the profession amplifies the achievements' of the GIC (Larson, 1993: 102). These outlets are important vehicles that enable Rogers (no other Rogers team member is ever mentioned) to heighten his status as an authority on planning the 'high-tech' city of the future, even though his plans had minimal impact on the actual development of Lujiazui. The professional media in particular tends to focus on the purity of concepts underlying the plan, while disregarding the context in which they would have to be implemented. Chiow's (1994: 30–1) article, for example, speaks of the plan as if the Rogers team 'has managed to tackle successfully the complex issue of reducing city energy consumption', while also providing a 'foundation which also manages to foster a sense of community'.

---

[33] I should note that Rogers, like most architects, approaches the issue of sustainable development from a very narrow, technocratic perspective (Taylor, 1997). 'Green' buildings (or even green districts) in financial centres that facilitate the plundering of China's natural resources (through e.g. the financing of massive new joint-venture automobile factories) are not helping to reduce natural resource usage. It is the broader issue of the development paradigm that needs to be altered (Friedmann, 1992; Marcuse, 1998).

For Shanghai, Chiow notes, Rogers 'provides the missing link. Shaking it from its dormant state, he has created an urban strategy well-prepared to help Shanghai take the great leap from a present and distant past into the next millennium'.

Rogers himself has used the media and lecture circuit to disseminate concepts and images associated with the LICP. In 1993, he gave a series of lectures across Europe titled 'Cities of Tomorrow' in which the Shanghai plan was used as a model city. His speaking engagements culminated in The Reith Lectures that were broadcast on BBC Radio (including the World Service) over five weeks during January and February 1995. The Reith Lectures, inaugurated in 1948 by Bertrand Russell, are closely followed in the English-speaking world. Former speakers include John Kenneth Galbraith and Edward Said. Rogers used this Sunday evening lecture series (that was reprinted on Mondays in the *Independent*) to argue for a rethinking of British urban development policy, and for a resurrection of the state as a patron of city planning initiatives. The Partnership's Shanghai plan was used as a counterpoint in relation to the London Dockland's development, and as a model approach to developing an 'environmentally sustainable community' (Rogers, 1995*b*). His text suggests that their plan *could* work if the Shanghai government chooses to pursue the proposals. As Rogers (1994: 2–3) remarks:

Our transport engineers calculated that with a broader mix of activities, and a greater emphasis on public transport the area taken up by roads could be reduced by as much as 60 per cent. Air pollution was dramatically reduced and we were able to transform single-use roads into multi-use public space—vastly expanding the network of pedestrian-biased streets, cycle paths, market places, avenues and making possible a substantial central park. These public spaces were carefully linked to create a single interconnected web of movement. The overall aim was to locate the community's everyday needs including public transport within comfortable walking distance and away from through traffic.

Here again we see flows of concepts and images being legitimated by the Shanghai experience, and then recirculated into ongoing debates about the nature of urbanism in Britain. While beyond the scope of this book, the other three élite architects also enabled the LICP output to be circulated within discursive fields associated with the discipline of architecture (e.g. Yanagisawa, 1993).

In all of these discursive activities—drawing, writing, speaking, teaching— Rogers (like all élite architects) 'proclaims the superiority of the idea over its realization' (Larson, 1993: 147). The intellectual purity of the plan is boosted by ignoring the reality that many buildings were being developed in 1992 when they were preparing their submission. After the completion of the LICP, Rogers also attempted to maintain the status of the plan's concepts by distancing them from the subsequent developments taking place in Lujiazui. By 1994 Rogers (1994) pulled back somewhat:

The Shanghai government was very enthusiastic about our proposals and in all our subsequent discussions, presenting their modifications, they have always maintained they are doing what we set out—adapting the flexible framework to their needs. But we have become anxious that in the process some of the basic principles have been lost.

You can see that they took pride in presenting 'our drawing interpreting what we think you are looking for', but it is completely contrary to what we were trying to say in emphasising the importance of the street.

I cannot be wholly optimistic about the future of the plans, and the frustrations are enormous, but being part of that major discussion is a fantastic opportunity to learn from past mistakes, and to communicate from those mistakes.

In his 1995 Reith Lectures on the BBC, Rogers (1995*b*) stated:

Whether Shanghai itself will pursue any of these proposals is an open question. Political and commercial pressures have already led to the sale of isolated sites. And the highest building in the East is to be erected in the very centre of our unbuilt park. This will lead to the construction of roads to service the new buildings and will generate the classic market-driven form of the modern commercial city.

And in his 1997 manifesto *Cities for a Small Planet*, Rogers (1997: 45) complained that development trends in Shanghai were now depressingly familiar to those being experienced in other large cities around the world. While 'our approach sought to avoid creating a private financial ghetto detached from the life of the city' through the establishment of 'sustainable local communities, convivial neighbourhoods that would also consume only half the energy of their conventionally planned counterparts, . . . slavish adherence to conventional market and transportation criteria had determined the form of the new area—a grid of stand alone buildings ringed by heavily congested streets'. The point was obviously taken: by the late 1990s the Rogers proposal for Lujiazui had become firmly viewed (within the architectural sphere) as a brilliant proposal marred by ineffective implementation (see e.g. Moore, 1999: 31).

It is only through a process of disconnection like this that Rogers can retain the value of his team's images and concepts. The ability to circulate these images and concepts ultimately depends on ensuring that they have purchase on meaning (versus reality) and a utopian ideal. Yet, the decontextualized rhetoric and images of Rogers also flow around legitimating material processes which he surely disagrees with (if I have read his material correctly). As with the architects and planners of Brasilia, the Rogers team has produced a plan that 'contradicted what was intended' in a most profound manner (Holston, 1989: 23). That such a situation could arise surely lies in the dependency of utopian dreamers on the processes that they so detest. The global flows of images and concepts that Rogers *et al.* create are derived when he (and his team) offer us 'the mystic's eye, soaring overhead like his buildings, transporting us momentarily from the mundane present into a glimmer of the future' (Pilkington, 1994: 39). While such inspirational dreams are always necessary in our world, this approach to urbanism is sure to fail unless the visionaries directly engage with the complexities of the multiple contexts in which they are operating. This is difficult though for an ultra-mobile élite who also have little experience and commitment to forming the extended social relations in East Asia that would enable them to operate à la Li Ka-shing and family.

6

Some Final Thoughts

Summary

In this book, I have sought to better understand the nature of the global actors behind the global flows of capital, ideas, and images that are propelling the production of new urban spaces such as Pacific Place in Vancouver, and Lujiazui Central Finance District in Shanghai. Rather than treating the transnational cultures associated with these projects as anonymous and homogeneous agents, controlled and/or controlling from afar, my approach has been to treat them as everyday human beings, with multiple and shifting identities, situated at the intersections of networks of asymmetrical social relations that are place-specific (in a plural sense). While the material and non-material resources that transnational cultures 'command' may be relatively large, they nevertheless operate within a rapidly changing context; one that opens up both opportunities and constraints. The achievement of goals is never a certainty (witness the failure of the Rogers team to achieve their stated objectives), and is always subject to considerable effort, coordination, and sometimes simple good luck. In other words, 'global reach' is a performative act, dependent upon a wide range of processes and forces operating at a variety of scales. In general though, the transnational cultures examined in this book have reached the status they are associated with via their successes, their triumphs, in constructing and exploiting networks of association (at various scales) in contingent (and distinctive) space-times.

Given such inclinations, I have attempted to develop a conceptual framework inspired by Arjun Appadurai's (1990a, 1990b, 1996) concept of the five 'scapes' (ethnoscape; mediascape; technoscape; finanscape; ideoscape) that make up the global cultural economy; the overlapping disjunctive scapes through which global flows pass. As noted throughout this text, these global flows are inextricably bound to the perspectives and imaginations of historically and geographically situated actors. I also drew upon complementary insights from socio-economic literature (in geography and sociology) to explain how the actors driving global flows are 'situated' and 'embedded' in multiple networks and institutions associated with a global city milieu for the most part. In short, the production of global flows is a form of social action, a social construct that can be more subtly analysed through provisional accounts focused on specific actors, institutions, and events; actors, institutions, and events likely to be sited in various types of global cities.

In developing such an approach to the analysis of globalization and urban change in a Pacific Rim context I have pursued theoretically informed multi-locale empirical field work. One key problem of much of contemporary globalization literature is that it quickly degenerates into a needlessly 'high level of abstraction' as Janet Abu-Lughod (1991) complains. Aihwa Ong (1999: 3) also raises this point, criticizing traditional political economy for failing to deal with 'human agency and its production and negotiation of cultural meanings within the normative milieus of late capitalism'. In other words, while not seeking to deny the importance of abstraction, theorization, and structural forces, there is a need for *global* research that 'captures the ambiguities and nuances of the concrete, as they are embodied in the lives of people' (Abu-Lughod, 1991: 131). The question is, how to do so, but in a manner that also factors in the insights gained via the application of urban political-economy.

The tack I have taken is to use the urban mega-project as a 'lens' through which to explore the workings of contemporary globalization processes as they unfold in two very different cities on the Pacific Rim—Vancouver, Canada, and Shanghai, China—in the late 1980s and early 1990s. The approach of using one urban site as lens is akin to that adopted by David Harvey in Paris (1985), David Ley (1987) in Vancouver, Andrew Merrifield in Baltimore (1993), and Darrel Crilley (1993*a*, 1993*b*), Susan Fainstein (1994), or Sharon Zukin (1992*a*, 1992*b*) in New York and London—all essays focused on monumental urban structures or urban development processes, albeit from differing theoretical perspectives. As Harvey (1994*b*: 5) notes:

I've always taken the view that any microcosm—a particular incident that appears as an anecdote—will always contain processes which are part of the macrocosm, and that therefore it's not a matter of the microcosm reflecting the macrocosm, the microcosm is the macrocosm. So the purpose of an anecdote is to try to capture what you think are the fundamental forces at work in creating that situation.

The examination of a tangible UMP permits one to weave 'the most local detail with the most global structures in such a way as to bring both into view simultaneously' (Geertz, 1983, cited in Anderson, 1988: 145). Globalization processes 'assume concrete localized form' in the city (Sassen, 1994: 123), though in my opinion they can be analysed with increased clarity at the smaller spatial scale of the mega-project. The adoption of what is effectively a case study approach enables me to perform theoretically informed empirical research in the attempt to analyse the detail, complexity, context, and key processes associated with *globalizing* cities, the 'unavoidably incomplete city' (Beauregard and Haila, 1997).

While the main geographic settings for the book are Vancouver, Shanghai, and Hong Kong, the main focus of attention has been the transnational cultures which have the largest impact in shaping the global networks that constitute global flows (of both a material and non-material nature). This is because analyses which seek to examine socially and culturally embedded economic processes operating at a global scale must focus on the 'micro-situation' in order to collect suitable data (A. Smart, 1994: 11; Ong, 1999). Macro-analysis at the level of annual FDI flows from Hong Kong to Canada, for example, cannot provide the type of relevant data that can be acquired from detailed case studies of international business transactions. Yeung's recent work (1998) at the level of the firm is the largest scale possible to pull out what I am deeming relevant data, yet even Yeung bases his findings on personal interviews with individual actors representing the Hong Kong-based TNCs he is studying.

In a world becoming more interdependent, greater attention needs to be focused on élites in their cultural and professional context(s)—these 'conduits' (Featherstone, 1990*a*) of diverse material and non-material flows—who have such powerful influences on the process of time–space convergence (King, 1990*b*; Sklair, 1995, 1997; Mitchell, 1997*b*; Olds, 1998*a*; Yeung and Olds, 2000). With the implementation of WTO regulations regarding services, and further global integration (particularly in legal and financial sectors), these transnational cultures will increasingly inscribe the city (for good and for bad), though in a manner strongly mediated by the state (hence my comments at the start of this chapter). While some bemoan the attention allocated to the new middle class (e.g. Chouinard, 1994), let alone multi-billionaires and celebrity architects, or else focus attention on communities fighting against mega-developers such as Olympia and York (Keith and Pile, 1993), a focus on relatively affluent people *vis-à-vis* their networks provides relevant information for the formation of more proactive community strategies and local government policies and practices. One of the first steps in strategy formation is to understand how and why these landscapes are produced—not by relaying yet another critique at the level of aesthetics, or a story of misery that ironically makes some academics feel useful (while local communities quietly bemoan the parasites from the ivory tower who come yet again to rifle through their disorganized filing cabinets).

With reference to the specific research questions outlined in Chapter 1, the main findings of this project are as follows.

1. What are the key factors leading these transnational cultures to extend their reach over space into these cities at this particular time? One of the key factors underlying the impetus to reach over space is the simple desire to take part in new and exciting initiatives. For the GIC, Shanghai was a glamorous city, linked to an exotic colonial past. The rapid changes in China during the reform era also added an important lustre to the city, and it made the architects feel they were playing an influential role in guiding the future transformation of one of China's most well-known cities. For the Hong Kong-based Chinese property developers, Vancouver was becoming an 'in' city. The ethnoscapes, mediascapes, and finanscapes which link up both sides of the Pacific had transformed Vancouver's social structure by the late 1980s, turning it into a relatively welcoming Western city for Asian investors. An open social structure was important, for it enabled the ethnic Chinese developers to become part of the business mainstream immediately. The basic point here is that both transnational cultures thrive in cosmopolitan settings, cities open to global flows.

Both UMPs also represented opportunities to further 'internal' goals. Pacific Place was used as an educational tool to enhance Victor Li's skills, reputation, and confidence in the large-scale property development industry. The acquisition of the site in 1988 enabled Victor to be 'groomed' in a non-Hong Kong locale for his eventual appointment as a senior Cheung Kong Group executive. In considerable contrast, the Lujiazui project in Shanghai was an effective tool for the advancement of Richard Rogers's élite status within autonomous professional *discourse*. Lujiazui represented an opportunity for Rogers to demonstrate the continued relevance of modernism as the leading architectural and urban planning paradigm, and his personal role in reconstructing the socially progressive Modern Movement via propagation of concepts associated with 'sustainable cities'.

Finally, simple material goals also inspired the global cultures to extend their reach over space. The Vancouver and Shanghai UMPs were vehicles to develop new opportunities for work in the short and long term. The Pacific Place project enabled the developers to diversify their property portfolios, while enjoying steady (if unspectacular by Asian standards) returns. The low cost of the land was an incentive to deepen links with Vancouver, but a stronger aim was to establish a long-term North American base. For the GIC, the Shanghai project represented a potential opportunity to build up contacts for subsequent work in Shanghai and the rest of China. Large firms such as the Richard Rogers Partnership are dependent upon the processes of economic development to afford them the opportunity to conduct work. For the Rogers Partnership, Lujiazui was a high-profile pilot project which would theoretically lead to subsequent work opportunities. It is worth noting that the Rogers team has not returned to work in China since the practical failure of their initiative. However, Rogers and his acolytes continue to return to Shanghai (in a metaphorical sense) as they profile their plan's theoretical contributions via the discursive spaces of the architectural press.

2. How did the global cultures extend their reach and control over space in order to formulate and activate the global flows associated with these two UMPs? In the Pacific Place case, flows of capital from Hong Kong were channelled along networks of social relations that revolved around the Li family. These flows were guided by a myriad of trusted relations with people living and working in

Vancouver (including Victor Li). These networks of social relations enabled the family to acquire relevant and timely information on the potential investment decision, while also identifying a team of 'expert systems' (especially Stanley Kwok) to implement the family's goals. The decision-making process was enhanced through the historical relations Li Ka-shing had built up with people and institutions in Canada.

In strong contrast to the ethnic Chinese investors in Vancouver, the GIC had no previous links with people or institutions in Shanghai. They used their existing knowledge base to develop universal solutions for what they deemed to be universal problems. The knowledge base that the GIC drew from was heavily technocratic (e.g. engineers, computer programmers), with no recognition of political, cultural, economic, or even administrative difference. Once the international consultation planning process was initiated, key officials from the Shanghai Municipal Government provided the GIC with additional information: however, the GIC team did not commit any additional resources to enhancing their understanding of the local context.

3. What is the role of the state in each of the UMP development processes? More specifically, what is the role of the state in enabling, structuring, or contesting the global flows associated with these global cultures? In the Vancouver case, the state played a variety of enabling roles which directly and indirectly supported flows of capital from Hong Kong to Vancouver. First, federal government immigration regulations enabled considerable numbers of Hong Kong immigrants to flow to Canada (including key actors such as Stanley Kwok, Victor Li, and Terry Hui). This regulatory regime hooked Canada (and Vancouver in particular) up to flows of ethnic Chinese migrants, and ultimately provided the window through which the development capital and expertise flowed to Vancouver, thereby underlying the production of space. Secondly, various arms of the state have encouraged the formation of a plethora of 'Pacific Rim' institutions and initiatives. These institutions, many of which are funded with state capital, encouraged the formation of greater linkages between Vancouver, Hong Kong, and the broader Asia-Pacific region. These linkages helped structure a supportive 'atmosphere' in which the Chinese developers could operate. Thirdly, the provincial government transferred land from the public to private sector during the midst of a privatization initiative. The land on which Pacific Place is being developed was sold to the Hong Kong financiers at a 'fire sale' price to speed up the privatization process. And fourthly, the local state has ensured that the development process proceeds with certainty, while also attempting to extract some benefits in the form of amenities and services.

In Shanghai, the state played a strongly developmental role in association with Lujiazui Central Finance District. State capital is funding infrastructure schemes; state regulations are encouraging flows of capital into the district through the provision of various incentives; state powers are being used to guide key financial institutions (such as the Shanghai Stock Exchange) to locate in the district; and state capital is directly and indirectly funding the construction of a large proportion (some 60 to 70 per cent) of the initial buildings going up on the site. On a broader scale, central government policies and regulations have encouraged the formation of commoditized land markets, and the restructuring of China's economy (which propels the growth of the tertiary sector, leading to increased demand for office space). All of these initiatives underlie the flows of images and expertise that the GIC were asked to provide during the Lujiazui International Consultation Process.

4. What roles does the global city play in the activities of the global cultures in general, and in these initiatives in particular? For the Hong Kong-based Chinese property tycoons who were active in Vancouver, the global city represents a key node through which global flows pass. By positioning themselves in these cities, large Chinese conglomerates are able to access the international financial system (Olds and Yeung, 1999). Capital is extracted via equity and bond markets, and then used to finance business activity around the world. Relatedly, access to these flows of capital must be tapped through the means of 'expert systems'. A global city such as Hong Kong harbours large numbers of professionals (e.g. accountants, lawyers) who can be used to enhance the economic performance of the Chinese business firms. Global cities also provide enhanced access to family, friends, colleagues, and acquaintances. The tycoons are able to maintain face to face contact with a large number of relations, and build up social networks. And finally, dynamic global cities such as Hong Kong have a large enough population base to support the provision of mass housing complexes, telecommunication systems, retail outlets, transportation systems—the exact sectors Chinese business firms thrive in (Yeung and Olds, 2000). Global cities such as Hong Kong are also the source of considerable flows of immigrants that the firms seek to exploit (through e.g. the provision of housing on the Pacific Place site).

For the GIC who were active in Shanghai, the global city provides enhanced opportunities to generate employment, primarily by working on large-scale projects. Large institutional structures and corporate headquarters are virtually all situated in the global city. Apart from providing work, these types of structures can elevate the status of architects if they are designed with panache, and they receive the concentrated attention of the cognoscenti. The global city is the base for the professional media, and professional institutions such as the Royal Institute of British Architects. The GIC can maintain and enhance their élite status by building up contacts and relations with representatives based in these institutions. The global city is also the base of the premier educational institutions, and the GIC need to tap into these schools to acquire labour, and to disseminate their ideas, images, and theories on architecture and the future of the profession.

Reflections

In November 1989 I attended yet another public hearing regarding the Official Development Plan for the North Shore of False Creek in Vancouver, Canada. I met a good friend in the auditorium and we sat listening to the expected: disgruntled activists voicing their concerns about the social impacts of the project, and supportive (and better-dressed) defenders of Concord Pacific's plans for the site. The eventual vote (eight to three in favour) was also expected, for Mayor Campbell's NPA majority outweighed the minority COPE representatives by the same proportion.

On the sidelines, also listening to the debate (more closely than I), were representatives of Concord Pacific Developments Ltd. While Concord's staff tried not to appear too ecstatic when the eventual vote was cast, it was obvious they were pleased that the lengthy ODP public hearing process was finally over. To those of us in the audience who were concerned about the negative social impacts the project would have in the low-income community bordering the site, the City's vote merely enhanced these impacts. While many City officials (and some politicians) expressed genuine concerns about the impact of the redevelopment project, those of us with community links were unimpressed. Over one-sixth of Vancouver's downtown core was about to be redeveloped, and the City had not even conducted a social impact assessment study (though considerable effort had been devoted to aesthetic issues). The frustrations of working in such a context can be quite draining, and over time lead to feelings of ineffectiveness.

This type of mundane experience provided much of the inspiration to conduct the research that this book is derived from. Its origins lay in my background as an interested citizen in Vancouver's development, and in my experiences of assisting inner city community groups in Vancouver address the housing impacts of various mega-projects affecting them. Since 1984 I have been attempting (with mixed success) to conduct research on processes shaping the development of Vancouver's Downtown Eastside community. This area of the city is one of the lowest income communities in Canada, and residents there have been actively contesting external representations of their community as 'Skid Row' (Ley, 1994; Blomley, 1998; Sommers, 1998). Over the years I have attempted to frame several of the research projects I have been involved with (see Olds, 1988, 1998b; Hulchanski, 1989; Hulchanski *et al.*, 1991) to assist the representatives of the community in their goal of implementing 'people in place prosperity'.

While it is clearly important to keep involved in the fine-grained detail of local politics, it is also important to stand back sometimes, and open up a wider view onto the situation you are involved in. I do not mean to imply that standing back provides the *full* view; rather, new perspectives simply have the capacity to provide new insights, and potentially help in the aim of formulating better strategy (whatever the 'project' may be). One has to understand the processes generating the issues being dealt with, or else risk formulating and implementing less effective (and perhaps detrimental) policies, programmes, and projects.

A case in point is the sale of the North Shore of False Creek (one-sixth of the downtown core of Vancouver) to the Li family for a discounted sum of C$145 million—a miniscule amount of money for one of the world's ten richest families. Unfortunately the politicians representing the Province of British Columbia, and the politicians and planners representing the City of Vancouver, knew little about the Li family, nor about the complex network of firms they control, nor about the institutional environment (centred in Hong Kong) that these firms are embedded in. If the City had bothered to devote one week's worth of staff time conducting research on the nature of the family and the firms, they would have realized how significant the site and the development project were to a critically important (for Hong Kong's highest profile Chinese family firm) management succession process. In doing so considerably more community benefits could have been leveraged out of Concord Pacific at various stages in the development process. However, issues related to aesthetics took much higher priority: it is a sad fact that more staff time was devoted to planning the width and surfacing material on the site's waterfront walkway, than was devoted to identifying exactly who backed Concord Pacific, why they were 'reaching' across the Pacific into Vancouver (and this particular site) at this particular time, and how the Cheung Kong Group commonly interacts with government officials and politicians. My general point is that as cities become integrated into an evolving global system, the politicians and bureaucrats allocated with the responsibility for representing citizens (and taxpayers) need to become less focused on locality (the local) and more on multi-scalar social, economic, and political dynamics and relations. To use an anthropological analogy, politicians and planners need to rework their approach to understanding change; they need to retheorize and move from 'spatial sites to political locations' (Gupta and Ferguson, 1997: 35). To use a geographical analogy, they need to develop a more 'progressive sense of place'; one which recognizes that the 'character' of place is constructed out of the formation of an evolving constellation of linkages between that place and places beyond (Massey, 1993, 1994). Of course politicians and planners in rapidly developing cities everywhere are overworked, but the strategic allocation of 'evaluative' resources with respect to context (in business school speak 'the strategic environment facing modern managers') needs to prioritize enhancing understandings of the world beyond narrow administratively defined boundaries.

Academics, of course, can play a key role in assisting officials, politicians, and community groups in understanding the nature of the multi-scalar processes that underlie the production of urban space. The question is 'how to do so in an effective manner?' After working for several years on this research project, I would like to reflect on this matter *vis-à-vis* some simple insights generated while analysing two forms of transnational cultures which are dependent upon conducting their own research and analysis in the process of work.

It seems to me that the Rogers Partnership (at least exemplified in Shanghai) is the perfect model of how *not* to work across space and time—a form of research that is increasingly required in the social sciences. While the Rogers Partnership operates according to worthwhile ethical principles, their method of operation suggests that they can offer a satellite utopian view, free of local clutter and context. Like an increasing number of academics today, they roam the world, acting as 'jet set quick dip experts', applying decontextualized theoretical frameworks as they seek to shape the production of urban space. They produce the abstract city, stylish, theoretically equitable and sustainable, yet curiously void. IMF economists adopt similar totalizing approaches to analysis and prescription. When academics adopt such approaches to addressing the topic of globalization and urban change, they contribute little to generating knowledge that can be acted upon at the local level. Such knowledge is too abstract, and frequently difficult for non-academics to understand. Such knowledge also has greater potential in unwittingly abstracting from view segments of society: witness the hundreds of thousands of people forcibly relocated from Lujiazui Central Finance District, people who were invisible in the Rogers plan.

In contrast, the Li family effectively established a research process that was grounded in the machinations of life (including politics) in the city. They collaborated in a long-term project, bringing together a diverse array of knowledges, skills, linguistic abilities, cultural backgrounds, and interests. Their adopted approach was obviously global in scope, yet exceedingly local (multi-locale to be more precise) in practice, blending trusted inputs in the codetermination of an ideal path to follow. Translated into academic terms, what I witnessed was a long-term, multi-disciplinary collaborative research project between people of like minds; a project that was certainly not the product of an isolated armchair theorist.

The success of such a research model (in achieving stated objectives within ever-changing contexts) jars, however, when considering how much collaborative research is still denigrated in academia, despite considerable institutional rhetoric to the contrary. This is particularly the case because collaborative research leads to the production of jointly authored texts. Academic institutions in many countries continue to prioritize the 'brilliant' insights of the lone academic, following a period of splendid isolation and reflection. In many cases, 'brilliant' is also equated with 'difficult to understand'; writings associated with theoretical gymnastics.

For me, the contrast between the insights generated by the Li team and the Rogers team holds many lessons. The most basic one of all, however, is that academics interested in analysing the processes globalizing cities need to become more collaborative in nature, interdisciplinary inclined, and excited at the prospects of working both *in* and *on* the city versus just *on* the city. We need to pull in complementary skills (including languages), cultural backgrounds, interests, and approaches in the pursuit of more *grounded research* in multiple locales, directly engaging with vibrant and evolving social formations. Such an approach to the global space of flows suggests a relatively higher level of provisionality in analysis, one that rejects representations of 'the forces of globalization' as monolithic, absolute, and homogenous in nature (Thrift, 1995: 35). That said, a focus on transnational practices and networks must also 'embed the theory of practice within, not outside of or against, political-economic forces' (Ong, 1999: 5). In practice, this means enhancing our understandings of the structural forces reshaping societies and economies. At the same time (not literally of course) this means conducting multi-locale research to become entangled within the 'stretched out' social relations that play a key role in constituting the global space of flows. In doing so we might be able to better identify strategies and plans for developing more humane cities. In turn, we might also be able to prevent the degeneration of academic discourses on the global into the forms of defeatist 'global babble' that Janet Abu-Lughod (1991) and Aihwa Ong (1999) so rightly worry about.

APPENDIX A:
NOTES ON METHODOLOGY

This appendix is a review of the research methodology I adopted in collecting and analysing data for this book. While a considerable number of studies on globalization processes (and globalizing cities) have been published in the last several years, few of them address the issue of how to conduct research on the main phenomena of globalization—the 'stretching' and 'deepening' of interconnections between states and societies (Held *et al.*, 1999). Even rarer are discussions of research on globalization processes that are reflexive in identifying the author's positionality, and how this shapes the unique opportunities and constraints faced by the researcher 'in the field'.

Given all of the above factors, this research project (and this book) should be considered as a learning exercise and an exposition about both substantive issues (the processes which underlie the production of new urban spaces on the Pacific Rim) *and* methodological issues (the specific practices which are employed to understand the nature of globalization processes *vis-à-vis* urban change). As a consequence, this appendix is relatively lengthy in comparison to most appendices in research monographs. That said, while I believe it is important to be somewhat 'reflexive' in the book (and this appendix), I feel that some of the 'critical ethnographies' inspired by Clifford and Marcus (1986) and Marcus and Fischer (1986) are excessive to the point of self-indulgent navel gazing. The approach of Holston (1989) in his 'critical ethnography of modernism' (the city of Brasilia) strikes a better balance in my opinion.

Acquiring and Understanding Data

The analysis in this book draws from three main stages of research: first, relevant pre-Ph.D. experience in Vancouver from 1984 to 1992 when I was both a student and urban planner for the City of Vancouver; secondly, during the three years (1992 to 1995) I was registered at the University of Bristol as a doctoral candidate; and thirdly, during the last four years while working at universities in Vancouver, Bristol, and now Singapore. These three stages are interdependent, and knowledge gained during all periods informs the construction of this book. The earliest phase, in particular, was key for it enabled me to form trusted social networks with Vancouver-based actors; networks that I subsequently drew upon during the second and third phases of research.

There were three main forms of local involvement in Vancouver. First, I worked for the City of Vancouver Planning Department in 1987 and 1988, and this employment provided me with the opportunity to form contacts and friends who were interviewed during the Ph.D. research process. Secondly, as a community activist I attended many open houses and public hearings regarding the City of Vancouver's processing of the Pacific Place development proposals. Thirdly, employment at the UBC Centre for Human Settlements (1989–92) included a research project under contract with the City of Vancouver Planning Department related to the potential housing impacts of the Pacific Place project (see Hulchanski, 1989). At UBC I was also involved with a Canadian International Development Agency-funded project which led to the development of a collaborative research project on urban planning issues in Shanghai with the

College of Architecture and Urban Planning, Tongji University—my host department while I was in Shanghai. In short, this research project is bound up in innumerable ways, and dependent upon, my pre-Ph.D. life.

Multi-Locale Field Work

In contrast to the traditional 'developing country' geographical research that tends to be done in one locale (e.g. Forbes, 1988), or else a 'developed country' research focused on one locale or region, the vast majority of the data for this book was collected during *multi-locale* field work.

In a globalizing world, where mobility is a central feature of contemporary societies, researchers in disciplines including geography (Thrift, 1993*b*; Gregory, 1994; Murdoch, 1997; Whatmore and Thorne, 1997), sociology (M.P. Smith, 1994; Portes *et al.*, 1999), and anthropology (Appadurai, 1990*a*; Clifford, 1992; Hannerz, 1992*a*, 1996; Marcus, 1992, 1997; Gupta and Ferguson, 1997; Ong, 1999) have started to extol the virtues of multi-locale ethnographies, or multi-locale field work in general. Until recently, the vast majority of traditional 'field research' (particularly anthropological ethnographies) reflected the valuation and virtues of 'localized *dwelling*'—'mini-immigration' to an exotic site for an extended period where the 'field worker is "adopted," "learns" the culture and the language' and produces detailed objective texts full of insightful truths (Clifford, 1992: 98–9; emphasis in original; also see Gupta and Ferguson, 1997). However, anthropologists such as Akhil Gupta and George Marcus have thrown out a challenge— a challenge often written about (positively or negatively) yet rarely performed—that 'innovative forms of multi-locale ethnography [research] may be necessary to do justice to transnational political, economic, and cultural forces that traverse and constitute local or regional worlds' (Clifford, 1992: 102, drawing on Marcus and Fischer, 1986). Or, as Appadurai (1991: 191, 196; cited in Gupta and Ferguson, 1997: 3) puts it:

As groups migrate, regroup in new locations, reconstruct their histories, and reconfigure their ethnic 'projects,' the *ethno* in ethnography takes on a slippery nonlocalized quality, to which descriptive practices of anthropology will have to respond. The landscapes of group identity—the ethnoscapes—around the world are no longer familiar anthropological objects, insofar as groups are no longer tightly territorialised, spatially bounded, historically self-conscious, or culturally homogeneous. . . . The task of ethnography now becomes the unraveling of a conundrum: what is the nature of locality, as a lived experience, in a globalized, deterritorialized world?

Now the 'representational challenge is seen to be the portrayal and understanding of local/global historical encounters, co-productions, dominations, and resistances' where 'one needs to focus on hybrid, cosmopolitan experiences as much as on rooted, native ones' (Clifford, 1992: 101). It implies a shift from focus on 'spatial sites' to 'the interlocking of multiple social-political sites and locations' (Gupta and Ferguson, 1997: 37). As a point of caution, however, the point is not simply that new forms of research on 'interconnected cosmopolitanisms' may involve 'literal travel' during the research process; rather, we should also develop an ontology of mobility, hybridity, and flow when we conceptualize our research subjects and objects, in order to focus on interconnections, interdependencies, and extended social relations of an uneven nature (Clifford, 1992: 103; also see Appadurai, 1990*a*; Thrift, 1994). Field work becomes decentred, involving geographically positioned research (e.g. in Shanghai and

Vancouver), as well as research in strategic socio-political sites such as Hong Kong (source of investment flows into Vancouver and Shanghai; sources of knowledge about Chinese business conglomerates) and Paris (the cultural centre of élite architectural production in Europe).

Multi Locale Local: Global Flows and Global Cities

If global space is the space of flows and 'qualitative community research becomes literally "displaced" from the local to the global [multi-locale] scale' as M.P. Smith (1994: 20) suggests, what is global research and how do we conduct it? Janet Abu-Lughod's fascinating book *Before European Hegemony: The World System A.D. 1250–1350* provides us with some useful insights. Her study of the 'system of world trade circa 1300 A.D.' examines the extent to which the world was linked into a common commercial network of production and exchange' (1989: 13). However, as she, Allen and Hamnett (1995) and Massey (1993) all note, the world system is not global 'in the sense that all parts articulate evenly with one another, regardless of whether the role they play is central or peripheral' (Abu-Lughod, 1989: 32). Today, as in the thirteenth and fourteenth centuries, the world system is composed of distinct and overlapping subsystems linked together by uneven material and non-material flows. While each of these subsystems has its own core and hegemonic state, 'whose economy sets the terms of trade for its "satellites"', the socio-spatial formation which links the subsystems to the world system is the 'world city' (Friedmann, 1986; Friedmann and Wolff, 1982; Sassen, 1991, 1994, 1998). Abu-Lughod (1989: 32–3) is worth quoting at length on this matter:

In the thirteenth century, also, there were subsystems (defined by language, religion, empire) dominated by imperial or core cities as well as mediated by essentially hinterlandless trading enclaves. Their interactions with one another, although hardly as intense as today, defined the contours of the larger system. Instead of airlines, these cities were bound together by sea lanes, rivers, and great overland routes, some of which had been in use since antiquity. Ports and oases served the same function as air terminals, bringing goods and people together from long distances.

Given the primitive technologies of transport that existed during the earlier time, however, few world cities at opposite ends of the system did business directly with one another. The journey had to be broken geographically, with centres between flanking places serving as 'break-in-bulk' and exchange points for goods destined for more distant markets.

To analyse the world system at this time in history, composed as it was by eight inter-linked subsystems within three larger circuits, Abu-Lughod conducts empirical research on the 'archipelago' of cities (following Braudel and Haëpke). She focuses on cities as 'nodal points' in order to 'trace the connections among the highpoints of the archipelagos themselves' (1989: 13–14).

Abu-Lughod's archival analysis of the restructuring of the 13th century global space of flows is a deeply urban analysis. Her approach is certainly appropriate, reconfigured of course, for the study of the contemporary global space of flows. For, as Appadurai (1990*a*, 1990*b*), Giddens (1990), Simon (1992), M.P. Smith (1994), Hamnett (1995), and Sassen (1991, 1994, 1998) all note, the nexus of global–local relations are extended social relations which are constituted *in*, and stretched out *between*, global cities.

Given the subject matter of this book, a 'particular geography to the networks of social interaction' (Hamnett, 1995: 126) was identified by myself. The multi-locale research for this book is profoundly bound to the human and academic resources available in five different types of global cities—Hong Kong, London, Paris, Shanghai, and Vancouver. Given the contemporary nature of my topic, and adequate research funding, I was able to spend sufficient time in all these cities.

Hong Kong was identified as the hinge for both case studies, though again, the two cases are interrelated yet non-comparative. While there are similar types of flows between Hong Kong, Vancouver, and Shanghai (e.g. property development capital, property development models), these flows can be differentiated in terms of pace, form, and goal(s). This should not be unexpected, for as Allen and Hamnett (1995: 235) note, 'even if places are tied in globally, it does not follow that everywhere is moving in the same direction, along the same path of development, with the same prospects' and convergences.

The most concentrated stretch of field work for this book took place between September 1993 and May 1994 when I spent time in five Asian and Canadian cities (see Table A.1). In addition, short visits (up to one week long) to collect data in London and Paris took place both before and after this major trip. In total, over 44,000 airmiles were travelled during the seven month concentrated field research phase.

As I noted above, since 1994, follow-up research and reconceptualization has been undertaken over the last several years while working at universities in Vancouver, Bristol, and now Singapore. During this phase I have been fortunate in receiving financial and intellectual support from a range of institutions and people in all three places.

The timing of the heaviest stage of this research project was opportune in that the 1993 to 1994 field work period was marked by historically unprecedented FDI flows into China and Shanghai; flows of migrants to Shanghai reached record levels as approximately 3 million unregistered people resided in the city; Hong Kong was literally throbbing with economic and social activity as international financial services firms used the city as a base to control activities in China and the rest of the Asia-Pacific region; Hong Kong's Hang Seng index was peaking as a result of global flows of capital to the Stock Exchange of Hong Kong; Hong Kong's property markets (commercial, residential, industrial) were spiralling out of control; immigration into Canada and Vancouver from Hong Kong continued at relatively strong levels; and Vancouver's property market boom of the late 1980s and early 1990s was just beginning to level off. While these trends added an inspirational if dizzying level of excitement to the research process, they reinforced the validity of Harvey's (1989*a*) argument about the 'annihilation of space through time' through the expansion of the capitalist system, albeit one grounded in very distinct local practices ('local capitalisms') in the Asia-Pacific case (Pred and Watts, 1992; Hamilton, 1996; Smart, 1998).

Conducting Multi-Locale Research

Setting up Shop on the Road

There are a number of relevant factors which should be briefly addressed in the discussion of field work. First, hosts were arranged beforehand in each city to assist me during the research process in matters personal and academic. Arranging for a host is an absolutely critical factor in conducting efficient multi-locale field work. In my case, the

Table A.1. Multi-locale field work details

City	Dates	Main host	Research objectives
Hong Kong	22 Sept.–7 Oct. 1993	Chinese University of Hong Kong	To set up base for 1994 visit.
Shanghai	7 October–22 Nov.	Tongji University	To conduct research on the Lujiazui International Consultation Process.
Hong Kong	22–4 Nov.	Brief stop over	n/a
Manila	24 Nov.–2 Dec.	Asian Development Bank (ADB)	To conduct research in the ADB library, interview ADB staff regarding their Shanghai initiatives, and meet with Manila NGOs active in urban redevelopment struggles.
Bangkok	2 Dec. 1993–14 Jan. 1994	Chulalongkorn University	To conduct research at the Economic and Social Commission for Asia and the Pacific (ESCAP), and to have a mid-trip/Christmas break.
Vancouver	14 Jan.–28 Mar.	University of British Columbia	To conduct research on issues related to Pacific Place, on China's position in the world economy, and on Chinese property market issues.
Hong Kong	2 Apr.–1 May	Chinese University of Hong Kong	To conduct research on issues related to Hong Kong as the hinge for both case studies, on the Hong Kong financiers of Pacific Place, and on development trends in Shanghai.
Paris	24–8 Oct. 1994	n/a	To conduct research on the Lujiazui International Consultation Process, the role of the French authorities in organizing the process, and on La Défense.

most common hosts were university departments of either geography, architecture, or urban planning disciplines. These arrangements were made quickly and with appropriate people and institutions through my past association with the UBC Centre for Human Settlements (CHS). To formalize and reciprocate, I restarted an official relationship with CHS and became an 'Affiliated Researcher', complete with business card. In return for a variety of assistance (opening doors; 'in kind' contributions such as office space; a small contribution towards expenses) I offered to contribute to their research project in the form of written work. CHS was coordinating a multi-year collaborative research project on urbanization issues with three universities in China (including Tongji University in Shanghai), one in Thailand (Chulalongkorn University), and one in Indonesia. This project was funded by the Canadian International Development Agency (CIDA) through a national 'International Centre of Excellence' programme. The formation of my temporary links with these partner universities, with the Chinese University of Hong Kong, and with the Asian Development Bank, were all facilitated by Professor Aprodicio Laquian, Director of CHS. Dr Laquian is a master of networking, and he has a long association with senior people working for academic and multilateral institutions in the Pacific Rim. Other contacts in Shanghai were generously facilitated by Dr Richard Kirkby of the University of Liverpool, a well-connected China urbanization expert (see Kirkby, 1985).

The pragmatic difficulties of conducting multi-locale research in these cities was eased by previous travel experience (for extended periods) in Hong Kong, Manila, and Bangkok. Research in Shanghai was also facilitated by my hosts, the College of Architecture and Planning, Tongji University, and the Parisian organizers of the Lujiazui International Consultation process. The College of Architecture and Planning is China's oldest and most respected university department of this type, and their graduates are senior officials of the Pudong New Area Administration and the Shanghai Municipal Government. Benefits from my association with Tongji included access to knowledgeable and friendly staff and students, an excellent translator when required, affordable housing, administrative support, and assistance in connecting with their relevant former graduates. A whole host of reciprocal offerings were made while I was in Shanghai such as offering assistance to staff and students wishing to apply to North American universities, and commenting on their research projects. In terms of language—my lack of Putonghua skills certainly changed the nature of my research, but most of the key officials I needed to interview spoke clear English. English was also the main language used for the planning exercises for the Lujiazui Central Finance District and all documentation was prepared in English and Chinese.

Research in Vancouver, my former (long-term) home, was relatively simple in comparison to Shanghai. In fact, living away from Vancouver in Bristol and Singapore brings (I think) a beneficial degree of perceived 'distance' to my research project. The friendly reception I received from various research subjects in Vancouver would have been less welcoming if I had been based at UBC, since I would likely have been viewed as a biased participant in debates over this controversial development project. Realizing this early in the research process enabled me to accentuate my Bristol or Singapore base in Vancouver through verbal references and the use of business cards.

The time spent living and travelling in England and Asia also left me feeling different about development issues in Vancouver. The city never quite felt like home and I experienced 'a feeling of detachment, perhaps irritation with those committed to the local common sense and unaware of its arbitrariness' (see Hannerz (1990: 248) on feelings that are linked to long-term residence away from 'home'). From a research perspective I feel this new perspective helped me better identify and understand development issues in Vancouver.

Accessing Information

The ability to establish and manoeuvre through tight and loose social networks in multi-locale field work is an important skill; a skill dependent upon the formation of trusting relationships with diverse people. Trust enables relevant information to flow across space quickly in a disembedded (non-local context): trust also enables the analyst to conduct research on sensitive issues by acquiring data which are not present in any written form (be it published or unpublished), and to create what I would term a *trust cascade*—a widening and deepening network of people who are willing and able to supply you with relevant contacts and information. The term cascade is meant to evoke the feeling of increasing speed, as one contact leads to another to another to another, and many contacts begin to offer to open doors for you during the research process. The main methods used to build trust *and* interest in my research project include:

- the use of respected contacts to open doors;
- the ability to maintain a contact's reputation, and my willingness to save their 'face';
- the ability to reciprocate in the short and long term;
- the ability to present myself in a 'professional' confident manner, appropriate to their standards, through the use of clothing, voice, body language, business cards, letterhead, and common sense of timeliness;
- the use of an academic base which effectively enabled me to ask questions which no other distanced person could ever ask;
- the formation of associations with a variety of 'respected' educational institutions (University of Bristol, University of British Columbia, National University of Singapore, and my host institution in each temporary base);
- the ability to create and emphasize a 'cosmopolitan' nature through the use of business cards from several countries, discussion of flights and travel, and knowledge of appropriate issues in a variety of countries;
- the ability to highlight 'code words' which emphasize my understanding of specific issues few others (apart from myself and my interviewee) understand;
- the ability to identify a somewhat controversial subject which is sufficiently contested that my contacts seek to express 'their side of the story', but not so controversial that they do not want to discuss the issue;
- the ability to recognize and reject the use of academic jargon;
- the reputation of my funding agencies;
- the ability to convince contacts that I will produce publications for international distribution in which their names and reputations will be discussed.

Research Methods and Data Sources

The narrative that this book is composed of is primarily based upon qualitative data, supplemented by some quantitative data which addresses the background macroeconomic context. Qualitative data is the main form of data which can be used to highlight the social processes and extended social relations which underlie globalization processes. Qualitative data, provided it is extracted from a multiple of relevant and well-placed sources, is incredibly rich in detail, and it enables the analyst to engage in deeper levels of abstraction (Sayer, 1992).

Research methods consisted of literature searches, company searches, formal open-ended interviews, informal interviews, gossip, and drawing from pre-Ph.D. participant observation in Vancouver (see above on this last point). The main sources of qualitative data during all stages of the research programme are noted below:

- Formal open-ended interviews with sixty-eight people in the six cities noted above from 1993–5, and fourteen people from 1996–8. The vast majority of the interviews were conducted in person, and the interviewees included senior representatives of the transnational cultures active in Vancouver and Shanghai; the French organizers of the LICP; senior, mid-level, and junior government officials in both cities; municipal politicians in Vancouver; and an assortment of lawyers, bankers, journalists, academics, chartered surveyors, and community representatives.

- Informal 'off the record' open-ended personal interviews with knowledgeable participants in the development processes, and general observers of both the development processes and the global actors. Several of these people wished to remain anonymous because of fears that their reputations would be tarnished (in the Vancouver case), or that they would face political persecution (in the Shanghai case).

- Observation, gossip, and casual 'chit-chat' in person and over the telephone with knowledgeable participants in the development processes, and general observers of both the development processes and the global actors. Some of this data was acquired at events such as the International Urban Development Association INTA 17—New Town Experience Joint Conference and the World Property Market Exhibition held in Hong Kong (26–30 Sept. 1993). I was able to attend this extremely expensive event by offering to write a review of the conference and exhibition (see Olds, 1994) for the event organizers.

- Written correspondence with developers, architects, international organizations, and government officials involved with the planning and development of UMPs throughout the world. Over 450 letters were written to directly and indirectly acquire relevant data.

- Secondary materials including academic articles and books, unpublished security and financial services company reports, official company reports, brochures, analyses of the listed firms active in Vancouver, unpublished confidential reports from multilateral agencies. With respect to the *Vancouver* case study, the City of Vancouver Planning Department provided me with all relevant reports and documentation on the Pacific Place planning process; Concord Pacific Developments Ltd. provided me with many of their brochures and background materials; the Pacific Place Design Consortium provided me with volumes of planning and design material on the project; and the government of British Columbia and the government of Canada supplied me with published and unpublished data. With respect to the *Shanghai* case study, the French organizers of the international consultation process supplied me with all of the background and evaluation reports written on the process, and with all of the conceptual plans prepared by the architectural firms; academic and non-academic contacts in Shanghai and Hong Kong contacts supplied me with important documentation on the LICP, and on urban development trends in Shanghai; and international financial firms and chartered surveyors in Hong Kong and Shanghai provided me with company research reports on relevant issues in Hong Kong, Shanghai, and the broader Asia-Pacific region.

A wide variety of methods was used in order to 'triangulate' the research findings given that there are weaknesses in each method, however rigorously applied (Babbie, 1979: 110). Or, as Schoenberger (1992: 217) highlights, 'different methods tend to miss different things and that is why access to a range of research strategies is useful'. The emphasis on different methods changed depending on which locale I was working in, and as my knowledge of issues increased over time.

The most significant method overall is the personal interview. As noted above, I formally interviewed sixty-eight people in six cities from 1993 to 1995 and fourteen people from 1996 to 1998. In addition, I have a 'resource person' list of approximately sixty people who informally assisted me during various stages of the research process. The majority of these contacts were male, the majority of interviewees were white-collar professionals. Many of the dynamics associated with interviewing élites, as discussed in Cassell (1988), Schoenberger (1991, 1992), McDowell (1992, 1998), Herod (1993, 1999), Ostrander (1993), Markusen (1994), Thomas (1993), Woods (1998), and Ward and Jones (1999), were confronted. These included gaining access, the process of interviewing (these are 'people accustomed to being in control and exerting authority over others' (Schoenberger, 1991: 182)), power relations between myself and the interviewee (i.e. my low status in their eyes), and the uneven quality (reliability) of the interview data.

I addressed the issue of interview data reliability through three main techniques. First, I spoke to as many relevant people as possible who had different insights on the same topic. As the number of interviews increased, certain patterns started to appear in the responses. These patterns enable the interviewer to discern when the response of some interviewees is 'suspect' or incomplete. Secondly, in occasional cases where I was uneasy about data reliability, I used existing relationships with relevant people who would 'decode' the responses of my interviewees. My decoders would identify the discrepancies in the responses of the interviewees, as well as the likely rationale for these discrepancies. Thirdly, I relied most heavily upon the responses of interviewees I knew before (and trusted), or interviewees who were favourably judged by people I knew and trusted.

The issue of access was generally resolved through the production of trust (as noted above) and through the use of social networks to open doors for me. In the rare cases when I was unable to have someone provide an introduction, I used two alternative techniques: (1) identifying an appropriate name through newspaper coverage of the issue, and contacting them directly; and (2) visits, telephone calls, and faxes to relevant institutions to identify the 'most relevant person to discuss the following issue'. Given time constraints I often simply identified the appropriate person to contact during field work and wrote to them upon returning to my base city. Pure luck also played a role during the research process as the occasionally chance meeting with well-placed individuals at bars and condominium barbecues in Hong Kong provided me with excellent data on the Hong Kong financiers of Pacific Place.

In every case, the importance of my research project to these busy actors was reinforced by accentuating its pure academic ('100 per cent educational') nature, the relevance of its findings for policy-makers dealing with these unique urban redevelopment projects, the fact that I was going to publish my findings, and the mention of interviews with other people (knowing that they would then be interested in getting across their points).

My access to these people, and the dynamics of the subsequent interviews, was affected positively in virtually all cases by my middle-class white Canadian status, by my ability to build trust and interest in the research project (as outlined above), and by my gender. Property development at the international level is an enormously masculine venture as noted by Fainstein (1994: 4): one only needs to skim popular press coverage of property developers such as Donald Trump, George Soros, or the Reichmanns to recognize this. Interviews with developers and other contacts associated with finance or property in this research project were punctuated by aggressive banter, and 'tall stories' (see Herod, 1993: 308), and I learned to accentuate certain personal characteristics to encourage such expressions (expressions less likely to be unveiled, in my opinion, in the presence of female researchers given the Asian context). Story-telling is a sign of relaxation and trust on the part of the interviewee and when I encouraged such forms of personal expression, relevant information was released. In short, gender relations simply contoured the dynamics of the interviews differently, and they underlie the quality and form of data I collected throughout application of the personal interview method.

To summarize, the multi-locale research for this dissertation involved a variety of methods. However, the key factor underlying the acquisition of insightful data was the ability to identify and then insert myself into evolving networks of power, and using what 'social capital' and 'cultural capital' I possess or could accrue during the course of the research process. Unless the researcher becomes entangled within these networks, critical social relations—the nexus of the global–local dialectic—will remain out of reach from academic discourses on the global.

Telling Stories: Narratives of a Decentred and Partial Nature

Even with a complex research strategy, a broad informational base, and a focus on the *global*, the analysis presented in this book is partial, and it represents one decentred perspective on the nature of globalization processes and urban change today. For too long social scientists have claimed to 'see all'; a claim bound up with, in Gillian Rose's (1993: 70–1) view, the assumption of a 'vantage point far removed from the embodied social world, and this transcendent, distanced gaze reinforces the dominant Western masculine subjectivity in all its fear of embodied attachment and in all its universal pretensions'. As Gregory (1994: 9) points out, it is impossible to claim a stable vantage point, since perspectives are formed in a world 'in which the observers and the observed are in ceaseless, fluid and interactive motion'.

This book is my construction of a deeply perspectival analysis of the global space of flows as they relate to the production of urban space on the Pacific Rim in the late twentieth century. Provided the reader is aware of the author's subject position, and that this account, like *all* accounts, is value-impregnated (Duncan and Ley, 1993; Ley, 1993*a*), these partial perspectives, these incisions into our continually evolving world-system, can shed some light on why our cities are developing the way they are. In short, there is no 'final vocabulary' (Thrift and Olds, 1996).

Given the above points, an explicit writing style has been adopted in this book. In general, narrative style (and first person form where appropriate) is used throughout the book. The research process outlined above, and the various forms of data I collected over the years, have been constructed by me into this text. In contrast to the 'logo-scientific' mode of knowing and presenting, I have chosen to acknowledge the abundant presence of narratives and have them inform my analysis rather than 'picking them up when nobody was looking in order to take them home and beat them into scientific shape' (Czarniawska-Joerges, 1995: 14; also see Czarniawska, 1997, 1998). Interestingly, the vast majority of the interview data took the form of short stories in the form of narratives—their answers expressed a 'narrative form of knowing' (Czarniawska-Joerges, 1995: 13).

The rationale for this style of presentation is based upon a conceptualization of research as a complex and messy process infused with personal subjectivities, practical constraints, and opportunities; a process unable to claim the title of 'objective'. More specifically, I am first seeking to position myself as a researcher and writer by rejecting the distanced and transcendent approach to many studies of globalization; and secondly, I am attempting to highlight the many dilemmas and quandaries that emerge when attempting to conduct multi-locale empirical research on global processes.

The narrative style has increasingly been adopted in the era of more reflexive modes of knowing and presentation. It is also very common in the case study form of research where field work is involved. The narrative form 'relies on sequentiality to determine plot and its power as a story. In other words, the temporal ordering of events suggests some causality . . . whose plausibility will be judged by the recipients of the story' (Czarniawska-Joerges, 1995: 12). While chronology is used as the main organizing device, narratives are also characterized by a 'recognizable repertoire of plots, unpredictability (suspense) and a moral point', where 'action—accounted for in terms of intentions, deeds and consequences—is commonly given central place', and where 'explanation and interpretation not only sit side by side, they are often . . . confused'. Finally, 'action' can be associated with both humans and non-humans (e.g. a master plan; an architectural monograph) leading some (e.g. Bruno Latour) to favour the term 'actant' (Czarniawska-Joerges, 1995: 15–16; Murdoch, 1995, 1997). In effect, the researcher takes part in a complex and iterative *ordering* process as he or she becomes more knowledgeable about the research topic and subsequently when the research findings are constructed into a text.

In the urban context, for example, Budd (1992) adopts the narrative form. He constructs a 'narrative' regarding the City of London in order to highlight the 'particular material circumstances' which 'have given rise to distinctive forms of urban development, social practice and behavior'—in other words, 'each urban community has its own story to tell' even though cities are being impacted by broader (global) imperatives (ibid. 261–2). The 'urban narrative' approach is similar to the spatial narrative approach of Harvey (1985) in his analysis of the building of the Basilica of Sacré-Coeur in Paris.

In the institutional context, John Law (1994) has provided insightful analysis of both his substantive object of study, and of the narrative form. In *Organizing Modernity*, he addresses the process of organizing and ordering our 'complex', messy, and heterogeneous social world'—the 'plural processes of socio-technical ordering' through the performance of the 'social' (talk, bodies, texts, machines, architectures, and so on). While Law's research examines the management and organization of a scientific laboratory, his approach offers useful insights in terms of the conceptualization of the research process and the presentation of research findings. Law (1994: 2) recognizes that researchers and writers are 'caught up in ordering too':

When we write about ordering [the development of an UMP] there is no question of standing apart and observing from a distance. We're participating in ordering too. We're unavoidably involved in the modern reflexive project of monitoring, sensemaking and control. But since we participate in this project, we're also, and necessarily, caught up in its uncertainty, its incompleteness, its plurality, a sense of fragmentation.

He attempts to face this issue by weaving together four stories including an organizational ethnography of ordering in the laboratory, an analysis of the process of ordering through the application of theory, a story about the political context, and a story about the process of ethnography and writing (1994: 3–4).

Law's four-layered approach is written in narrative form, to 'tell tales', an approach which, in his mind, enables him to convey the 'complex and messy' social world which academics study and which our subjects work in (1994: 5); he also emphasizes the importance of attempting to tell 'sufficiently modest' stories about our ordering to avoid the creation of yet another form of 'hegemonic monotheism' (1994: 8). Stories enable us to develop symmetrical and non-reductionist approaches to analysis where *everything* deserves explanation, and to reject approaches that privilege and render invisible certain classes of phenomena (1994: 9–12). Law uses the example of the distinction between micro-social and macro-social phenomena which some theories prioritize over the other. Instead, adopting the principles of symmetry and non-reductionism leads the researcher to focus on the questions of 'how the macro-social *got* to be the macro-social' and to focus on 'size as a product or an effect, rather than something given in the nature of things' (ibid.). This is a relational approach where 'there are no privileged places, no dualisms' (e.g. the post-Fordist city), 'no a priori reductions'; we now conceive of 'conditional and uncertain processes, not something that is achieved for ever' (1994: 11–13; also see Boden, 1994; Thrift, 1996, 1999*b*).

Law suggests that we can locate a more modest form of analysis and focus on *process* by the telling of 'stories'. However, he is not suggesting an approach which wallows in undifferentiated 'thick description' uncoupled from an examination of theory, the narrative form critiqued by Sayer (1992: 258–66). Rather, these stories should attempt to 'suggest that some effects are generated in a more rather than less stable manner', and to 'explore how it is that divisions that look like dualisms come to look that way'. Yet, while the stories inevitably discuss contingent matters (case studies), 'there are patterns in that contingency', and the stories offer clues to patterns, ranking and causality (preferably in a 'non-dogmatic manner') (Law, 1994: 14, 19). These stories can be applied to powerful transnational cultures, the élite actors shaping the networks guiding global flows. However, these 'captains of industry', and their 'organizations',—will be seen as 'more or less precarious recursive outcomes' and 'we will burrow into them, taking them apart, seeing how they were achieved, and exploring their hurts that were done along the way' (ibid. 15). By recursion he means (following Anthony Giddens) the social actors are participants in self-generating processes—they are mediums and outcomes of socio-technical processes.

To summarize then, this book is *my* narrative about the production of global flows associated with the development of UMPs in Vancouver and Shanghai in the late twentieth century. I am attempting to create an analysis which does justice to the complexity of the processes that structure the nature of these global flows, though I explicitly recognize that I can only offer one decentred and partial analysis of these processes. However, by conducting multi-locale field work, and by using a myriad of techniques to insert myself into the stretched out and tangled social relations that guide global flows across space, I believe that this partial perspective cuts into the core issues.

APPENDIX B:
LIST OF RESOURCE
PERSONS AND INSTITUTIONS

The research that this book is based upon was primarily conducted between October 1992 and September 1995, with follow up research conducted between January 1996 hierarchically categorized and November 1999. A wide variety of people and institutions have assisted me, either through formal interviews, semi-formal interviews, casual gossip, correspondence, or through the supply of resources and contacts. All of this assistance is of equal importance. For this reason, I have not hierarchically categorized the people I formally interviewed in this appendix (as is common in many social science research projects).

Please note that I have not included the names of people who specifically asked to remain anonymous. Moreover, the opinions expressed in this book are mine alone, and none of the following resource people or institutions should be held responsible for what I write.

The Vancouver Case Study
BC Tel
Bob Chambers; Fares Salloum.

Cheung Kong (Holdings) Ltd.
George Magnus.

The City of Vancouver
John Atkin; Jonathon Barrett; Larry Beasley; Coralys Cuthbert; Jill Davidson; Michel Desrochers; Ken Dobell; Nathan Edelson; Tom Fletcher; Michael Gordon; Cameron Gray; Ronda Howard; Richard Johnson; Gordon Price; Ian Smith; Pat Wotherspoon.

Concord Pacific Developments Ltd.
Blair Hagkull; Terry Hui; Jon Markoulis; Stanley Kwok.

Hong Kong Bank of Canada
David Bond; Martin Glynn.

Pacific Place Design Consortium
Barry Downs; Rick Hulbert; Graham McGarva.

Miscellaneous Institutions
Asia-Pacific Foundation of Canada; British Columbia Assessment Authority; BC Trade; BC Stats; Canada and Hong Kong Project (York University); Canadian High Commission in Hong Kong; Citizenship and Immigration Canada; Cathay Pacific

Airways; CEF Holdings Limited; Colliers Jardine; Pacific Place Remediation Project; Province of British Columbia.

Miscellaneous People

Michael Beazley; Nick Blomley; Rick Carlton; Tung Chan; Nellie Cheng; Maurice Copithorne; Don DeVoretz; Andrea Eng; Matt Farish; Michael Goldberg; John Gray; Jim Green; Gary Hamilton; Dan Hiebert; Frank Ip; Roslyn Kunin; David Ley; Peter Maddocks; Kevin Murphy; Alan Nymark; Gordon Redding; Marino Piombini; Ronald Skeldon; Ray Spaxman; Judy Tutchener; Brian Woolley.

The Shanghai Case Study

Asian Development Bank

J. Warren Evans; Bong Koo Lee; Bruce Murray; Richard Ondrik; Ernesto Pernia; Min Tang.

Hong Kong- and China-Based Architects and Chartered Surveyors

Nicholas Brooke; Sam Crispin; Alan Dalgleish; Tony Darwell; Tao Ho; C.Y. Leung; Simon Lim.

Jiaotong University

Lu Qiang; Jin Wei.

Shanghai Lujiazui International Planning and Urban Design Consultation Process Participants

Laurie Abbott; Gilles Antier; Giovanni Bellavati; Joseph Belmont; Jacques Guaran; Philip Gumuchdjian; Huang Fuxiang; Huang Ji Ming; Luxia Xiong; Rémi Masson; Kazutoshi Morita; Ove Arup Partnership; Alan Penn; Wang Rong-ding.

Shanghai Municipal Government

Li Jianeng; Xia Zhongguang; Zhu Wen Jing.

Tongji University

Cui Hongbin; Lancelot Lake; Li Dehua; Peng Zhenwei; Wang Bo Wei; Yang Guiqing; Zhao Min; Zheng Shiling.

World Bank

Scott Guggenheim; Tova Solo; Lee Travers.

Miscellaneous Institutions

The Ecologist magazine; HongkongBank China Services Ltd.

Miscellaneous Institutions in Shanghai

American Consulate; British Council; Lujiazui Finance and Trade Zone Development Corporation; Pudong New Area Administration; Shanghai Centre; Shanghai Securities Exchange; Shanghai Foreign Investment Commission; Shanghai Urban Planning and Design Institute.

Miscellaneous People

Terry Cannon; Stephen Kidd; Dingfa Zhang; Richard Graham; Sandy Hirshen; Kerrie MacPherson; Reg McLemore; Martin Pawley; Deyan Sudjic; Jack Williams; Jianming Xu; Zhang Huijun.

Miscellaneous Assistance

Financial Institutions

Baring Securities; Daewoo Securities; Goldman Sachs; Hang Seng Bank; Hongkong Bank; ING Barings; Jardine Fleming; Kleinwort Benson; KPMG Peat Marwick; Morgan Grenfell; Morgan Stanley; Nippon Credit Bank; Nomura; Nomura Research Institute; Salomon Brothers; Towa Securities; UBS Securities.

Miscellaneous Institutions

Asian Coalition for Housing Rights; Economic and Social Commission for Asia and the Pacific; Government of Hong Kong; Hong Kong Monetary Authority; Hong Kong Trade Development Council; Japan Local Government Centre; Kings Cross Railway Lands Group; Kop van Zuid; Kuala Lumpur City Centre; Nation Fender Architects, Bankok; Nomura City Development Wien Ges.m.b.H; Royal Institute of British Architects; Royal Institute of Chartered Surveyors; Stock Exchange of Hong Kong; Suntec City; United Nations Centre for Regional Development; UNDP (Beijing).

Miscellaneous People

John Allen; Joe Berridge; Roger Borromeo; Graeme Bristol; Tim Bunnell; Neil Coe; Denis Cosgrove; Maurice Daly; Michael Douglass; David Edgington; Michael Edwards; Paul Goodwin; C. Michael Hall; Peter Hall; Rob Harris; Ilse Helbrecht; You-tien Hsing; David Hulchanski; Thomas Hutton; Margo Huxley; Michael Keith; Philip Kelly; Peter Kershaw; Sakchai Kirinpanu; Richard Kirkby; Lily Kong; Aprodicio Laquian; Michael Leaf; Scott Leckie; Christopher Leo; Colin Lizieri; Patrick Loftman; Lui Siu Yun; Richard Marshall; Doreen Massey; Terry McGee; Andy Merrifield; David Meyer; Katharyne Mitchell; Nick Oatley; Daj Oberg; Phillip O'Neill; Steve Pile; Peter Rimmer; Victor Savage; David Simon; Alan Smart; Josephine Smart; Teo Siew Eng; Nipan Vichiennoi; Brahm Wiesman; Brenda Yeoh; Henry Wai-chung Yeung; Yue-man Yeung; Karen Zeller; Elizabeth Zook.

REFERENCES

ABU-LUGHOD, J. (1989) *Before European Hegemony: The World System A.D. 1250–1350*, Oxford: Oxford University Press.
——(1991) 'Going beyond global babble', in King (1991): 131–8.
AGREST, D., CONWAY, P., and WEISMAN, L. K. (eds) (1996) *The Sex of Architecture*, New York: Harry N. Abrams.
AHMED, M., and GOOPTU, S. (1993) 'Portfolio investment flows to developing countries', *Finance and Development*, Mar.: 9–15.
AHRENTZEN, S., and ANTHONY, K. (1993) 'Sex, stars, and studios: a look at gendered educational practices in architecture', *Journal of Architectural Education*, 27(1): 11–29.
AKYÜZ, Y. (1993) 'Financial liberalization: the key issues', *UNCTAD Discussion Paper*, No. 56, Mar (available from United Nations Sales Section, Palais des Nations, 1211 Geneva 10, Switzerland).
ALEXANDER, J. (1994) 'HK top 10 urged to expand their horizons', *Eastern Express*, 5 Apr.: 21.
ALLEN, J. (1995a) 'Global worlds', in J. Allen and D. Massey (eds), *Geographical Worlds*, Oxford: Open University and Oxford University Press, 105–42.
——(1995b) 'Crossing borders: footloose multinationals', in Allen and Hamnett (1995): 55–102.
——and HAMNETT, C. (eds) (1995) *A Shrinking World?* Oxford: Open University and Oxford University Press.
——MASSEY, D., and PRYKE, M. (eds) (1999) *Unsettling Cities: Movement/Settlement*, London: Routledge.
AMIN, A. (1999) 'An institutionalist perspective on regional economic development', *International Journal of Urban and Regional Research*, 23(2): 365–78.
——and HAUSNER, J. (eds) (1997) *Beyond Market and Hierarchy: Interactive Governance and Social Complexity*, Cheltenham: Edward Elgar.
——and THRIFT, N. (1992) 'Neo-Marshallian nodes in global networks', *International Journal of Urban and Regional Research*, 16(4): 571–87.
————(eds) (1994) *Globalization, Institutions, and Regional Development in Europe*, Oxford: Oxford University Press.
————(1995a) 'Institutional issues for European regions: from markets and plans to socioeconomics and powers of association', *Economy and Society*, 24(1): 41–66.
————(1995b) 'Globalisation, institutional "thickness" and the local economy', in P. Healey, S. Cameron, S. Davoudi, S. Graham, and A. Madani-Pour (eds), *Managing Cities: The New Urban Context*, Chichester: John Wiley & Sons, 91–108.
AMSDEN, A. (1989) *Asia's Next Giant: South Korea and Late Industrialization*, Oxford: Oxford University Press.
'An "inside" Asian investor's view of Canada', *Invest Canada*, Nov.: 8–9.
ANDERSON, B. (1983) *Imagined Communities: Reflections on the Origin and Spread of Nationalism*, London: Verso.
ANDERSON, K. (1988) 'Cultural hegemony and the race-definition process in Chinatown, Vancouver: 1880–1980', *Environment and Planning D: Society and Space*, 6(2): 127–49.

——(1991) *Vancouver's Chinatown: Racial Discourse in Canada, 1875–1980*, Montreal and Kingston: McGill-Queen's University Press.

ANDERSON, R., and WACHTEL, E. (eds) (1986) *The Expo Story*, Madeira Park, BC: Harbour Publishing.

ANG, I. (1994) 'On not speaking Chinese: postmodern ethnicity and the politics of diaspora', *New Formations*, 24: 1–18.

——and STRATTON, J. (1996) 'Asianising Australia: notes towards a critical transnationalism in cultural studies', *Cultural Studies*, 10(1): 16–36.

APPADURAI, A. (1990*a*) 'Disjuncture and difference in the global cultural economy', *Public Culture*, 2(2): 1–24.

——(1990*b*) 'Disjuncture and difference in the global cultural economy', *Theory, Culture and Society*, 7: 295–310.

——(1991) 'Global ethnoscapes: notes and queries for a transnational anthropology', in R. Fox (ed.), *Recapturing Anthropology: Working in the Present*, Santa Fe, N. Mex.: School of American Research Press, 191–210.

——(1996) *Modernity at Large: Cultural Dimensions of Globalization*, London: University of Minnesota Press.

APPELBAUM, R., and HENDERSON, J. (eds) (1992) *States and Development in the Asian Pacific Rim*, London: Sage.

APPLEYARD, B. (1986) *Richard Rogers: A Biography*, London: Thames and Hudson.

Architectural Review (1993) 192(1151), Jan.

ARMSTRONG, W., and McGEE, T. G. (1985) *Theatres of Accumulation: Studies in Asian and Latin American Urbanization*, New York: Methuen.

ARNOLD, W. (1992) 'Japan and the development of Shanghai's Pudong area', *The Pacific Review*, 5(3): 241–9.

ASH, R., and QI, L. (1998) 'Economic development', in Hook (1998): 147–80.

Asian Development Bank (1993) 'Pudong: a dragon's head pulling the body', *ADB Quarterly Review*, Jan.: 4–5.

ATASH, F., and WANG, X. (1990) 'Satellite town development in Shanghai, China: an overview', *The Journal of Architectural and Planning Research*, 7(3): 245–57.

AUGÉ, M. (1995) *Non-Places: Introduction to an Anthropology of Supermodernity*, London: Verso.

BABBIE, E. (1979) *The Practice of Social Research*, Belmont, Calif.: Wadsworth.

BADCOCK, B. (1984) *Unfairly Structured Cities*, Oxford: Basil Blackwell.

BADEN-POWELL, F. (1993) *Building Overseas*, Oxford: Butterworth Architecture.

BAKER, A. (1997) 'Asia/Pacific region heads world construction growth', *AIArchitect*, Feb.: 4.

BALFOUR, A. (1993) 'Land Rush in Berlin', *Blueprint*, Apr.: 26–9.

Bank for International Settlements (1992) *62nd Annual Report*, Basle: BIS.

——(1995) *65th Annual Report*, Basle: BIS.

——(1996) *66th Annual Report*, Basle: BIS.

——(1997) *67th Annual Report*, Basle: BIS.

——(1998) *68th Annual Report*, Basle: BIS.

Baring Securities (1995*a*) *Macro Monitor: Asian Regional Research, May–June 1995*, Hong Kong: Baring Securities.

——(1995*b*) *Stock Market Review: End of the Tunnel?* Hong Kong: Baring Securities.

——(1995*c*) *Stock Market Review: Interest Rates: The Spark*, Hong Kong: Baring Securities.

BARNA, J. W. (1992) *The See-Through Years: Creation and Destruction in Texas Architecture and Real Estate 1981–1991*, Houston: Rice University Press.

BARNES, T., EDGINGTON, D., DENIKE, K., and McGEE, T. G. (1992) 'Vancouver, the province and the Pacific Rim', in Wynn and Oke (1992): 171–99.

——and HAYTER, R. (1992) '"The little town that did": flexible accumulation and community response in Chemainus, British Columbia', *Regional Studies*, 26(7): 647–63.

BAUM, A., and SCHOFIELD, A. (1991) 'Property as a global asset', Working Papers in European Property, Centre for European Property Research, University of Reading, Mar.

BC Stats (1997), Special Feature: Immigration from APEC Members <http://www.bcstats.gov.bc.ca/-DATA/POP/mig/imm972sf.pdf>, accessed 18 Nov. 1999.

——(1999) Feature Article: B.C. Migration—Outlook for 1999, April, <http://www.bcstats.gov.bc.ca/DATA/POP/mig/mig984fa.pdf>, accessed 18 Nov. 1999.

BEAUREGARD, R. (1995) 'Theorizing the global-local connection', in P. Knox and P. Taylor (eds), *World Cities in a World System*, Cambridge: Cambridge University Press, 232–48.

——and HAILA, A. (1997) 'The unavoidable incompleteness of the city', *American Behavioral Scientist*, 41(3): 327–41.

BEAZLEY, M. (1994) 'Public participation in urban mega-project planning: a case study of Pacific Place, Vancouver B.C.', unpublished Ph.D. dissertation, School of Community and Regional Planning, University of British Columbia, Vancouver.

BECK, U., GIDDENS, A., and LASH, S. (1994) *Reflexive Modernization: Politics, Tradition and Aesthetics in the Modern Social Order*, Cambridge: Polity.

BEERS, D. (1994) 'We're no angels', *Vancouver*, Apr.: 41–50.

BENNETT, W. (1980) 'Speaking notes for Premier Bennett', Four Seasons Hotel, Vancouver, 29 Jan.

BERGER, M., and BORER, D. (eds) (1997) *The Rise of East Asia: Critical Visions of the Pacific Century*, London: Routledge.

BERGER, P., and LUCKMANN, T. (1966) *The Social Construction of Reality: A Treatise in the Sociology of Knowledge*, Garden City, NY: Doubleday.

BERMAN, M. (1982) *All that is Solid Melts into Air: The Experience of Modernity*, New York: Simon and Schuster.

BERRY, M. (1994) 'Japanese property development in Australia', *Progress in Planning*, 41(2): 113–201.

——and HUXLEY, M. (1992) 'Big build: property capital, the state and urban change in Australia', *International Journal of Urban and Regional Research*, 16(1): 35–59.

BESHER, A. (1993) 'British-designed, futuristic minicity on Shanghai's investment menu', *Orange County Register*, 24 Jan.: 109.

BIERSTEKER, THOMAS (1995) 'The "triumph" of liberal economic ideas in the developing world', in Barbara Stallings (ed.), *Global Change, Regional Response: The New International Context of Development*, Cambridge: Cambridge University Press, 174–96.

BINGHAM, N. (1996) 'Object-ions: from technological determinism towards geographies of relations', *Environment and Planning D: Society and Space*, 14: 635–57.

BIRD, J., CURTIS, B., PUTNAM, T., ROBERTSON, G., and TICKNER, L. (eds) (1993) *Mapping the Futures: Local Cultures, Global Change*, London: Routledge.

BLAIN, J. (1990) 'Expo cleanup best estimate, McCarthy says', *Vancouver Sun*, 12 Jan., p. A12.

BLOCK, F. (1990) *Postindustrial Possibilities: A Critique of Economic Discourse*, Berkeley: University of California Press.

BLOMLEY, N. (1998) 'Landscapes of property', *Law & Society Review*, 32(3): 567–612.

BODEN, D. (1994) *The Business of Talk: Organizations in Action*, Cambridge: Polity.

BONNETT, A. (1996) 'Constructions of race, place and discipline: geographies of racial identity and racism', *Ethnic and Racial Studies*, 19: 864–83.

BOREHAM, G. (1993) 'Revisiting China's banking reforms', *Canadian Banker*, 100(1): 26–9.

BOWLES, P., and DONG, X. Y. (1994) 'Current successes and future challenges in China's economic reforms', *New Left Review*, 208: 49–76.

BOYLE, M., FYFE, N., and MCNEILL, D. (1999) 'From critic to practitioner: an interview with Deyan Sudjic', *Environment and Planning A*, 31: 951–8.

BRADBURY, N. (1993) 'Playing lean and mean in Canada', *Euromoney*, Nov.: 92–4.

British Columbia Place and the City of Vancouver (1982) 'B.C. Place issues paper', 16 June.

Brooke Hillier Parker (1995) *Lujiazui Finance and Trade Zone: Economic and Demographic Report*, Hong Kong: BHP.

BROWNILL, S. (1990) *Developing London's Docklands: Another Great Planning Disaster?* London: Paul Chapman Publishing Ltd.

BUDD, L. (1992) 'An urban narrative and the imperatives of the City', in Budd and Whimster (1992): 260–81.

——and WHIMSTER, S. (eds) (1992) *Global Finance and Urban Living: A Study of Metropolitan Change*, Andover, Hants: Routledge, Chapman and Hall.

BUELL, F. (1994) *National Culture and the New Global System*, Baltimore: Johns Hopkins University Press.

BUNNELL, T. (1999) 'Revisioning Malaysia: landscape, national identity and the Petronas Twin Towers', *Singapore Journal of Tropical Geography*, 20(1): 1–23.

BURDETT, R. (ed.) (1996) *Richard Rogers Partnership: Works and Projects*, New York: The Monacelli Press.

BURKINSHAW, R. (1984) 'False Creek: history, images and research sources', Occasional Paper No. 2, City of Vancouver Archives.

BURNINGHAM, K., and COOPER, G. (1999) 'Being constructive: social constructionism and the environment', *Sociology*, 33(2): 297–316.

BUSINESS IMMIGRATION BRANCH, PROVINCE OF BRITISH COLUMBIA (1993) 'Program statistics, 1993', mimeo.

CAHILL, K., KIRWIN, P., and SIEGLE, E. (1993) 'Tory money: the unexplained millions that elected three governments', *Business Age*, May: 40–8.

CANNON, T., and JENKINS, A. (eds) (1990) *The Geography of Contemporary China: The Impact of Deng Xiaoping's Decade*, London: Routledge.

CANNON, T., and ZHANG, L.-Y. (1996) 'Inter-region tension and China's reforms', in I. Cook, M. Doel, and R. Li (eds), *Fragmented Asia: Regional Integration and National Disintegration in Pacific Asia*, Aldershot: Avebury, 75–101.

CARLINE, J. (1986) 'Planning B.C. Place: sweeter the second time', *Quarterly Review* (City of Vancouver Planning Department), Jan.: 15.

CARRANZA, L. (1994) 'Le Corbusier and the problems of representation', *Journal of Architectural Education*, 48(2): 70–81.

CARTIER, C. (1999) 'The state, property development and symbolic landscape in high-rise Hong Kong', *Landscape Research*, 24(2): 185–208.

CASSELL, J. (1988) 'The relationship of observer to observed when studying up', *Studies in Qualitative Methodology*, 1: 89–108.

CASTELLS, M. (1989) *The Informational City*, Oxford: Blackwell.

——(1992) 'Four Asian tigers with a dragon head: a comparative analysis of the state, economy and society in the Asian Pacific Rim', in Appelbaum and Henderson (1992): 33–70.

——(1993a) 'The informational economy and the new international division of labor', in M. Carnoy, M. Castells, S. Cohen, and F. H. Cardosa, *The New Global Economy in the Information Age*, University Park, Pa.: The Pennsylvania State University Press, 15–43.

——(1993b) 'European cities, the informational society, and the global economy', *Tijdscrift voor Econ. en Soc. Geographie*, 84(4): 247–57.

——(1996) *The Rise of the Network Society*, Oxford: Blackwell.

——and HENDERSON, J. (1987) 'Techno-economic restructuring, socio-political processes and spatial transformation: a global perspective', in Henderson and Castells (1987): 1–17.

CAZAL, D. (1994) 'Ethics and global competitiveness: confucianism in Korean companies', in Schütte (1994): 22–32.

CERNEA, M. (1993) *The Urban Environment and Population Relocation*, World Bank Discussion Paper 152, Washington, DC: The World Bank.

——(1994) 'Population resettlement and development', *Finance and Development*, Sept.: 46–9.

——and MCDOWELL, C. (eds) (2000) *Risks and Reconstruction: Experiences of Resettlers and Refugees*, Washington: World Bank.

CHAN, A. (1996) *Li Ka-shing: Hong Kong's Elusive Billionaire*, Toronto: Macmillan.

CHAN, E. (1995) 'Rehousing city's poor needs $6.4b', *South China Morning Post International Weekly*, 22 Apr.: 12.

CHEN, X. (1993) 'China's growing integration with the Asia-Pacific economy', in A. Dirlik (ed.), *WHAT IS IN A RIM? Critical Perspectives on the Pacific Region Idea*, Oxford: Westview Press, 89–119.

CHENG, E. (1990) 'The east is ready', *Far Eastern Economic Review*, 31 May: 57.

——(1992) 'Shanghai surprise', *Far Eastern Economic Review*, 18 June: 64–5.

'Cheung Kong puts forward a new image', *South China Morning Post*, 25 May 1993.

China Economic News (1993) 'Shanghai has 1,762 financial institutions', *China Economic News*, No. 7, 22 Feb.

——(1993) 'Shanghai's road to develop tertiary industry', *China Economic News*, No. 9, 8 Mar.: 5–6.

China News Analysis (1994a) 'The land market', *China News Analysis*, 1503, 1 February.

——(1994b) 'The price of economic reforms: central-local tensions', *China News Analysis*, 1508, 15 Apr.

China Trade Report (1992) 'Financial breakthrough', *China Trade Report*, Mar.: 5.

CHIOW, S. (1994) 'Shanghai's great leap forward: a new master plan for Pudong', *Competitions*, 4(2): 26–32.

CHOUINARD, V. (1994) 'Reinventing radical geography: is all that's Left Right?' *Environment and Planning D: Society and Space*, 12(1): 2–6.

Citizenship and Immigration Canada (1997) *Facts and Figures 1996: Immigration Overview*, <http://www.cic.gc.ca/english/pub/facts96/index_e.html>, accessed 17 Nov. 1999.

——(1999) *Facts and Figures 1998: Immigration Overview*, <http://cicnet.ci.gc.ca/-english/pdffiles/pub/facts98e.pdf>, accessed 17 Nov. 1999.

CLEATHERO, J., and LEVENS, B. (1993) *Environmental Scan of the Lower Mainland: A Compilation of Socio-Economic Trends: Part One: Population Data*, Burnaby, Canada: United Way.

——(1994) *Environmental Scan of the Lower Mainland: A Compilation of Socio-Economic Trends: Part Two: Socio-Economic Trends*, Burnaby, Canada: United Way.

CLIFFORD, J. (1992) 'Traveling cultures', in L. Grossberg, C. Nelson, and P. Treichler (eds), *Cultural Studies*, London: Routledge, 96–116.

——and MARCUS, G. (eds) (1986) *Writing Culture: The Poetics and Politics of Ethnography*, Berkeley: University of California Press.

CLIFFORD, N. (1991) *Spoilt Children of the Empire: Westerners in Shanghai and the Chinese Revolution of the 1920s*, Hanover: University Press of New England.

CLOKE, P., PHILO, C., and SADLER, D. (1991) *Approaching Human Geography: An Introduction to Contemporary Theoretical Debates*, New York: Guilford.

COAKLEY, J. (1994) 'The integration of property and financial markets', *Environment and Planning A*, 26: 697–713.

COCHRANE, A., and JONAS, A. (1999) 'Reimagining Berlin: world city, national capital or ordinary place?' *European Urban and Regional Studies*, 6(2): 145–64.

COHEN, R. B. (1981) 'The new international division of labour, multinational corporations and urban hierarchy', in M. Dear and A. Scott (eds), *Urbanization and Urban Planning in Capitalist Society*, London: Methuen, 287–315.

COLLIERS JARDINE (1997) *Asia Pacific Property Trends: Conditions and Forecasts*, 11th, edn. Hong Kong: Colliers Jardine.

COLOMINA, B. (1994) *Privacy and Publicity: Modern Architecture as Mass Media*, London: MIT Press.

——*et al.* (eds) (1992) *Sexuality & Space*, New York: Princeton Architectural Press.

CONSTANTINEAU, B. (1992) 'Banking on it', *Vancouver Sun*, 11 June, p. D1.

——and POWER, B. (1988) 'Expo land buyer deals quietly', *Vancouver Sun*, 30 Apr., pp. A1, A10.

COOKE, K. (1993) 'New tiger will pace the east bank', *Financial Times*, 2 June: 33.

CORBRIDGE, S., and THRIFT, N. (1994) 'Introduction and overview', in Corbridge *et al.* (1994): 1–25.

——and MARTIN, R. (eds) (1994) *Money, Power, and Space*, Oxford: Blackwell.

COX, K. (1992) 'The politics of globalization: a sceptic's view', *Political Geography*, 11(5): 427–9.

——(ed.) (1997) *Spaces of Globalization: Reasserting the Power of the Local*, London: Guilford.

CRAWFORD, M. (1991) 'Can architects be socially responsible?' in Ghirardo (1991): 27–45.

CRILLEY, D. (1993a) 'Megastructures and urban change: aesthetics, ideology and design', in Knox (1993): 127–64.

——(1993b) 'Architecture as advertising: constructing the image of redevelopment', in Kearns and Philo (1993): 231–52.

CROTHALL, G. (1994) 'The new Shanghai goldrush', *South China Morning Post International Weekly*, 12–13 Feb.: 10–11.

CUFF, D. (1989*a*) 'Mirrors of power: reflective professionals in the neighborhood', in J. Wolch and M. Dear (eds), *The Power of Geography: How Territory Shapes Social Life*, Boston: Unwin Hyman, 331–50.

——(1989*b*) 'The social production of built form', *Environment and Planning D: Society and Space*, 7: 433–47.

——(1991) *Architecture: The Story of Practice*, Cambridge, Mass.: MIT Press.

——(1999) 'The political paradoxes of practice: political economy of local and global architecture', *Practice*, 3(1): 77–88.

CYBRIWSKY, R., LEY, D., and WESTERN, J. (1986) 'The political and social construction of revitalized neighbourhoods: Society Hill, Philadelphia, and False Creek, Vancouver', in N. Smith and P. Williams (eds), *Gentrification of the City*, London: Allen & Unwin, 92–120.

CZARNIAWSKA, B. (1997) 'A four times told tale: combining narrative and scientific knowledge in organization studies', *Organization*, 4(1): 7–30.

——(1998) *A Narrative Approach in Organization Studies*, Thousand Oaks, Calif.: Sage.

CZARNIAWSKA-JOERGES, B. (1995) 'Narration or science?: collapsing the division in organization studies', *Organization*, 2(1): 11–33.

Daewoo Securities (1995) *China & India: Third Quarter 1995*, Hong Kong: Daewoo Securities.

DANIELS, P. (1993) *Service Industries in the World Economy*, Oxford: Blackwell.

DAVIES, C. (1988) *High Tech Architecture*, London: Thames and Hudson.

——(1992) 'On being big in France', *World Architect*, 18: 34–7.

DAVIS, H. C., and HUTTON, T. (1992) 'Structural change in the British Columbia economy: regional diversification and metropolitan transition', paper prepared for the B.C. Round Table on the Environment and Economy, mimeo.

————(1994) 'Marketing Vancouver's producer services to the Asia Pacific', *The Canadian Geographer*, 38(1): 18–28.

DAVIS, M. (1991) 'The infinite game: redeveloping downtown L.A.', in Ghirardo (1991): 77–113.

——(1992) *City of Quartz: Excavating the Future in Los Angeles*, New York: Vintage.

DEMERITT, D. (1996) 'Social theory and the reconstruction of science and geography', *Transactions of the Institute of British Geographers*, 21: 484–503.

DESFOR, G., GOLDRICK, M., and MERRENS, R. (1988) 'Redevelopment on the North American water-frontier: the case of Toronto', in B. Hoyle, D. Pinder, and M. Husain (eds), *Revitalizing the Waterfront: International Dimensions of Dockland Redevelopment*, London: Belhaven Press, 92–113.

DEUTSCHE, R. (1996) *Evictions: Art and Spatial Politics*, Cambridge, Mass.: MIT Press.

DICKEN, P. (1992) *Global Shift: The Internationalization of Economic Activity*, 2nd edn., London: Paul Chapman.

——(1998) *Global Shift: Transforming the World Economy*, 3rd edn., London: Paul Chapman.

——PECK, J., and TICKELL, A. (1997) 'Unpacking the global', in Lee and Wills (1997): 158–66.

——and THRIFT, N. (1992) 'The organization of production and the production of organization: why business enterprises matter in the study of geographical industrialization', *Transactions of the Institute of British Geographers*, 17: 279–91.

DiMaggio, P. (1994) 'Culture and economy', in Smelser and Swedberg (1994*b*): 27–57.

Dirlik, A. (ed.) (1993) *WHAT IS IN A RIM? Critical Perspectives on the Pacific Region Idea*, Oxford: Westview Press.

——(1995) 'Confucius in the borderlands: global capitalism and the reinvention of confucianism', *boundary*, 2(22): 229–73.

——(1997) 'Critical reflections on "Chinese capitalism" as paradigm', *Identities*, 3: 303–30.

——(1999) 'Globalism and the politics of place', in Olds *et al.* (1999): 39–56.

Douglass, M. (1987) 'Transnational capital and urbanization in Japan', in M. Douglass and J. Friedmann (eds), *Transnational Capital and Urbanization on the Pacific Rim*, Los Angeles: Center for Pacific Rim Studies.

——(1989) 'The future of cities on the Pacific Rim', in M. P. Smith (ed.), *Pacific Rim Cities in the World Economy: Comparative Urban and Community Research* ii, New Brunswick and London: Transaction Publishers, 9–67.

——(1994) 'The "developmental state" and the newly industrialised economies of Asia', *Environment and Planning A*, 26: 543–66.

——(1998*a*) 'A regional network strategy for reciprocal rural-urban linkages', *Third World Planning Review*, 20(1): 1–33.

——(1998*b*) 'World city formation on the Asia Pacific Rim: poverty, "everyday" forms of civil society and environmental management', in M. Douglass and J. Friedmann (eds), *Cities for Citizens*, Chichester: John Wiley & Sons, 107–37.

Dowall, D. (1993*a*) 'Establishing urban land markets in the People's Republic of China, *American Planning Association Journal*, 59(2): 182–92.

——(1993*b*) 'Urban redevelopment in the People's Republic of China', *Housing Finance International*, Mar.: 25–35, 41.

——(1994) 'Urban residential redevelopment in the People's Republic of China', *Urban Studies*, 31(9): 1497–516.

Dresdner Bank (1994) *Investing in China*, Frankfurt: Dresdner Bank AG.

Duckett, J. (1998) *The Entrepreneurial State in China: Real Estate and Commerce Departments in Reform-Era Tianjin*, London: Routledge.

Duncan, J., and Ley, D. (eds) (1993) *Place/Culture/Representation*, London: Routledge.

East Asia Analytical Unit (1995) *Overseas Chinese Business Networks in Asia*, Parkes, Australia: Department of Foreign Affairs and Trade.

Ecologist (1994) *Evicted! The World Bank, British Aid and Forced Resettlement*, Dec., Sturminster Newton: The Ecologist.

Economist (1992) 'A driving force', 18 July: 21–4.

——(1993) 'Television's final frontier', 31 July: 59.

——(1994) 'A survey of Asian finance', 12 Nov.

——(1995*a*) 'A Survey of Multinationals', 24 June.

——(1995*b*) 'Hung up', 22 July: 76–7.

Economist Intelligence Unit (1994) *The China Connection: Shaping a Business in Shanghai*, London: EIU.

——(1997) *Global Direct Investment and the Importance of Real Estate*, London: EIU/RICS.

Edgington, D. (1992) *Japanese Direct Investment in Canada: Recent Trends and Prospects*, B.C. Geographical Series, No. 49, Vancouver: Department of Geography, University of B.C.

EDGINGTON, D. (1994) 'The new wave: patterns of Japanese direct foreign investment in Canada during the 1980s', *The Canadian Geographer*, 38(1): 28–36.

——and GOLDBERG, M. (1990) 'Vancouver and the emerging network of Pacific Rim global cities', Paper No. ULE008, Canadian Real Estate Research Bureau, Faculty of Commerce and Business Administration, University of British Columbia.

————(1992) 'Vancouver: Canada's gateway to the Rim', in E. Blakely and R. Stimson (eds), *New Cities of the Pacific Rim*, Oct., Monograph 43, IURD, University of California at Berkeley.

EDWARDS, I. (1992) 'Quiet clout', *Business in Vancouver*, 8–14 Dec.: 8–9.

EMIRBAYER, M. (1997) 'Manifesto for a relational sociology', *American Journal of Sociology*, 103(2): 281–317.

ENRIGHT, M., SCOTT, E., and DODWELL, D. (1997) *The Hong Kong Advantage*, Hong Kong: Oxford University Press.

Euromoney (1994a) Asian Issuers and Capital Markets Supplementary Issue.

——(1994b), 'Roots and fruits of the family tree . . . and other sturdy branches', Oct.: 104–12.

——(1995) 'Investors play hard-to-get', Feb.: 72–5.

EVANS, M. (1994) 'CIBC Asian jewel a low-key winner', *Financial Post*, 20 Apr.: 42.

EVANS, P. (1992) 'The emergence of Eastern Asia and its implications for Canada', *International Journal*, 47(3): 504–28.

FAINSTEIN, S. (1994) *The City Builders*, Oxford: Blackwell.

Far Eastern Economic Review (1993) 'A bearish voice', 11 Nov.: 5.

——(1994) 'Singapore: try life', 19 May: 62.

FAROUK, O. (1995) 'Shanghai: the new dragon of East China', *Insight* (International Public Affairs Branch, Department of Foreign Affairs and Trade, Government of Australia), 30 May: 3–4.

FARROW, M. (1991) 'Iron Lady falls for city's beauty', *Vancouver Sun*, 18 Mar., p. B1.

FEATHERSTONE, M. (1990a) 'Global culture: an introduction', in Featherstone (1990b): 1–14.

——(ed.) (1990b) *Global Culture: Nationalism, Globalization and Modernity*, London: Sage.

——LASH, S., and ROBERTSON, R. (eds) (1995) *Global Modernities*, London: Sage.

Financial Times (1995) 'Cultural wall falls to DM's incursion', 27 July: 19.

'Fire hits controversial Shanghai area', *The Globe and Mail* (Toronto), 11 Mar., p. A11.

First Pacific Davies (1997) 'Pudong property focus—the East is nearly ready', *Asia Property Focus*, Aug.

FOLKES, S. (1989) 'Citizen participation and the redevelopment of urban land: a case study of the North Shore of False Creek', unpublished MA thesis, School of Community and Regional Planning, University of British Columbia.

FORBES, D. (1988) 'Getting by in Indonesia: research in a foreign land', in J. Eyles (ed.), *Research in Human Geography: Introductions and Investigations*, Oxford: Blackwell, 100–20.

——(1993) 'Towards the "Pacific century": integration and disintegration in the Pacific Basin', in *The Far East and Australasia 1993*, 24th edn., London: Europa Publishing Ltd., 23–9.

——(1996) *Asian Metropolis: Urbanisation and the Southeast Asian City*, Melbourne: Oxford University Press.

——(1997) 'Metropolis and megaurban region in Pacific Asia', *Tijdschrift voor Economische en Sociale Geografie*, 88: 457–68.

——(1999) 'Globalisation, postcolonialism and new representations of the Pacific Asian metropolis', in Olds *et al.* (1999): 238–54.

Forbes Magazine, <http://www.forbes.com>, accessed 22 Nov. 1999.

FORD, L. (1998) 'Midtowns, megastructures, and world cities', *The Geographical Review*, 88(4): 528–47.

FOSTER, H., LAI, D., and ZHOU, N. (eds) (1998) *The Dragon's Head: Shanghai, China's Emerging Megacity*, Victoria, BC: Western Geographical Press.

FPD Savills Research (1999) *Infrastructure Briefing*, Hong Kong: FPD Savills, Nov.

FRAMPTON, K. (1992) *Modern Architecture: A Critical History*, London: Thames and Hudson.

FRIEDMAN, J. (1997) 'Global crises, the struggle for cultural identity and intellectual porkbarrelling: cosmopolitans versus locals, ethnics and nationals in an era of de-hegemonisation', in P. Werbner and T. Modood (eds), *Debating Cultural Hybridity: Multicultural Identities and the Politics of Anti-racism*, London: Zed Books, 70–89.

FRIEDMANN, J. (1986) 'The world city hypothesis', *Development and Change*, 17: 69–83.

——(1992) *Empowerment: The Politics of Alternative Development*, Oxford: Blackwell.

—— and WOLFF, G. (1982) 'World city formation: an agenda for research and action', *International Journal of Urban and Regional Research*, 6: 309–44.

FUNG, K. I., YAN, Z. M., and NING, Y. M. (1992) 'Shanghai: China's world city', in Yeung and Hu (1992*b*): 124–52.

GEERTZ, C. (1983) *Local Knowledge*, New York: Basic Books.

GENG, Y. (1993) 'A brief introduction to the adjustment made in the overall planning of the City of Shanghai', paper presented at the International Workshop on the Planning and Development of Metropolitan Regions, Shanghai, 11–14 Oct.

GEREFFI, G. (1996) 'Commodity chains and regional divisions of labour in East Asia', *Journal of Asian Business*, 12(1): 75–112.

——(1999) 'International trade and industrial upgrading in the apparel commodity chain', *Journal of International Economics*, 48(1): 37–70.

—— and HAMILTON, G. (1991) 'Modes of incorporation in an industrial world: the social economy of global capitalism', Working Paper No. 34, Program in East Asian Business and Development, Institute of Governmental Affairs, University of California at Davis.

GHIRARDO, D. (ed.) (1991) *Out of Site: A Social Criticism of Architecture*, Seattle: Bay Press.

GIBSON-GRAHAM, J. K. (1996) *The End of Capitalism (As We Knew It): A Feminist Critique of Political Economy*, Cambridge, Mass.: Blackwell Publishers.

GIDDENS, A. (1990) *The Consequences of Modernity*, Stanford, Calif.: Stanford University Press.

——(1991) *Modernity and Self-Identity*, Cambridge: Polity.

——(1994) *Beyond Left and Right: The Future of Radical Politics*, Oxford: Polity.

GITTINGS, L. (1993) 'Peasants in the path of power', *Guardian*, 14 May: 18–19.

GLEN, J., and PINTO, B. (1994) 'Emerging capital markets and corporate finance', *Columbia Journal of World Business*, 29(2): 31–41.

GOLD, T. (1991) 'Can Pudong deliver?' *China Business Review*, Nov.–Dec.: 22–9.

GOLDBERG, M. (1985) *The Chinese Connection: Getting Plugged in to Pacific Rim Real Estate, Trade and Capital Markets*, Vancouver: University of British Columbia Press.

——(1989) 'Foreign capital flows and the U.S. property market: a view primarily from Asia', Research Papers in International Business, Trade and Finance, IBTF 90-042, Faculty of Commerce and Business Administration, University of British Columbia.

——(1991*a*) 'The evolving Pacific property market: a view from North America', Research Papers in International Business, Trade and Finance, IBTF 92-102, Faculty of Commerce and Business Administration, University of British Columbia.

——(1991*b*) 'Vancouver: a Pacific Rim city in the making', *UBC Alumni Chronicle*, winter: 22–4.

——(1993) 'The evolving Pacific property market: a view from North America', in Yeung (1993): 25–46.

GOODMAN, D., and SEGAL, G. (eds) (1994) *China Deconstructs: Politics, Trade and Regionalism*, London: Routledge.

GOTTDIENER, M. (1995) *Postmodern Semiotics: Material Culture and the Forms of Postmodern Life*, Oxford: Blackwell.

GRABHER, G. (ed.) (1993) *The Embedded Firm: On the Socioeconomics of Industrial Networks*, London: Routledge.

—— and STARK, D. (eds) (1997) *Restructuring Networks in Post-Socialism: Legacies, Linkages, and Localities*, Oxford: Oxford University Press.

GRANOVETTER, M. (1985) 'Economic action and social structure: the problem of embeddedness', *American Journal of Sociology*, 91: 481–510.

—— and SWEDBERG, R. (eds) (1992) *The Sociology of Economic Life*, Boulder, Colo.: Westview Press.

Greater Vancouver Regional District (1999) *Greater Vancouver Key Facts: A Statistical Profile of Greater Vancouver*, Canada, Burnaby, BC: GVRD.

GREENHALGH, S. (1994) 'De-Orientalizing the Chinese family firm', *American Ethnologist*, 21(4): 746–75.

GREGORY, D. (1994) *Geographical Imaginations*, Oxford: Blackwell.

Groupe Français D'Appui au développement de Shanghai-Pudong (1992) 'Shanghai, L'Aménagement du Quartier Central de Lu Jia Zui a Pudong: Resultats de la Consultation International', mimeo.

GRUNDY-WARR, C., PEACHEY, K., and PERRY, M. (1999) 'Fragmented integration in the Singapore-Indonesian border zone: Southeast Asia's "growth triangle" against the global economy', *International Journal of Urban and Regional Research*, 23(2): 304–28.

Guardian (1994) 'Top tycoon', 31 May: 10.

GUPTA, A., and FERGUSON, J. (eds) (1997) *Anthropological Locations: Boundaries and Grounds of a Field Science*, Berkeley: University of California Press.

GUTSTEIN, D. (1986) 'The impact of Expo on Vancouver', in R. Anderson and E. Wachtel (eds), *The Expo Story*, Madeira Park, BC: Harbour Publishing, 65–100.

——(1990) *The New Landlords: Asian Investment in Canadian Real Estate*, Victoria, BC: Press Porcépic Limited.

HAAS, P. (1992) 'Introduction: epistemic communities and international policy coordination', *International Organization*, 46(1): 1–36.

HAGGARD, S. (1990) *Pathways from the Periphery: The Politics of Growth in the Newly Industrializing Countries*, Ithaca, NY: Cornell University Press.

HAILA, A. (1997) 'The neglected builder of global cities', in O. Kalltorp *et al.* (eds), *Cities in Transformation—Transformation in Cities: Social and Symbolic Change of Urban Space*, Aldershot: Avebury, 1–64.

——(1999) 'City building in the East and West: United States, Europe, Hong Kong and Singapore compared', *Cities*, 16(4): 259–67.

HALL, P. (1995) 'Towards a general urban theory', in J. Brotchie, M. Batty, E. Blakely, P. Hall, and P. Newton (eds), *Cities in Competition: Productive and Sustainable Cities for the 21st Century*, Melbourne: Longman Australia, 3–31.

HALL, T., and HUBBARD, P. (eds) (1998) *The Entrepreneurial City: Geographies of Politics, Regime and Representation*, London: Routledge.

HAMILTON, G. (1988) 'Questions raised over Li legacy', *Vancouver Sun*, 17 Dec., pp. B1, B2.

——(1991*a*) 'The organizational foundations of Western and Chinese commerce: a historical and comparative analysis', in Hamilton (1991*b*): 48–65.

——(ed.) (1991*b*) *Business Networks and Economic Development in East and Southeast Asia*, Hong Kong: Centre of Asian Studies, University of Hong Kong.

——(1992) 'Overseas Chinese capitalism', Working Paper No. 42, Program in East Asian Business and Development, Institute of Governmental Affairs, University of California at Davis.

——(1994) 'Civilizations and the organization of economics', in Smelser and Swedberg (1994*b*): 183–205.

——(1996) 'Overseas Chinese capitalism' in Tu, W.-M. (ed.), *Confucian Traditions in East Asian Modernity: Moral Education and Economic Culture in Japan and the Four Mini-Dragons*, Harvard: Harvard University Press, 328–42.

——(2000) 'Reciprocity and control: the organization of Chinese family-owned conglomerates', in Yeung and Olds (2000): 55–74.

HAMNETT, C. (1994) 'Social polarisation in global cities', *Urban Studies*, 31(3): 401–24.

——(1995) 'Controlling space: global cities', in Allen and Hamnett (1995): 103–42.

Hang Seng Bank (1994) 'Foreign direct investment in China—trends and prospects', *Hang Seng Economic Monthly*, Dec.

——(1995) 'Rationalization of the services industries', *Hang Seng Economic Monthly*, Aug.

HANNERZ, U. (1990) 'Cosmopolitans and locals in world culture', in Featherstone (1990*b*): 237–52.

——(1992*a*) *Cultural Complexity: Studies in the Social Organization of Meaning*, New York: Columbia University Press.

——(1992*b*) 'The cultural role of world cities', in N. AlSayyad (ed.), *Forms of Dominance: On the Architecture and Urbanism of the Colonial Enterprise*, Aldershot, UK: Avebury, 67–84.

——(1992*c*) *Culture, Cities and the World*, Amsterdam: Centrum voor Grootstedelijk Onderzoek.

——(1996) *Transnational Connections*, London: Routledge.

HARRIS, C. (1992) 'The Lower Mainland, 1820–81', in Wynn and Oke (1992): 38–68.

HARRIS, N. (1986) *The End of the Third World: Newly Industrializing Countries and the Decline of an Ideology*, Harmondsworth: Penguin.

HARRIS, N. (1993) 'Transportation and the economic survival of cities', *The Urban Age*, fall: 3.

HARVEY, D. (1982) *The Limits to Capital*, Oxford: Blackwell.

——(1985) *Consciousness and the Urban Experience*, Oxford: Blackwell.

——(1989*a*) *The Condition of Postmodernity*, Oxford: Blackwell.

——(1989*b*) 'From managerialism to entrepreneurialism: the transformation of urban governance in late capitalism', *Geografiska Annaler*, 71: 3–17.

——(1994*a*) 'The invisible political economy of architectural production', in O. Bouman and R. van Toorn (eds), *The Invisible in Architecture*, London: Academy Editions, London, 420–7.

——(1994*b*) 'Towards reclaiming our cities: experience and analysis', *Regenerating Cities*, 6: 3–8.

HASSEMER, V. (1993) 'What is Berlin's position today? planning and building in the metropolis', speech at the International Urban Development Association INTA 17–New Town Experience Joint Conference and the World Property Market Exhibition, 29 Sept., Hong Kong.

HÄUBERMANN, H., and STROM, E. (1994) 'Berlin: the once and future capital', *International Journal of Urban and Regional Research*, 18(2): 335–46.

HAWKINS, F. (1989) *Critical Years in Immigration: Canada and Australia Compared*, Kingston: McGill-Queen's University Press.

HAYTER, R., and SUN, S. H. (1998) 'Reflections on China's open door policy towards foreign direct investment', *Regional Studies*, 32(1): 1–16.

HEALEY, P. (1991) 'Models of the land development process: a review', *Journal of Property Research*, 8: 219–38.

HELD, D. (1991) 'Democracy, the nation-state and the global system', *Economy and Society*, 20: 138–72.

——(1993) 'Democracy: from city-states to a cosmopolitan order?', in D. Held (ed.), *Prospects for Democracy: North, South, East, West*, Cambridge: Polity Press, 13–52.

——(1996) *Models of Democracy*, 2nd edn., Cambridge: Polity.

——McGREW, A., GOLDBLATT, D., and PERRATON, J. (1999) *Global Transformations: Politics, Economics and Culture*, Cambridge: Polity Press.

HELLEINER, E. (1992) 'States and the future of global finance', *Review of International Studies*, 18: 31–49.

HENDERS, S., and PITTIS, D. (1993) 'Is Canada losing Hong Kong investment', *Canada and Hong Kong Update*, 10, summer: 13–14.

HENDERSON, J. (1989) *The Globalisation of High Technology Production*, London: Routledge.

——(1999) 'Uneven crises: institutional foundations of East Asian economic turmoil', *Economy and Society*, 28(3): 327–68.

——and CASTELLS, M. (eds) (1987) *Global Restructuring and Territorial Development*, London: Sage.

HENRIOT, C. (1993) *Shanghai, 1927–1937: Municipal Power, Locality and Modernization*, Berkeley: University of California Press.

HEROD, A. (1993) 'Gender issues in the use of interviewing as a research method', *Professional Geographer*, 45(3): 305–17.

——(1999) 'Reflections on interviewing foreign elites: praxis, positionality, validity, and the cult of the insider', *Geoforum*, 30(4): 313–28.

——Ó TUATHAIL, G., and ROBERTS, S. (eds) (1998) *An Unruly World? Globalization, Governance and Geography*, London: Routledge.

HERTZ, E. (1998) *The Trading Crowd: An Ethnography of the Shanghai Stock Market*, Cambridge: Cambridge University Press.

HEWETT, G. (1994) 'Sun Hung Kai tops blue chip survey', *South China Morning Post International Weekly*, 17–18 Sept., p. B3.

HIEBERT, D. (1994) 'Canadian immigration: policy, politics, geography', *The Canadian Geographer*, 38(3): 254–8.

——(1999) 'Immigration and the changing social geography of Greater Vancouver', *BC Studies*, 121: 35–82.

HILLIER, B., and PENN, A. (1992) 'Dense civilisations: the shape of cities in the 21st century', *Applied Energy*, 43: 41–66.

————HANSON, J., GRAJEWSKI, T., and XU, J. (1993) 'Natural movement: or, configuration and attraction in urban pedestrian movement', *Environment and Planning B: Planning and Design*, 20: 29–66.

Hillier Parker (1995) *International Property Bulletin*, London: Hillier Parker.

HIRST, P., and THOMPSON, G. (1992) 'The problem of "globalization": international economic relations, national economic management and the formation of trading blocs', *Economy and Society*, 21(4): 357–96.

————(1996) *Globalization in Question*, Cambridge: Polity.

HO, D. (1993) 'Key legal issues concerning China property investment', *The Securities Journal* (Hong Kong), Nov.: 8–12.

HO, L. D. (1998) 'The Lu Jia Zui, Shanghai (1992)', *Arca plus*, 5(3): 48–57.

HODDER, R. (1996) *Merchant Princes of the East: Cultural Delusions, Economic Success, and the Overseas Chinese in Southeast Asia*, New York: J. Wiley.

HODGSON, G. M. (ed.) (1994) *The Economics of Institutions*, Aldershot: Edward Elgar.

HOLBERTON, S. (1993) 'HK's superman finds warmer winds from China', *Financial Times*, 23 June: 30.

——(1995) 'Mr Li sets Hong Kong a puzzle', *Financial Times*, 6 June: 26.

——and WALKER, T. (1994) 'The generals' big offensive', *Financial Times*, 28 Nov.: 19.

HOLSTON, J. (1989) *The Modernist City: An Anthropological Critique of Brasília*, Chicago: University of Chicago Press.

HOLTON, R. (1992) *Economy and Society*, London: Routledge.

Hong Kong Monetary Authority (1995) *1994 Annual Report*, Hong Kong: Hong Kong Monetary Authority.

Hong Kong Trade Development Council (1991) *Vancouver: Hong Kong's Trading Partner in North America*, Hong Kong: HKTDC.

——(1993) *Investment Environment of Pudong, Shanghai*, Hong Kong: HKTDC.

HOOK, B. (ed.) (1998) *Shanghai and the Yangtze Delta: A City Reborn*, Hong Kong: Oxford University Press.

HORNIK, R. (1994) 'Bursting China's bubble: the muddle kingdom?' *Foreign Affairs*, 73(3): 28–42.

HSING, Y.-T. (1993) 'Transnational networks of Taiwan's small business and China's local governments: a new pattern of foreign direct investment', Unpublished Ph.D. dissertation, City and Regional Planning, University of California at Berkeley.

——(1994) 'Blood thicker than water: networks of local Chinese bureaucrats and Taiwanese investors in Southern China', Asian Urban Research Network Working Paper, UBC Centre for Human Settlements, Vancouver, Canada.

——(1998) *Making Capitalism in China: The Taiwan Connection*, New York: Oxford University Press.

Hu, Y. (1993) *China's Capital Market*, Hong Kong: The Chinese University of Hong Kong.

Huang, F. X. (1993) '21st Century Shanghai CBD—The finalization and refining of Lujiazui Cental Area planning', paper presented at the Second International Conference of Aquapolises, Shanghai, 15–19 Nov.

Hulchanski, J. D. (1989) 'Low rent housing in Vancouver's central area: policy and program options', report prepared for the Central Area Division, City of Vancouver, Sept.

——Eberle, M., Olds, K., and Stewart, D. (1991) *Solutions to Homelessness: Vancouver Case Studies*, Vancouver: UBC Centre for Human Settlements, and Ottawa: Canada Mortgage and Housing Corporation.

Hume, M. (1988) 'Ex-insiders caught in Expo land fray', *Vancouver Sun*, 8 Apr., p. A3.

Hutchinson, M. (1994) 'Donald Trump', *Architectural Design*, 64(11–12), pp. viii–xi.

Hutton, T. (1994a) 'Vancouver', *Cities*, 11(4): 219–39.

——(1994b) 'Visions of a 'post staples economy: structural change and adjustment issues in British Columbia', Policy Issues and Planning Responses paper PI No. 3, Centre for Human Settlements, University of British Columbia.

——(1998) *The Transformation of Canada's Pacific Metropolis: A Study of Vancouver*, Montreal: IRPP.

Huus, K. (1994) 'No place like home: Beijing is remaking itself, but for whose benefit?' *Far Eastern Economic Review*, 28 July: 72–3.

Huxtable, A. L. (1984) *The Tall Building Artistically Reconsidered*, New York: Pantheon Books.

Hyslop, J. (1990) 'The spatial structure of Shanghai city proper', in G. Linge and D. Forbes (eds), *China's Spatial Economy: Recent Developments and Reforms*, Hong Kong: Oxford University Press, 144–59.

Ibelings, H. (1998) *Supermodernism: Architecture in the Age of Globalization*, Rotterdam: Netherlands Architecture Institute.

Imai, S. (1993) 'The Tumen River Area Special International Economic Zone', *JETRO China Newsletter*, 104: 14–23.

ING Barings (1997) *Macro Monitor*, Aug., Hong Kong: ING Barings.

Institut d'Aménagement et d'Urbanisme de la Région Ile de France (IAURIF), and the Etablissement Public d'Aménagement de La Défense (EPAD) (1991) 'Shanghai: international consultation on the Lu Jia Zui business centre in Pu Dong', mimeo.

International Chamber of Commerce and UNCTAD (1998) <http://www.unicc.org/unctad/en/pressref/bg9802en.htm>, accessed 13 May 1998.

International Monetary Fund (1992) *Measurement of International Capital Flows*, Sept., Washington: IMF.

——(1994a) *International Capital Markets: Developments, Prospects, and Policy Issues*, Washington: IMF.

——(1994b) *World Economic Outlook*, May, Washington: IMF.

——(1995) *World Economic Outlook*, May, Washington: IMF.

Jackson, P. (1993) 'Changing ourselves: a geography of position', in R. Johnston (ed.), *The Challenge for Geography: A Changing World: A Changing Discipline*, Oxford: Blackwell, 198–214.

——(1998) 'Constructions of "whiteness" in the geographical imagination', *Area*, 30(2): 99–106.

——and PENROSE, J. (eds) (1993) *Constructions of Race, Place and Nation*, London: UCL Press.

JACOBS, J. (1961) *The Death and Life of Great American Cities*, New York: Vintage.

——(1994) 'The battle of bank junction: the contested iconography of capital', in S. Corbridge, R. Martin, and N. Thrift (eds), *Money, Power and Space*, Oxford: Blackwell, 356–82.

JACOBS, J. B., and HONG, L. (1994) 'Shanghai and the lower Yangzi Valley', in Goodman and Segal (1994): 224–52.

JAMESON, F. (1984) 'Postmodernism, or the cultural logic of late capitalism', *New Left Review*, 146: 59–92.

JANELLE, D. (1969) 'Spatial reorganization: a model and concept', *Annals of the Association of American Geographers*, 59: 348–64.

Jardine Fleming (1995) 'A monetary dilemma', *Economic Research* (Jardine Fleming Broking Limited, Hong Kong), May.

JAY, M. (1992) 'Scopic regimes of modernity', in Lash and Friedman (1992): 178–95.

JENCKS, C. (1991) *The Language of Post-Modern Architecture*, London: Academy Editions.

——(n.d.) 'Aphorisms on power', *Architectural Design Review*, 114: 21–3.

JESSOP, B. (1999) 'Reflections on globalisation and its (il)logic(s)', in Olds *et al.* (1999): 19–38.

JOHNSON, G. (1994) 'Hong Kong immigrants and the Chinese community in Vancouver', in Skeldon (1994*b*): 120–38.

JOHNSTON, R., TAYLOR, P., and WATTS, M. (eds) (1995) *Geographies of Global Change: Remapping the World in the Late Twentieth Century*, Oxford: Blackwell.

JONES, A. (1998) 'Re-theorising the core: a "globalized" business elite in Santiago, Chile', *Political Geography*, 17(3): 295–318.

JONES, G. W. (1991) 'Urbanization issues in the Asian-Pacific region', *Asian-Pacific Economic Literature*, 5(2): 5–33.

Jones Lang Wootton (1993*a*) *JLW Asia Property 1993*, Hong Kong: JLW.

——(1993*b*) *Shenzhen Property—A Guide for Foreign Investors*, Hong Kong: JLW.

——(1993*c*) *Shanghai Property—An Analysis of the Grade A Office Market*, Hong Kong: JLW.

——(1994) *Shanghai Renaissance—An International Financial and Trading Centre Re-emerges*, Hong Kong: JLW.

JONES, R., KING, R., and KLEIN, M. (1993) 'Economic integration between Hong Kong, Taiwan and the coastal provinces of China', *OECD Economic Studies*, 20: 115–44.

KAHN, J. (1993) 'In China's cities, growth takes its toll', *Wall Street Journal*, 22 Dec., p. A8.

——(1994*a*) 'Jews return to Shanghai, a refuge far from Nazis', *Asian Wall Street Journal*, 25 Apr.: 5.

——(1994*b*) 'Unwelcome blossoms: Shanghai attempts to nip spring dissent in the bud', *Asian Wall Street Journal*, 28 Apr.: 1.

——(1997) 'Shanghai reconstructs grandiose legacy', *Asian Wall Street Journal*, 16 May: 1.

KARMEL, S. (1994) 'Emerging securities markets in China: capitalism with Chinese characteristics', *The China Quarterly*, 140: 1105–20.

KAYATEKIN, S., and RUCCIO, D. (1998) 'Global fragments: subjectivity and class politics in discourses of globalization', *Economy and Society*, 27(1): 74–96.

KEARNS, G. (1993) 'The city as spectacle: Paris and the Bicentenary of the French Revolution', in Kearns and Philo (1993): 49–101.

——and PHILO, C. (eds) (1993) *Selling Places: The City as Cultural Capital, Past and Present*, Oxford: Pergamon.

KEITH, M., and PILE, S. (1993) 'Introduction part 1: the politics of place . . .', in M. Keith and S. Pile (eds), *Place and the Politics of Identity*, London: Routledge, 1–21.

KELLY, P. (1997) 'Globalization, power and the politics of scale in the Philippines', *Geoforum*, 28(2): 151–72.

——(1999) 'The geographies and politics of globalization', *Progress in Human Geography*, 23(3): 379–400.

——and OLDS, K. (1999) 'Questions in a crisis: the contested meanings of globalisation in the Asia-Pacific', in Olds *et al.* (1999): 1–16.

KENNEDY, S. (1995) 'Beijing sheds some weight', *The Banker*, Mar.: 48–50.

KESWICK, M., OBERLANDER, J., and WAI, J. (1990) *In a Chinese Garden: The Art & Architecture of the Dr Sun Yat-Sen Classical Chinese Garden*, Vancouver: The Dr Sun Yat-Sen Classical Chinese Garden Society.

KIM, S. J. (1993) 'Tumen River Area Development Project and inter-Korean economic cooperation', *East Asian Review*, 5(2): 65–86.

KING, A. (1990*a*) *Global Cities*, London: Routledge.

——(1990*b*) 'Architecture, capital and the globalization of culture', in Featherstone (1990*b*): 397–411.

——(ed.) (1991) *Culture, Globalization and the World-System*, London: Macmillan.

——(1993) 'Identity and difference: the internationalization of capital and the globalization of culture', in Knox (1993*b*): 83–110.

——(1996) 'Worlds in the city: Manhatten transfer and the ascendance of spectacular space', *Planning Perspectives*, 11: 97–114.

KIRKBY, R. (1985) *Urbanization in China: Town and Country in a Developing Economy, 1949–2000AD*, New York: Columbia University Press.

KNOX, P. (1993*a*) Capital, material culture and socio-spatial differentiation', in Knox (1993*b*): 1–34.

——(ed.) (1993*b*) *The Restless Urban Landscape*, Englewood Cliffs, NJ: Prentice Hall.

——(1995) 'World cities and the organization of global space', in Johnston *et al.* (1995): 232–47.

KOBAYASHI, A. (1994) 'Coloring the field—gender, race, and the politics of fieldwork', *Professional Geographer*, 46(1): 73–80.

KOHUT, J. (1993) 'Pudong's great joint adventure', *South China Morning Post*, 16 Jan.

KOOLHAUS, R., and MAU, B. (1995) *Small, Medium, Large, Extra-Large*, Rotterdam: 010 Publishers.

KPMG Peat Marwick Stevenson & Kellog/Peat Marwick Thorne (1992) 'British Columbia financial review: The issue of disposal and valuation of assets', report to the Province of British Columbia, 5 Mar.

KRAAR, L. (1992*a*) 'A billionaire's global strategy', *Fortune*, 13 July: 106–9.

——(1992*b*) 'The legend of Li Ka Shing', *Asiaweek*, 17 July: 56–67.

——(1999) 'Inside Li Ka-Shing's empire', *Fortune*, 29 Mar.: 30–6.

KRANGLE, K. (1988) 'City staff gave Li site advice', *Vancouver Sun*, 29 Apr., pp. A1, A2.

KRÄTKE, S. (1992) 'Berlin: the rise of a new metropolis in a post-Fordist landscape', in M. Dunford and G. Kafkalas (eds), *Cities and Regions in the New Europe: the Global-Local Interplay and Spatial Development Strategies*, London: Belhaven, 213–38.

KUEH, Y. Y. (1992) 'Foreign investment and economic change in China', *The China Quarterly*, Sept., No. 131: 637–90.

LANGDON, F. (1995) 'Canada's goal in the Asia Pacific', *The Pacific Review*, 8(2): 383–400.

LANGDON, P. (1995) 'Asia bound', *Progressive Architecture*, Mar.: 43–9.

LARDY, N. (1992) *Foreign Trade and Economic Reform in China, 1978–1990*, Cambridge: Cambridge University Press.

——(1994) *China in the World Economy*, Washingon: Institute for International Economics.

——(1998) *China's Unfinished Economic Revolution*, Washington: Brookings Institution Press.

LARSON, M. S. (1993) *Behind the Postmodern Facade: Architectural Change in Late Twentieth Century America*, Berkeley: University of California Press.

——(1994) 'Architectural competitions as discursive events', *Theory and Society*, 23: 469–504.

LARY, D. (1994) 'Regional variations in settlement of Hong Kong immigrants, *Canada and Hong Kong Update*, No. 12, spring: 5–6.

LASH, S. (1993) 'Berlin's second modernity', in Knox (1993b): 237–54.

——(1994) 'Reflexivity and its doubles: structure, aesthetics and community', in Beck *et al.* (1994): 110–73.

—— and FRIEDMAN, S. (eds) (1992) *Modernity and Identity*, Oxford: Blackwell.

—— and URRY, J. (1987) *Disorganized Capitalism*, Madison: University of Wisconsin Press.

————(1994) *Economies of Signs and Space*, London: Sage.

LATOUR, B. (1993) *We Have Never Been Modern*, London: Harvester Wheatsheaf.

LAW, J. (1994) *Organizing Modernity*, Oxford: Blackwell.

LEAF, M. (1994) 'Urban Planning and urban reality in post-reform China', paper presented at the 36th Annual Meeting of the Association of Collegiate Schools of Planning, Phoenix, Arizona, 4 Nov.

——(1995) 'Inner city redevelopment in China: implications for the city of Beijing', *Cities*, 12(3): 149–62.

——(1998) 'Urban planning and urban reality under Chinese economic reforms', *Journal of Planning Education and Research*, 18: 145–53.

LECKIE, S. (1994a) *Destruction by Design: Housing Rights Violations in Tibet*, Utrecht, The Netherlands: Centre on Housing Rights and Evictions.

——(1994b) 'Social engineering, occupying powers and evictions; the case of Lhasa, Tibet', *Environment and Urbanization*, 6(1): 74–88.

——(1995) *When Push Comes to Shove*, Utrecht, The Netherlands: Centre on Housing Rights and Evictions.

LE CORBUSIER (1957/1941) *La Charte d'Athenes*, Paris: Editions de Minuit, 1957; 1st pub. 1941.

——(1967/1933) *The Radiant City: Elements of a Doctrine of Urbanism to be Used as the Basis of Our Machine Age Civilization*, New York: Orion Press, 1967; 1st pub. 1933.

LEE, J. (1988) 'Lands have long development history', *Vancouver Sun*, 28 Apr., p. G1.

——(1994) 'Mayor's party outspent COPE by 2 to 1', *Vancouver Sun*, 23 Mar., p. B1.

LEE, L. O.-F. (1999) *Shanghai Modern: The Flowering of a New Urban Culture in China, 1930–1945*, Cambridge, Mass.: Harvard University Press.

LEE, R., and SCHMIDT-MARWEDE, U. (1993) 'Interurban competition? Financial centres and the geography of financial production', *International Journal of Urban and Regional Research*, 17(4): 492–515.

——and WILLS, J. (eds) (1997) *Geographies of Economies*, London: Edward Arnold.

LEE, W. N., and TSE, D. (1994) 'Becoming Canadian: understanding how Hong Kong immigrants change their consumption', *Pacific Affairs*, 67(1): 70–95.

LEES, L., and DEMERITT, D. (1998) 'Envisioning the livable city: the interplay of "Sin City" and "Sim City" in Vancouver's planning discourse', *Urban Geography*, 19(4): 332–59.

LEFEBVRE, H. (1991) *The Production of Space*, Oxford: Blackwell.

LEMAN, E. (1994*a*) 'Foreign investment in China: some upcoming challenges', *Canada China Business Forum*, Sept./Oct.: 15–21.

——(1994*b*) 'Shanghai: re-emergence of a world metropolis', *Canada China Business Forum*, July/Aug.: 21–4.

——(1995*a*) 'Recent trends in China's Yangtze Delta Market', *Canada China Business Forum*, Mar./Apr.: 21–4.

——(1995*b*) 'Market potentials in the Yangtze Delta megalopolis', *Canada China Business Forum*, May/June: 17–20.

LESLIE, G. (1991) *Breach of Promise: Scored Ethics Under Vander Zalm*, Madeira Park, BC: Harbour Publishing.

LEY, D. (1980) 'Liberal ideology and the postindustrial city', *Annals, Association of American Geographers*, 70: 238–58.

——(1987) 'Styles of the times: liberal and neo-conservative landscapes in inner Vancouver, 1968–1986', *Journal of Historical Geography*, 14: 40–56.

——(1989*a*) 'Modernism, post-modernism and the struggle for place', in J. Agnew and J. Duncan (eds), *The Power of Place*, Boston: Unwin Hyman, 44–65.

——(1989*b*) 'Fragmentation, coherence, and the limits to theory in human geography', in A. Kobayashi and S. Mackenzie (eds), *Remaking Human Geography*, Boston: Unwin Hyman, 227–44.

——(1993*a*) 'Postmodernism, or the cultural logic of advanced intellectual capital', *Tijdschrift voor Econ. en Soc. Geografie*, 84(3): 171–4.

——(1993*b*) 'Gentrification in recession: social change in six Canadian cities, 1981–1986', *Urban Geography*, 13(3): 230–56.

——(1994) 'The Downtown Eastside: "One hundred years of struggle"', in S. Hasson and D. Ley, *Neighbourhood Organizations and the Welfare State*, Toronto: University of Toronto Press, 172–204.

——(1995) 'Between Europe and Asia: the case of the missing sequoias', *Ecumene*, 2(2): 185–210.

——(1996) *The New Middle Class and the Remaking of the Central City*, Oxford: Oxford University Press.

——(1999) 'Myths and meanings of immigration and the metropolis', *Canadian Geographer*, 43(1): 2–19.

——HIEBERT, D., and PRATT, G. (1992) 'Time to grow up? From urban village to world city 1966–91', in Wynn and Oke (1992): 234–66.

——and HUTTON, T. (1987) 'Vancouver's corporate complex and producer services sector: linkages and divergence within a provincial staple economy', *Regional Studies*, 21: 413–24.

——and MILLS, C. (1993) 'Can there be a postmodernism of resistance in the built environment', in Knox (1993b): 255–78.

——and OLDS, K. (1988) 'Landscape as spectacle: world's fairs and the culture of heroic consumption', *Environment and Planning D: Society and Space*, 6: 191–212.

————(1992) 'World's Fairs and the culture of consumption in the contemporary city', in K. Anderson and F. Gale (eds), *Inventing Places: Studies in Cultural Geography*, Melbourne: Longman Chesire, 178–93.

LEYSHON, A. (1997) 'True stories? Global dreams, global nightmares, and writing globalization', in Lee and Wills (1997): 133–46.

——and THRIFT, N. (1992) 'Liberalisation and consolidation: the Single European Market and the remaking of European financial capital', *Environment and Planning A*, 24: 49–81.

————(1996) *Money/Space: Geographies of Monetary Transformation*, New York: Routledge.

————(1999) 'Lists come alive: electronic systems of knowledge and the rise of credit-scoring in retail banking', *Economy and Society*, 28(3): 434–66.

————and DANIELS, P. (1987) 'Large commercial property firms in the U.K.: the operational development and spatial expansion of general practice firms of chartered surveyors', Working Paper on Producer Services No. 5, Department of Geography, University of Bristol and University of Liverpool.

LI, F., and LI, J. (1999) *Foreign Investment in China*, London: Macmillan.

LI, V. T. K. (1992) 'Why we invest in Canada', *Dialogue* (Asia Pacific Foundation of Canada), 6(1), Feb.: 3, 8.

LIN, G. C.-S. (1994) 'Changing theoretical perspectives on urbanisation in Asian developing countries', *Third World Planning Review*, 16(1): 1–23.

LINDORFF, D. (1993) 'Financing China's capitalist revolution', *Global Finance*, Feb.: 42–5.

LIZIERI, C., and DOBLIAS, G. (1995) 'Financial services, innovation and real estate markets: urban change & systemic risk', paper presented to the 11th Annual Meeting of the American Real Estate Society, Hilton Head, South Carolina, 30 Mar.

——and FINLAY, L. (1995) 'International property portfolio strategies: problems and opportunities', *Journal of Property Valuation and Investment*, 13(1): 6–21.

LO, F.-L., and YEUNG, Y.-M. (eds) (1996) *Emerging World Cities in Pacific Asia*, Tokyo: United Nations University Press.

LOGAN, J. (1993) 'Cycles and trends in the globalization of real estate', in Knox (1993b): 35–54.

LUCAS, L. (1995) 'Net for China: no smut, no politics, no decadent culture', *Financial Times*, 10 July: 13.

LUKE, T. (1997) 'Localized spaces, globalized places: virtual community and geo-economics in the Asia-Pacific', in Berger and Borer (1997): 241–59.

MCDOWELL, L. (1992) 'Valid games? a response to Erica Schoenberger', *Professional Geographer*, 44(2): 212–15.

McDowell, L. (1998) 'Elites in the City of London: some methodological considerations', *Environment and Planning A*, 30: 2133–46.

McGee, T. G. (1976) 'The persistence of the proto-proletariat', *Progress in Geography*, 9: 1–38.

——(1989) 'Urbanisasi or Kotadesasi?: evolving patterns of urbanization in Asia', in F. Costa, A. Dutt, L. Ma, and A. Noble (eds), *Urbanization in Asia: Spatial Dimensions and Policy Issues*, Honolulu: University of Hawaii Press, 93–108.

——(1991) 'Presidential address: Eurocentrism in geography—the case of Asian urbanization', *The Canadian Geographer*, 35(4): 332–44.

——(1994) 'The future of urbanisation in developing countries: the case of Indonesia', *Third World Planning Review*, 16(1), pp. iii–xii.

——and Robinson, I. M. (eds) (1995) *The Mega-Urban Regions of Southeast Asia*, UBC Press: Vancouver.

McGrew, A. (1992a) 'A global society', in S. Hall, D. Held, and T. McGrew (eds), *Modernity and Its Futures*, Oxford: Polity and The Open University, 61–116.

——(1992b) 'Conceptualizing global politics', in A. McGrew and P. Lewis (eds), *Global Politics: Globalization and the Nation State*, Cambridge: Polity, 1–30.

Machimura, T. (1992) 'The urban restructuring process in Tokyo in the 1980s: transforming Tokyo into a world city', *International Journal of Urban and Regional Research*, 16(1): 114–28.

——(1998) 'Symbolic use of globalization in urban politics in Tokyo', *International Journal of Urban and Regional Research*, 22(2): 183–94.

Mackie, J. (1992) 'Overseas Chinese entrepreneurship', *Asian-Pacific Economic Literature*, 6(1): 41–64.

McLaughlin, G. (1993) 'The broker to billionaires', *The Financial Post Magazine*, June: 16–24.

McLemore, R. (1995) 'Shanghai's Pudong: a case study in strategic planning', *Plan Canada*, Jan.: 28–32.

MacPherson, K. (1994) 'The head of the dragon: the Pudong New Area and Shanghai's urban development', *Planning Perspectives*, 9: 61–85.

Magnusson, W. (1990) 'Regeneration and quality of life in Vancouver', in D. Judd and M. Parkinson (eds), *Leadership and Urban Regeneration: Cities in North America and Europe*, Newbury Park: Sage, 171–87.

Majury, N. (1994) 'Signs of the times—Kerrisdale, a neighborhood in transition', *Canadian Geographer*, 38(3): 265–70.

Marcus, G. (1992) 'Past, present and emergent identities: requirements for ethnographies of late twentieth century modernity worldwide', in Lash and Friedman (1992): 309–30.

——(1995) 'Ethnography in/of the world system: the emergence of multi-sited ethnography', *Annual Review of Anthropology*, 25: 95–117.

——(1997) 'Spatial practices: fieldwork, travel and the disciplining of Anthropology', in Gupta and Ferguson (1997): 185–222.

——and Fischer, M. (eds) (1986) *Anthropology as Cultural Critique: An Experiential Moment in the Human Sciences*, Chicago: University of Chicago Press.

Marcuse, P. (1997a) 'Glossy globalization: unpacking a loaded discourse', in P. Droege (ed.), *Intelligent Environments: Spatial Aspects of the Information Revolution*, Amsterdam: Elsevier, 29–47.

——(1997*b*) 'The enclave, the citadel, and the ghetto: what has changed in the post-fordist U.S. city', *Urban Affairs Review*, 33(2): 228–64.

——(1998) 'Sustainability is not enough', *Environment and Urbanization*, 10(2): 103–11.

MARKUSEN, A. (1994) 'Studying regions by studying firms', *The Professional Geographer*, 46(4): 477–90.

MARRIAGE, P., and MILITANTE, G. (1992) 'Plan to take over Shanghai ports', *South China Morning Post Weekly*, 31 July–6 Aug., p. B3.

MARTON, A. (2000) *China's Spatial Economic Development: Regional Transformation in the Lower Yangzi Delta*, London: Routledge.

——McGEE, T., and PATERSON, D. (1995) 'Northeast Asian economic cooperation and The Tumen River Area Development Project', *Pacific Affairs*, 68(1): 8–33.

MASON, G., and BALDREY, K. (1989) *Fantasyland: Inside the Reign of Bill Vander Zalm*, Toronto: McGraw-Hill Ryerson.

MASSEY, D. (1992) 'A place called home?', *New Formations*, 17, summer: 3–15.

——(1993) 'Power-geometry and a progressive sense of place', in Bird *et al.* (1993): 59–69.

——(1994) *Space, Place and Gender*, Cambridge: Polity, 146–56.

——(1995) 'Imagining the world', in J. Allen and D. Massey (eds), *Geographical Worlds*, Oxford: Oxford University Press and The Open University, 5–52.

——ALLEN, J., and PILE, S. (eds) (1999) *City Worlds*, London: Routledge.

————and SARRE, P. (eds) (1999) *Human Geography Today*, Cambridge: Polity Press.

MATAS, R. (1989*a*) 'Mystery, unanswered questions remain about B.C.'s land deal of the century', *The Globe and Mail*, 17 June, pp. A1, A7.

——(1989*b*) 'BC government lost millions in rush to sell waterfront land', *The Globe and Mail*, 20 June, pp. A1, A8.

——(1989*c*) 'Unidentified partners joined billionaires in buying Expo lands', *The Globe and Mail*, 21 June.

——(1994) 'Mud flying in Expo '86 cleanup', *The Globe and Mail*, 31 Jan., p. A4.

——and YORK, G. (1989) 'Expo site project rolling on fast track', *The Globe and Mail*, 19 June, pp. A1, A8.

MERRIFIELD, A. (1993) 'The struggle over place: redeveloping American Can in Southeast Baltimore', *Transactions of the Institute of British Geographers*, 18(1): 102–21.

MEYER, D. (1997) 'Expert managers of uncertainty: intermediaries of capital in Hong Kong', *Cities*, 14(5): 257–63.

MILLS, C. (1988) ' "Life on the upslope": the postmodern landscape of gentrification', *Environment and Planning D: Society and Space*, 6: 169–89.

——(1993) 'Myths and meanings of gentrification', in Duncan and Ley (1993): 149–70.

MITCHELL, K. (1993*a*) 'Facing capital: cultural politics in Vancouver', unpublished Ph.D. dissertation, Department of Geography, University of California, Berkeley.

——(1993*b*) 'Multi-culturalism, or the united colors of capitalism', *Antipode*, 25(4): 263–94.

——(1995), 'Flexible circulation in the Pacific Rim: capitalism in cultural context', *Economic Geography*, 71(4): 364–82.

MITCHELL, K. (1996) 'The Hong Kong immigrant and the urban landscape: shaping the transnational cosmopolitan in the era of Pacific Rim capital', in A. Ong and D. Nonini (eds), *Crossing the Edges of Empires: Culture, Capitalism, and Identity in Modern Chinese Transnationalism*, London: Routledge, 228–56.

—— (1997a) 'Transnational discourse: bringing Geography back in', *Antipode*, 29(2): 101–14.

—— (1997b) 'Different diasporas and the hype of hybridity', *Environment and Planning D: Society and Space*, 15: 533–53.

—— and OLDS, K. (2000) 'Chinese business networks and the globalization of property markets in the Pacific Rim', in Yeung and Olds (2000): 195–219.

MITTELMAN, J. (1996) *Globalization: Critical Reflections*, Boulder, Colo.: Lynne Rienner.

MOLOTCH, H. (1993) 'The political economy of growth machines', *Journal of Urban Affairs*, 15(1): 29–53.

MONTAGNON, P. (1994) 'Intermediaries find role under threat in Asia', *Financial Times*, 6 Dec.: 21.

—— and WALKER, T. (1995) 'Shanghai suffers the pain of youth', *Financial Times*, 18 May: 25.

MOORE, R. (1999) 'Vertigo: the strange new world of the contemporary city', in R. Moore (ed.), *Vertigo: The Strange New World of the Contemporary City*, London: Laurence King in association with Glasgow, 8–58.

MORGAN STANLEY (1994) 'China property', Investment Research, Japan & Asia/Pacific Memorandum, 3 Nov.

MUELLER, G. (1992) 'Watching global real estate markets', *Urban Land*, Mar.: 30–2.

MULLINS, P. (1991) 'Tourism urbanization', *International Journal of Urban and Regional Research*, 15(3): 321–42.

MURDOCH, J. (1995) 'Actor-networks and the evolution of economic forms: combining description and explanation in theories of regulation, flexible specialization, and networks', *Environment and Planning A*, 27: 731–57.

—— (1997) 'Towards a geography of heterogeneous associations', *Progress in Human Geography*, 21(3): 321–37.

MURPHEY, R. (1980) *The Fading of the Maoist Vision: City and Country in China's Development*, London: Methuen.

NASH, A. (1993) 'Hong Kong's business future: the impact of Canadian and Australian business migration programmes', in Yeung (1993): 309–39.

NAUGHTON, B. (1995) *Growing out of the Plan: Chinese Economic Reform, 1978–1993*, New York: Cambridge University Press.

NAUGHTON, T. (1999) 'The role of stock markets in the Asia-Pacific region', *Asian-Pacific Economic Literature*, 13(1): 22–5.

NEWMAN, P. (1993) 'The master builder', *Vancouver Magazine*, Sept.: 34–42.

NG, M. K. (1999) 'Political economy and urban planning: a comparative study of Hong Kong, Singapore and Taiwan', *Progress in Planning*, 51(5): 1–90.

—— and TANG, W.-S. (1999) 'Land use planning in "one country, two systems": Hong Kong, Guangzhou and Shenzhen', *International Planning Studies*, 4(1): 7–27.

NICOLL, A. (1993) 'Zhu heeds foreign advice to slow China's growth', *Financial Times*, 25 Aug.: 3.

—— (1994) 'Captivation with China by proxy', *Financial Times*, 3 May: 28.

NISSE, J., and POOLE, T. (1993) 'When the stardust finally settled', *The Independent on Sunday*, 1 Aug.: 6–7.

NONINI, D., and ONG, A. (1997) 'Introduction: Chinese transnationalism as an alternative modernity', in A. Ong and D. Nonini (eds), *Ungrounded Empires: The Cultural Politics of Chinese Transnationalism*, London: Routledge, 3–33.

NORTH, R., and HARDWICK, W. (1992) 'Vancouver since the Second World War: an economic geography', in Wynn and Oke (1992): 200–34.

NUTT, R. (1989) 'Institute expands city's list of Asia-oriented facilities', *Vancouver Sun*, 5 Oct., p. F3.

O'BRIEN, R. (1992) *Global Financial Integration: The End of Geography*, London: Royal Institute of International Affairs.

O'CONNOR, K., and SCOTT, A. (1991) 'The impact of changes in air services on airports in the Pacific Rim 1947–1990', paper presented at the 3rd Annual Pacific Rim Council on Urban Redevelopment Conference, Vancouver.

OECD (1992) 'Foreign direct investment flows: recent developments and prospects', *Financial Market Trends*, 52, June: 13–29.

——(1993) 'Recent developments in foreign direct investment: a sectoral analysis', *Financial Market Trends*, 54, Feb.: 67–85.

OLDS, K. (1988) 'Planning for the housing impacts of hallmark events: a case study of Expo 86', unpublished MA thesis, School of Community and Regional Planning, University of British Columbia.

——(1994) 'Conference Reports: INTA 17 New Town Experience Joint Conference and the World Property Market Exhibition, Hong Kong, 26 to 30 September 1993', *Land Use Policy*, 11(3): 234–6.

——(1995) 'Globalization and the production of new urban spaces: Pacific Rim mega-projects in the late 20th century', *Environment and Planning A*, 27: 1713–43.

——(1997) 'Globalizing Shanghai: the "global intelligence corps" and the building of Pudong', *Cities*, 14(2): 109–23.

——(1998a) 'Globalization and urban change: tales from Vancouver via Hong Kong', *Urban Geography*, 19(4): 360–85.

——(1998b) 'Hallmark events, evictions and housing rights: the Canadian case', *"Current Issues in Tourism*, 1(1): 2–46. A version of this is also accessible on the World Wide Web at <http://www.crdi.ca/books/focus/861/chapt1.html>.

——DICKEN, P., KELLY, P., KONG, L., and YEUNG, H. (eds) (1999) *Globalisation and the Asia-Pacific: Contested Territories*, London: Routledge.

——and YEUNG, H. (1999) 'Reshaping "Chinese" business networks in a globalising era', *Environment and Planning D: Society and Space*, 17(5): 535–55.

OLSON, S., and KOBAYASHI, A. (1993) 'The emerging ethnocultural mosaic', in L. Bourne and D. Ley (eds), *The Changing Social Geography of Canadian Cities*, Montreal and Kingston: McGill Queen's University Press, 138–52.

ONG, A. (1997) '"A momentary glow of fraternity": narratives of Chinese nationalism and capitalism', *Identities—Global Studies in Culture and Power*, 3(3): 331–66.

——(1999) *Flexible Citizenship: The Cultural Logics of Transnationality*, Durham: Duke University Press.

——CHENG, L., and EVANS, L. (1992) 'Migration of highly educated Asians and global dynamics', *Asian and Pacific Migration Journal*, 1(3–4): 543–67.

ORAM, R. (1994) 'A consuming interest in China', *Financial Times*, 28 Sept.: 25.

OSTRANDER, S. (1993) ' "Surely you're not in this just to be helpful": Access, rapport, and interviews in three studies of elites', *Journal of Contemporary Ethnography*, 22(1): 7–27.

Ó TUATHAIL, G. (1997*a*) 'At the end of geopolitics? reflections on a plural problematic at the century's end', *Alternatives*, 22: 35–55.

——(1997*b*) 'Emerging markets and other simulations: Mexico, the Chiapas revolt and the geofinancial panoptican', *Ecumene*, 4(3): 300–17.

PADERANGA, C. (1999) 'Globalisation and the limits to national economic management', in Olds *et al.* (1999): 163–80.

PAGE, J. (1994) The East Asian miracle: an introduction', *World Development*, 22(4): 615–25.

PALMER, V. (1990) 'Expo lands: Plan A was a better idea', *Vancouver Sun*, 2 Mar., p. A16.

PAN, L. (1990) *Sons of the Yellow Emperor: The Story of the Overseas Chinese*, London: Mandarin.

——(1993) *Shanghai: A Century of Change in Photographs, 1843–1949*, Hong Kong: Hai Feng Publishing Co.

PARSONAGE, J. (1992) 'Southeast Asia's "growth triangle": a subregional response to global transformation', *International Journal of Urban and Regional Research*, 16(2): 307–17.

PAWLEY, M. (1992*a*) 'Living in the past', *World Architecture*, 18: 31.

——(1992*b*) 'Sir Richard Rogers: global architect', *World Architecture*, 18, July: 32–55.

——(1998) *Terminal Architecture*, London: Reaktion Books.

PE-PUA, R., MITCHELL, C., IREDALE, R., and CASTLES, S. (1996) *Astronaut Families and Parachute Children: The Cycle of Migration between Hong Kong and Australia*, Canberra: Australian Government Publishing Service.

PECK, J. (1995) 'Moving and shaking: business élites, state localism and urban privatism', *Progress in Human Geography*, 19(1): 16–46.

PEPCHINSKI, M. (1993) 'Report from Berlin', *Progressive Architecture*, 11: 78–84.

PERRAULT, D. (1996) *Dominique Perrault*, Paris: Sens & Tonka.

——(1999) *Dominique Perrault architect*, Basel: Birkhauser.

PERRY, E. (1993) *Shanghai on Strike: The Politics of Chinese Labour*, Stanford, Calif.: Stanford University Press.

PERSKY, S. (1989) *Fantasy Government: Bill Vander Zalm and the Future of Social Credit*, Vancouver: New Star Books.

PETIT, B. (1992) 'Zoning the market, and the single family landscape: neighbourhood change in Vancouver, Canada', unpublished Ph.D. dissertation, School of Community and Regional Planning, University of British Columbia.

PHILLIPS, D., and YEH, A. G.-H. (1990) 'Foreign investment and trade: impact on spatial structure of the economy', in Cannon and Jenkins (1990): 224–48.

PILKINGTON, E. (1994) 'Ghetto blaster', *Guardian*, 4 June: 34 (*Guardian Weekend*).

PORTES, A., GUARNIZO, L., and LANDOLT, P. (1999) 'The study of transnationalism: pitfalls and promise of an emergent research field', *Ethnic and Racial Studies*, 22(2): 217–37.

——and SENSENBRENNER, J. (1993) 'Embeddedness and immigration—notes on the social determinants of economic action', *American Journal of Sociology*, 98(6): 1320–50.

POTTER, P. (1995) 'Foreign investment law in the People's Republic of China: Dilemmas of state control', *The China Quarterly*, 141: 155–85.

POWELL, W. (1990) 'Neither market nor hierarchy: network forms of organisation', *Research in Organisational Behaviour*, 12: 295–336.

——and DiMAGGIO, P. (eds) (1991) *The New Institutionalism in Organizational Analysis*, London: University of Chicago Press.

PRED, A., and WATTS, M. (1992) *Reworking Modernity: Capitalisms and Symbolic Discontent*, New Brunswick, NJ: Rutgers University Press.

PROCTOR, J. (1998) 'The social construction of nature: relativist accusations, pragmatist and critical realist responses', *Annals of the Association of American Geographers*, 88(3): 352–76.

Province of British Columbia (1993*a*) *BC STATS*, Feb., Issue 92-3, Central Statistics Branch, Population Section, Victoria, Canada.

——(1993*b*) *BC STATS*, Nov., Issue 93-2, Central Statistics Branch, Population Section, Victoria, Canada.

PRYKE, M. (1999) 'City rhythms: neo-liberalism and the developing world', in Allen *et al.* (1999): 321–38.

Pudong Development Office of Shanghai, Municipal People's Government, The People's Construction Bank of China (eds) (1991) *Guide to the Development and Investment of Pudong Shanghai*, Hong Kong: Economic Information and Agency of Hong Kong.

PYE, L. W. (1991) *China: An Introduction*, New York: Harper Collins.

RAFFERTY, K. (1989) *City on the Rocks: Hong Kong's Uncertain Future*, London: Viking.

RAMBERT, F. (1997) *Massimiliano Fuksas*, Paris: Éditions du Regard.

RAMO, J. C. (1998) 'The Shanghai bubble', *Foreign Policy*, 111: 64–75.

REDDING G. (1990) *The Spirit of Chinese Capitalism*, Berlin: Walter de Gruyter.

——(1994) 'Determinants of the competitive power of small business networking: the Overseas Chinese case', in Schütte (1994): 101–17.

——(1995) 'Overseas Chinese networks: understanding the enigma', *Long Range Planning*, 28(1): 61–9.

RENDELL, J., PENNER, B., and BORDEN, I. (eds) (2000) *Gender Space Architecture: An Interdisciplinary Introduction*, London: Routledge.

Richard Rogers Partnership (1992) 'Shanghai Lu Jia Zui: proposals for a new commercial centre; a nucleus for the development of Pu Dong', Nov.

RICS (1993) 'Understanding the property cycle', Working Paper Two, The Royal Institution of Chartered Surveyors, London, Mar.

RIMMER, P. (1991*a*) 'The global intelligence corps and world cities: engineering consultancies on the move', in P. Daniels (ed.), *Services and Metropolitan Development: International Perspectives*, London: Routledge, 66–106.

——(1991*b*) 'Megacities, multilayered networks and development corridors in the Pacific economic zone: the Japanese ascendency', plenary paper presented at the 3rd Annual Pacific Rim Council on Urban Redevelopment Conference, Vancouver.

——(1991*c*) 'Exporting cities to the Western Pacific Rim: the art of the Japanese package', in J. Brotchie, M. Batty, P. Hall, and P. Newton (eds), *Cities of the 21st Century: New Technologies and Spatial Systems*, Melbourne: Longman Cheshire, 243–61.

RIMMER, P. (1993) 'Reshaping western Pacific Rim cities: exporting Japanese planning ideas', in K. Fujita and R. C. Hill (eds), *Japanese Cities in the World Economy*, Philadelphia: Temple University Press, 257–79.

——(1994) 'Regional economic integration in Pacific Asia', *Environment and Planning A*, 26(11): 1731–60.

ROBERTSON, R. (1992) *Globalization*, London: Sage.

ROBINS, K. (1991) 'Prisoners of the city: whatever could a postmodern city be?' *New Formations*, 15, winter: 1–22.

ROGERS, R. (1985) *Richard Rogers + Architects*, London: Academy Editions.

——(1991) *Architecture: A Modern View*, London: Thames and Hudson.

——(1994) 'Shanghai of the future', *Britain-China*, 51(1): 1–3.

——(1995a) 'Learning to live with the city', *Independent*, 13 Feb.: 18.

——(1995b) 'Looking forward to the Compact City', *Independent*, 20 Feb.: 18.

——(1995c) 'The imperfect form of the new', *Independent*, 27 Feb.: 18.

——(1995d) 'Let London live again, for all our sakes', *Independent*, 6 Mar.: 18.

——(1995e) 'Building cities to move the spirit', *Independent*, 13 Mar.: 18.

——(1997) *Cities for a Small Planet*, London: Faber and Faber.

——and FISHER, M. (1992) *A New London*, Harmondsworth: Penguin.

ROSE, G. (1993) 'Some notes on thinking about the spaces of the future', in Bird *et al.* (1993): 70–86.

Rosehaugh Stanhope Developments (1991) *Broadgate in the World Context*, London: Rosehaugh Stanhope Developments.

RUGGIE, J. (1993) 'Territoriality and beyond: problematizing modernity in international relations', *International Organization*, 47(1): 139–74.

RUSH, R. (1995) 'Shanghai: home of the handmade highrise', *Progressive Architecture*, Mar.: 35–6.

Salomon Brothers (1993) 'Residential property', Hong Kong Equity Research Report, Sept.

SARTI, R. (1988) 'Residents' organizer fears new evictions', *Vancouver Sun*, 27 Oct., p. A3.

SASSEN, S. (1988) *The Mobility of Labor and Capital: A Study in International Investment and Labour Flow*, New York: Cambridge University Press.

——(1991) *The Global City*, Princeton: Princeton University Press.

——(1994) *Cities in a World Economy*, Thousand Oaks, Calif.: Pine Forge Press.

——(1996) *Losing Control? Sovereignty in an Age of Globalization*, New York: Columbia University Press.

——(1998) 'Hong Kong: strategic site/new frontier', in C. Davidson (ed.), *Anyhow*, Cambridge/New York: MIT Press/Anyone Corp., 130–7.

——(1999) 'Servicing the global economy: reconfigured states and private agents', in Olds *et al.* (1999).

SAVITCH, H. (1988) *Post-Industrial Cities: Politics and Planning in New York, Paris and London*, Princeton: Princeton University Press.

SAYER, A. (1992) *Method in Social Science: A Realist Approach*, London: Routledge.

SCHOENBERGER, E. (1991) 'The corporate interview as a research method in economic geography', *Professional Geographer*, 43(2): 180–9.

——(1992) 'Self-criticism and self-awareness in research: a reply to Linda McDowell', *Professional Geographer*, 44(2): 215–18.

SCHÜTRE, H. (ed.) (1994) *The Global Competitiveness of the Asian Firm*, New York: St Martin's Press.

SEAGRAVE, S. (1995) *Lords of the Rim: The Invisible Empire of the Overseas Chinese*, London: Bantam Press.

'Secrets of the Arup Archipelago', *World Architect*, 18, July 1992: 76–81.

SEEK, N. H. (1996) 'Institutional participation in Asia Pacific real estate markets: Are the benefits worth the risks?' *Real Estate Finance*, 12(4): 51–8.

SEGAL, G. (1993) *The Fate of Hong Kong*, London: Simon & Schuster.

SENDER, H. (1993) 'Just like Hong Kong', *Far Eastern Economic Review*, 12 Aug.: 71–2.

——(1994) 'Passion for profit', *Far Eastern Economic Review*, 23 June: 54–6.

SHALE, T. (1993) 'Zhu Rongji's big gamble', *Euromoney*, Aug.: 32–6.

Shanghai Foreign Investment Commission (1995) *Guide to Investment in Shanghai*, Shanghai: Shanghai Foreign Investment Commission.

Shanghai Lujiazui Central Area International Planning and Urban Design Consultation Committee (1992*a*) 'Invitation of the Shanghai Lujiazui Central Area International Planning and Urban Design Consultation', 26 May, mimeo.

——(1992*b*) 'Shanghai: International Consultation of Planning and Urban Design, Lujiazui Central Area, Pudong', May, mimeo.

Shanghai Municipal Government (1993) *The Foreign Economic Statistical Yearbook of Shanghai, 1993* (in Chinese), Shanghai: Shanghai Municipal Yearbook.

Shanghai Municipal People's Government (1991) *The Developing Shanghai Finance*, Shanghai: Shanghai Municipal People's Government.

Shanghai Pudong New Area Administration (1993) *Shanghai Pudong New Area Handbook*, Shanghai: Shanghai Far East Publishers.

Shanghai Star (1995) 'Financial operations hit 2,500', *Shanghai Star*, 14 Feb.: 6.

SHAW, G. (1993) 'It's back to the drawing board for Stanley Kwok', *Vancouver Sun*, 18 Sept., p. C6.

SHAYLER, J. (1986) 'Expo 86: the social impact on its backdoor neighbourhood', *City Magazine*, 8(2): 32–5.

SHIRK, S. (1993) *The Political Logic of Economic Reform in China*, Berkeley: University of California Press.

SHURMER-SMITH, P., and HANNAM, K. (1994) *Worlds of Desire, Realms of Power: A Cultural Geography*, London: Edward Arnold.

SIDAWAY, J., and PRYKE, M. (2000) 'The strange geographies of "emerging markets"', *Transactions of the Institute of British Geographers* 25(2): 187–202.

SILVER, N. (1994) *The Making of Beauberg: A Building Biography of the Centre Pompidou, Paris*, London: MIT Press.

SIMON, D. (1992) *Cities, Capital and Development: African Cities in the World Economy*, London: Belhaven.

——(1993) 'The world city hypothesis: reflections from the periphery', CEDAR Research Paper No. 7, Royal Holloway, University of London.

SIRAT, M. (1997) 'Globalization of economic activity and the changing landscape of Kuala Lumpur Central Planning Area', *Asian Geographer*, 16(1–2): 37–58.

——and GHAZALI, S. (1999) *Globalisation of Economic Activity and Third World Cities: A Case Study of Kuala Lumpur*, Kuala Lumpur: Utusan Publications.

SITO, P., and FUNG, W-K. (1995) 'Li maintains confidence in HK despite offshore share trust', *South China Morning Post*, 17 May: 1.

SKELDON, R. (1994*a*) 'Hong Kong in an international migration system', in Skeldon (1994*b*): 21–51.

——(ed.) (1994*b*) *Reluctant Exiles?: Migration from Hong Kong and the New Overseas Chinese*, New York: M. E. Sharpe.

——(1995) 'Recent changes in migratory movements and policies', *Asian and Pacific Migration Journal*, 4(4): 543–54.

SKLAIR, L. (1991) *Sociology of the Global System*, Hertfordshire: Harvester Wheatsheaf.

——(1995) 'Social movements and global capitalism', *Sociology*, 29(3): 495–512.

——(1997) 'Social movements for global capitalism: the transnational capitalist class in action', *Review of International Political Economy*, 4(3): 514–38.

SMART, A. (1994) 'Economic transformation in socialist and post-socialist societies: property regimes and social relations', paper presented at the American Anthropological Association, Nov., Atlanta.

——(1995) 'Local capitalisms: situated social support for capitalist production in China', Occasional Paper No. 121, Mar., Department of Geography, The Chinese University of Hong Kong.

——(1997) 'Capitalist story-telling and hegemonic crises: some comments', *Identities*, 3: 399–412.

——(1998) 'Economic transformation in China: property regimes and social relations', in J. Pickles and A. Smith (eds), *Theorising Transition: The Political Economy of Post-Communist Transformations*, London: Routledge, 428–49.

—— and SMART, J. (1996) 'Monster homes: Hong Kong immigration to Canada, urban conflicts, and contested representations of space', in J. Caulfield and L. Peake (eds), *City Lives and City Forms: Critical Research and Canadian Urbanism*, Toronto: University of Toronto Press, 33–46.

————(2000) 'Failures and strategies of Hong Kong firms in China: an ethnographic perspective', in Yeung and Olds (2000): 244–71.

SMART, B. (1993) *Postmodernity*, London: Routledge.

SMART, J. (1994) 'Business immigration to Canada: deception and exploitation', in Skeldon (1994*b*): 98–119.

—— and SMART, A. (1991) 'Personal relations and divergent economies: a case study of Hong Kong investment in South China', *International Journal of Urban and Regional Research*, 15: 216–33.

SMELSER N. J., and SWEDBERG, R. (1994*a*) 'The sociological perspective on the economy', in Smelser and Swedberg (1994*a*): 3–26.

————(eds) (1994*b*) *The Handbook of Economic Sociology*, Princeton and New York: Princeton University Press and Russell Sage Foundation.

SMITH, A. (1990) 'Towards a global culture?', in Featherstone (1990*b*): 171–92.

SMITH, M. P. (1994) 'Transnational migration and the globalization of grassroots politics', *Social Text*, 39, summer: 15–34.

SMITH, P. (1992) 'The making of a global city: the case of Vancouver 1943–1992', *Canadian Journal of Urban Research*, 1(1): 90–112.

SMITH, S. (1993) 'Immigration and nation-building in Canada and the United Kingdom', in Jackson and Penrose (1993): 50–77.

SOJA, E. (1994) 'Heterotopologies: a rememberances of other spaces in the Citadel-LA', in S. Watson and K. Gibson (eds), *Postmodern Cities and Spaces*, Oxford: Blackwell, 13–34.

SOMMER, D., STÖCHER, H., and WEIBER, L. (1994) *Ove Arup & Partners: Engineering the Built Environment*, Berlin: Birkhäuser Verlag.

SOMMERS, J. (1998) 'Men at the margin: masculinity and space in downtown Vancouver, 1950–1986', *Urban Geography*, 19(4): 287–310.

SORKIN, M. (ed.) (1992) *Variations on a Theme Park: The New American City and the End of Public Space*, New York: Noonday Press.

Statistics Canada (1999) Statistical Profile Highlights: Vancouver (Census Metropolitan Area), British Columbia, <http://ww2.statcan.ca/english/profil/Details /details1.cfm?PSGC=59&SGC=93300&LANG=E&Province=59&PlaceName=Van couver&CMANAME=Vancouver&CMA=933>, accessed 19 Nov.

STINE, S. (1993) 'The dragon's head', *ASIA, INC*, Dec.: 40–3.

Stock Exchange of Hong Kong (1995) *Stock Exchange Fact Book 1994*, Hong Kong: The Stock Exchange of Hong Kong.

——(1996) *Stock Exchange Fact Book 1995*, Hong Kong: The Stock Exchange of Hong Kong.

——(1997) *Stock Exchange Fact Book 1996*, Hong Kong: The Stock Exchange of Hong Kong.

STOFFMAN, D. (1989) 'Asia comes to lotusland', *The Globe and Mail Report on Business Magazine*, Nov.: 123–37.

STRANGE, S. (1988) *States and Markets*, London: Pinter Publishers.

STROM, E. (1996) 'In search of the growth coalition—American urban theories and the redevelopment of Berlin', *Urban Affairs Review*, 31(4): 455–81.

SUDJIC, D. (1986) *Norman Foster, Richard Rogers, James Stirling: New Directions in British Architecture*, London: Thames and Hudson.

——(1992*a*) *The 100 Mile City*, London: André Deutch.

——(1992*b*) 'Birth of the brave new city', *Guardian*, 2 Dec.: 2–3.

——(1993*a*) 'Their love keeps lifting us higher', *Telegraph Magazine*, 15 May: 17–25.

——(1993*b*) 'Bangkok's instant city', *Blueprint*, 99, July–Aug.: 16–19.

——(1994*a*) 'Tomorrow's man today', *Guardian*, 15 Nov., p. Arts 4–5.

——(1994*b*) *The Architecture of Richard Rogers*, London: Fourth Estate and Wordsearch Ltd.

——(1995) 'The city that François built', *Guardian*, 12 May, p. Arts 19.

SUN, H. (1998*a*) *Foreign Direct Investment and Economic Development in China: 1979–1996*, Singapore: Ashgate.

——(1998*b*) 'Macroeconomic impact of direct foreign investment in China, 1979–96', *World Economy*, 21(5): 675–94.

——(1994) 'China's land market: current situation, problems and development trends', mimeo.

SUNG, Y. W. (1993) 'China's impact on the Asian Pacific regional economy', *Business & The Contemporary World*, spring: 105–28.

SUTCLIFFE, A. (1993) *Paris: An Architectural History*, New Haven: Yale University Press.

SUTCLIFFE, B. (1994) 'Migration, rights and illogic', *Index on Censorship*, 3: 27–37.

SWEDBERG, R., and GRANOVETTER, M. (1992) 'Introduction', in Granovetter and Swedberg (1992): 1–26.

SWYNGEDOUW, E. (1989) 'The heart of the place: the resurrection of locality in an age of hyperspace', *Geographiska Annaler*, 71B(1): 31–42.

SWYNGEDOUW, E. (1997) 'Neither global nor local: "glocalization" and the politics of scale', in Cox (1997): 137–66.

SZE, J. (1993) 'The allure of B shares', *The China Business Review*, Jan.–Feb.: 42–8.

TAN, A., and LOW, L. (1999) 'Shanghai world financial center: love and rockets in the spree economy', in R. Moore (ed.), *Vertigo: The Strange New World of the Contemporary City*, London: Laurence King in association with Glasgow 1999.

TANG, W. S. (1989) 'The Shanghai Master Plan: rational planning or social making', paper presented at the 31st Annual Conference of the Collegiate Schools of Planning, Portland, Oregon, USA, 4–7 Oct.

——CHU, D., and FAN, C. (1993) 'Economic reform and regional development in China in the 21st century', in Yeung (1993): 105–33.

TAYLOR, D. (1997) 'Rogers accused of hypocrisy over sustainable development by FOE [Friends of the Earth]', *Architects' Journal*, 206(13): 19.

TAYLOR, M. (1992) 'Have cash, will travel', *Far Eastern Economic Review*, 5 Mar.: 56–60.

THOMAS, R. (1993) 'Interviewing important people in big companies', *Journal of Contemporary Ethnography*, 22(1): 80–96.

THORNLEY, A. (1993) 'Ideology and the by-passing of the planning system: case studies of Canary Wharf, London, and the Globe, Stockholm', *European Planning Studies*, 1(2): 199–216.

THORNTON, E. (1995) 'The rush to modernize', *Far Eastern Economic Review*, 6 Apr.: 38–44.

THRIFT, N. (1986) 'The internationalisation of producer services and the integration of the Pacific Basin property market', in M. Taylor and N. Thrift (eds), *Multinationals and the Restructuring of the World Economy*, London: Croom Helm, 142–92.

——(1987) 'The fixers: the urban geography of international commercial capital', in Henderson and Castells (1987): 203–33.

——(1993a) 'An urban impasse?', *Theory, Culture and Society*, 10: 229–38.

——(1993b) 'For a new regional geography', *Progress in Human Geography*, 17(1): 92–100.

——(1994) 'Inhuman geographies: landscapes of speed, light and power', in P. Cloke, M. Doel, D. Matless, M. Phillips, and N. Thrift, *Writing the Rural: Five Cultural Geographies*, London: Paul Chapman, 191–248.

——(1995) 'A hyperactive world', in Johnston *et al.* (1995): 18–35.

——(1996) *Spatial Formations*, London: Sage.

——(1997) 'The still point: resistance, expressive embodiment and dance', in S. Pile and M. Keith (eds), *Geographies of Resistance*, London: Routledge, 124–51.

——(1999a) 'The globalisation of the system of business knowledge', in Olds *et al.* (1999): 57–71.

——(1999b) 'Steps to an ecology of place', in Massey *et al.* (1999): 295–322.

——and OLDS, K. (1996) 'Refiguring the economic in economic geography', *Progress in Human Geography*, 20(3): 311–37.

TIERNEY, B. (1987) 'Mr. Moneybags', *The Vancouver Sun*, 14 Nov., pp. B1–B2.

——(1989) 'Li Ka-shing', *The Vancouver Sun*, Oct., n.p.

TIME, 17 Nov. 1997.

TIMEWELL, S. (1994) 'Shanghai's renaissance', *The Banker*, May: 34–8.

'Top sources of business immigration', *Pacific Post*, 27 Jan. 1995: 17.

TSANG, S. K. (1994) 'Hong Kong's economic prospect in a changing relationship with China: a speculative essay', BRC Papers on China, Business Research Centre, Hong Kong Baptist College, Feb.

'Tycoon Li grooms Victor as successor', *South China Morning Post*, 14 Jan. 1994.

UBS Global Research (1994) 'Cheung Kong (Holdings) Ltd.—a big gun loaded with firepower', Hong Kong Equities research report, Apr.

——(1995) 'New World Development: taking the China road', Hong Kong Equities research report, July.

United Nations Centre for Human Settlements (1996) *An Urbanizing World: Global Report on Human Settlements, 1996*, Oxford: Oxford University Press/ UNCHS.

United Nations Conference on Trade and Development (1994) *World Investment Report 1994: Transnational Corporations, Employment and the Workplace*, Geneva: UNCTAD.

——(1996) *World Investment Report 1996: Investment, Trade and International Policy Arrangements*, Geneva: UNCTAD.

——(1998) *World Investment Report 1998. Trends and Determinants*, Geneva. UNCTAD.

United Nations Development Programme (1999) *Human Development Report*, New York: Oxford University Press.

Urban Task Force (1999) *Towards an Urban Renaissance*, London: UK Department of Environment, Transport and the Regions.

'Vancouver: Asia's new capital', *TIME*, 17 Nov. 1997, pp. 28–9.

VAN HALM, R. (1988) 'Catching the Pacific wave', *BC Business*, 16(3): 22–7.

VIRILIO, P. (1991) *The Lost Dimension*, New York: Semiotext(e).

——(1994) *The Vision Machine*, London: British Film Institute.

Vista, Oct. 1989: 35–45.

WALKER, A. (1991) *Land, Property and Construction in the People's Republic of China*, Hong Kong: Hong Kong University Press.

——WING, C. K., and CHUNG, L. L. W. (1995) *Hong Kong in China: Real Estate in the Economy*, Hong Kong: Brooke Hillier Parker.

WALKER, T. (1993) 'A creaking infrastructure', *Financial Times*, 2 June: 30.

——(1994*a*) 'Dragon with an eye on its futures', *Financial Times*, 2–3 April: 10.

——(1994*b*) 'From abacus to automation', *Financial Times*, 7 July: 21.

——and COOKE, K. (1993) 'Centrist at a golden crossroad', *Financial Times*, 17 May: 28.

——PEEL, Q., and GAPPER, J. (1995) 'Way clear for five banks to open in Beijing', *Financial Times*, 7 June: 4.

WALLERSTEIN, I. (1974) *The Modern World System: Capitalist Agriculture and the Origins of the European World-Economy in the Sixteenth Century*, New York: Academic Press.

——(1979) *The Capitalist World-Economy*, Cambridge: Cambridge University Press.

——(1983) *Historical Capitalism*, London: Verso.

WALTON, J. (1995) 'How real(ist) can you get?', *Professional Geographer*, 47(1): 61–5.

WANG, G., and WONG, S.-L. (eds) (1997) *Dynamic Hong Kong: Business and Culture*, Hong Kong: Centre for Asian Studies, University of Hong Kong.

WARD, K., and JONES, M. (1999) 'Researching local elites: reflexivity, situatedness and political-temporal contingency', *Geoforum*, 30(4): 301–12.

WATERS, M. (1995) *Globalization*, London: Routledge.

WEBER, M. (1978) *Economy and Society*, 2 vols., Berkeley: University of California Press.

WEI, B. P-T. (1990) *Shanghai: Crucible of Modern China*, Oxford: Oxford University Press.

——(1993) *Old Shanghai*, Oxford: Oxford University Press.

WEYLAND, P. (1993) *Inside the Third World Village*, London: Routledge.

WHATMORE, S. (1999) 'Hybrid geographies: rethinking the "human" in human geography', in Massey *et al.* (1990): 22–40.

——and THORNE, L. (1997) 'Nourishing networks: alternative geographies of food', in M. Watts and D. Goodman (eds), *Postindustrial Nature: Culture, Economy and the Consumption of Food*, London: Routledge, 287–303.

WHITE, G. (1993) *Riding the Tiger: The Politics of Reform in Post-Mao China*, London: Macmillan.

WHITLEY, R. (1991) 'The social construction of business systems in East Asia', *Organization Studies*, 12(1): 1–28.

——(1992a) *Business Systems in East Asia: Firms, Markets and Societies*, London: Sage.

——(1992b) 'The social construction of organizations and markets: the comparative analysis of business recipes', in M. Reed and M. Hughes (eds), *Rethinking Organization: New Directions in Organization Theory and Analysis*, London: Sage, 120–43.

——(1994) 'Dominant forms of organization in market economies', *Organization Studies*, 15(2): 153–82.

——(1999) *Divergent Capitalisms: The Social Structuring and Change of Business Systems*, Oxford: Oxford University Press.

WILIAMSON, R. K. (1991) *American Architects and the Mechanics of Fame*, Austin: University of Texas Press.

——(1990) 'Our verandha is crowded, but the view is still hazy', *Business in Vancouver*, 8 Jan.: 9.

WILLIAMS, R. (1976) *Keywords: A Vocabulary of Culture and Society*, London: Fontana.

WILLIAMSON, R. (1992) 'Kwok's connections open doors to Asia', *The Globe and Mail*, 6 Apr., pp. B1–B2.

——(1994) 'West Coast condo king breaks ground', *The Globe and Mail*, 7 Nov., pp. B1, B3.

WILSON, K. (1993) 'High-tech city set to rise out of Shanghai's shadow', *South China Morning Post*, 9 January, p. 3.

WINTERBOURNE, E. (n.d.) 'Architecture and the politics of culture in Mitterrand's France', *Architectural Design Profile*, 114: 24–9.

WONG, L. (1993) 'Immigration as capital accumulation: the impact of business immigration to Canada', *International Migration*, 31(1): 171–87.

WONG, S. L. (1991) 'Chinese entrepreneurs and business trust', in Hamilton (1991b): 13–29.

WONG, S.-L. (1988) *Emigrant Entrepreneurs: Shanghai Industrialists in Hong Kong*, Hong Kong: Oxford University Press.

——(2000) 'Transplanting enterprises in Hong Kong', in Yeung and Olds (2000): 153–66.

Woo-Cumings, M. (ed.) (1999) *The Developmental State*, Ithaca, NY: Cornell University Press.

Woods, L. (1994) 'The Asia-Pacific policy network in Canada', *The Pacific Review*, 7(4): 435–45.

Woods, M. (1998) 'Rethinking elites: networks, space, and local politics', *Environment and Planning A*, 30: 2101–19.

World Architecture (n.d.) 'Child of Bombay', 27: 76–8.

—— (n.d.) 'An abecedario: Jean Nouvel', 31: 26–7.

World Bank (1991) *Urban Policy and Economic Development: An Agenda for the 1990s*, Washington: The World Bank.

—— (1992) *Reforming Urban Land Policies and Institutions in Developing Countries*, Washington: The World Bank.

—— (1993a) *Global Economic Prospects and the Developing Countries*, Washington: World Bank.

—— (1993b) *China: Urban Land Management in an Emerging Market Economy*, Washington: The World Bank.

—— (1993c) *The East Asian Miracle: Economic Growth and Public Policy*, Oxford: Oxford University Press.

—— (1994a) *Global Economic Prospects and the Developing Countries*, Washington: World Bank.

—— (1994b) *Resettlement and Development: The Bankwide Review of Projects Involving Involuntary Resettlement, 1986–1993*, Washingon: Environment Department, The World Bank.

—— (1996a) *Global Economic Prospects and the Developing Countries*, Washington: World Bank.

—— (1996b) *Managing Capital Flows in East Asia*, Washington: World Bank.

—— (1997a) *World Development Report 1997: The State in a Changing World*, Washington: World Bank.

—— (1997b) *China Engaged: Integration with the Global Economy*, Washington: World Bank.

Wright, G. (1991) *The Politics of Design in French Colonial Urbanism*, Chicago: University of Chicago Press.

—— (1996) 'Modernism and the specifics of place', in P. Yaeger (ed.), *The Geography of Identity*, Ann Arbor: University of Michigan Press, 307–33.

Wu, F. (1999) 'The "game" of landed-property production and capital circulation in China's transitional economy, with reference to Shanghai', *Environment and Planning A*, 31(10): 1757–71.

—— (2000) 'The global and local dimensions of place-making: remaking Shanghai as a world city'. *Urban Studies*, 37(2): 1359–77.

Wu, J. (1993) 'The historical development of Chinese urban morphology', *Planning Perspectives*, 8: 20–52.

—— (1994) 'Property market brisk', *Shanghai Star*, 1 Nov.: 4.

Wu, V. (1998) 'The Pudong Development Zone and China's economic reforms', *Planning Perspectives*, 13: 133–65.

Wu, Y., and Xu, T. (1993) 'Shanghai replays role as an oriental metropolis', *Beijing Review*, 2–9 May: 12–18.

Wynn, G. (1992) 'The rise of Vancouver', in Wynn and Oke (1992): 69–145.

—— and Oke, T. (eds) (1992) *Vancouver and its Region*, Vancouver: UBC Press.

XIAO, J. (1994) 'Hub goal assessed', *Shanghai Star*, 24 May: 1.

XIAO, Z. (1995) 'Rewards begin to roll in', *Shanghai Star*, 12 May: 6.

YABUKI, S. (1995) *China's New Political Economy: The Giant Awakes*, Boulder, Colo.: Westview Press.

YAO, S. (1997) 'The romance of Asian capitalism: geography, desire and Chinese business', in Berger and Borer (1997): 221–40.

YANAGISAWA, J. (1993) 'Shanghai Lujiazui central area international planning and urban design consultation', *JA Library*, 1 Summer: 116–21.

YEE, P. (1988) *Saltwater City: An Illustrated History of the Chinese in Vancouver*, Vancouver: Douglas & McIntyre.

YEH, A. (1992) 'Land leasing and urban planning', working paper, Centre of Urban Planning and Environmental Management, University of Hong Kong, Jan.

——and WU, F. (1999) 'The transformation of urban planning system in midst of economic reform in PRC', *Progress in Planning*, 51(3): 167–252.

——XU, X., and YAN, X. (eds) (1997) *Urban Planning Education Under Economic Reform in China*, Hong Kong: Centre for Urban Planning and Environmental Management.

YEUNG, W. C. H. (1998) *Transnational Corporations & Business Networks: Hong Kong Firms in the ASEAN Region*, New York: Routledge.

——and OLDS, K. (eds) (2000) *The Globalisation of Chinese Business Firms*, London: Macmillan.

YEUNG, Y. M. (ed.) (1993) *Pacific Asia in the 21st Century: Geographical and Developmental Perspectives*, Hong Kong: The Chinese University Press.

——and HU, X. W. (1992*a*) 'China's coastal cities as development and modernization agents: an overview', in Yeung and Hu (1992*b*): 1–23.

————(eds) (1992*b*) *China's Coastal Cities: Catalysts for Modernization*, Honolulu: University of Hawaii Press.

YIN, R. (1989) *Case Study Research: Design and Methods*, Newbury Park, Calif.: Sage.

YOUNG, M. (1991) 'Canada's immigration program', Background Paper BP-190E, Research Branch, Library of Parliament, Government of Canada.

YUSUF, S., and WU, W. (1997) *The Dynamics of Urban Growth in Three Chinese Cities*, Oxford: Oxford University Press (for the World Bank).

ZHANG, D. (n.d.) 'Spatial structure and change in the service industries of the P.R. China', mimeo.

ZHANG, Y. (1994) 'Look out New York', *Shanghai Star*, 8 Apr.: 1.

——(1995*a*) 'Pudong beats Shenzen in real estate', *Shanghai Star*, 31 Mar.: 4.

——(1995*b*) 'Pudong turns 5', *Shanghai Star*, 18 Apr.: 1.

——(1995*c*) 'Pudong unique', *Shanghai Star*, 28 Apr.: 1.

ZHANG, Y. C., and YU, D. (1994) 'China's emerging securities markets', *Columbia Journal of World Business*, 29(2): 113–21.

ZHANG, Z. (1993) 'From West to Shanghai: architecture and urbanism in Shanghai from 1840 to 1940', *A+U—Architecture and Urbanism*, 273: 69–100.

ZHAO, M. (1993) 'Understanding metropolitan Shanghai', in A. Laquian (ed.), *Planning and Development of Metropolitan Regions: Proceedings of an International Workshop, Bangkok, 29 June–July 3 1992*, Vancouver: UBC Centre for Human Settlements.

ZHENG, J. (1995*a*) 'New era, new face', *Shanghai Star*, 17 Feb.: 1.

——(1995*b*) 'Take lead, Jiang says', *Shanghai Star*, 26 May: 1.

ZUKIN, S. (1991) *Landscapes of Power: From Detroit to Disney World*, Berkeley: University of California Press.

——(1992*a*) 'Postmodern urban landscapes: mapping culture and power', in Lash and Friedman (1992): 221–47.

——(1992*b*) 'The city as a landscape of power: London and New York as global financial capitals' in Budd and Whimster (1992): 195–223.

——and DiMAGGIO, P. (eds) (1990) *Structures of Capital: The Social Organization of the Economy*, Cambridge: Cambridge University Press.

INDEX